P9-CEQ-196

Thomas Merton

SPIRITUAL DIRECTION & MEDITATION

The Liturgical Press
Collegeville, Minnesota

Cover photo: Courtesy of Gethsemani Archives, Abbey of Gethsemani, Trappist, Kentucky
Cover design: Cathleen Casey

Nihil obstat ex parte Ordinis: Fr. M. Thomas Aquinas Porter; Fr.
M. Paul Bourne; Fr. M. Shane Regan. *Imprimi potest:* Fr. M. Gabriel
Sortais, Abbot General. January 16, 1960.

Nihil obstat: John Eidenschink, O.S.B., J.C.D., *Censor deputa-
tus. Imprimatur:* ✠ Peter W. Bartholome, D.D., Bishop of St
Cloud. December 14, 1959.

CONTENTS

PREFACE

This booklet contains a revised and considerably expanded version of material on spiritual direction and meditation which appeared, in installments, in the magazine *Sponsa Regis*. The first part is addressed to the Christian, particularly to the religious, who seeks a director or who has one, and who desires to take full advantage of his opportunities. At the same time, it is hoped that some priests who are too shy to regard themselves as potential "spiritual directors" may, by reading these pages, learn to overcome their natural hesitations and, relying on the help of God, be emboldened to give advice and encouragement in the confessional when there is time to do so.

At the same time it is hoped that some over-rigid and stereotyped ideas about direction may be partially dispelled by one of the points made in these pages, namely, that the director is not to be regarded as a magical machine for solving cases and declaring the holy will of God beyond all hope of appeal, but a trusted friend who, in an atmosphere of sympathetic understanding, helps and strengthens us in our groping efforts to correspond with the grace of the Holy Spirit, who alone is the true Director in the fullest sense of the word.

It is also emphasized that, since grace builds on nature, we can best profit by spiritual direction if we are encouraged to develop our natural simplicity, sincerity, and forthright spiritual honesty, in a word to "be ourselves" in the best sense of the expression. In this way, a healthy and widespread use of this important means to perfection will help Christians to keep in vital contact with the reality of their vocation and of their life, instead of losing themselves in a maze of abstract devotional fictions.

The second part of the book is made up of notes on meditation which were written in 1951 as a kind of companion to *What is Contemplation?* After they had been typed out, they were laid aside and forgotten. They are now being printed with additions and corrections. You cannot learn meditation from a book. You just have to *meditate*. However, we can all agree that a few hints at the right time and in the right words may make a great deal of difference.

We hope that these few pages may help someone who has not been able to find what he needed in the other books on the subject. That is sufficient reason for their publication, assuming that there is nothing radically wrong with our approach. There should not be. It is perfectly traditional and familiar. The only striking characteristic of this approach is its informality and its aversion to conventional and rigid systems. Not that there is anything wrong with systems of meditation — and certainly an aversion to systems must not be interpreted as a repugnance for discipline. Discipline is most important, and without it no serious meditation will ever be possible. But it should be *one's own* discipline, not a routine mechanically imposed from the outside.

Here, then, are these pages which do not pretend to be complete, thorough or exhaustive. They simply touch on a few of the important points that anyone needs to understand before he can really meditate well. Nowhere in these notes have I insisted that meditation is important, and nowhere have I tried to sell anyone the idea of meditating. That is because all this is taken for granted. This book is not for people who do not want to meditate. It is only for those who are already interested, and who would like to meditate every day.

The factor of *desire* is, of course, extremely important. One of the main reasons why people who take up meditation fail to get anywhere in it is that they go about it halfheartedly, without any serious interest. It should be taken as obvious that a man who has no real desire to meditate will certainly not succeed; for here is one place, before all others, where you have to do the job yourself, aided by the grace of God. Nobody else is going to do it for you.

Abbey of Gethsemani
Fall, 1959

SPIRITUAL DIRECTION
AND MEDITATION

SPIRITUAL DIRECTION

1. *The Meaning and Purpose of Spiritual Direction*

The original, primitive meaning of spiritual direction suggests a particular need connected with a special ascetic task, a peculiar vocation for which a professional formation is required. In other words, spiritual direction is a monastic concept. It is a practice which was unnecessary until men withdrew from the Christian community in order to live as solitaries in the desert. For the ordinary member of the primitive Christian community there was no particular need of personal direction in the professional sense. The bishop, the living and visible representative of the apostle who had founded the local Church, spoke for Christ and the apostles, and, helped by the presbyters, took care of all the spiritual needs of his flock. The individual member of the community was "formed" and "guided" by his participation in the life of the community, and such instruction as was needed was given first of all by the bishop and presbyters, and then, through informal admonitions, by one's parents, spouse, friends and fellow Christians.

But when the first solitaries retired to the desert, they separated themselves from the Christian community. Their departure into the wilderness was approved and, in a sense, canonized by no less a bishop than St. Athanasius, soon followed by many others. But they lived solitary and dangerous lives, far from any church, and rarely participating even in the Mystery of the Eucharist. Yet they had gone into the wilderness to seek Christ. They had, like Christ, been "led by the Spirit into the wilderness to be tempted." And, like the Lord Himself, they were to be tempted by the evil one. Hence the need for "discernment of spirits" — and for a director.

We look back after many centuries upon the desert fathers and interpret their vocation in the light of our own. After all, they were the "first religious." We do not see how very different, in many ways, were their lives from ours. In any event, their deliberate withdrawal from the normal life of the visible Church was a very perilous spiritual adventure and an innovation of a type that would undoubtedly be considered out of the question by many today. In this adventure, certain safeguards were absolutely essential, and the most obvious and important of these was the training and guidance of the novice by a "spiritual father." In this case, the spiritual father replaced the bishop and presbyter as representative of Christ. And yet there was a difference because there was nothing hierarchical about his function. It was purely and simply charismatic. It was sanctioned by the father's own personal holiness. The greatest "abbots" in the Egyptian and Syrian deserts were generally not priests.

The *Apothegmata* or "Sayings of the Fathers" remain as an eloquent witness to the simplicity and depth of this spiritual guidance. Disciples travelled often for miles through the wilderness just to hear a brief word of advice, a "word of salvation" which summed up the judgment and the will of God for them in their actual, concrete situation. The impact of these "words" resided not so much in their simple content as in the inward action of the Holy Spirit which accompanied them, in the soul of the hearer. This of course presupposes an ardent faith, and a deep hunger for the word of God and for salvation. This spiritual appetite, this need for light, had in its turn been generated by tribulation and compunction. "Direction" then was God's answer to a need created in the soul by trial and compunction, and communicated through a charismatic representative of the Mystical Body, the *Abbas*, or spiritual Father.

This brings us to the root meaning of spiritual direction. It is a continuous process of formation and guidance, in which a Christian is led and encouraged *in his special vocation*, so that by faithful correspondence to the graces of the Holy Spirit he may attain to the particular end of his vocation and to union with God. This union with God signifies not only the vision of God in heaven but, as Cassian specifies, that perfect purity of heart which, even on earth, constitutes sanctity and attains to an obscure experience of heavenly things. Spiritual direction was, then, one of the essential means to monastic perfection.

This description of spiritual direction brings out certain important differences between direction and counselling, or direction and psychotherapy. Spiritual direction is not merely the cumulative effect of encouragements and admonitions which we all need in order to live up to our state in life. It is not mere ethical, social or psychological guidance. It is *spiritual*.

But it is important for us to understand what this word "spiritual" means here. There is a temptation to think that spiritual direction is the guidance of one's spiritual activities, considered as a small part or department of one's life. You go to a spiritual director to have him take care of your spirit, the way you go to a dentist to have him take care of your teeth, or to a barber to get a haircut. This is completely false. The spiritual director is concerned with the *whole person*, for the spiritual life is not just the life of the mind, or of the affections, or of the "summit of the soul" — it is the life of the whole person. For the spiritual man (*pneumatikos*) is one whose whole life, in all its aspects and all its activities, has been spiritualized by the action of the Holy Spirit, whether through the sacraments or by personal and interior inspirations. Moreover, spiritual direction is concerned with the whole person not simply as an individual human being, but as a son of God, another Christ, seeking to recover the perfect likeness to God in Christ, and by the Spirit of Christ.

The spiritual man is one who, "whether he eats or drinks or whatever else he does, does all for the glory of God" (1 Cor. 10:31). Again, this does not mean that he merely registers in his mind an abstract intention to glorify God. It means that in all his actions he is free from the superficial automatism of conventional routine. It means that in all that he does he acts freely, simply, spontaneously, from the depths of his heart, moved by love.

Originally, as we have said, the concept of the "spiritual father" is linked up with the idea of a special vocation, and very particular risks. But of course, all through the history of monasticism, we see evidence that the monk tends to become, in certain cases, the spiritual father to all comers, and to give advice about everything. This was quite common for example among the Cistercian laybrothers in 12th century England, some of whom acquired a great reputation for their ability to read and guide souls. Perhaps there was some element of nonsense in this sudden popular craze: the same kind of credulity that led people to frequent the recluses and anchoresses immured near village churches, who, though doubtless quite pious, had a universal reputation for being gossips. Nevertheless, we must not judge these manifestations of popular piety too harshly. There is no doubt that the Lord has, in the past, reached souls very effectively in this way, and we must not make the mistake of thinking that direction is a luxury reserved for a special elite. For if, as Eric Gill said, "every man is a special kind of artist" it is perhaps true that every man has a special and even perilous vocation to complete the supreme work of art which is his sanctification. Hence the apt saying of a Russian *Staretz* who was criticized for spending time seriously advising an old peasant woman about the care of her turkeys. "Not at all," he replied, "her *whole life* is in those turkeys." Direction, then, speaks to the whole man, in the concrete circumstances of his life, however simple they may be. It is not a question of discussing the relative merits of the discipline and the hairshirt, and determining whether or not one has reached the "prayer of quiet."

The whole purpose of spiritual direction is to penetrate beneath the surface of a man's life, to get behind the façade of conventional gestures and attitudes which he presents to the world, and to bring out his inner spiritual freedom, his inmost truth, which is what we call the likeness of Christ in his soul. This is entirely a supernatural thing, for the work of rescuing the inner man from automatism belongs first of all to the Holy Spirit. The spiritual director cannot do such a work himself. His function is to verify and to encourage what is truly spiritual in the soul. He must teach others to "discern" between good and evil tendencies, to distinguish the inspirations of the spirit of evil from those of the Holy Spirit. A spiritual director is, then, one who helps another to recognize and to follow the inspirations of grace in his life, in order to arrive at the end to which God is leading him. And this, as we have said, originally presupposed a special vocation. A spiritual director was necessary, above all, for one who had been called to seek God by an unusual and perilous road. It must not be forgotten that the spiritual director in primitive times was much more than the present name implies. He was a spiritual father who "begot" the perfect life in the soul of his disciple by his instructions first of all, but also by his prayer, his sanctity and his example. He was to the young monk a kind of "sacrament" of the Lord's presence in the ecclesiastical community.

In the earliest days of Christian monasticism the spiritual father did much more than instruct and advise. The neophyte lived in the same cell with him, day and night, and did what he saw his father doing. He made known to the father "all the thoughts that came into his heart" and was told, on the spot, how to react. In this way he learned the whole spiritual life in a concrete and experimental way. He literally absorbed and reproduced in his own life the life and spirit of his "father in Christ."

The same concept of spiritual fatherhood persists

today in Asia, for example in Yoga, where the difficult and complex disciplines can only be properly learned from a *guru* who is considered not only an expert in his professional field, but a representative and instrument of God. Russian literature of the nineteenth century introduces us to the figures of remarkable spiritual directors, *startzi*, holy monks who exercised a great influence in the life of the time, not only on the poor and humble, as we have just seen, but also on the intelligentsia.

It is important that we recover the full idea of spiritual direction and rescue the concept from its impoverished condition — according to which the director is merely one to whom we apply for quasi-infallible solutions to moral and ascetic "cases." If this is what we mean by a director, we will find that our understanding will be perverted by a kind of magic and pragmatic conventionalism. The "director" is thought to be one endowed with special, almost miraculous, authority and has the power to give the "right formula" when it is asked for. He is treated as a machine for producing answers that will work, that will clear up difficulties and make us perfect. He has a "system," or rather, he has become an expert in the workings of somebody else's system — which, having been approved by the Church, is devoutly believed to be infallible in every case, no matter how it is applied, and even if it is used arbitrarily with supreme disregard for individual circumstances.

Such spiritual direction is mechanical, and it tends to frustrate the real purpose of genuine spiritual guidance. It tends to reinforce the mechanisms and routines with which the soul is destroying its own capacity for a spontaneous response to grace.

The first thing that genuine spiritual direction requires in order to work properly is a normal, spontaneous human relationship. We must not suppose that it is somehow "not supernatural" to open ourselves easily to a director and converse with him in an atmosphere of pleasant and easy familiarity. This aids the work of grace : another example of grace building on nature.

It is a paradox that those who are the most rigidly "supernatural" in their theory of the spiritual life are sometimes the most "natural" in practice. To imagine that faith can only operate in a situation that is humanly repugnant, and that the "supernatural" decisions are only those which the penitent finds revolting or practically impossible, is to frustrate the whole purpose of direction. Some directors, under pretext of acting entirely according to "supernatural principles," are tyrannical and arbitrary. They allow themselves to ignore or overlook the individual needs and weaknesses of their penitents. They have standard answers which are "hard sayings" that admit of no exception and no mitigation and are always the same, no matter how the case may be altered by circumstances. Thus they take satisfaction in secretly indulging their aggressive instincts.

Obviously, we must be prepared to be told things we do not like and we must meet demands that are supremely exacting. We must be ready for sacrifice. And a good director will not hesitate to impose a sacrifice when he believes that it is the will of God. But the trouble is that a certain type of spirituality is arbitrary and unfeeling as a matter of deliberate policy. It assumes as a basic axiom of the spiritual life that every soul needs to be humiliated, frustrated and beaten down; that all spontaneous aspirations are suspect by the very fact that they are spontaneous; that everything individual is to be cut away, and that the soul is to be reduced to a state of absolute, machine-like conformity with others in the same fantastic predicament. Result: a procession of robot "victim souls" moving jerkily from exercise to exercise in the spiritual life, secretly hating the whole business and praying for an early death, meanwhile "offering it up" so that the whole may not be lost.

Obviously, no direction at all is preferable to such direction as this. It is the bane of the religious life.

The seventeenth-century Benedictine mystic, Dom Augustine Baker, who fought a determined battle for the interior liberty of contemplative souls in an age ridden by autocratic directors, has the following to say on the subject: "The director is not to teach his own way, nor indeed any determinate way of prayer, but to instruct his disciples how they may themselves find out the way proper for them. . . . In a word, he is only

God's usher, and must lead souls in God's way, and not his own."

2. *Is Direction Necessary?*

The answer to this question has been prepared by the opening paragraphs of our study. Strictly speaking, spiritual direction is not necessary for the ordinary Christian. But wherever there is *a special mission or vocation* a certain minimum of direction is implied by the very nature of the vocation itself. Let us clarify.

First, let us briefly consider the place of direction in the life of the ordinary Christian layman. Strictly speaking, the ordinary contacts of the faithful with their pastor and confessor are sufficient to take care of their needs. But, of course, this implies that they are known to their pastor and that they have a regular confessor. In a very large parish, where contacts with the pastor may perhaps be at a minimum or even non-existent, then certainly one should at least have a regular confessor to whom he is known, even though the confessor may not be formally and explicitly a "spiritual director." The reason for this is that confession itself implies a certain minimum of spiritual direction. The confessor is bound to instruct and direct the penitent at least to the extent that this is necessary for a fruitful reception of the sacrament of penance. But where one is habitually sinning gravely, advice and special instructions are certainly necessary if the penitent is to take effective steps to avoid sin. And if he is not prepared to take such steps, can it be said that he is fruitfully receiving the sacrament? Hence, even ordinary confession should involve *some spiritual direction*. It is very unfortunate that many busy priests have come to forget or to neglect this obligation; but perhaps in some cases it is morally impossible to fulfill.

However, this kind of "direction" which is inseparable from the sacrament of penance is not really what we mean by spiritual direction in the present study. It does not go deep enough, and it does not aim at the orientation of one's whole life, with a special ascetic vocation or apostolic mission in view.

One might suppose that because the layman is not in a "state of perfection" he does not need this kind of direction. But certainly, wherever a layman has a special work to do for the Church, or is in a situation with peculiar problems, he certainly ought to have a director. For instance, workers in Catholic action, college students, professional men, or couples preparing for matrimony need some spiritual direction.

So much for the layman. For the religious, direction is a much more serious matter. It would seem that spiritual direction is morally necessary for a religious. Anyone who freely adopts certain professional means for attaining to union with God naturally needs to receive a special formation. He or she needs to be taught the meaning of his vocation, its spirit, its aims and its characteristic problems.

This means something much deeper than a mere exterior formation — learning how to keep the rules, how to carry out the various rites and observances of community life. From the moment one enters into a strictly institutionalized life, in which everything is regulated down to the minutest detail, intimate personal direction becomes a morally necessary *safeguard against deformation*. It is false to imagine that mere external observance of the rules of a religious community is sufficient to educate the novice interiorly and give him the proper spiritual orientation demanded by his new state. Unless, in personal direction, the rules and observances are explained, unless they are applied to the actual circumstances of the life of the individual, they will infallibly produce a spirit of uncomprehending and lifeless routine. Without a really interior and sensitive direction during the crucial period of formation, a young religious is likely to be placed in a very delicate situation, and, indeed, his whole life may be turned into a meaningless pantomime of perfection. Happiness in the religious life really depends on wise direction, especially during the period of formation. Of course, a religious can be "saved" without a good director. That is not the point. The question is, can he lead a fruitful, happy, intelligent spiritual life? Without at least some direction, this is hardly possible. But of course, the direction of a priest, of a theologian, or a specialist is not necessarily indicated here. Where sisters are concerned, a wise prioress or a good novice mistress should be capable of some direction in this sense.

Even after the period of formation the professed religious needs direction. In some cases the more serious problems are not met with until after one has made profession. It is then that direction is most of all necessary, in certain circumstances. It is very important for all newly professed religious to enjoy, if possible, a guidance that is fairly continuous, though not necessarily frequent. What is most to be desired is the intimate direction of someone who knows and understands them, in an atmosphere of informality and trust which perhaps may not be easy to achieve with the superior. Those who have years of experience in the religious life are presumably able to direct themselves — but even they sometimes need to consult a wise spiritual guide. No religious should assume that he has absolutely no need, at any time, of spiritual direction.

It will be noticed that we by no means assume the same need for spiritual direction in all religious. The young need it more than the old, but in fact everything depends on the individual case. In general, however, we might profitably reiterate the statement that a mature religious should normally be able to direct himself. Certainly anyone with a position of responsibility or with a difficult assignment finds that he has to make many decisions for which he alone is accountable in the presence of God. He may even have to solve problems which it is impossible to refer to the judgment of any other human being. This places him in a truly dreadful solitude. Some religious and priests are filled with terror at the very thought of such decisions. And yet that is an error. We should not flee from responsibility, and we should not make such a fetish out of spiritual direction that, even though we are mature and responsible clerics, we refuse to move an inch without being "put under obedience"—in other words without someone else assuming responsibility for us. Needless to say, the concept that we are to "obey" a director in all things is another error, as will be explained later on. The normal religious ought to develop the virtue of prudence, in line with his religious formation, and guide himself when he cannot or need not seek guidance from another. This implies trust in God and a sincere abandonment to the Holy Spirit, from whom we can at any time rely on the light of divine Counsel, provided that we are conscientious religious and try to be men of prayer.

It is not necessary to add that through the course of the ages spiritual direction has become a special function, separate from that of the superior and even from that of the confessor. In early organized monasticism the abbot was at the same time not only the canonical superior of all the monks, but at the same time their spiritual director and confessor. Today the superior is forbidden to hear the confession of his subjects except in certain rare cases. He can, however, be their spiritual director. Very often spiritual direction is separated from confession, and "direction" is given by a specially qualified priest, perhaps on rare occasions. Today most people are lucky if they can find someone who can "give them direction" when they are burdened by accumulated problems. The ideal would be for everyone to have a father to whom he or she could go for regular direction. Superiors will always be ready to grant permission for conscience letters to be sent to a qualified director. The code guarantees access to any confessor with faculties.

However, spiritual directors are not easy to find, even in the religious life. Even where there are several priests at hand, this does not mean that they are all suitable as "directors." The scarcity of really good spiritual directors for religious may perhaps account for the magnitude of the problems in certain communities. Sometimes religious do not receive a really adequate formation, and they are nevertheless professed with unfortunate consequences. After profession, the effects of a good novitiate may vanish into thin air, through lack of a director to continue the work that was well begun. No doubt many losses of vocation could have been prevented by a really solid and firm spiritual direction in the first years after the novitiate.

Those who are firmly grounded and who can share their knowledge and their strength with others receive in this process lights which are of inestimable value for their own religious lives. Nevertheless, even for a superior, a timely conference with a good director may resolve many apparently hopeless problems and open one's eyes to unsuspected dangers, thereby preventing a disaster.

At all times, spiritual direction is of the greatest value to a religious. Even though it may not be strictly necessary, it is always useful. In many cases the absence of direction may mean the difference between sanctity and mediocrity in the religious life. Naturally, one who has sought direction and not found it will not be held responsible for its lack, and God Himself will make up to the soul what is wanting to it in His own way.

We have said above that good directors are rare. This, in fact, is a rather important matter. If we really desire spiritual directors for our communities and for others, let us seek them. We can at least pray for this intention! In the last ten years there has been an amazing growth in the publishing of spiritual books and in the study of the spiritual life. This growth has come at a time when it was needed and desired by the faithful. If it is realized that there is not only a need for spiritual direction, but also a very real hunger for it on the part of religious, directors will soon begin to be more numerous, for God will send them. He will raise up priests who will desire to give themselves to this kind of work, in spite of the difficulties and sacrifices involved. But there is always a danger that the priest qualified to seriously direct religious will be overwhelmed by the demand for his services. His first duty, **if he wants to be an effective director, is to see to his own interior life and take time for** prayer and meditation, since he will never be able to give to others what he does not possess himself.

3. *How to Profit by Direction*

Setting aside this urgent problem, let us suppose that one has found a director. How can he make the best use of this grace? In the first place, those who have regular spiritual direction ought to realize that this is a gift of God, and even though they may not be thoroughly satisfied, they should humbly appreciate the fact that they have direction at all. This will enable them to take advantage of what they have, and they may perhaps see that supernaturally they are much better off than they realized. Gratitude will make them more attentive to the direction they receive and will attune their faith to possibilities which they had overlooked. Even if their director is not another St. Benedict or St. John of the

Cross, they may come to realize that he is nevertheless speaking to them in the name of Christ and acting as His instrument in their lives.

What are we normally entitled to expect from spiritual direction ? It is certainly very helpful, but we must not imagine that it works wonders. Some people, and especially some religious who ought to know better, seem to think that they ought to be able to find a spiritual director who with one word can make all their problems vanish. They are not looking for a director but for a miracle-worker. In point of fact, we very often depend on someone else to solve problems that we ought to be able to solve, not so much by our own wisdom as by our generosity in facing the facts and obligations that represent for us the will of God. Nevertheless, human nature is weak, and the kindly support and wise advice of one whom we trust often enables us to *accept* more perfectly what we already know and see in an obscure way. A director may not tell us anything we do not already know, but it is a great thing if he helps us to overcome our hesitations and strengthens our generosity in the Lord's service. However, in many cases, a director will reveal to us things which we have hitherto been unable to see, though they were staring us in the face. This, too, is certainly a great grace, for which we should be thankful.

One thing a good director will not do is make our ill-defined, unconscious velleities for perfection come true with a wave of the hand. He will not enable us to attain the things we "wish" for, because the spiritual life is not a matter of "wishing" for perfection. Too often people think that all they need to turn a "wish" into the "will of God" is to have it confirmed by a director. Unfortunately, this kind of alchemy does not work, and one who seeks to practice it is in for disappointment.

It often happens, as a matter of fact, that so called "pious souls" take their "spiritual life" with a wrong kind of seriousness. We should certainly be serious in our search for God — nothing is more serious than that. But we ought not to be constantly observing our own efforts at progress and paying exaggerated attention to "our spiritual life." Some who lament the fact that they cannot find a director actually have all the opportunities for direction they really need, but they are not pleased with the available director because he does not flatter their self-esteem or cater to their illusions about themselves. In other words, they want a director who will confirm their hope of finding pleasure in themselves and in their virtues, rather than one who will strip them of their self-love and show them how to get free from preoccupation with themselves and their own petty concerns, to give themselves to God and to the Church.

This does not mean that all that passes for spiritual direction is really adequate. On the contrary, very often the "direction" given after confession is nothing more than a short, impersonal homily delivered to each penitent individually. It may be doctrinally correct, and perfectly good as a sermon. But direction is, by its very nature, something *personal*. It is quite obvious that a sister who knows she is receiving exactly the same vague, general exhortation as the twenty who went before her to confession hardly feels that she is receiving spiritual direction. Of course she is not.

Even then, she should try to make the best of it. If she is humble enough to accept at least this, she will find that the Lord has His message for her in it all. And the message will be personal.

On the other hand, a priest who might be glad to give direction pertinent to the individual case is sometimes unable to do so because the penitent has not made a sufficiently clear manifestation of conscience.

4. *Manifestation of Conscience and Direction*

The manifestation of conscience, which is *absolutely necessary* for spiritual direction, is something apart from sacramental confession of sins. In actual fact, sometimes our real problems are not very closely connected with the sinful acts which we submit to the power of the keys. Or if they are connected, the mere confession of the sins does nothing to make the connection apparent.

Actually, sin usually presents itself to the confessor as something rather impersonal — genus and species are the same in everyone. In consequence, the best he can do is to respond with advice that is more or less general and universal. It may be good advice in itself and perfectly in accordance with moral theology, and yet not get anywhere near the real root of the concrete, personal problem in the soul of the penitent.

Those who have never stopped to make a distinction between confession and direction may, when the time comes to have a director, fail to take advantage of the situation because they do not know how to make a manifestation of conscience. This is perhaps because they have a vaguely professional and technical idea of spiritual direction — the sort of thing we have outlined and perhaps caricatured in the first chapter. Direction for them is a strange, efficient, magical system. One comes to the director with complex ascetic problems and he resolves them with appropriate technical solutions. Hence the temptation to falsify the whole thing from the very start by coming in with an "interesting problem" or a "new case" — just to show how important and how different we are. This can sometimes happen. But usually we are so unimaginative that we simply cannot work up this kind of material, and we become discouraged. Naturally this is all very foolish.

If we are to take advantage of spiritual direction we must, on the one hand, avoid inertia and passivity —

simply saying nothing and waiting for the "magic" director to read our minds and apply spiritual balm — and, on the other, we must not falsify and dramatize the situation by the creation of fictitious "problems."

What we need to do is bring the director into contact with our real self, as best we can, and not fear to let him see what is false in our false self. Now this right away implies a relaxed, humble attitude in which we *let go* of ourselves and renounce our unconscious efforts to maintain a façade. We must let the director know that we really think, what we really feel, and what we really desire, even when these things are not altogether honorable. We must be quite frank about our motives insofar as we can be so. The mere effort to admit that we are not as unselfish or as zealous as we pretend to be is a great source of grace. Hence, we should approach direction in a spirit of humility and compunction, ready to manifest things of which we are not proud! This means that we must abandon all pugnacity about ourselves and get rid of our instinct for self-defence and self-justification, which is, in itself, the greatest obstacle to grace in our relations with a director.

The manifestation of conscience supposed by ordinary spiritual direction implies an atmosphere of unhurried leisure, a friendly, sincere and informal conversation, on a basis of personal intimacy.

The director is one who knows and sympathizes, who makes allowances, who understands circumstances, who is not in a hurry, who is patiently and humbly waiting for indications of God's action in the soul. He is concerned not just with this or that urgent problem, this or that sin, but with the whole life of the soul. He is not interested merely in our actions. He is much more interested in the basic attitudes of our soul, our inmost aspirations, our way of meeting difficulties, our mode of responding to good and evil. In a word, the director is interested in our very self, in all its uniqueness, its pitiable misery and its breathtaking greatness. A true director can never get over the awe he feels in the presence of a person, an immortal soul, loved by Christ, washed in His most Precious Blood, and nourished by the sacrament of His Love. It is, in fact, this respect for the mystery of personality that makes a real director : this, together with common sense, the gift of prayer, patience, experience, and sympathy.

Of course, as St. Theresa points out, he ought to be a theologian. But no amount of theological study can give a man spiritual discernment if he lacks the sense of respect for souls in their uniqueness, which is a gift of humility and love.

Manifestation of conscience in the deep sense of the word is often very difficult. It may be even more difficult than the confession of sins. One feels an inexpressible shame and embarrassment in laying open the inmost depths of his soul, even when there is nothing there to be ashamed of.

As a matter of fact, it is often harder to manifest the good that is in us than the evil. But that is precisely the thing about direction. We have to be able to lay bare the secret aspirations which we cherish in our hearts because they are the dear refuge to which we can escape from reality. We must be able to lay them bare, knowing well enough that even in manifesting them we run the risk of seeing them in a different light — in which they lose their mystery and their magic. The director has to know what we really want, for only then will he know what we really are.

The trouble is that very often we ourselves do not know what we "really want." And this brings us to an important but very delicate subject: the attitude of religious and of Christians in general toward *the will of God*.

Too often a legalistic concept of the will of God leads to a hypocritical falsification of the interior life. Do we not often unconsciously take it for granted that God is a harsh lawgiver, without interest in the thoughts and desires of our own hearts, seeking only to impose upon us the arbitrary dictates of His own inscrutable, predetermined plans? And yet, as St. Paul has said, we are called to *collaborate* with God. "We are God's coadjutors" (1 Cor. 3:9). As sons of God, we are called to use our freedom *to help God create His likeness in our own souls*. And of course, we help Him also to build His kingdom in the world. In this work of collaboration we are not mere passive and mechanical instruments. Our freedom, our love, our spontaneous contribution to God's work is itself the choicest and most precious effect of His grace. To frustrate this active participation in the work of God is *to frustrate what is most dear to His will.*

This means concretely that in spiritual direction it will be very important to discover what holy and spiritual desires in the soul of the penitent really represent a possibility of *a special, spontaneous and personal gift which he alone can make to God.* If there is some gift which he alone can give, then almost certainly God asks that gift from him, and a holy, humble, and sincere desire may be one of the signs that God asks it!

But this is where a certain unconscious hypocrisy comes in. We are afraid to make this spontaneous gift, afraid of spontaneity itself because we have been so warped by the idea that everything spontaneous is "merely natural" and that for a work to be supernatural it has to go against the grain, it has to frustrate and disgust us. The truth is, of course, quite different. It is necessary for us to frustrate and overcome our sensual, selfish and exterior self, the compulsive and automatic self that is really incapable of true love. But when we do this we set free our interior, simple self, our godlike self, the image of God, "Christ in us," and we become able to love God with spiritual liberty and make Him, in all simplicity, the gift that He asks of us.

But when we fear spontaneity, we tend to mask our desires and to present them by denying them as it were. We feel that the director will automatically reject anything that we really desire. We believe that both God and the director are predisposed, in advance, against everything spontaneous. Hence, rather than simply manifest what we really feel, or really desire, we say something else that we imagine we are expected to feel, expected to desire, and we give the impression that we do not desire what we secretly desire. This, for all our good intentions, is plain hypocrisy. The consequences are really quite dangerous, because if this is our concept of the interior life, then we are saying, in effect, that God wills a façade. And we concentrate on building this façade in our own life and perhaps even in the lives of others. The result is the falsification of the whole religious life of our community.

No, we must be perfectly open and simple, without prejudices and without artificial theories about ourselves. We must learn to speak according to our own inner truth, as far as we can perceive it. We must learn to say what we really mean in the depths of our souls, not what we think we are expected to say, not what somebody else has just said. And we must be prepared to take responsibility for our desires, and accept the consequences. This is neither hard nor unnatural, since every man coming into the world is born with this simplicity. It is the simplicity of the child, which we all unfortunately lose before we have a chance to make good use of it.

Incidentally, this childlike simplicity has nothing to do with the artificially cultivated effrontery of the average teen-ager today. Cynicism is not a deep conviction with him (he has no deep convictions). It is only a pose which he adopts because he is insecure and is afraid to lose the approval of his group.

True simplicity implies love and trust — it does not expect to be derided and rejected, any more than it expects to be admired and praised. It simply hopes to be accepted on its own terms. This is the kind of atmosphere which a good director tries to produce : an atmosphere of confidence and friendliness in which the penitent can say anything that is on his mind with the assurance that it will be dealt with *frankly and honestly*. If in trying to be sincere the penitent simply poses, then he must be prepared to take the consequences. But anything he says that is genuine, that really comes from his heart, will be understood and accepted by a wise director. Such real, genuine aspirations of the heart are sometimes very important indications of the will of God for that soul — and sometimes they must be sacrificed.

This gives us a clue to what the director is really seeking to find out from us. He does not merely want to know our problems, our difficulties, our secrets. And that is why one should not think that a direction session that does not tackle a problem has not been a success. The director wants to know our inmost self, our *real* self. He wants to know us not as we are in the eyes of men, or even as we are in our own eyes, but as we are in the eyes of God. He wants to know the inmost truth of our vocation, the action of grace in our souls. His direction is, in reality, nothing more than a way of leading us to see and obey our real Director — the Holy Spirit, hidden in the depths of our soul. We must never forget that in reality we are not directed and taught by men, and that if we need human "direction" it is only because we cannot, without man's help, come into contact with that "unction (of the Spirit) which teaches us all things" (1 John 2:20).

In manifesting our inmost aspirations and trials, we should strive above all to be perfectly frank and clear. Direction will school us in being true to ourselves and true to the grace of God. *The discipline of sincerity and simplicity which a good director will discreetly impose, perhaps by indirect means, is one of the most vitally necessary things in the interior life of religious today.*

Sometimes it seems that the so called "interior life" is little more than a web of illusion, spun out of jargon and pious phrases which we have lifted from books and sermons and with which we conceal, rather than reveal, what is in us. How often the director, listening to seemingly admirable religious souls, is saddened and chilled by the sense that a smug, unconscious complacency, armed with the cliches of pious authors, stands before him fully prepared to resist every advance of humility and truth. His heart is contracted by a kind of hopelessness, a feeling that there is no way of breaking through and setting free the real person who remains buried and imprisoned under the false front that has been acquired, unfortunately, as a result of religious malformation.

Perhaps unwise direction is itself to blame for this spiritual "warping" of the person. Such souls are really unable to manifest what is in them, because they have blinded themselves completely to what is there and put something else in its place. Yet they are in perfect good faith, and in a sense they have a kind of peace, based on the rigid structure of artificiality which they have erected precisely as a bulwark against anxiety. Perhaps sometimes a little anxiety can be a good thing!

In any case, the director must be on his guard against the unconscious spiritual vanity which makes virtuous souls seek to shine, in a subtle way, in his eyes and capture his approval. Where there is good, he should certainly approve and encourage it, in all simplicity. Artificial humiliations are not necessary to keep the soul humble. But the simplicity of the director and perhaps a gentle sense of humor will be alert to detect anything that savors of a pious "act" on the part of the penitent. Nothing does so much harm in direction as the acceptance by the director of an unconscious pretense of perfection in place of the real thing.

There is perhaps no more difficult and delicate task for the director than the guidance of Christians called to a life of interior prayer. This is rendered all the more arduous by the fact that there is so much pious nonsense written, printed, and said, about "mystics," "victim souls" and other such categories. Direction is very important in the life of prayer, but at the present time the situation is such that a director who is not very simple and very wholesome can do great harm to someone who might be quite close to God in prayer. The whole trouble comes from the inordinate reflection upon self that is generated by the consciousness of "degrees of prayer" and steps on the ascent of the "mountain of love." Actually, when a person begins to take his prayer life overseriously and thinks of it as something requiring especially earnest direction, he tends to undermine it by reflection. He starts looking at himself, judging his reactions, and worse still, deciding whether or not to make them known to the director. This of course is fatal to genuine prayer, and even in the long run leads to the ruin of perfectly good contemplative vocations. It would seem that most of the pseudo-technical questions that seem to require consideration in direction are completely useless and should be forgotten. What possible good can be done for a monk by deciding whether or not his contemplation is "infused"? Even those who are still interested in the defunct argument, acquired vs. infused contemplation, agree that in practice it makes little difference in the direction of a person whose prayer is simple and contemplative in a general way. A contemplative is not one who takes his prayer seriously, but one who takes God seriously, who is famished for truth, who seeks to live in generous simplicity, in the spirit. An ardent and sincere humility is the best protection for his life of prayer. A director who can encourage simplicity and faith will find many genuine, simple contemplatives responding to his guidance, with little or no nonsense about ligature, prayer of quiet, prayer of full union and so on. The trouble is not that such things are unimportant or unreal, but rather that the verbiage that tends to surround them actually gets between the contemplative and reality, between the soul and God. The most dangerous thing about this kind of reflexive self-consciousness in prayer is that the soul turns into an opaque mirror in which the contemplative looks no longer at God but at himself. Such technical folly, together with the worse folly of visions and locutions that are taken seriously without sufficient reason, ends by the sanctuary of the spirit becoming a kind of abomination of desolation in which the voice of God cannot be heard because on all sides the walls re-echo with clichés from "spiritual authors."

An artificial gruffness and the use of deliberate humiliations will do nothing to remedy this state of affairs, if the director himself, even secretly, adopts the same false standard of values and declares implicitly, by the very way in which he "humbles" his penitent, that these are great graces capable of turning anyone's head. This is just another way of making the same mistake. Neither the director nor the one directed should become obsessed with the problem of gifts and graces, but should concern themselves with God the Giver, not with His gifts. The important thing is the will of God and His love. The more objective one can be about this, the better. Graces and gifts are never going to turn the head of anyone who keeps his attention fixed on God, instead of on himself, and the more truly contemplative a state of prayer is, the more will it be obscure and transparent and unaware of itself.

What has been said about graces of prayer applies in equal measure to trials and passive purifications. The important thing is to quietly reassure the soul that seems to be anxious and upset, to create a proper understanding of spiritual trials without overdramatizing the "night" of the soul. In reality, there is just as much danger of self-contemplation in trials as in consolations, provided that the trials themselves are not really severe. A lot of darkness in prayer that glorifies itself as "passive purification" is perhaps in large measure a matter of boredom due to confusion and fixation upon the subjective and accessory aspects of the spiritual life. Let the soul get back into full contact with reality and the dryness will probably clear up to a great extent. Unfortunately, the routine and spirituality encouraged in certain contemplative communities tend to invite frustration and to glorify every form of infantile moodiness as a spiritual night. The victims of this kind of system are encouraged in masochism and self-pity on the ground that this has something to do with "contemplation." Actually, this is an evasion of grace and a pure pretense of spirituality. In the long run, it leads to various forms of escape, for example useless and futile activities, unnecessary work projects, etc., which are dreamed up more or less deliberately to break the spell of obsession with self. But they do not accomplish their effect, producing only a different kind of anxiety and a new frustration. What is really required is a normal, realistic and completely simple grasp of what the contemplative life is, in all its simplicity, with its humble, spontaneous activities, its genuine, if rustic, satisfactions, and the legitimate diversion that can come from a variety of reading and a broadening of healthy human interests, not at all incompatible with a life of prayer.

It is certainly not necessary to break up an unhealthy fixation on experiences in prayer by going to the other extreme and launching the bewildered subject into a round of parties and secular diversions, as too many directors might be prone to do. We must be careful to seek a happy and balanced medium. This consists neither in the extreme of self-conscious asceticism or the opposite extreme of self-abandoned sociability and conviviality, but rather in the recovery of a simple and wholesome ordinary life, lived at a moderate and humanly agreeable tempo, with a few very humble satisfactions and joys of a more or less primitive character. Manual labor (especially outdoor work) plays a very important part in this readjustment, not purely as a penance but also as a way of relaxing and refreshing the mind.

In summary, one of the most important benefits a director can bring to the prayer life of his contemplative penitents is to help them reintegrate their whole existence, as far as possible, on a simple, natural and ordinary level on which they can be fully *human*. Then grace can work on them and make them fully sons of God.

5. *Special Problems*

Once we have opened the depths of our soul to him, the director penetrates our motives and sees, though "through a glass darkly," to what extent they correspond to the truth and grace of God. The value of a director lies in the clarity and simplicity of his discernment, in sound judgment, rather than in the exhortation he gives. For if his exhortation is based on a wrong judgment, then it is of little value. In fact it may do harm. This faculty of supernatural discernment is a grace; in fact, it is a charismatic gift, a grace of a high order, given especially by God for the sake of souls. And such charismata are by no means as rare as one might imagine. The Holy Spirit still works powerfully in His Church, though His power is more hidden than it was in the first centuries! Have we any reason to doubt it?

Sometimes the light of truth given to the director pierces, in spite of us, through our unconscious armor. He may say something that troubles us deeply. We may rebel at first. We may imagine that he has made a serious error and does not understand us. We argue that everything he says ought to bring us peace — and this new statement of his brings profound disturbance! We may be tempted to reject his decision and disregard his advice, even to leave him altogether.

At such a time we must be on our guard. We may be resisting the light of God. We may be refusing to accept a grace which will transform our whole lives. We may be hesitating and turning back on the threshold of one of those "conversions" which lead to a whole new level of spirituality and to deeper intimacy with Christ. Let us be very careful when we are angry with our director. Let us see if we cannot accept what he has said, no matter how wrong it may seem. Let us at least try to go along with him and see what comes of it.

A little good will, a little faith and a humble prayer to God may enable us to do what seemed to be impossible, and we may be surprised to find that an almost miraculous change has suddenly come over our life. Even when the director himself was clumsy or high-handed, God may reward our humility and good will with great graces.

Of course, as we have indicated above, it is quite possible that we have a director who does not understand us. There is no such thing as a perfect director, and even the most enlightened and sensitive spiritual guide can fail to respond to the delicate resonances which reveal the true inner secret of one's character. There are people who simply do not "click." The situation may be serious enough for a change of director to be indicated. For instance, if a director simply refuses to listen to our sincere views and rejects all serious discussion of them, it may be a reason to change. However, do not be too hasty. Give the matter time and thought. Have you really sufficient reason for changing? Supposing he does not understand you thoroughly: supposing there is a kind of wall between you: can you say that even then he has not revealed to you many important things that no one else has yet told you? If that is the case, then God is using him as an instrument, and you should stay with your director, unless it is quite clear that another and more understanding director is available. In any case, a change of director should be made only with prudent consideration, and if possible after consultation with a wise friend, a competent superior, or an alternate confessor — for example at the time of annual retreat or of extraordinary confessions.

What is the value of direction by mail? It should not be overestimated. An occasional letter from some spiritual guide who knows you well, and is a good theologian or a deeply spiritual person — this may be of some value. But direction by mail is seriously handicapped by one important thing : the lack of direct personal contact. In oral spiritual direction, much is communicated without words, even in spite of words. The direct person-to-person relationship is something that cannot be adequately replaced. Christ Himself said, "Where two or three are gathered together in My Name, there am I in the midst of them." There is a special spiritual presence of Christ in direct personal conversation, which guarantees a deeper and more intimate expression of the whole truth.

Of course, letters from a really good director are perhaps better than direct contact with a bad one. But most good directors have very little time to write long letters. They have too many other things to do.

One must not imagine that one owes strict obedience to the spiritual director. A director is not a superior. Our relation to him is not that of a subject to a divinely constituted juridical authority. It is rather the relation of a friend to an advisor. Hence, the virtue to be exercised in direction is docility rather than obedience, and docility is a matter of prudence. Obedience is a matter of justice. To ignore the guidance of a director may be imprudent, but it is not a sin against justice or against the vow of obedience.

We might add that theologians today discourage any such thing as a private vow of obedience to the director. However, in the case of people with scruples, they must follow to the letter the instructions given by the director and not quibble over words; it will be, in practice, a kind of obedience. But in this case the scrupulous person is incapable of practicing prudence, and consequently he must obey the director. He is in the position of a child who has to obey his parents since he cannot yet trust his own prudence.

One final point. The director is not a psychoanalyst. He should stick to his divinely given mission, and avoid two great mistakes. First, he should not become an amateur in psychotherapy. He should not try to concern himself directly with unconscious drives and emotional problems. He should know enough about them to recognize their presence. He should have a deep respect for man's unconscious, instinctual nature. He should not make the mistake of giving a direction that reinforces unconscious and infantile authoritarian trends. At the same time he should not be too easy and too soothing, giving approval to every whim, no matter how unreasonable.

Secondly, he should realize that psychological problems are very real and that when they exist they are beyond the range of his competency. He should not be one of those who derides psychiatry on principle and pretends that all emotional problems can be solved by ascetic means. He should know when to refer someone to a psychiatrist for proper treatment. He should not try to "cure" a neurotic by bluffing him, or jollying him along, still less by jumping on him!

We have taken a brief glance at some of the advantages of spiritual direction and at some of its problems. Inevitably, such a treatment as this lacks perspective. It gives the impression that there is always a great deal going on between the director and the one being directed. It creates the idea that the director has to be always on his toes to avoid being deceived — as if every direction session turned into a battle between light and darkness.

This is by no means the case. Once the director and his penitent get to know each other, the direction generally goes on peacefully and uneventfully from month to month and from year to year. Great problems seldom arise. Difficulties are few. When they come up, they are handled simply and peacefully, without much fuss. There may be rare moments of difficulty and stress, but they pass by. One is tempted to think that all this is too tame, too quiet, too safe. It almost looks as if direction were a waste of time, as if it amounted to nothing more than a friendly chat about the trivial events of the season.

However, if we are wise, we will realize that this is precisely the greatest value of direction. The life that is peaceful, almost commonplace in its simplicity, might perhaps be quite a different thing without these occasional friendly talks that bring tranquility and keep things going on their smooth course. How many vocations would be more secure if all religious could navigate in such calm, safe waters as these!

WHAT IS MEDITATION?

To meditate is to exercise the mind in serious reflection. This is the broadest possible sense of the word "meditation." The term in this sense is not confined to religious reflections, but it implies serious mental activity and a certain absorption or concentration which does not permit our faculties to wander off at random or to remain slack and undirected.

From the very start it must be made clear, however, that reflection here does not refer to a purely intellectual activity, and still less does it refer to mere reasoning. Reflection involves not only the mind but also the heart, and indeed our whole being. One who really meditates does not merely think, he also loves, and by his love — or at least by his sympathetic intuition into the reality upon which he reflects — he enters into that reality and knows it so to speak from within, by a kind of identification.

St. Thomas and St. Bernard of Clairvaux describe meditation (*consideratio*) as "the quest for truth." Nevertheless their "meditation" is something quite distinct from study, which is also a "quest for truth."

Meditation and study can, of course, be closely related. In fact, study is not spiritually fruitful unless it leads to some kind of meditation. By study we seek the truth in books or in some other source outside our own minds. In meditation we strive to absorb what we have already taken in. We consider the principles we have learned and we apply them to our own lives. Instead of simply storing up facts and ideas in our memory, we strive to do some original thinking of our own.

In study we can be content with an idea or a concept that is true. We can be content to know *about* truth. Meditation is for those who are not satisfied with a merely objective and conceptual knowledge *about* life, *about* God — *about* ultimate realities. They want to enter into an intimate contact with truth itself, with God. They want to experience the deepest realities of life by *living* them. Meditation is the means to that end.

And so, although the definition of meditation as a quest for truth (*inquisitio veritatis*) brings out the fact that meditation is above all a function of the intelligence, nevertheless it implies something more. St. Thomas and St. Bernard were speaking of a kind of meditation which is fundamentally religious, or at least philosophical, and which aims at bringing our whole being into communication with an ultimate reality beyond and above ourselves. This unitive and loving knowledge begins in meditation but it reaches its full development only in contemplative prayer.

This idea is very important. Strictly speaking, even religious meditation is primarily a matter of thought. But it does not end in thought. Meditative thought is simply the beginning of a process which leads to interior prayer and is normally supposed to culminate in contemplation and in affective communion with God. We can call this whole process (in which meditation leads to contemplation) by the name *mental prayer*. In actual practice, the word "meditation" is quite often used as if it meant exactly the same thing as "mental prayer." But if we look at the precise meaning of the word, we find that meditation is only a small part of the whole complex of interior activities which go to make up mental prayer. Meditation is the name given to the earlier part of the process, the part in which our heart and mind exercise themselves in a series of interior activities which prepare us for union with God.

When thought is without affective intention, when it begins and ends in the intelligence, it does not lead to prayer, to love or to communion. Therefore it does not fall into the proper pattern of mental prayer. Such thought is not really meditation. It is outside the sphere of religion and of prayer. It is therefore excluded from our consideration here. It has nothing to do with our subject. We need only remark that a person would be wasting his time if he thought reasoning alone could satisfy the need of his soul for spiritual meditation. Meditation is not merely a matter of "thinking things out," even if that leads to a good ethical resolution. Meditation is more than mere practical thinking.

The distinctive characteristic of religious meditation is that it is a search for truth which springs from love and which seeks to possess the truth not only by knowledge but also by love. It is, therefore, an intellectual activity which is inseparable from an intense consecration of spirit and application of the will. The presence of *love* in our meditation intensifies and clarifies our thought by giving it a deeply affective quality. Our meditation becomes charged with a loving appreciation of the *value* hidden in the supreme truth which the intelligence is seeking. This affective drive of the will, seeking the truth as the soul's highest good, raises the soul above the level of speculation and makes our quest for truth a prayer full of reverential love and adoration striving to pierce the dark cloud which stands between us and the throne of God. We beat against this cloud with supplication, we lament our poverty, our helplessness, we adore the mercy of God and His supreme perfections, we dedicate ourselves entirely to His worship.

Mental prayer is therefore something like a sky-rocket. Kindled by a spark of divine love, the soul streaks heavenward in an act of intelligence as clear and direct as the rocket's trail of fire. Grace has released all the deepest energies of our spirit and assists us to climb to new and unsuspected heights. Nevertheless, our own faculties soon reach their limit. The intelligence can climb no higher into the sky. There is a point where the mind bows down its fiery trajectory as if to acknowledge its limitations and proclaim the infinite supremacy of the unattainable God.

But it is here that our "meditation" reaches its climax. Love again takes the initiative and the rocket "explodes" in a burst of sacrificial praise. Thus love flings out a hundred burning stars, acts of all kinds, expressing everything that is best in man's spirit, and the soul spends itself in drifting fires that glorify the Name of God while they fall earthward and die away in the night wind!

That is why St. Albert the Great, the master who gave St. Thomas Aquinas his theological formation at Paris and Cologne, contrasts the contemplation of the philosopher and the contemplation of the saints:

The contemplation of philosophers seeks nothing but the perfection of the one contemplating and it goes no further than the intellect. But the contemplation of the saints is fired by the love of the one contemplated: that is, God. Therefore it does not terminate in an act of the intelligence but passes over into the will by love.

St. Thomas Aquinas, his disciple, remarks tersely that for this very reason the contemplative's knowledge of God is arrived at, on this earth, by the light of burning love: *per ardorem caritatis datur cognitio veritatis.* (Commentary on St. John's Gospel, Chapter 5.)

The contemplation of "philosophers," which is merely intellectual speculation on the divine nature as it is reflected in creatures, would be therefore like a sky-rocket that soared into the sky but never went off. The beauty of the rocket is in its "death," and the beauty of mental prayer and of mystical contemplation is in the soul's abandonment and total surrender of itself in an outburst of praise in which it spends itself entirely to bear witness to the transcendent goodness of the infinite God. The rest is silence.

Let us never forget that the fruitful silence in which words lose their power and concepts escape our grasp is perhaps the perfection of meditation. We need not fear and become restless when we are no longer able to "make acts." Rather we should rejoice and rest in the luminous darkness of faith. This "resting" is a higher way of prayer.

MEDITATION IN SCRIPTURE

We read in Genesis that Isaac went out into the field in the evening to meditate (Gen. 24:63). What was he meditating about? The patriarchs were men very close to God, men to whom He spoke familiarly. He was always close at hand in the lives of Noe, Abraham, Isaac, Jacob. When the Jews invoked the God of Abraham, Isaac and Jacob, they invoked Him whom their fathers *knew*, Him who had promised salvation to them through their fathers. Although man was expelled from paradise, a few chosen persons still enjoyed something of the intimacy with God which had belonged to the old days when Adam and Eve heard His voice as He walked in the Garden of Eden in the early evening.

One reason why the Law was given to Moses on Sinai was that the Chosen People were afraid to speak directly with God or have Him speak to them.

And all the people saw the voices and the flames, and the sound of the trumpet, and the mount smoking: and being terrified and struck with fear, they stood afar off, saying to Moses: Speak thou to us, and we will hear; let not the Lord speak to us, lest we die! (Exodus 20:18–19).

Meditation on the Law of the Lord was now a valid substitute for the intimate familiarity with God which had been the joy and light of the patriarchs. How could this be so if meditation on the Law did not lead to a union of minds and wills with God, if meditation did not bear fruit in a holy and supernatural conversation with God, sanctified by filial fear, and consecrated by reverence, obedience and self-sacrificing love? The reward of this meditation was the light of supernatural prudence, a wisdom which penetrated the meaning of the Law. This meditation on the Law meant that men not only externally fulfilled its prescriptions but understood their import, saw them in relation to God's purposes for man. This understanding brought man face to face with the power and mercy of God, reflected in His promises to the holy nation and in His designs for them. The fruit of understanding was indefectible moral strength, supernatural courage.

Take courage therefore, and be very valiant: that thou mayst observe and do all the law, which Moses my servant hath commanded thee: turn not from it to the right hand or to the left, that thou mayst understand all things which thou dost. Let not the book of his law depart from thy mouth: but thou shalt meditate on it day and night, that thou mayst observe and do all things that are written in it: then shalt thou direct thy way, and understand it (Josue 1:7, 8).

This meditation must accompany the reading and

recitation of the Law : its words make some sense when they are in our mouths, but they only make complete sense if they are at the same time fulfilled in our lives. Meditation on the Law means therefore not only thinking about the Law, studying the Law, but living it with a full, or relatively full, understanding of God's purpose in manifesting to us His will.

But what is this purpose ? We shall see that God's real intentions for man are contained not only in the Law of His justice but also and especially in the promise of His mercy. All God's love for us was already implicitly contained in His promises to Abraham. The "just man lives by faith" in those promises.

The psalms everywhere sing of this "meditation" on the Law of God. But above and beyond the Law, the psalmists are carried out of themselves by their experience of God's mercy, by their realization of His *fidelity to His promises: Misericordias Domini in aeternum cantabo*! The psalms meditate not only on the goodness and beauty of the Law of God, and on the happiness of a life set in order by that Law, but above all on a supreme and ecstatic happiness which is the pure gift of God's mercy to the poor, to the *Anawin* — to those who, because they have no human hope, greatness or support, are therefore shielded and loved with a special power and compassion on the part of God. Meditation on the psalms, inspired by love, is the key to the great mystery of the divine compassion.

Hence the psalmist often sees himself raised above the level at which one finds God only through the medium of an outward expression of His will. Often the psalms bring us close to God Himself, the merciful God, the God who has promised justice to the oppressed, mercy and salvation to His people. The meditation of which the psalms are constantly singing often rises to the level of a penetrating experience of God's everlasting mercies. Then the psalmist breaks out into praise; for this experience of God's mercy is above all an experience that He is the supreme and transcendent Reality, and that He, the Lord who is above all gods, loves those to whom He has manifested His love and their salvation.

The mercies of the Lord I will sing forever.
I will show forth thy truth from generation to generation.
For thou hast said: mercy shall be built up forever in the
    heavens:
thy truth shall be prepared in them (Ps. 88:1–3).

It is clear, then, that the way of meditation is the way to perfect happiness, because it leads to the knowledge of the living God, to an experience of who He really is!

Blessed is the man who hath not walked in the counsel of
    the ungodly, nor stood in the way of sinners, nor sat in
    the chair of pestilence.
But his will is in the law of the Lord, and on his law he
    shall meditate day and night.
And he shall be like a tree which is planted near the run-

ning waters, which shall bring forth its fruit in due season. And his leaf shall not fall off: and all whatsoever he shall do shall prosper.

Not so the wicked, not so: but like the dust, which the wind driveth from the face of the earth.

Therefore the wicked shall not rise again in judgment: nor sinners in the council of the just.

For the Lord knoweth the way of the just: and the way of the wicked shall perish (Ps. 1).

Monks meditate on the psalms when they sing them. But St. Benedict in his Rule provides for a time when this meditation on the psalms is carried on outside of choir. The meditation can have various degrees. For beginners it means simply learning them by heart. For those further advanced it means the intelligent penetration of their meaning.

However this penetration of the meaning of the psalms was not just a matter of studying them with the aid of a commentary. It was a question of "savoring" and "absorbing" the meaning of the psalms in the depths of one's own heart, repeating the words slowly, thoughtfully, prayerfully in the deepest center of one's being, so that the psalms gradually come to be as intimate and personal as one's own reflections and feelings. Thus the psalms "form" the mind and the heart of the monk according to the mind and heart of Christ. Even the perfect monk does not abandon his *meditatio psalmorum* as if it were a mere exercise for beginners.

Contemplatives keep these holy words, as did Mary,

pondering them in their hearts so that they re-live the deep experiences of the psalmist, and in so doing are touched by the finger of God, raised to contemplation, and penetrate deeply into the mystery of Christ, which overshadows the whole Old Testament like the luminous cloud on Thabor. Christ is everywhere in the psalms, the Law and the Prophets. To find Him in them is to experience their perfect fulfillment because we find Him who is the life and meaning of the psalms, living within ourselves.

Jesus gave His disciples the sacrifice and sacrament of the Eucharist. This tremendous gift, containing in itself all the wisdom of God in mystery, sums up in itself all the mighty works of God, and is the greatest of them all. In this sacrament we are intimately united to Him, and bless Him who has "visited His people." The mystery of God's merciful love is revealed in the pierced Heart of Christ, the *magnum pietatis sacramentum*.

Meditation on this mystery, is, in some sense, essential to the Eucharistic sacrifice since Jesus said, "Do this in memory of me." The Mass is a memorial of Christ's sacrifice, not in the sense of an exterior commemoration, but as a living and supremely efficacious re-presentation of that sacrifice, pouring out into our hearts the redemptive power of the Cross and the grace of the resurrection, which enables us to live in God. Our participation in the Eucharistic sacrifice and our entrance with burning hearts into the mystery of Christ assumes in our lives the place which belonged to "meditation of the Law" in the lives of the Old Testament saints.

Nevertheless, as the New Testament does not do away with the Old, neither do we cease to meditate on the Law of the Lord. But our meditation is now nourished by the *memoria Christi* — the consciousness, the awareness, the experience of Jesus hidden in the Old Testament which He has now fulfilled.

This is what meditation meant to St. Paul: the finding of ourselves in Christ, the penetration of the Scriptures by divinely enlightened love, the discovery of our divine adoption and the praise of His glory.

Let us meditate on the Scriptures, which, as St. Paul says, were all written to fill us with the knowledge of God's promises and the hope of their fulfillment. "For what things soever were written, were written for our learning: that through patience and the comfort of the scriptures, we might have hope" (Romans 15:4). Believing in what we meditate, we are sealed, transformed, consecrated: "Signed with the Holy Spirit of promise." And to what purpose?

That the God of our Lord Jesus Christ, the Father of glory, may give unto you the spirit of wisdom and of revelation, in the knowledge of him: the eyes of your heart enlightened, that you may know what the hope is of his calling, and what are the riches of the glory of his inheritance in the saints. And what is the exceeding greatness of his power towards us, who believe according to the operation of the might of his power . . ." (Ephesians 1:17–19).

MEDITATION — ACTION
AND UNION

All comparisons are defective in some respect. Our image of the sky-rocket might perhaps mislead imaginative minds. Meditation does not have to be colorful or spectacular. The effectiveness of our mental prayer is not to be judged by the interior fireworks that go off inside us when we pray. On the contrary, although sometimes the fruit of a good meditation may be an ardent sensible love springing from vivid insights into the truth, these so-called "consolations of prayer" are not to be trusted without reserve or sought for their own sake alone. We should be deeply grateful when our prayer really brings us an increase of clear understanding and felt generosity and we should by no means despise the stimulation of sensible devotion when it helps us to do whatever we have to do, with greater humility, fidelity and courage.

Nevertheless, since the fruit of mental prayer is harvested in the depths of the soul, in the will and in the intelligence, and not on the level of emotion and instinctive reactions, it is quite possible that a meditation that is apparently "cold," because it is without feelings, may be most profitable. It can give us great strength and spiritualize our interior life, lifting it above the level of the senses and teaching us to guide ourselves by reason and the principles of faith.

Sometimes a potentially good meditation can even be spoiled by emotion. The spiritual effect of grace may be frustrated, the will may remain inert while the germinating idea is sterilized by sentimentality.

This is one of the points at which ignorance makes progress in mental prayer difficult or even impossible. Those who think that their meditation must always culminate in a burst of emotion fall into one of two errors. Either they find that their emotions run dry and that their prayer seems to be "without fruit." Therefore they conclude that they are wasting their time and give up their efforts, in order to satisfy their craving for sensations in some other way.

Or else they belong to the category of those whose emotions are inexhaustible. They can almost always weep at prayer. They can quite easily produce sentiments of fervor, with a little concentration and the right kind of effort, whenever they desire them. But this is a dangerous form of success. Emotional versatility is a help at the beginning of the interior life, but later on it may be an obstacle to progress. At the beginning, when our senses are easily attracted to created pleasures, our emotions will keep us from turning to God unless they themselves can be given some enjoyment and awareness of the value of prayer. Thus the taste for spiritual things has to start out with a humble and earthly beginning, in the senses and in feeling. But if our prayer always ends in sensible pleasure and interior consolation we will run the risk of resting in these things which are by no means the end of the journey.

There is always a danger of illuminism and false mysticism when those who are easily swayed by fancy and emotion take too seriously the vivid impulses they experience in prayer, and imagine that the voice of their own exalted feeling is really the voice of God.

The proper atmosphere of meditation is one of tranquillity and peace and balance. The mind should be able to give itself to simple and peaceful reflection. Intellectual brilliance is never required. The will should find itself directed toward the good and strengthened in its desire for union with God. It does not have to feel itself enkindled with raptures of ardent love. A good meditation may well be quite "dry" and "cold" and "dark." It may even be considerably disturbed by involuntary distractions. St. John of the Cross says somewhere that "The best fruit grows in land that is cold and dry." But this arid meditation nevertheless fills the soul with humility, peace, courage, and the determination to persevere in negotiating the obstacles to our spiritual progress. Our meditations may be habitually quite prosaic and even a little dull. That does not matter, if they succeed in bringing the depths of our intelligence and will into a direct focus upon the things of God, no matter how obscure our spiritual vision may happen to be.

A good meditation does not necessarily give us an absolutely clear perception of the spiritual truth that we are seeking. On the contrary, as we progress in the interior life our grasp of divine things, in mental prayer, tends to become somewhat indefinite because our minds find themselves in the presence of mysteries too vast for human comprehension. It is necessarily impossible for the human mind on this earth to have a clear, comprehensive perception of the things of God as they really are in themselves. The contemplative "experience" of divine things is achieved in the darkness of "pure faith," in a certitude that does not waver, though it cannot grasp any clear human evidence for its support.

This cannot be understood unless we remember one absolutely fundamental truth : that the power of meditation is generated not by *reasoning* but by *faith*. It can be said, without fear of error, that our meditation is as good as our faith. Hence the aim we should keep in view, when we meditate, is not so much the penetration of divine truths with our intelligence, as the firm grasp of faith which enables us to embrace these truths with our entire being. This does not mean that intelligence is excluded from mental prayer, and replaced by a kind of pietistic obscurantism. For faith is after all an act of the intelligence, as well as of the will, elevated to a supernatural level by the light of divine grace. Everyone who meditates should realize the full import of St. Anselm's dictum: *credo ut intelligam*, "I believe in order that I may understand." Only firm faith can bring any real spiritual light to our life of prayer. In order to practice this faith, we need to concentrate upon certain sayings of Christ Our Lord in the Gospel, or other words of the divinely inspired Scriptures, and reaffirm our faith and our conviction that these are, in all truth, the words of salvation, the treasure hidden in the field, for which we must sell everything else, abandon every other truth, in order that we may come to God. We should let these "words of salvation" sink deeply into our hearts and take full possession of them. It is precisely when our prayer is dry that we can most fruitfully exercise our faith in this manner. And remember that faith can at times require much struggle and effort. Above all if it is honest. For we may have to face great difficulties and human uncertainties, and face them with sincere minds. Faith is a risk and a challenge, and it is most pure when we have to pay for it with effort and spiritual sacrifice. Such effort and sacrifice have their place in meditation.

If our mental vision of God and of the way to God tends to lose its sharp outlines in the "cloud of un-

knowing," there should never be any real confusion
as to the object we are seeking: union with God.
Mental prayer need not make us *see* the God we seek,
but it should always confirm us in our determination to
seek Him and no other. It may not always show us
clearly the way to find Him; but it should always leave
us more and more convinced that there is nothing else
worth finding. Therefore, although the object of our
prayer may be hidden in darkness, meditation nevertheless makes it ever more and more clear that this
object is the one goal of all our efforts. In this sense God
and the way to God become more and more perfectly
"defined" as we advance in mental prayer.

*   *   *

Writers on mental prayer often stress the fact that
meditation should bear fruit in particular virtues and
other immediate, practical results. And it is quite true
that meditation has a practical purpose since it must
enlighten our actions and make them all bear fruit in
communion with God.

Meditation can therefore be considered in relation to
two ends, one of which leads to the other. The immediate end of our mental prayer may be the understanding
of some particular truth, the resolution to embrace a
particular course of action, the solution of a spiritual
problem, all of which prepare us for the reception of a
very definite and particular grace necessary for the
practical fulfillment of our daily duties.

But the ultimate end of all mental prayer is communion with God. Of course it is quite true that meditation disposes us for an immediate practical end on earth, with a view to our future union with God in heaven. But what I mean to emphasize here is that every meditation, every act of mental prayer, even if it may have some immediate practical purpose, should also bring us into direct communion with God. This is the true fruit of meditation. Every other immediate practical purpose is secondary and subordinate to this one principle and all important end.

Let me take an example. Suppose that I meditate upon the patience of our Lord Jesus Christ in His Passion. Suppose that I do so with an immediate practical end: to help myself practice patience in a difficult situation which confronts me. My interior vision will be concentrated upon the Redeemer who, without anger or contempt, without rancor or perturbation, silently and with supreme interior tranquillity accepted the gravest injustice and ingratitude, not to mention the most painful of physical and moral suffering. I will see that He was able to undergo all this with a pure and disinterested mercy for all men, including those who put Him to death.

I will also realize that in doing so He was not merely leaving me an example to admire from a distance. By virtue of my baptismal vows I am *obliged* to follow that example and to reproduce in myself something of

His patience, meekness and tranquillity under suffering. Jesus Himself said, "He who does not take up his cross and come after me cannot be my disciple" (Luke 14:27).

Therefore, with all this before my mind, I will begin to desire with all the power of my will to practice this same patience according to my capacity in my own trials. Knowing at the same time the weakness and imperfection of my own soul fettered by attachments, I will above all pray earnestly and humbly for the grace without which I can never hope to conquer my impatience, irritability, aggressiveness and self-righteous impulses to judge and punish other men.

Such a meditation is directly ordered to an immediate practical end. It is aimed at the practice of patience. It seeks the grace that will make me strong enough to be meek. Meekness and non-violent resistance to evil both require the highest kind of fortitude, a fortitude which can come to me only from the cross of Christ!

If well made, my meditation will bear fruit in an increase of fortitude in patience. My patience will help me to endure trials in such a way that my soul will be purified of many imperfections and obstacles to grace. I will learn to know better the sources of anger in myself. I will then grow in charity, and since charity is the source of supernatural merit, I will merit a higher degree of union with God in heaven.

Also, of course, I will be a more charitable and virtuous person here on earth. But that alone is not what I mean by the ultimate end of meditation. The ultimate end of meditation should be a more intimate communion with God not only in the future *but also here and now*.

Therefore, in order to make a really deep and mature meditation on the Passion of Christ, I must become *spiritually identified* with Christ in His Passion. This recalls what has been said above about our union with Christ in the Mass and especially at Holy Communion. The words of Pius XII concerning the liturgy might equally well be applied to Christian meditation; its function is to "reproduce in our hearts the likeness of the divine Redeemer through the mystery of the Cross."

Not that we must never meditate on any other mystery than the Passion; but since all grace flows from the pierced side of Christ on the Cross, the Passion of Christ is in fact the meritorious and efficient principle of our union with God and of our supernatural transformation. This is clear in the second chapter of St. Paul's Epistle to the Ephesians in which the Apostle declares that Christ on the Cross restored peace between man and man as well as between mankind and God. Christ has in fact taken all our enmities and "killed them in Himself upon the Cross," so that He is our "peace" and in Him we are all united, in one Spirit, with God the Father (Ephesians 2:11–22). Clearly the Cross and Resurrection of Christ are the very center of Christian mysticism.

This great theological truth makes it unnecessary to inquire, at great length, in what our "communion" or "identification" with Jesus in mental prayer must consist.

This communion is not merely a psychological identification, a matter of emotional sympathy in which we stir up in our hearts what we imagine to have been the sentiments of the Redeemer on the Cross. Nor is this communion simply a moral one, in which we strive by our mind and will to produce in ourselves His ethical dispositions. Our identification with Jesus is spiritual and should, in many cases, also be sacramental or quasi-sacramental.

I mean by this that it is a union or identification in the order of grace or love. Grace comes to us above all by the use of prayer, the sacramentals and the sacraments. I have adopted the term "quasi-sacramental" to cover situations in which our mental prayer prolongs and develops our fruitful reception of the sacraments or in which, for instance, we meditate with the help of such sacramentals as the Bible, the Way of the Cross, or the rosary.

Grace is the principle of supernatural and spiritual life. It makes us sons of God. That is to say, it makes us live spiritually by the divine life itself. Nor is this divine life in our souls merely a figure of speech. Life expresses itself in vital activities. The supernatural life of grace not only vivifies the whole organism of the Mystical

Body of Christ but also produces, in each of its living members, the activities of virtue and the life of contemplation which are the manifestation of God's special presence in the soul.

Now this life of grace is the life of Christ, the true Son of God. We share God's life through the merits of the Passion of Christ. By participating mystically in His Passion and death we become sons of God by adoption as He is the Son of God by nature. Our adoptive sonship is immersed, as it were, in the divine life which Jesus possesses by His own right as the Second Person of the Blessed Trinity. St. Thomas holds that Christ, as the "Head" of the Mystical Body, has the power to pour out grace into all the members of that Body, and this is not merely a theologian's opinion. The Church teaches us that in actual fact Jesus constantly sends forth the life-giving streams of grace into the souls of all those who are united to Him.

This very brief outline is sufficient to enable anyone to understand the one big principle upon which our identification with Christ in contemplative prayer must depend. Here is the principle. All the members of the Mystical Body of Christ have, in actual fact, the divine life of Christ within them and are "mystically" identified with Him in a broad sense of the word. This identification is effected by the reception of baptism or by any act of faith or contrition vivified by perfect charity. The identification is real, and it is in fact our supernatural life. However, *we are not conscious of it*. The identification which we seek to effect in mental prayer is therefore *a conscious realization of the union that is already truly effected between our souls and God by grace.*

This is the secret of mental prayer, as it is also the secret of contemplation. Unless our mental prayer does something to awaken in us a consciousness of our union with God, of our complete dependence upon Him for all our vital acts in the spiritual life, and of His constant loving presence in the depths of our souls, it has not achieved the full effect for which it is intended.

Contemplative souls generally have a special attraction to the presence of God within them, or to some other form of consciousness of God's nearness to their intimate being. This is a grace which, though quite normal in the spiritual life, is not shared by all. But even those who do not have this particular attraction ought to realize that the function of their mental prayer is to bring them somehow into conscious communion with the God who is the source of their natural and supernatural life and the principle of all the good that is in them.

HOW TO MEDITATE

Meditation is really very simple and there is not much need of elaborate techniques to teach us how to go about it. But that does not mean that mental prayer can be practiced without constant and strict interior discipline. This is especially true in our own time when the intellectual and moral flabbiness of a materialistic society has robbed man's nature of its spiritual energy and tone. Nevertheless, the necessity for discipline does not imply the obligation for all men to follow one identical and rigid system. There is a difference between being strict and being rigid. The well-disciplined soul, like a well-disciplined body, is agile, supple and adaptable. A soul that is not pliable and free is incapable of progress in the ways of prayer. An unwise rigidity may seem to produce results at first, but it only ends by paralyzing the interior life.

There are however certain universal requirements for the sane practice of mental prayer. They cannot be neglected.

Recollection

In order to meditate, I have to withdraw my mind from all that prevents me from attending to God present in my heart. This is impossible unless I recollect my senses. But it is almost useless to try to recollect myself at the moment of prayer if I have allowed my senses and imagination to run wild all the rest of the day. Consequently the desire to practice meditation implies the effort to preserve moderate recollection throughout the day. It means living in an atmosphere of faith and with occasional moments of prayer and attention to God. The world in which we live today presents a tantalizing problem to anyone who wants to acquire habits of recollection.

The price of true recollection is a firm resolve to take no wilful interest in anything that is not useful or necessary to our interior life. The world we live in assails us on every side with useless appeals to emotion and to sense appetite. Radios, newspapers, movies, television, billboards, neon-signs surround us with a perpetual incitement to pour out our money and our vital energies in futile transitory satisfactions. The more we buy the more they urge us to buy. But the more they advertise the less we get. And yet, the more they advertise the more we buy. Eventually all will consist in the noise that is made and there will be no satisfaction left in the world except that of vain hopes and anticipations that can never be fulfilled.

I say this in order to show that very much of what we read in magazines or newspapers or see and hear in movies or elsewhere, is completely useless from every point of view. The first thing I must do if I want to practice meditation is to *develop a strong resistance to the futile appeals which modern society makes to my five senses.* Hence I will have to mortify my desires.

I do not speak here of extraordinary ascetic practices; merely of self-denial required to live by the standards of reason and of the Gospels. In present-day America, such self-denial is apt to require heroism. In practice it may mean giving up many or most of the luxuries which I have come to regard as necessities, at least until I have acquired sufficient self-control to use these things without being enslaved by them.

The Sense of Indigence

In order to make a serious and fruitful meditation we must enter into our prayer with a real sense of our need for these fruits. It is not enough to apply our minds to spiritual things in the same way as we might observe some natural phenomenon, or conduct a scientific experiment. In mental prayer we enter a realm of which we are no longer the masters and we propose to ourselves the consideration of truths which exceed our natural comprehension and which, nevertheless, contain the secret of our destiny. We seek to enter more deeply into the life of God. But God is infinitely above us, although He is within us and is the principle of our being. The grace of close union with Him, although it is something we can obtain by prayer and good works, remains nevertheless His gift to us.

One who begs an alms must adopt a different attitude from one who demands what is due to him by his own right. A meditation that is no more than a dispassionate study of spiritual truths indicates no desire, on our part, to share more fully in the spiritual benefits which are the fruit of prayer. We have to enter into our meditation with a realization of our spiritual poverty, our complete lack of the things we seek, and of our abject nothingness in the sight of the infinite God.

The Prodigal Son in the parable can serve as our model. Having wasted his patrimony in a distant country, he was starving to death, unable even to get his hands on a few of the husks which were thrown to the swine he tended. But he "entered into himself." He meditated on his condition. His meditation was brief and to the point. He said to himself: "Here I am dying of hunger, while at home in my father's house the servants have plenty to eat. I will return to my own country and to my father and say to him: Father, I have sinned against heaven and against you, and I am no longer worthy to be called your son. Will you take me in as one of your hired servants?"

The Fathers of the Church saw that every one of us

is more or less like the Prodigal, starving in a distant land, far from our Father's House. This is the common condition of mankind exiled from God and from Paradise by an inordinate preoccupation with perishing things and by a constant inclination to self-gratification and sin. Since this is in fact our position, and since our mental prayer is a journey from time into eternity, from the world to God, it follows that we cannot make a good meditation unless we realize, at least implicitly, the starting point of our journey.

This is true in one way or another on every level of the spiritual life. The saints are, as a matter of fact, much more keenly aware of the gulf between themselves and God than are those who live always on the periphery of sin. As we advance in the interior life it generally becomes less and less necessary for us to stir up in ourselves this feeling of exile and of spiritual need. The soul that is only dimly enlightened by God has very little conception of its own indigence. The most serious faults seem to it to be quite harmless.

Habitual self-complacency is almost always a sign of spiritual stagnation. The complacent no longer feel in themselves any real indigence, any urgent need for God. Their meditations are comfortable, reassuring and inconclusive. Their mental prayer quickly degenerates into day-dreaming, distractions or plain undisguised sleep. For this reason trials and temptations can prove to be a real blessing in the life of prayer, simply because they force us to pray. It is when we begin to find out our need for God that we first learn how to make a real meditation.

The Proper Atmosphere of Prayer

One who has reached a certain proficiency in the interior life can normally practice some form of mental prayer anywhere and under almost any conditions. But beginners and proficients alike need to devote some part of the day to formal meditation. This means choosing a time and place propitious for mental prayer, and the exclusion of all possible obstacles to meditation. It should not be necessary to remark that we can best meditate in silence and retirement — in a chapel, in a garden, a room, a cloister, a forest, a monastic cell.

Religious communities have a set time for the practice of mental prayer. Sometimes the meditation degenerates into a dreary routine of "points" read from a pious book followed by intervals of silence and communal wool-gathering. Discouraging as this procedure may sometimes be, there is nothing in it that makes a good meditation essentially impossible. The very superficiality of the "points" may well awaken in us an acute sense of spiritual indigence and make us seek the living God with deep anguish and humility!

The trouble is however that human nature yields

easily to exasperation under the pressure of mechanical routine. Exasperation foments interior rebellion, which is an obstacle to good mental prayer. Nevertheless there will always be docile and humble spirits who will quietly recollect themselves and listen to the "points" and receive with deep gratitude the slightest suggestion they may offer. Such souls are capable of progress in spite of the apparent mediocrity of their environment.

Nevertheless, passive acceptance of mediocrity is an obstacle to progress in prayer. The chief trouble with pre-digested meditations imposed mechanically upon a whole group is that they tend to bring meditation into disrepute — especially in seminaries where the victims of this system do not hesitate to detect the faintest shadow of stupidity or artificiality and make it the subject of frivolous comment.

The religious orders have their mental prayer in common but systematization and routine are usually foreign to their spirit. Communal mental prayer presents no unusual problems in a contemplative monastery, provided the rule is kept and the proper conditions of silence and good order are maintained.

Everyone should try to set aside some part of the day in which he can pray under conditions which seem to be most favorable for himself. This does not mean that we should try to gratify ourselves even in spiritual things, but it is legitimate and even in some cases necessary for us to seek an atmosphere that really helps us to pray. Anyone who seriously wants to meditate should be allowed reasonable liberties in this regard.

Naturally speaking, the best position for meditation is a seated one. The sitting position is favored by a certain type of contemplative, and a quotation from that charming fourteenth-century mystic, Richard Rolle, may be adduced in witness to the fact: He says (in the *Form of Perfect Living*)

I have loved for to sit: for no penance, nor fantasy, nor that I wished men to talk of me, nor for no such thing: but only because I knew that I loved God more and longer lasted within the comfort of love than going, or standing, or kneeling. For sitting I am most at rest, and my heart most upward. But therefore peradventure it is not best that another should sit, as I did and will do to my death, save he were disposed in soul as I was.

Religious custom makes it easy for Catholics to meditate on their knees. It is usually better to remain quiet, to be still. But there is no reason why one should not also meditate walking up and down in a garden. In short, there is an almost infinite variety of places and positions that can be adopted in mental prayer. They are all accidental. The most important thing is to seek silence, tranquillity, recollection and peace.

The only thing that remains to be added, before we pass on, is a reminder of the importance of leisure in the life of prayer. Leisure is so poorly understood by some religious people that it is regarded as almost synonymous with idleness. Without making any distinction between fruitful and sterile leisure, these busybodies condemn all desire for leisure as a sin. They believe that a man who is not always on the move is wasting precious time. They do not realize the meaning of St. Thomas's definition of laziness. Laziness, says the Angelic Doctor, is a weariness of and distaste *for what is good*. He does not say that laziness is distaste for work, because he is careful not to identify work, as such, with what is simply "good." Yet it is true that our fallen nature needs to labor and suffer in order to arrive at its highest good, spiritual good. It follows that in most cases our laziness is, in fact, a distaste for the labor that is required if we are to procure this good for ourselves. Nevertheless, the fact remains that the highest spiritual good is an action which is so perfect that it is absolutely free of all labor, and is therefore at the same time perfect action and perfect rest. And this is the contemplation of God.

Now the Fathers of the Church well understood the importance of a certain "holy leisure" — *otium sanctum*. We cannot give ourselves to spiritual things if we are always swept off our feet by a multitude of external activities. Business is not the supreme virtue, and sanctity is not measured by the amount of work we accomplish. Perfection is found in the purity of our love for God, and this pure love is a delicate plant that grows best where there is plenty of time for it to mature.

holy leisure

This truth rests on an obvious natural foundation. Someone has said, "It takes time to be a genius." Many promising artists have been ruined by a premature success which drove them to overwork themselves in order to make money and renew again and again the image of themselves they have created in the public mind. An artist who is wise thinks more than he paints and a poet who respects his art burns more than he publishes. So too, in the interior life, we cannot hope to pray well unless we allow ourselves intervals of silent transition between work and formal prayer. In trying to turn out too much work for God we may well end up by doing nothing for Him at all and losing our interior life at the same time. St. Therese of Lisieux wisely reminds us that "God has no need of our works: He has need of our love."

The ideal of the contemplative life is not, however, the exclusion of all work. On the contrary, total inactivity would stultify the interior life just as much as too much activity. The true contemplative is one who has discovered the art of finding leisure even in the midst of his work, by working with such a spirit of detachment and recollection that even his work is a prayer. For such a one the whole day long is *otium sanctum*. His prayer, his reading, his labor all alike give him recreation and rest. One balances the other. Prayer makes it easy to work, work helps him to return with a mind refreshed for prayer. These conditions are well fulfilled in the sane, quiet round of St. Benedict's monastic day of liturgy, meditative reading and manual work in the fields.

Sincerity

Mental prayer is by its nature personal and individual. In common vocal prayer, and in the liturgy, it is understood that the words we utter with our lips may not necessarily express the spontaneous feelings of our heart at the moment. When we unite with others in liturgical prayer, we put aside our sentiments of the moment in order to unite with the thoughts and desires of the community, expressed in the liturgical prayers. These then become our own sentiments and raise us above our individual level, to the level of the mystical Christ, praying in the liturgy.

In mental prayer, it is still the mystical Christ who prays in us, but in a different way. The private prayer of an individual is still in some sense a prayer of the Church, but it has no official and public character. Yet it is the prayer of the Holy Spirit in a member of Christ, in one who is by his baptism "another Christ." The desires and sorrows of our heart in prayer rise to the heavenly Father as the desires and sorrows of His Son, by virtue of the Holy Spirit who teaches us to pray, and who, though we do not always know how to pray as we ought, prays in us, and cries out to the Father in us.

For you have not received the spirit of bondage again in fear; but you have received the spirit of adoption of sons, whereby we cry Abba, (Father). For the Spirit Himself giveth testimony to our spirit that we are the sons of God. And if sons, heirs also; heirs indeed of God and joint heirs with Christ: yet so, if we suffer with Him, that we may be glorified with Him. . . .

Likewise the Spirit also helpeth our infirmity. For we know not what we should pray for as we ought; but the Spirit Himself asketh for us with unspeakable groanings. And He that searcheth the hearts knoweth what the Spirit desireth; because He asketh for the saints according to God.

(Romans 8:15–17, 26, 27.)

It can therefore be said that the aim of mental prayer is to awaken the Holy Spirit within us, and to bring our hearts into harmony with His voice, so that we allow the Holy Spirit to speak and pray within us, and lend Him our voices and our affections that we may become, as far as possible, conscious of His prayer in our hearts.

This implies a difficult and constant attention to the sincerity of our own hearts. We should never say anything in mental prayer that we do not really mean, or at least sincerely desire to mean. One of the reasons why our mental prayer easily grows cold and indifferent is that we begin with aspirations that we do not feel or cannot really mean at the moment. For instance, we fall on our knees out of habit, and without directing our attention to God we begin to tell Him that we love

Him, in a more or less exterior and mechanical fashion, hardly even aware of what we are saying. It is true, that we have a more or less habitual desire to love God, and if we attend to what we are doing we are capable of "purifying our intention" more or less as if we were using a mental windshield-wiper, wiping away juridical specks of self-love. We don't really *want* things that go contrary to God and to His will.

Nevertheless, is it quite sincere for us to express deep sentiments of love which we do not feel? Especially if in actual fact our hearts are quite cold and our minds are pretty much taken up with distractions which, though we do not formally will them, are nevertheless in almost complete possession of our hearts at the moment?

Here sincerity excludes spiritual laziness. At such a time, the sincere thing to do is to regret one's distracted state, and to make an honest effort to pray while admitting that really one has begun without any desire to pray and has just started out of routine.

Sincerity demands that we do what we can to break the grip of routine on our souls, even if it means being a little unconventional. If we really do not feel like praying, it seems at least more honest to recognize that fact before God than to assure Him that we are burning up with fervor. If we admit the truth, we will start out on a basis of humility, recognize the need for effort, and perhaps we will be rewarded with a little of the grace of compunction, which is the most precious of all helps in mental or any other kind of prayer.

Compunction is simply an awareness of our indigence and coldness and of our need for God. It implies faith, sorrow, humility and above all hope in the mercy of God. For the man without compunction, prayer is a cold formality in which he remains centered on himself. For the man who has a sense of compunction, prayer is a living act which brings him face to face with God in an I-Thou relationship which is not imaginary but real, spiritual and personal; and the basis of this reality is our sense of our need for God, united with faith in His love for us.

If we compare the sobriety of the liturgy with the rather effusive emotionalism of books of piety which are supposed to help Christians to "meditate," we can see at once that liturgical prayer makes sincerity much easier. The liturgy takes man as he is: a sinner who seeks the mercy of God. The book of piety sometimes takes him as he is only on very rare occasions: on fire with exalted and heroic love, ready to lay down his life in martyrdom, or on the point of feeling his heart pierced by the javelin of mystical love. Most of us, unfortunately, are not ready to lay down our lives in martyrdom most days at six o'clock in the morning or whenever our mental prayer may occur, and most of us have little or nothing to do with javelins of mystical love.

Mental prayer should be affective, it should be a work of love. But it should not be operatic, or a work of spiritual melodrama. The super-affective quality of some pious literature is a remnant of the baroque piety and mysticism of past centuries — a piety and mysticism peculiar to Italy, France and Spain in the 17th and 18th centuries. This particular form of piety was, perhaps, a result of the vulgarization of the spirituality of several great modern saints who exercised a decisive influence on Catholic piety during the period.

One should be able to rise above mere fashions in piety, especially when these fashions wear themselves out. If we go back to the saints themselves, we find a much more pure, sober and virile spirituality than in their more superficial followers.

In reaction against the over-enthusiastic affectivity of such piety, there is perhaps a tendency, in modern America especially, to become colloquial and informal in the extreme. One chats amicably with "Jesus" and "Mary." Our Lady becomes "Mom." St. Joseph is "Dad." And we "just tell them all about ourselves, all day long." This can, in the long run, become even more artificial and obnoxious than the worst flights of baroque opera. Some people may feel as if this sort of thing is "spontaneous" because it happens to flow easily and without effort. But it may simply be a kind of pose they have picked up from what we might call the "comic book school of spirituality." It flourishes today in the popular religious press.

Concentration and Unity

We have already seen that progress in the life of prayer means the emergence of one dominant attraction — a concentration of the interior life on one objective, union with God. We have remarked that this objective is usually obscure to our experience. The desire for God becomes more intense and more continual, and at the same time our knowledge of Him, rising above precise and definite concepts, becomes "dark" and even confused. Hence the anguish of the mystic who seeks God in the night of pure faith, above the level of human ideas, knowing Him not by light but by darkness. Contemplative prayer apprehends God by love rather than by positive knowledge. But this union of love, which gives the soul an "experience" of God, is effected in the soul by the action of the Holy Spirit, not by the soul's own efforts.

At the beginning of the life of prayer it would be a manifest error to seek this simple and obscure unification of our faculties in God by simply abandoning all efforts to think, to reason, or to meditate discursively. Meditation is the normal path to contemplative prayer. We have to start out with certain simple concepts. Med-

itation makes use of definite theological and philosophical ideas of God. It deals with ideas and principles
which, when the soul is enlightened by faith and moved
to action by charity, bear fruit in deep supernatural
convictions.

The success of meditative prayer depends on our
ability to apply our faculties to these revealed truths
collectively referred to as "The Word of God." Therefore, meditation must have a definite subject. In the
beginning of the life of prayer, the more definite and
concrete we are in our meditations the better off we will
be. The discipline of concentrating on a particular,
clear-cut subject tends to unify the faculties and thus
to dispose them remotely for contemplative prayer.

The Subject of Meditation

The choice of a subject is obviously important in
meditation. And it is immediately evident that since
meditation is a personal and intimate form of spiritual
activity, the choice should be personal. Most people do
not meditate well on a "topic" imposed by someone
else, especially if it is something abstract.

The normal subject of meditation, according to the
Christian ascetic tradition, will be some mystery of the
Christian faith. There is a difference between a mystery
and a dogma. A dogma of the faith is a more abstract,

authoritative statement of the truth to be believed, couched in its official formulation. Meditation on a dogma, in this technical sense, is bound to be a little cold and abstract, though there are minds that might thrive on it.

A mystery is not just the distilled and decanted formulation of a revealed truth, but that whole truth in all its concrete manifestation : in the mysteries of the faith we see God Himself, generally in one of those great theandric actions in which He has revealed Himself to us in a concrete and tangible form, has carried out the work of our redemption, communicated to us a share in His divine life and united us to Himself.

To meditate on a mystery of the faith in this sense means first of all to perceive it externally as it is presented to us, as part of the Church's experience. The Church's experience of the mysteries, if such a phrase may be permitted, is handed down from age to age in tradition. Tradition is the *renewal,* in each Christian generation and society, of the experiential knowledge of the mysteries of the faith. Each new age of Christendom renews its faith and its grasp of the mystery of salvation, the mystery of man united to God in Christ, and each age renews this fundamental experience of the Christian mystery in its own characteristic way.

To enter into the mysteries of the faith by meditation, guided by the spirit of the Church, especially by the spirit of the liturgy and of Christian art, is to renew in oneself the Church's experience of those mysteries by participating in them. And of course the full participation of the Christian in the mystery of Christ is sacramental, public, liturgical: in the sacraments and at Mass. Hence the close relationship between private meditation and the public worship of the Church.

Suppose we meditate on the Incarnation.

The obvious approach to this subject is first of all to *see* the mystery as the Church sees it: hence, we meditate on the Gospel of the Annunciation, or the Gospel account of the Nativity — especially in the liturgical context of the Masses for Christmas or of the Annunciation. Christian meditation on the Incarnation is nourished by the sacramental *experience* of this mystery, as it is lived and celebrated liturgically by the Church.

This "external" grasp of the mystery involves activity of the senses, the imagination, the emotions, the feelings, the affections. A Christian, by meditation and by participating in liturgical worship, comes to feel and act as if he had been present among the shepherds at Bethlehem. Bethlehem is part of his life. He is completely familiar with the Nativity as though it were an event in his own history. And indeed it is, though on a mystical and invisible level. The function of meditation is first of all then to enable us to *see* and *experience* the mysteries of the life of Christ as real and present factors in our own spiritual existence.

To make this experience deeper and more personal,

meditation seeks to read the *inner meaning* beneath the surface of the exterior, and also, (most important of all) to *relate the historical events given us in the Gospels with our own spiritual life here and now.*

In simple terms, the Nativity of Christ the Lord in Bethlehem is not just something that I make present by fantasy. Since He is the eternal Word of God before whom time is entirely and simultaneously present, the Child born at Bethlehem "sees" me here and now. That is to say, I "am" present to His mind "then." It follows that I can speak to Him as to one present not only in fantasy but in actual reality. This spiritual contact with the Lord is the real purpose of meditation.

From this simple example we see, once again, that the real function of meditation is to enable us to *realize* and to *actualize* in our own experience the fundamental truths of our faith.

But there are other subjects for meditation.

Our own life, our own experience, our own duties and difficulties, naturally enter into our meditations. Actually, a lot of "distractions" would vanish if we realized that we are not bound at all times to *ignore* the practical problems of our life when we are at prayer. On the contrary, sometimes these problems actually *ought to be* the subject of meditation. After all, we have to meditate on our vocation, on our response to God's will in our regard, on our charity towards other people, on our fidelity to grace. This enters into our meditations on Christ and His life; for He desires and intends to live in us. The Christ-life has, as its most important aspect for each of us, *His actual presence and activity in our own lives.*

Meditation that ignores this truth easily tends to be aimless and confused.

Hence we cannot help sometimes meditating on our own lives, on what we have done, on what has happened to us, on what we intend to do. But in the event that these things intrude upon our prayer unexpectedly, we should tie them in with our faith in Christ and in Divine Providence. We should try to see our lives in the light of His providential will for us and for mankind. And by the same token we must sometimes meditate on the events of the history of our time and try to penetrate their terrible significance.

I would be inclined to say that a nun who has meditated on the Passion of Christ but has not meditated on the extermination camps of Dachau and Auschwitz has not yet fully entered into the experience of Christianity in our time. For Dachau and Auschwitz are two terrible, indeed apocalyptic, presentations of the *reality* of the Passion renewed in our time. Many pious people might be inclined to think that such things were "distractions" and attempt to exclude them from their minds. If such a revulsion were elevated to a level of strict principle and unvarying policy, it would lead to a complete lack of realism in the spiritual life. Such things should be known, thought about, understood in prayer. Indeed, the contemplative above all should ruminate on these terrible realities which are so symptomatic, so important, so prophetic.

The only reservation to be made here is with regard to one's approach to these things. Obviously the newspapers or news magazines give only a superficial and generally slanted view of events, and a view so shallow and secularized that it cannot possibly lend itself to "meditation" or serious thought at all. One has to see these things with a little depth, and without partisan prejudice. Otherwise one's meditation will be nothing but a jumble of absurd political clichés and self-complacent rationalizations which will be worse than useless, and will of course really prove harmful to the inner life.

Let us not forget the importance of meditation in the life of a man like Gandhi, one of the few really outstanding spiritual figures who had a part to play in modern political life. With him, it was a religious and spiritual obligation to understand, by meditation, the inner significance of events and political pressures, not in order to gain power but in order to liberate and defend man, the image of God.

Fundamentals

In order to understand even the trivial events of our

own lives, we need to *create a religious perspective* in which to view everything that happens. This perspective demands first of all that we frequently renew the realization of the fact that we must die and that our life must pass through the inexorable light of judgment. One who never thinks of the hour of his death cannot make really spiritual decisions during his life. He will never be anything more than a short-sighted opportunist whose decisions will have no lasting value.

Above all, our life should always be seen in the light of the Cross. The Passion, Death and Resurrection of Christ the Lord have entirely changed the meaning and orientation of man's existence and of all that he does. One who cannot realize this will spend his life building a spider's web that has no substance and no real reason for existence.

A meditation that passes superficially over many topics ends by being no meditation at all. It only weakens and dissipates our faculties, leaving them slack and unprofitable. They have been incited to work, but no work has been done.

In order to learn to gather our faculties on one point it is well to begin meditating with the help of a book. I do not mean that one must necessarily use a book of formally prepared meditations. Any serious book about the things of God and the spiritual life can provide us with matter on which to concentrate our minds. But in order to focus our minds on any truth, we normally need the help of our senses. Therefore, at the beginning of the spiritual life, it is usually best to meditate on truths that present themselves under some concrete form, for instance in a parable or in some graphic saying or action of one of the saints, or of Christ our Lord.

All the ancient philosophies and all the higher forms of religious thought have made use of parables and simple imaginative figures to convey the deepest truths, and nowhere is this more true than in the Bible. Here God has revealed to us His mysteries with a graphic simplicity and concreteness which makes them accessible to every race and century. There is therefore no better book of meditations than the Bible, and especially the New Testament. *Lectio Divina,* or the meditative reading of Sacred Scripture, was considered by the Fathers of the Church to be the normal foundation for an interior life of meditation and prayer.

An even simpler and more helpful approach to meditation is to make a deep reflective reading of the liturgical texts from the Old and New Testaments as they are presented to us, for instance, Sunday by Sunday, in the Missal. In this way our meditations can be perfectly co-ordinated with the liturgical cycle. This has the advantage of bringing our minds and hearts into a more perfect union with the prayer of the whole Church and thus disposing us to receive in greater abundance the graces which God pours out upon the world in answer to that prayer.

Here it might be worthwhile to outline the simple essentials of meditative prayer, in schematic form.

1) *Preliminary*: a sincere effort of recollection, a realization of what you are about to do, and a prayer of petition for grace. If this beginning is well made, the rest ought to follow easily.

2) *Vision*: — the attempt to see, to focus, to grasp what you are meditating on. This implies an effort of *faith*. Keep working until faith is clear and firm in your heart (not merely in your head).

3) *Aspiration*: — From what you "see" there follow certain practical consequences. Desires, resolutions to act in accordance with one's faith, to live one's faith. Here, an effort of *hope* is required — one must believe in the *possibility* of these good acts, one must hope in the fulfilment of good desires, with the help of God. Above all, one must have a sincere hope in the possibility of divine union.

4) *Communion*: — here the prayer becomes simple and uncomplicated. The realization of faith is solid, hope is firm, one can rest in the presence of God. This is more a matter of simple repose and intuition, an embrace of simple *love*. But if activity is required, let love have an active character, in which case the prayer is more like the last level (3). Or love may take rather the form of *listening* to the Beloved. Or the form of *praise*. More often than not, we can be content to simply rest, and float peacefully with the deep current

of love, doing nothing of ourselves, but allowing the Holy Spirit to act in the secret depths of our souls. If the prayer becomes confused or weak, we can return to one of the earlier stages, and renew our vigilance, our faith, our love.

We can end with a brief and sincere prayer of thanksgiving.

TEMPERAMENT AND MENTAL PRAYER

The precise way in which each individual makes his meditation will depend in large measure upon his temperament and natural gifts. An intellectual and analytic mind will break down a text into its component parts, and follow the thought step by step, pausing in deep reflection upon each new idea, in order to examine it from different points of view and draw forth all its hidden implications, both speculative and practical.

But analysis must not go too far. The mind must ascend, by reasoning, to the threshold of intuition. Meditation enters into its full swing, for an intellectual, when his mind can grasp the whole content of the subject in one deep and penetrating gaze. Then he rests in this intuition, letting the truth sink in and become a part of himself. Above all, intuition, setting the intelligence temporarily at rest, should leave the will free to adapt itself to the practical consequences of the truth thus seen and to direct our whole life in accordance with it.

Such minds as these — which are a minority — can fruitfully meditate on an article of the *Summa Theo-*

logica or on any other theological text. But even they cannot always be contented with an intellectual approach to supernatural things. For a theologian, in practice, mental prayer should become a kind of refuge from his speculative study, an oasis of affectivity to which he can retire to rest after his intellectual labor. In any case, the prayer of love is always higher than mere mental considerations. All mental prayer, whatever may be its beginnings, must terminate in love.

Other less speculative minds approach the truth with a more immediate intuition, apprehending it in its wholeness as beauty rather than as truth. The radiance that pours forth from a spiritual intuition of the real is a pure light that captivates the whole soul. Sensible beauty loses its grip on the mind that finds itself momentarily under the spell of that *splendor veritatis*, the radiance of truth, the "beauty ever ancient and ever new" which finally brought peace to the soul of St. Augustine.

The majority of men need to practice a way of meditation that is more firmly rooted in the senses. For these, concentration depends on a mental picture and an important element in their mental prayer will be the exercise which St. Ignatius Loyola calls "application of the senses." In other words, they must take a concrete religious subject — a scene from the Gospels — and try to make all its sensible elements vividly real to their imagination.

This imaginative realization of a religious subject has a very definite practical purpose. It is supposed to pave the way for living spiritual contact with God. Meditating on the Gospels, we place ourselves, as far as we can, in the presence of Jesus. We arouse in our hearts the dispositions that we would hope to have if we were speaking with Him or listening to His words. We act interiorly just as if we were talking with our divine Redeemer. What Jesus said twenty centuries ago is also addressed to us now. He may not be physically present to me, here and now, as man, but He is present as God. His divinity, which is the center and source of my own being, is also the very Being of His Humanity. Consequently the Christ who lives and speaks in the Gospel is much more truly present to me than the persons around me with whom I speak and deal in my daily life.

It is therefore by no means a mere play of fancy to place ourselves in the presence of Christ in a scene from the New Testament. However, it must be remembered above all that the function of this technical device is to incite us to acts of the theological virtues of faith, hope and charity, which are the principles of Christ's supernatural presence in our souls.

The true end of Christian meditation is therefore practically the same as the end of liturgical prayer and the reception of the sacraments: a deeper union by grace and charity with the Incarnate Word who is the only Mediator between God and man, Jesus Christ.

The peculiar value of mental prayer however is that it is completely personal and favors a spiritual development along lines dictated by our own particular needs. The interior life demands of us a heroic struggle to practice virtue and to detach ourselves from inordinate love of temporal, created things. We cannot possibly bring our souls to renounce our most powerful natural desires unless we somehow have a real and conscious appreciation of our contact with something better. The love of God remains a cold and abstract thing unless we can bring ourselves to realize its deeply intimate and personal character. We can never hope, on earth, to achieve anything like a clear realization of what it means to be loved by the three divine Persons in one divine nature. But it is very easy to appreciate the love of God when we see it concretized in the human love of Jesus Christ for us. This is the best and most logical foundation for a life of faith and therefore this above all should be the primary object of meditation.

SUMMARY AND CONCLUSION

Meditation is spiritual work, sometimes difficult work. But it is a work of love and of desire. It is not something that can be practiced without effort, at least in the beginning. And the sincerity, humility and perseverance of our efforts will be proportionate to our desire. This desire in turn is a gift of grace. Anyone who imagines he can simply begin meditating without praying for the desire and the grace to do so, will soon give up. But the desire to meditate, and the grace to begin meditating, should be taken as an implicit promise of further graces. In meditation, as in anything else in the Christian life, everything depends on our correspondence with the grace of the Holy Spirit.

Meditation is almost all contained in this one idea: the idea of *awakening* our interior self and attuning ourselves inwardly to the Holy Spirit, so that we will be able to respond to His grace. In mental prayer, over the years, we must allow our interior perceptivity to be refined and purified. We must attune ourselves to unexpected movements of grace, which do not fit our own preconceived ideas of the spiritual life at all, and which in no way flatter our own ambitious aspirations.

We must be ready to cooperate not only with graces that console, but with graces that humiliate us. Not only with lights that exalt us, but with lights that blast our self-complacency. Much of our coldness and dryness in prayer may well be a kind of unconscious defence against grace. Without realizing it, we allow our nature to de-sensitize our souls so that we cannot perceive graces which we intuitively foresee may prove to be painful.

Meditation is then always to be associated in practice with abandonment to the will and action of God. It goes hand in hand with self-renunciation and with obedience to the Holy Spirit. Meditation that does not seek to bring our whole being into conformity with God's will must naturally remain sterile and abstract. But any sincere interior prayer that really seeks this one all important end — our conformity to God's will in our regard — cannot fail to be rewarded by grace. It will prove, without question, to be one of the most sanctifying forces in our lives. And St. Teresa of Avila believed that no one who was faithful to the practice of meditation could possibly lose his soul.

VITAL SIGNS

Dr. Cook explores the frightening possibilities of experimental fertilization—the passion to create life, and the power to destroy it...

"CONSTANT SUSPENSE . . . BELIEVABLE AND CHILLING."
—Houston Chronicle

"VINTAGE COOK . . . NONSTOP ACTION."
—Kirkus Reviews

HARMFUL INTENT

The explosive story of a doctor accused of malpractice—a fugitive on the run who pierces the heart of a shocking medical conspiracy...

"A REAL GRABBER!"
—Los Angeles Times

"TRULY EXCITING."
—Associated Press

MUTATION

On the forefront of genetic research, a brilliant doctor tries to create the son of his dreams—and invents a living nightmare...

"HOLDS YOU PAGE AFTER PAGE."
—Larry King, USA Today

"*REALLY* FRIGHTENING."
—Booklist

MORTAL FEAR

A major scientific breakthrough becomes the ultimate experiment in terror when middle-aged patients begin to die—of old age...

"A CHILLING ODYSSEY INTO THE ORIGINS OF LIFE—AND DEATH."
—*USA Weekend*

"COOK'S BEST BOOK SINCE *COMA*."
—*People*

OUTBREAK

Murder and mystery reach epidemic proportions when a devastating plague sweeps the country...

"HIS MOST HARROWING MEDICAL HORROR STORY."
—*New York Times*

"THE ULTIMATE NIGHTMARE . . . SPINE-TINGLING INTRIGUE AND FEVER-PITCHED ACTION."
—Associated Press

CONTAGION

His thriller based on medical fact—a battle for survival waged in the hot zone of a deadly new virus...

"EACH OF HIS THRILLERS HAS DEALT WITH A DIFFERENT ISSUE OR CONTROVERSY IN MEDICINE."
—*Milwaukee Journal*

Titles by Robin Cook

INVASION

ROBIN COOK

BERKLEY BOOKS, NEW YORK

INVASION

A Berkley Book / published by arrangement with
the author

PRINTING HISTORY
Berkley edition / April 1997

The Putnam Berkley World Wide Web site address is
http://www.berkley.com/berkley

ISBN: 0-425-15540-4

BERKLEY®
Berkley Books are published by The Berkley Publishing Group,
200 Madison Avenue, New York, New York 10016.
BERKLEY and the "B" design
are trademarks belonging to Berkley Publishing Corporation.

PRINTED IN THE UNITED STATES OF AMERICA

10 9 8 7 6 5 4 3 2

INVASION

PROLOGUE

IN THE FRIGID VASTNESS OF INTERSTELLAR SPACE A PIN-
point of matter–antimatter fluctuated from the void, creating
an intense flash of electromagnetic radiation. To the human
retina, the phenomena would have appeared as the sudden
emergence and expansion of a blip of colors representing
the full spectrum of visual light. Of course, the gamma rays,
the X rays, and even the infrared and radio waves would
not have been visible to a human's limited vision.

Simultaneous with the burst of colors, the human witness
would have seen the emergence of an astronomical number
of atoms in the form of a rotating, black disciform concretion. The phenomenon would have appeared like a video
run in reverse of the object falling into a crystalline pool
of fluid whose ripples were the warping of space and time.

Still traveling at nearly the speed of light, the huge number of coalesced atoms rocketed into the distant reaches of
the solar system, streaking past the orbits of the bloated
outer gaseous planets of Neptune, Uranus, Saturn, and Ju-
piter. By the time the concretion reached the orbit of Mars
its rotation and velocity had slowed significantly.

The object could now be seen for what it was: an intergalactic spaceship whose gleaming outer surface looked
like highly polished onyx. The only deformity of its disciform shape was a series of bulges along the top surface
of its outer edge. The contours of each of these bulges

mirrored the silhouette of the massive mother ship. There
were no other distortions of the outer skin: no portholes or
exhaust vents or antennae. There weren't even any struc-
tural seams.

Streaking into the outer fringes of the earth's atmosphere,
the outside temperature of the space ship soared. A burning
tail appeared to light up the night sky behind the ship as
the heat-excited atmospheric atoms gave off photons in protest.

The ship continued to slow both in terms of rotation and
velocity. Far below, the twinkling lights of an unsuspecting
city appeared. The preprogrammed ship ignored the lights;
it was by luck that the impact occurred in a rocky, boulder-
strewn, arid landscape. Despite the relatively slow speed it
was more of a controlled crash than a landing, sending
rock, sand, and dust billowing into the air. When the craft
finally came to a stop, it was half buried in earth. Debris
sent skyward in the impact rained down on its polished
topside.

After the surface temperature had fallen below two hundred degrees centigrade, a vertical slitlike opening appeared
along the ship's outer edge. It was not like a mechanical
door. It was as if the molecules themselves worked in concert to create the penetration of the ship's seamless exterior.

Vapor escaped through the slit, evidence that the interior
of the craft was deep-space frigid. Inside, banks of computers busily ran automatic sequences. Samples of the
earth's atmosphere and soil were hauled inside to be ana-
lyzed. These automated procedures functioned as planned,
including the isolation of prokaryotic life forms (bacteria)
from the dirt. Analysis of all the samples, including the
DNA contained therein, confirmed that the proper destination had been reached. The arming sequence was then in-
itiated. Meanwhile, an antenna was extended up into the
night sky to prepare for quasar frequency transmission to
announce that Magnum had arrived.

1

"HEY, HELLO!" CANDEE TAYLOR SAID AS SHE TAPPED JONathan Sellers on the shoulder. At the moment Jonathan was busily kissing her neck. "Earth to Jonathan, come in please!" Candee added while she began rapping on Jonathan's head with her knuckles.

Both Candee and Jonathan were seventeen and juniors at Anna C. Scott High School. Jonathan had recently gotten his driver's license, and although he was not yet permitted to use the family car, he'd been able to borrow Tim Appleton's VW. Despite it being a school night, Candee and Jonathan had managed to sneak out and drive up to the bluff overlooking the city. Each had eagerly anticipated this first visit to the school's favorite "lover's lane." To help set the mood, as if they'd needed any help, the radio was tuned to KNGA, home of nonstop top forty hits.

"What's the matter?" Jonathan questioned while probing the tender spot on the top of his head. Candee had had to hit him pretty hard to divert his attention. Jonathan was tall for his age and thin. His adolescent growth spurt had been all vertical, much to his basketball coach's delight.

"I wanted you to see the shooting star." As a gymnast, Candee was significantly more physically developed than Jonathan. Her body was the source of the admiration of the boys and the envy of the girls. She could have dated almost anyone, but she chose Jonathan because of a combination of his cuddly good looks and his interest in and abilities with computers. Computers happened to be one of her interests as well.

"So what's the big deal about a shooting star?" Jonathan whined. He glanced up at the stars but quickly returned his gaze to Candee. He couldn't be sure of it, but he thought that one of the buttons of her blouse that had been buttoned when they'd arrived was now mysteriously unbuttoned.

"It went all the way across the sky," Candee said. She traced her index finger across the windshield for emphasis. "It was awesome!"

In the half-light of the car's interior, Jonathan could just make out the imperceptible rise and fall of Candee's breasts with her breathing. He found that more awesome than any stars. He was about to lean over and try to kiss her when the radio seemingly self-destructed.

First the volume jumped to an ear-splitting level, followed instantly by a loud popping and hissing noise. Sparks leaped out of the dashboard and smoke billowed up.

"Shit!" Jonathan and Candee screeched in unison as they reflexively tried to push themselves away from the sparking receiver. Both leaped from the car. From the safety of the exterior they peered back inside, half expecting to see flames. Instead the sparking stopped as abruptly as it had started. Straightening up, they eyed each other across the top of the car.

"What the hell am I going to tell Tim?" Jonathan moaned.

"Look at the antenna!" Candee said.

Even in the darkness Jonathan could see that its tip was blackened.

Candee reached out and touched it. "Ouch!" she exclaimed. "It's hot."

Hearing a babble of voices, Jonathan and Candee looked around them. Other kids had gotten out of their cars as well. A pall of acrid smoke hung over the scene. Every radio that had been on, whether playing rap music, rock, or classical, had blown its fuse. At least that's what everybody was saying.

10:15 P.M.

DR. SHEILA MILLER LIVED IN ONE OF THE CITY'S FEW RESidential high-rises. She liked the view, the breezes from the desert, and the proximity to the University Medical Center. Of the three, the last was the most important.

At age thirty-five, she felt as if she'd been through two lives. She married early in college to a fellow premed student. They'd had so much in common. Both thought that medicine was to be their consuming interest and that they should share the dream. Unfortunately, reality had been brutally unromantic because of their arduous schedules. Still, their relationship might have survived if George hadn't had the irritating idea that his career as a surgeon was more valuable than Sheila's path, first in internal medicine and then in emergency medicine. As far as domestic responsibility was concerned, it had all fallen on her shoulders.

George's undiscussed decision to accept a two-year fellowship in New York had been the straw that broke the camel's back. The idea that George expected her to follow him to New York when she'd recently accepted the position of head of the University Medical Center emergency department showed Sheila how mismatched they were. What romance had once been between them had long since evaporated, so with little argument and no passion they divided up their collection of CDs and back issues of medical journals and went their separate ways. As far as Sheila was concerned, the only legacy was a mild bitterness about assumed male prerogatives.

On that particular night like most nights Sheila was busy reading her unending pile of medical journals. At the same time she was taping a TV presentation of an old movie classic with the idea of watching it over the weekend. Consequently her apartment was quiet save for the occasional tinkle of her wind chimes on her patio.

Sheila did not see the shooting star that Candee saw, but at the same moment Candee and Jonathan were startled by the destruction of Tim's car radio, Sheila was equally shocked by a somewhat similar catastrophe with her VCR. Suddenly it began to spark and whir as if it were about to launch into orbit.

Startled from the depths of concentration, Sheila still had the presence of mind to yank out the power cord. Unfortunately that maneuver had little effect. It wasn't until she disengaged the cable line that the machine fell silent although it continued to smoke. Gingerly Sheila felt the top of the console. It was warm to the touch but certainly not about to catch fire.

Silently cursing, Sheila went back to her reading. She vaguely toyed with the idea of bringing the VCR to the hospital the following day to see if one of the electronic technicians could fix it. She justified the idea with her busy schedule. There was no way she could take the time to schlep the thing to the appliance store where she'd bought it.

10:15 P.M.

PITT HENDERSON HAD BEEN SLOWLY EASING HIMSELF down so that he was now practically horizontal. He was sprawled on the threadbare couch squeezed into his third-floor dorm room on campus in front of his black-and-white thirteen-inch TV. His parents had given him the set on his previous birthday. The screen might have been tiny, but the reception was good, and the image was clear as a bell.

Pitt was a senior at the university and scheduled to graduate that year. He was premed and had majored in chemistry. Although he'd been only a slightly above average student, he'd been able to snare a position in the medical school by evidencing hard work and commitment. He was the only chemistry major who had opted for the work-study program and had been working in the University Medical Center since his freshman year, mostly in the labs. Currently he was on a work rotation and clerking in the emergency department. Over the years Pitt had developed a habit of making himself useful wherever in the hospital he was assigned.

A huge yawn brought tears to his eyes and the NBA game he was watching began to fade as his mind began to drift toward sleep. Pitt was a stocky, muscular twenty-one-year-old who'd been a star football player in high school but had failed to make the team in college. He'd weathered the disappointment and turned it into a positive experience by concentrating that much more on his goal of becoming a doctor.

Just when Pitt's eyelids touched, the picture tube of his beloved TV blew up, scattering shards of glass over his abdomen and chest. It had been at the same instant that Candee and Jonathan's radio as well as Sheila's VCR had gone crazy.

For a second Pitt didn't move. He was stunned and confused, unsure if the disturbance that had shocked him awake had been external or internal, like one of the jerks he'd get on occasion just before falling asleep. After pushing his glasses up on the bridge of his nose and finding himself staring into the depths of a burned-out cathode ray tube, he knew that he'd not been dreaming.

"Holy crap!" he remarked as he heaved himself to his feet and gingerly brushed the thin shards of glass from his lap. Out in the hall he heard multiple doors creaking against their hinges.

Stepping out into the hall, Pitt glanced up and down the corridor. A number of students in all manner of dress, male and female, were looking at each other with dazed expressions.

"My computer just blew a fuse," John Barkly said. "I was on the Internet." John lived in the room right next to Pitt's.

"My freakin' TV exploded," announced another student.

"My Bose clock-radio practically caught fire," said another student. "What the hell's going on? Is this some sort of prank?"

Pitt closed his door and eyed the sad remains of his beloved TV. Some prank, he mused. If he caught the guy responsible, he'd beat the crap out of him . . .

2

PULLING OFF MAIN STREET INTO COSTA'S 24-HOUR DINER, the right rear tire of Beau Stark's black Toyota 4Runner hit the curb and the vehicle bounced. Sitting in the front passenger seat, Cassy Winthrope's head bumped against the passenger-side window. She wasn't hurt, but the jolt had been unexpected. Luckily she had her seat belt on.

"My God!" Cassy exclaimed. "Where'd you learn to drive, Kmart?"

"Very funny," Beau said sheepishly. "I turned a little too soon, okay?"

"You should let me drive if you're preoccupied," Cassy said.

Beau drove across the crowded gravel parking lot and pulled to a stop in a slot in front of the diner. "How do you know I'm preoccupied?" he asked. He pulled on the brake and killed the engine.

"When you live with someone you begin to read all sorts of little clues," Cassy said as she undid her seat belt and alighted from the car. "Especially someone you're engaged to."

Beau did the same, but as his foot made contact with the ground, it slipped on a rock. He grabbed onto the open door to keep from falling.

"That settles it," Cassy said, having caught Beau's latest sign of inattentiveness and temporary lack of coordination. "After breakfast, I'm driving."

"I can drive fine," Beau said irritably as he slammed the car door and locked the car with his remote. He met up with Cassy at the rear of the car and they trudged toward the diner's entrance.

"Sure, just like you can shave fine," Cassy said.

Beau had a small forest of tissue paper plastered to the various nicks and cuts he'd inflicted on himself that morning.

"And pour coffee," Cassy added. Earlier Beau had dropped the pot of coffee and broken one of their mugs in the process.

"Well, maybe I am a little preoccupied," Beau reluctantly admitted.

Beau and Cassy had been living together for the last eight months. They were both twenty-one and seniors, like Pitt. They'd known of each other from their freshman year, but had never dated, each certain that the other was always involved with someone else. When they'd finally been brought together inadvertently by their mutual friend, Pitt, who'd been casually dating Cassy at the time, they'd clicked as if their relationship were meant to be.

Most people thought they resembled each other and could almost be brother and sister. Both had thick, dark brown hair, flawless olive-complected skin, and shockingly crystalline blue eyes. Both were also athletically inclined and frequently worked out together. Some people had joked that they were a brunette version of Ken and Barbie.

"Do you really think that you are going to hear from the Nite people?" Cassy asked as Beau held the door open for her. "I mean, Cipher is only the largest software company in the world. I think you are just setting yourself up for big-time rejection."

"No question that they'll call," Beau said confidently, entering the restaurant behind Cassy. "After the resume I sent, they'll be calling any minute." He pulled aside his

Cerruti jacket to flash the tip of his cellular phone stuck in his inner pocket.

Beau's snappy attire that morning was no accident. He made it a point to dress nattily every day. It was his feeling that looking successful bred success. Luckily, his professional parents were able and willing to indulge his inclinations. To his credit he was a hard worker, studied diligently, and got outstanding grades. Confidence was not something he lacked.

"Hey, guys!" Pitt called from a booth beneath the front windows. "Over here!"

Cassy waved and wormed her way through the crowd. Costa's Diner, affectionately labeled the "greasy spoon," was a popular university hangout, especially for breakfast. Cassy slid into the seat across from Pitt. Beau did likewise.

"Did you have any trouble with your TV or radio last night?" Pitt asked excitedly before any hellos were exchanged. "Did you have anything turned on around ten-fifteen?"

Cassy made an expression of exaggerated disdain.

"Unlike other people," Beau said with feigned haughtiness, "we study on school nights."

Pitt unceremoniously bounced a piece of wadded-up napkin off Beau's forehead. He'd been nervously toying with the paper while waiting for Beau and Cassy to arrive.

"For those of you nerds who have no idea of what's going on in the real world, last night at quarter past ten a whole shitload of radios and TVs were knocked out all over the city," Pitt said. "Mine included. Some people think it was a prank by some guys in the physics department, and I'll tell you, I'm steamed."

"It would be nice if it happened over the entire country," Beau said. "Within a week of no TV the national average IQ would probably go up."

"Orange juice for everyone?" Marjorie the waitress asked. She'd appeared at the tableside. Before anyone could answer she began pouring. It was all part of the normal morning ritual. Then Marjorie took their orders and barked them in Greek over the counter to the two short-order cooks.

While everyone was enjoying their juice, Beau's cellular phone's muted ring could be heard under the fabric of his jacket. In his haste to get to it, he knocked over his juice glass. Pitt had to react instinctively to avoid a lap full of OJ.

Cassy shook her head captiously as she pulled out a half-dozen napkins from the holder and blotted up the spilled juice. She rolled her eyes for Pitt's benefit and mentioned that Beau had been pulling off equivalent stunts all morning.

Beau's expression brightened when he realized his hopes had been answered: the call was coming from Randy Nite's organization. He even made certain to pronounce the name, Cipher, very clearly for Cassy's benefit.

Cassy explained to Pitt that Beau was looking for employment with the Pope.

"I'd be happy to come for an interview," Beau was saying with studied calmness. "It would be my pleasure indeed. Whenever Mr. Nite would like to see me, I'd be happy to fly east. As I indicated in my cover letter, I'll be graduating next month, and I'd be available to begin work . . . well, really any time thereafter."

" 'Thereafter!' " Cassy sputtered. She choked on her orange juice.

"Yeah," Pitt chimed in. "Where'd that word come from? That doesn't sound like the Beau I've learned to love."

Beau waved them off and shot them a dirty look. "That's correct," he said into the phone. "What I'm looking for is some permutation of the role of personal assistant to Mr. Nite."

"Permutation?" Cassy questioned, suppressing a laugh.

"What I like is the muted but fake English accent," Pitt said. "Maybe Beau should go into acting and forget computers."

"He is a rather good actor," Cassy said, tickling his ear. "This morning he was pretending to be a klutz."

Beau batted away her hand. "Yes, that would be fine," he said into the phone. "I'll make arrangements to be there. Please tell Mr. Nite I look forward to meeting him with great alacrity."

" 'Alacrity'?" Pitt voiced, pretending to gag himself with his index finger.

Beau pressed the end button and flipped his cellular phone closed. He glared at both Cassy and Pitt. "You guys are like really mature. That was possibly the most important call in my life, and you're clowning around."

" 'Like really mature'! That sounds more like the Beau I know," Cassy said.

"Yeah, who was that other guy talking on the phone?" Pitt asked.

"He's the guy who's going to be working for Cipher come June," Beau said. "Mark my word. After that, who knows? While you, my friend, are going to be wasting another four years in medical school."

Pitt laughed out loud. "Waste four years in medical school?" he questioned. "Now that's a curious, albeit twisted perspective."

Cassy slid over next to Beau and started to nibble at his earlobe.

Beau pushed her away. "Jeez, Cass, there are professors in here that I know, people who might be writing me letters of recommendation."

"Oh, don't be so uptight," Cassy said. "We're just teasing you 'cause you're so wired. Actually I'm amazed Cipher called you. It's quite a coup. I'd imagine they'd get lots of job inquiries."

"It's going to be even more of a coup when Randy Nite offers me a job," Beau said. "The experience would be mindboggling. It's a dream job. The man is worth billions."

"It would also be demanding," Cassy said wistfully. "Probably twenty-five hours a day, eight days a week, fourteen months a year. That doesn't leave much time for us, especially if I'll be teaching here."

"It's merely a way to get a jump on a career," Beau

said. "I want to do well for us so that we can really enjoy our lives."

Pitt pretended to gag himself again and pleaded with his breakfast companions not to make him sick with mushy romantic stuff.

Once the food came, the threesome ate quickly. They all involuntarily glanced at their respective watches. They didn't have that much time.

"Anybody up for a movie tonight?" Cassy said as she drained her coffee. "I've got an exam today and I deserve a little relaxation."

"Not me, Pumpkin," Beau said. "I got a paper due in a couple of days." He turned and tried to get Marjorie's attention to get the check.

"How about you?" Cassy asked Pitt.

"Sorry," Pitt said. "I'm doing a double shift at the medical center."

"What about Jennifer?" Cassy asked. "I could give her a call."

"Well, that's up to you," Pitt said. "But don't do it on my account. Jennifer and I are on the outs."

"I'm sorry," Cassy said with feeling. "I thought you two guys were a great couple."

"So did I," Pitt said. "Unfortunately she seems to have found someone more to her liking."

For a moment Cassy's and Pitt's eyes held, then they both looked off, feeling a twinge of embarrassment and a mild sense of déjà vu.

Beau got the check and smoothed it out on the table. Despite all three having had various college math courses, it took them five minutes to figure out how much each owed once a reasonable tip had been added.

"You want a ride to the med center?" Beau asked Pitt as they pushed out into the morning sunshine.

"I suppose," Pitt said ambivalently. He was feeling a little depressed. The problem was that he still harbored romantic feelings toward Cassy despite the fact that she had spurned him and Beau was his best friend. He and Beau had known each other since elementary school.

Pitt was a few steps behind his friends. His inclination was to go around to the passenger side of Beau's car to hold the door for Cassy, but he didn't want to make Beau look bad. Instead he followed Beau and was about to climb into the backseat when Beau put his arm on his shoulder.

"What the hell is that?" Beau asked.

Pitt followed Beau's line of sight. Stuck in the dirt directly in front of the driver's door was a curious, round black object about the size of a silver dollar. It was symmetrically domed, smooth, and in the sunlight it had a dull finish that made it difficult to tell if it were metal or stone.

"I must have stepped on the damn thing when I got out of the car," Beau said. The indentation of a smudged footprint clearly angled off to one side from the object's rounded peak. "I wondered why I slipped."

"Do you think it dropped out from under your car?" Pitt asked.

"It's weird-looking," Beau said. He bent down and, with the side of his hand, brushed away some of the sand from the partially buried curiosity. When he did so he could see eight minute little domes symmetrically arrayed around the object's edge.

"Hey, come on, you guys!" Cassy called from inside the car. "I got to get to my student teaching assignment. I'm already late as it is."

"Just a sec," Beau answered. Then to Pitt he asked: "Any ideas what it is?"

"Not a clue," Pitt admitted. "Let's see if your car starts."

"It's not from my car, you lunkhead," Beau said. With his thumb and index finger of his right hand he tried to pick the object up. It resisted his efforts. "It must be the end of a buried rod."

Using both hands to scrape away the gravel and sand from around the object, Beau surprised himself by quickly upending it. It wasn't part of a rod. The underside was flat. Beau picked it up. At the height of the dome it was about a centimeter thick.

"Shit, it's heavy for its size," Beau said. He handed it

to Pitt, who hefted it in the palm of his hand. Pitt whistled and made an expression of amazement. He gave it back to Beau.

"What's it made of?" Pitt asked.

"Feels like lead," Beau said. With his fingernail he tried to scratch it, but it didn't scratch. "But it ain't lead. Hell, I bet it's heavier than lead."

"It reminds me of one of those black rocks you find once in a while at the beach," Pitt said. "You know, those rocks that get rolled around for years by the surf."

Beau hooked his index finger and thumb around the margin of the object and made a motion as if to throw it. "With this flat underside I bet I could skip this thing twenty times."

"Bull!" Pitt said. "With its weight it would sink after one or two skips."

"Five bucks says I could skip it at least ten times," Beau said.

"You're on," Pitt said.

"Ahhh!" Beau cried suddenly. Dropping the object, which again half buried itself in the sand and gravel, Beau grabbed his right hand with his left.

"What happened?" Pitt demanded with alarm.

"The damn thing stung me," Beau said angrily. By squeezing the base of his index finger, he caused a drop of blood to appear at the tip.

"Oh, wow!" Pitt said sarcastically. "A mortal wound!"

"Screw you, Henderson," Beau said, grimacing. "It hurt. It felt like a goddamn bee sting. I even felt it up my arm."

"Ah, instant septicemia," Pitt said with equal sarcasm.

"What the hell's that?" Beau demanded nervously.

"It would take too long to explain, Mr. Hypochondriac," Pitt said. "Besides, I'm just pulling your leg."

Beau bent down and retrieved the black disc. He carefully inspected its edge but found nothing that could have accounted for the sting.

"Come on, Beau!" Cassy called angrily. "I gotta go. What on earth are you two doing?"

"All right, all right," Beau said. He looked at Pitt and shrugged.

Pitt bent down and from the base of the latest indentation the object had made in the sand, lifted a slender shard of glass. "Could this have been stuck to it somehow and cut you?"

"I suppose," Beau said. He thought it unlikely but couldn't think of any other explanation. He'd convinced himself there was no way the object could have been at fault.

"Beauuuuu!" Cassy called through clenched teeth.

Beau swung himself up behind the wheel of his 4×4. As he did so he absently slipped the curious domed disc into his jacket pocket. Pitt climbed into the backseat.

"Now I'm going to be late," Cassy fumed.

"When was your last tetanus shot?" Pitt questioned from the backseat.

A MILE FROM COSTA'S DINER THE SELLERS FAMILY WAS IN the final stages of its morning routine. The family minivan was already idling thanks to Jonathan, who sat expectantly behind the wheel. His mother, Nancy, was framed by the open front door. She was dressed in a simple suit befitting her professional position as a research virologist for a local pharmaceutical company. She was a petite woman of five foot two with a Medusa's head of tight, blond curls.

"Come on, honey," Nancy called to her husband, Eugene. Eugene was stuck on the kitchen phone, talking with one of the local newspaper reporters whom he knew socially. Eugene motioned he'd be another minute.

Nancy impatiently switched her weight from one foot to the other and eyed her husband of twenty years. He looked like what he was: a physics professor at the university. She'd never been able to coax him out of his baggy corduroy pants and jacket, blue chambray shirt, and knitted tie. She'd gone to the extent of buying him better clothes, but they hung unused in the closet. But she'd not married Eugene for his fashion sense or lack of it. They'd met in graduate school, and she'd fallen hopelessly in love with his wit, humor, and gentle good looks.

Turning around, she eyed her son, in whose face she could definitely see both herself and her husband. He'd seemed defensive that morning when she'd asked him about what he'd been doing the night before at his friend Tim's house. Jonathan's uncharacteristic evasiveness worried her. She knew the pressures teenagers were under.

"Honest, Art," Eugene was saying loud enough for Nancy to hear. "There's no way such a powerful blast of radio waves could have come from any of the labs in the physics department. My advice is to check with some of the radio stations in the area. There are two besides the university station. I suppose it could have been some kind of prank. I just don't know."

Nancy looked back at her husband. She knew it was difficult for him to be rude with anyone, but everybody was going to be late. Holding up a finger she mouthed the words "one minute" to Eugene. Then she walked out to the car.

"Can I drive this morning?" Jonathan asked.

"I don't think this is the morning," Nancy said. "We're already late. Shove over."

"Jeez," Jonathan whined. "You guys never give me any credit for being able to do anything."

"That's not true," Nancy countered. "But I certainly don't think putting you in a situation of having to drive while we are in a hurry is appropriate."

Nancy got in behind the wheel.

"Where's Dad anyway?" Jonathan mumbled.

"He's talking with Art Talbot," Nancy said. She glanced at her watch. The minute was up. She beeped the horn.

Thankfully Eugene appeared at the door, which he turned to and locked. He ran to the car and jumped in the backseat. Nancy quickly backed out into the street and accelerated toward their first stop: Jonathan's school.

"Sorry to keep everybody waiting," Eugene said after they'd driven a short distance in silence. "There was a curious phenomenon last night. Seems that a lot of TVs, radios, and even garage door openers suffered damage in

the area around the university. Tell me, Jonathan. Were you
and Tim listening to the radio or watching TV around ten-
fifteen? As I recall the Appletons live over in that general
area.''

''Who, me?'' Jonathan questioned too quickly. ''No, no.
We were . . . reading. Yeah, we were reading.''

Nancy glanced at her son out of the corner of her eye.
She couldn't help but wonder what he really had been doing.

''WHOA!'' JESSE KEMPER SAID. HE MANAGED TO KEEP A
steaming cup of Starbucks coffee from splashing into his
lap as his partner, Vince Garbon, bottomed out their cruiser
on the lip of the driveway going into Pierson's Electrical
Supply. It was located a few blocks away from Costa's
Diner.

Jesse was in his middle fifties and was still athletic. Most
people thought he was no more than forty. He was also an
imposing man with a bushy mustache to offset the thinning
hair on the dome of his large head.

Jesse was a detective lieutenant for the city police and
was well liked by his colleagues. He'd been only the fifth
African-American on the force, but encouraged by his record, the city had commenced a serious recruiting effort toward African-Americans to the point that the department
now racially mirrored the community.

Vince pulled the unmarked sedan around the side of the
building and stopped outside an open garage door next to
a city squad car.

''This I got to see,'' Jesse said, alighting from the passenger seat.

Coming back from a coffee run, he and Vince had heard
on the radio that a repeat, small-time crook by the name of
Eddie Howard had been found after having been cornered
all night by a watchdog. Eddie was so well known at the
police station that he was almost a friend.

Allowing their eyes to adjust from the bright sunlight to
the dim interior, Jesse and Vince could hear voices off to
the right, behind a bank of massive floor-to-ceiling shelv-

ing. When they walked back there they found two uniformed policemen lounging as if on a cigarette break.
Plastered to a corner was Eddie Howard. In front of him
was a large black-and-white pit bull who stood like a statue.
The animal's unblinking eyes were glued to Eddie like two
black marbles.

"Kemper, thank God," Eddie said, holding himself rigid
while he spoke. "Get this animal away from me!"

Jesse looked at the two uniformed cops.

"We called and the owner's on his way in," one of them
said. "Normally they don't get here until nine."

Jesse nodded and turned back to Eddie. "How long have
you been in here?"

"All freakin' night," Eddie said. "Pressed up against
this wall."

"How'd you get in?" Jesse asked.

"Just walked in," Eddie said. "I was just hanging out
in the neighborhood and suddenly the garage door back
there opened by itself, like magic. So I came in to make
sure everything was okay. You know, to help out."

Jesse gave a short derisive laugh. "I guess Fido here
thought you had something else in mind."

"Come on, Kemper," Eddie moaned. "Get this beast
away from me."

"In due time," Jesse said with a chuckle. "In due time."
Then he turned back to the uniformed officers. "Did you
check the garage door?"

"Sure did," the second officer replied.

"Any sign of forced entry?" Jesse asked.

"I think Eddie was telling the truth about that," the officer said.

Jesse shook his head. "More weird stuff happened last
night than you can shake a stick at."

"But mostly in this part of the city," Vince added.

SHEILA MILLER PARKED HER RED BMW CONVERTABLE IN
her reserved spot near the emergency-room entrance. Flipping the front seat forward, she eyed her stricken VCR. She
tried to think of a way of getting it, her briefcase, and a

separate stack of folders into her office in one trip. It
seemed doubtful until she saw a black Toyota utility vehicle
pull up to the unloading bay and discharge a passenger.

"Excuse me, Mr. Henderson," Sheila called out when
she recognized Pitt. She made it a point to know everyone
by name who worked in her department, whether clerk or
surgeon. "Could I see you a moment?"

Although obviously in a hurry, Pitt turned when he heard
his name. Instantly he recognized Dr. Miller. Sheepishly he
reversed directions, descended the steps from the loading
dock, and came over to her car.

"I know I'm a tad late," Pitt said nervously. Dr. Miller
had a reputation of being a no-nonsense administrator. Her
nickname was "Dragon Lady" among the lower-escbelon
staff, particularly the first-year residents. "It won't happen
again," Pitt added.

Sheila glanced at her watch, then back at Pitt. "You're
slated to start medical school in the fall."

"That's true," Pitt answered with his pulse rising.

"Well, at least you're better-looking than most of the
ones in this year's crop," Sheila said, hiding a grin. She
could sense Pitt's anxiety.

Confused by the comment, which sounded like a compliment, Pitt merely nodded. In truth he didn't know what
to say. He had a sense she was toying with him but couldn't
be sure.

"I'll tell you what," Sheila said, nodding toward her
back seat. "If you carry that VCR into my office I won't
mention this egregious infraction to the dean."

Pitt was now reasonably certain that Dr. Miller was teas-
ing him, but he still felt it better to keep his mouth shut.
Without a word he reached in, lifted the VCR, and followed
Dr. Miller into the ER.

There was a moderate amount of activity, particularly
from a few early-morning fender-benders. Fifteen to twenty
patients were waiting in the waiting area, as well as a few
more back in the trauma section. The staff present at the
front desk greeted Dr. Miller with smiles but cast puzzled

looks at Pitt, particularly the person Pitt was scheduled to relieve.

They walked down the main corridor and were about to enter Sheila's office when she caught sight of Kerry Winetrop, one of the hospital's electronic technicians. Keeping all the hospital's monitoring equipment functioning was a full-time job for several people. Sheila called out to the man, and he obligingly came over.

"My VCR had a seizure last night," Sheila said, nodding toward the VCR in Pitt's hands.

"Join the club," Kerry said. "You and a bunch of other people. Apparently there was a surge in the TV cable line around the university area at quarter after ten last night. I've already seen a couple of players that people brought in early this morning."

"A surge, huh," Sheila remarked.

"My TV blew up," Pitt said.

"At least my TV's okay," Sheila said.

"Was it on when the VCR blew?" Kerry asked.

"No," Sheila said.

"Well, that's the reason it didn't pop," Kerry said. "If it had been on you would have lost your picture tube."

"Can the VCR be fixed?" Sheila asked.

"Not without essentially replacing most of the guts," Kerry said. "To tell you the truth it's cheaper to buy another one."

"Too bad," Sheila said. "I'd finally figured out how to set the clock on this one."

CASSY HURRIED UP THE STEPS OF ANNA C. SCOTT HIGH School and entered just as the bell announced the beginning of the first period. Reminding herself that getting freaked out was not going to help anything, she rushed up the main stairs and down the hall to her assigned class. She was in the middle of a month-long observation of a junior English class. This was the first time she'd been late.

Pausing at the door to brush hair from her face and smooth the front of her demure cotton dress, she couldn't help but hear the apparent pandemonium going on inside the room. She'd expected to hear Mrs. Edelman's strident voice. Instead there was a mishmash of voices and laughter. Cassy cracked the door and looked within.

Students were haphazardly sprinkled around the room. Some were standing, others were sitting on the radiator covers and on desks. It was a beehive of separate conversations.

Cracking the door further, Cassy could see why there was such chaos. Mrs. Edelman was not there.

Cassy swallowed hard. Her mouth had gone dry. For a second she debated what to do. Her experience with high-school kids was minimal. All her student teaching had been at the elementary-school level. Deciding she had little choice and taking a deep breath, she pushed through the door.

No one paid her any attention. Advancing to Mrs. Edelman's desk in the front of the room she saw a note in Mrs. Edelman's script. It said simply: *Miss Winthrope, I will be delayed for some minutes. Please carry on.*

With her heart accelerating Cassy glanced out at the scene in front of her. She felt incompetent and an imposter. She wasn't a teacher, not yet anyway.

"Excuse me!" Cassy called. There was no response. She called more loudly. Finally she yelled as loudly as she could, which brought forth a stunned silence. She was now graced with close to thirty pairs of staring eyes. The expressions ran the gamut from surprise to irritation at being interrupted to outright disdain.

"Please take your seats," Cassy said. Her voice wavered more than she would have liked.

Reluctantly the students did as they were told.

"Okay," Cassy said, trying to bolster her confidence. "I know what your assignment was, so until Mrs. Edelman arrives, why don't we talk about Faulkner's style in a general sense. Who'd like to volunteer to get us started?"

Cassy's eyes roamed the room. The students who moments earlier were the picture of animation now appeared as if cut from marble. The expressions of those who were still looking at her were blank. One impertinent red-headed boy puckered his lips into a silent kiss as Cassy's eyes briefly locked onto his. Cassy ignored the gesture.

Cassy could feel perspiration at her hairline. Things were not going well. In the back of the second row she could see a blond-headed boy engrossed with a laptop computer.

Stealing a glance at the seating chart in the middle of the desk blotter, Cassy read the boy's name: Jonathan Sellers.

Looking back up, Cassy tried again: "Okay, everyone. I know it's cool to kinda zone out on me. After all I'm just a student teacher and you all know a lot more about what goes on in here than I do, but . . ."

At that moment the door opened. Cassy turned, hoping to see the competent Mrs. Edelman. Instead the situation took a turn for the worse. In walked Mr. Partridge, the principal.

Cassy panicked. Mr. Partridge was a dour man and a strict disciplinarian. Cassy had only met him once when her group of student teachers was going through their orientation. He'd made it very clear that he was not fond of the student-teaching program and only agreed to it under duress.

"Good morning, Mr. Partridge," Cassy managed. "Can I help you in some way?"

"Just carry on!" Mr. Partridge snapped. "I'd been informed of Mrs. Edelman's delay, so I thought I'd stop by to observe for a moment."

"Of course," Cassy said. She turned her attention back to the stony students and cleared her throat. "Jonathan Sellers," she called out. "Perhaps you could start the discussion."

"Sure," Jonathan said agreeably.

Cassy let out an imperceptible sigh of relief.

"William Faulkner was a major American writer," Jonathan said, trying to sound extemporaneous.

Cassy could tell he was reading off his LCD screen, but she didn't care. In fact, she was grateful for his resourcefulness.

"He's known for his vivid characterizations and, like, his convoluted style . . ."

Tim Appleton sitting across from Jonathan tried vainly to suppress a laugh since he knew what Jonathan was doing.

"Okay," Cassy said. "Let's see how that applies to the story you all were asked to read for today." She turned to the blackboard and wrote "vivid characters" and next to it "complex story structure." Then she heard the door to the hall open and close. Glancing over she was relieved to see that gloomy Partridge had already departed.

Facing the class again she was pleased to see several hands up of people willing to get involved in a discussion. Before she called on one of them, Cassy gave Jonathan a tiny but grateful smile. She wasn't sure but she thought she caught a blush before the boy looked back down at his laptop.

3

OLGAVEE HALL WAS ONE OF THE LARGEST TIERED LECTURE halls in the business school. Although not a graduate student, Beau had been given special permission to take an advanced marketing course that was extremely popular with the business school students. In fact, it was so popular it needed the seating capacity of Olgavee. The lectures were exciting and stimulating. The course was taught in an interactive style with a different professor each week. The downside was that each class required a lot of preparation. One had to be prepared to be called on at any moment.

But Beau was finding it uncharacteristically hard to concentrate at today's lecture. It wasn't the professor's fault. It was Beau's. To the dismay of his immediate neighbors as well as himself, he couldn't stop fidgeting in his seat. He'd developed uncomfortable aches in his muscles that made it impossible to get comfortable. On top of that he had a dull headache behind his eyes. What made everything worse was that he was sitting in the center of the hall four rows back and directly in the line of sight of the lecturer. Beau always made it a point to get to lecture early to get the best seat.

Beau could tell that the speaker was getting annoyed, but he didn't know what to do.

It had started on his way to Olgavee Hall. The first symptom had been a stinging sensation somewhere up inside his nose causing a wave of violent sneezes. It wasn't long before he was blowing his nose on a regular basis. Initially he'd thought he'd caught a cold. But now he had to admit that it had to be more. The irritation rapidly progressed from his sinuses into his throat, which was now sore, especially when he swallowed. To make matters worse, he began to cough repeatedly, which hurt his throat as much as swallowing.

The person sitting directly in front of Beau turned and gave him a dirty look after Beau let out a particularly explosive cough.

As time dragged on, Beau became particularly bothered by a stiff neck. He tried to rub his muscles, but it didn't help. Even the lapel of his jacket seemed to be exacerbating the discomfort. Thinking that the leadlike object in his pocket might be contributing, Beau took it out and put it on the desk in front of him. It looked odd, sitting on his notes. Its perfectly round shape and exquisite symmetry suggested it was a manufactured piece, yet Beau had no idea if it was. For a moment he thought that perhaps it could have been a futuristic paperweight, but he dismissed the idea as too prosaic. More probable was that it was a tiny sculpture, but he truly wasn't sure. Vaguely he wondered if he should take it over to the geology department to inquire if it could be the result of a natural phenomenon like a geode.

Musing about the object made Beau examine the minute wound on the tip of his index finger. It was now a red dot in the center of a few millimeters of pale, bluish skin. Surrounding that was a two-millimeter halo of redness. To the touch it was mildly sore. It felt like a doctor had poked him with one of those strange little lancets they used to get a small blood sample.

A shaking chill interrupted Beau's thoughts. The chill was followed by a sustained bout of coughing. When he finally got his breath, he acknowledged the futility of attempting to last through the lecture. He wasn't getting anything out of it, and on top of that he was bothering his fellow students and the lecturer.

Beau gathered his papers, slipped his putative mini-sculpture back into his pocket, and stood up. He had to excuse himself multiple times to move laterally along the row. Because of the narrow space his exit caused a signif-cant commotion. One student even dropped his looseleaf notebook which opened and sent its contents wafting down into the pit.

When Beau finally got to the aisle, he caught a glimpse of the lecturer shielding his eyes so as to see who was making all the fuss. He was one person Beau wasn't going to ask for a letter of recommendation.

FEELING EMOTIONALLY AS WELL AS PHYSICALLY EX-hausted at the end of the school day, Cassy made her way down the main stairs of the high school and exited out into the horseshoe drive in front. It was pretty clear to her that from a teaching standpoint she liked elementary school much better than high school. From her perspective high-schoolers generally seemed too self-centered and too inter-ested in constantly challenging their boundaries. She even thought a number of them were downright mean. Give me an innocent, eager third-grader any day, Cassy reflected.

The afternoon sun felt warm on Cassy's face. Shielding her eyes with her hand, she scanned the multitude of ve-hicles in the drive. She was looking for Beau's 4×4. He insisted on picking her up each afternoon, and was usually waiting for her. Obviously today was different.

Looking for a place to sit, Cassy saw a familiar face waiting nearby. It was Jonathan Sellers from Mrs. Edel-man's English class. Cassy walked over and said hello.

"Oh, hi," Jonathan stammered. He nervously glanced around, hoping he wasn't being observed by any class-mates. He could feel his face blush. The fact of the matter was, he thought Cassy was the best-looking teacher they'd ever had and had told Tim as much after class.

"Thanks for breaking the ice this morning," Cassy said.

"It was a big help. For a moment I was afraid I was at a funeral, my funeral."

"It was just lucky I'd tried to see what it said about Faulkner in my laptop."

"I still think it took a bit of courage on your part to say something," Cassy said. "I appreciated it. It certainly got the ball rolling. I was afraid no one would speak."

"My friends can be jerks at times," Jonathan admitted.

A dark blue minivan pulled up to the curb. Nancy Sellers leaned across the front seat and popped open the passenger-side door.

"Hi, Mom," Jonathan voiced with a little self-conscious wave.

Nancy Sellers's bright, intelligent eyes jumped back and forth between her seventeen-year-old son and this rather sexy college-age woman. She knew his interest in girls had suddenly mushroomed, but this situation seemed a wee bit inappropriate.

"Are you going to introduce me to your friend?" Nancy asked.

"Yeah, sure," Jonathan said, eyeing the crack in the sidewalk. "This is Miss Winthrope."

Cassy leaned forward and stuck out her hand. "Nice to meet you, Mrs. Sellers. You can call me Cassy."

"Cassy it is then," Nancy replied. She shook Cassy's outstretched hand. There was a short but awkward pause before Nancy asked how long Cassy and Jonathan had known each other.

"Mommmm!" Jonathan moaned. He knew instantly what she was implying, and felt mortified. "Miss Winthrope is a student teacher in English class."

"Oh, I see," Nancy remarked with mild relief.

"My mom is a research virologist," Jonathan said to change the subject and help explain how she could say something so stupid.

"Really," Cassy said. "That's certainly an interesting and important field in today's world. Are you at the University Med Center?"

"No, I'm employed at Serotec Pharmaceuticals," Nancy

said. "But my husband is at the university. He runs the physics department."

"My goodness," Cassy said. She was impressed. "No wonder you have such a bright son here."

Over the top of the Sellerses' van Cassy caught sight of Beau turning into the horseshoe drive.

"Well, nice meeting you," Cassy said to Nancy. Then turning to Jonathan she said: "Thanks again for today."

"It was nothing," Jonathan insisted.

Cassy half skipped, half ran up to where Beau had pulled to the curb.

Jonathan watched her go, mesmerized by the motion of her buttocks beneath her thin cotton dress.

"Well, am I giving you a ride home or not?" Nancy questioned to break the spell. She was becoming concerned again that there was something going on she didn't know about.

Jonathan climbed into the front of the car after carefully depositing his laptop on the backseat.

"What was she thanking you for?" Nancy asked as they pulled away. She could see Cassy getting into a utility vehicle driven by an attractive male her own age. Nancy's concerns melted again. It was tough raising a teenager: one minute proud, the next concerned. It was an emotional roller coaster for which Nancy felt unequipped.

Jonathan shrugged. "Like I said, it was nothing."

"Good grief," Nancy said, frustrated. "Getting even a modicum of information from you reminds me of that saying about squeezing water out of a rock."

"Gimme a break," Jonathan said. As they drove past the black 4×4 he stole another glance at Cassy. She was sitting in the vehicle, talking with the driver.

"YOU LOOK TERRIBLE," CASSY SAID. SHE WAS TWISTED IN the seat so she could look directly into Beau's face. He was paler than she'd ever seen him. Perspiration stood on his forehead like tiny cabochon topazes. His eyes were red and rheumy.

"Thanks for the compliment," Beau said.

"Really," Cassy said. "What's the matter?"

"I don't know," Beau said. He covered his mouth while he coughed. "It came on me just before my marketing class, and it's getting worse. I guess I got the flu. You know, muscle aches, sore throat, runny nose, headache, the works."

Cassy stretched out her hand and felt his sweaty brow. "You're hot," she said.

"Funny because I feel cold," Beau said. "I've been having shivers. I even got into bed, but as soon as I was under the covers, I felt hot and kicked them off."

"You should have stayed in bed," Cassy said. "I could have bummed a ride with one of the other student teachers."

"There was no way to get in touch with you," Beau said.

"Men," Cassy voiced as she got out of the car. "You guys never want to admit when you're sick."

"Where are you going?" Beau questioned.

Cassy didn't answer. Instead she walked around the front of the car and opened Beau's door. "Shove over," she said. "I'm driving."

"I can drive," Beau said.

"No arguments," Cassy said. "Move!"

Beau didn't have the energy to protest. Besides, he knew it was probably best even though he wouldn't admit it.

Cassy put the car in gear. At the corner she turned right instead of left.

"Where the hell are you going?" Beau asked. With his head throbbing he wanted to get back to bed.

"You are going to the student infirmary at the University Med Center," Cassy said. "I don't like the way you look."

"I'll be all right," Beau complained, but he didn't protest further. He was feeling worse by the minute.

The entrance to the student infirmary was through the ER, and as Cassy and Beau walked in, Pitt saw them and came out from behind the front desk.

"Good grief!" Pitt said when he took one look at Beau. "Did the Nite organization cancel your interview or did you get run over by the women's track team?''

"I can do without your wisecracks," Beau mumbled. "I think I got the flu."

"You ain't kidding," Pitt said. "Here, come on into one of the ER bays. I don't think they want you down in the student walk-in clinic."

Beau allowed himself to be led into a cubicle. Pitt facilitated the visit by bringing in one of the most compassionate nurses and then by going out to get one of the more senior ER physicians.

Between the nurse and the doctor Beau was quickly examined. Blood was drawn and an IV started.

"This is just for hydration," the doctor said, tapping the IV bottle. "I think you have a bad case of the flu, but your lungs are clear. Still, I think it best for you to stay in the student overnight ward, at least for a few hours to see if we can't bring your fever down and control that cough. We'll also be able to take a look at your blood work in case there's something I'm missing."

"I don't want to stay in the hospital," Beau complained.

"If the doctor thinks you should stay, you're staying," Cassy said. "I don't want to hear any macho bull crap."

Pitt was again able to grease the skids, and within a half hour Beau was comfortably situated in one of the student overnight rooms. It looked like a typical hospital room with vinyl flooring, metal furniture, a TV, and a window that looked south over the hospital lawn. Beau was dressed in hospital-issue pajamas. His clothes were hung in the closet, and his watch, wallet, and the black mini-sculpture were in a metal valuables cabinet affixed to the top of the bureau. Cassy had programmed the combination lock with the last four digits of their home phone number.

Pitt excused himself to get back to the ER desk.

"Comfortable?" Cassy asked. Beau was lying on his back. His eyes were closed. He'd been given a cough suppressant which had already taken effect. He was exhausted.

"As comfortable as can be expected," Beau murmured.

"The doctor said I should come back in a few hours,"

Cassy said. "All the tests will be available and most likely I'll be able to take you home."

"I'll be here," Beau said. He was enjoying the sensation of a strange languid sleep settling over him like a welcome blanket. He didn't even hear Cassy close the door behind her when she left.

Beau slept more soundly than he'd ever slept. He didn't even dream. After several hours of this comalike trance his body took on a faint phosphorescence. Inside the locked valuables box the black disciform object did the same, particularly one of eight small domed excrescences arrayed around the object's rim. Suddenly the tiny disc detached itself and floated free. Its glow intensified until it became a pinpoint of light like a distant star.

Moving laterally the point of light contacted the side of the valuables box, but it didn't slow. With a muted hissing sound and a few sparks it traveled through the metal, leaving a tiny, perfectly symmetrical hole behind it.

Once free of the confined space, the point of light traveled directly to Beau, causing Beau's luminosity to intensify. It approached Beau's right eye and then hovered a few millimeters away. Slowly the intensity of the point of light decreased until it assumed its normal flat black color.

A few pulses of visible light traveled from the tiny object and impinged on Beau's eyelid. Instantly the eye opened while the other stayed shut. The exposed pupil was maximally dilated with just a bare band of iris visible.

Pulses of electromagnetic radiation were then dispatched into Beau's open eye, mostly in the visible light wavelength. It was one computer downloading to another, and it went on for almost an hour.

"HOW'S OUR FAVORITE PATIENT?" CASSY ASKED PITT when she came through the ER door. Pitt hadn't seen her until she'd spoken. The ER had been busy and he'd had his hands full.

"Fine as far as I know," Pitt said. "I looked in on him a couple of times, as did the nurse. Every time he was sleeping like a baby. I don't think he moved. He must have been exhausted.''

"Did his blood work come back?" Cassy asked.

"Yup, and it was pretty normal," Pitt said. "His white count was up slightly but only his mononuclear lymphocytes."

"Hey, remember you're talking to a layperson," Cassy said.

"Sorry," Pitt said. "The bottom line is that he can go home. Then it's the usual. You know: fluids, aspirin, rest, and some TLC."

"What do I have to do to get him released?" Cassy asked.

"Nothing," Pitt said. "I already did all the paperwork. We just have to get him out into the car. Come on, I'll give you a hand."

Pitt got leave from the head nurse to take a break. He found a wheelchair and started down the hall toward the student overnight ward.

"You think a wheelchair is necessary?" Cassy asked with concern.

"We might as well have it just in case," Pitt said. "His legs were pretty wobbly when you brought him in."

They got to the door, and Pitt knocked quietly. When there was no answer he cracked the door and peered inside.

"Just as I thought," Pitt said. He opened the door wide to push in the wheelchair. "Sleeping Beauty still hasn't moved."

Pitt parked the wheelchair and followed Cassy to the bed. Each went to a separate side.

"What did I tell you?" Pitt said. "The picture of tranquility. Why don't you kiss him and see if he turns into a frog."

"Should we wake him?" Cassy asked, ignoring Pitt's attempt at humor.

"It's going to be hard getting him home if we don't," Pitt said.

"He looks so peaceful," Cassy said. "He also looks a

hell of a lot better than he did earlier. In fact, his color looks normal.''

"I suppose," Pitt said.

Cassy reached out and gently shook Beau's arm while calling his name softly. When he didn't respond, she shook him harder.

Beau's eyes blinked open. He looked back and forth between his two friends. "Hey, how ya doing?" he asked.

"I think the question is how you are doing," Cassy said.

"Me, I'm fine," Beau said. Then his eyes made a rapid sweep around the room. "Where am I?"

"At the med center," Cassy said.

"What am I doing here?" Beau questioned.

"You don't remember?" Cassy asked with concern.

Beau shook his head. He yanked back the covers and threw his feet over the side.

"You don't remember getting sick in class?" Cassy asked. "You don't remember my bringing you here?"

"Oh, yeah," Beau said. "It's coming back. Yeah, I remember. I felt terrible." He looked at Pitt. "Jeez, what did you guys give me? I feel like a new man."

"Seems that you just needed some serious shuteye," Pitt said. "Except for a little hydration, we really didn't treat you."

Beau stood up and stretched. "I might have to come in for hydration more often," he said. "What a difference." He eyed the wheelchair. "Who's that contraption for?"

"You, in case you needed it," Pitt said. "Cassy came to take you home."

"I sure don't need any wheelchair," Beau said. He then coughed and made a face. "Well, my throat's still a little sore, and I still have a cough, but let's get out of here." He stepped over to the closet and grabbed his clothes. He retreated to the bathroom and pushed the door almost closed. "Cassy, could you get my wallet and watch out of that cabinet?" he called through the door.

Cassy stepped over to the bureau and entered the combination.

"If you guys don't need me, I'll head back to the desk," Pitt said.

Cassy turned as she stuck her hand into the valuables box. "You've been a dear," she said as her hand grasped Beau's wallet and watch. She pulled them out and shut the door. Stepping over to Pitt she gave him a hug. "Thanks for your help."

"Hey, any time," Pitt said self-consciously. He looked down at his feet, then out the window. Cassy had a way of making him feel flustered.

Beau came out from the bathroom still tucking in his shirt. "Yeah, thanks, buddy," he said. He gave Pitt a poke in the arm. "Really appreciate it."

"Glad you're feeling better," Pitt said. "See you around." Pitt grabbed the wheelchair and pushed it out the door.

"He's a good guy," Beau said.

Cassy nodded. "He'll make a good doctor. He really cares."

4

CHARLIE ARNOLD HAD BEEN WORKING FOR THE UNIVER-
sity Medical Center for thirty-seven years, ever since his
seventeenth birthday when he decided to drop out of
school. He'd begun with the Building and Grounds Department, mowing lawns, pruning trees, and weeding the
flower beds. Unfortunately an allergy to grass drove him
out of that line of work. But since he was a valued hospital
employee, the administration offered him a housekeeping
position instead. Charlie had accepted and enjoyed the
work. Particularly on hot days he enjoyed it more than being outside.

Charlie liked working on his own. The supervisor would
give him a list of the rooms to clean, and off he'd go. On
this particular night he had one more room to go: one of
the student overnight rooms. They were always easier than
a regular hospital room. In a regular room he never knew
what he was going to run into. It depended on the illness
of the previous occupant. Sometimes they could be pretty
bad.

Whistling under his breath, Charlie cracked open the
door, pushed in his mop bucket, and pulled in his cleaning
cart. With his hands on his hips he surveyed the room. As
he'd expected, it only needed a light disinfectant mopping

and dusting. He walked over to the bathroom and glanced in there. It didn't even look as if it had been used.

Charlie always started in the bathroom. After putting on his thick protective gloves, he scrubbed out the shower and the sink and disinfected the toilet. Then he mopped the floor.

Moving out into the room, he peeled off the bed linens and wiped down the mattress. He dusted all other horizontal surfaces, including the windowsill. He was about to start mopping when a glow caught his eye. Turning to face the bureau, he stared at the valuables safe. Although his mind told him it was preposterous, the box seemed to be glowing as if there was an enormously powerful light inside it. Of course that didn't make any sense, since the box was made out of metal, so no matter how bright a light was, even if there was one inside, it wouldn't shine through.

Charlie leaned his mop against the top edge of the bucket, and took a few steps toward the bureau, intending to open the door to the box. But he stopped about three feet away. The glow that surrounded the box had gotten brighter. Charlie even imagined he could feel a warmth on his face!

Charlie's first thought was to get the hell out of the room, but he hesitated. It was a confusing spectacle and mildly frightening, yet curious at the same time.

Then to Charlie's amazement a shower of sparks burst forth from the side of the box accompanied by a hissing sound similar to arc welding. Charlie's hands reflexively shot up to protect his face from the sparks, but they stopped almost the moment they began. From the point of sparking a luminous red spinning disc the size of a silver dollar emerged. It had seared through the metal, leaving a smoking slit.

Completely stunned by this phenomenon, Charlie couldn't move. The spinning disc slowly traveled laterally toward the window, coming within a foot of his arm. At the window it hovered as if it were appreciating the vista of the night sky. Then its color changed from red to white-hot and a corona appeared around it like a narrow halo.

Charlie's curiosity propelled him closer to this mysterious object. He knew no one was going to believe him when he described it. Holding out his hand, palm down, he waved it back and forth over the object to make sure there wasn't a wire or a string. He couldn't understand how it was hanging in the air.

Sensing its warmth, Charlie cupped his hands and slowly brought them closer and closer to the object. It was a peculiar warmth that tingled his skin. When his hands got within the corona, the tingling magnified.

The object ignored Charlie until he inadvertently blocked the object's view of the night sky. The moment he did so, the disc moved laterally, and before Charlie could react, it instantly and effortlessly burnt a hole through the center of his palm! Skin, bone, ligaments, nerves, and blood vessels were all vaporized.

Charlie let out a yelp more in surprise than pain. It had happened so quickly. He staggered back, gaping at his perforated hand in total disbelief and smelling the unmistakable aroma of burnt flesh. There was no bleeding since all the vessels had been heat-coagulated. In the next instant the corona around the luminous object expanded to a foot in diameter.

Before Charlie could react, a whooshing sound commenced and rapidly increased in volume until it was deafening. At the same time Charlie felt a force pulling him toward the window. Frantically he reached out with his good hand and grabbed the bed only to have his feet go out from underneath him. Gritting his teeth, he managed to hang on even though the bed itself moved. The violence of the sound and the movement lasted only seconds before being capped by a noise vaguely reminiscent of the closing of a central vac port.

Charlie let go of the bed and tried to get to his feet, but he couldn't. The muscles of his legs were like rubber. He knew something was horribly wrong and tried to cry out for help, but his voice was weak, and he was salivating so copiously that any speech was nearly impossible. Marshalling what strength he had, he attempted to crawl toward the door. But the effort was in vain. After moving only a few feet he started to retch. Moments later utter darkness descended as Charlie's body was racked by a series of rapidly fatal grand mal seizures.

5

AS FAR AS STUDENT APARTMENTS WENT, IT WAS RELA-
tively luxurious and spacious, and since it was located on
the second floor, it even had a view. Both Cassy's and
Beau's parents wanted their children to live in decent surroundings and had been accordingly willing to up their
kids' living allowances when they decided to move out of
their dorms. Part of the reason for the largesse was that
both had stellar academic records.

Cassy and Beau had found the apartment eight months
previously and had jointly painted and furnished it. The
furniture was mostly garage-sale acquisitions which had
been stripped and refinished. The curtains were bedsheets
in disguise.

The bedroom faced east which at times was a bother
because of the intensity of the morning sun. It wasn't a
bedroom that invited late sleeping. But at a little after two
in the morning, it was dark save for a swath of light that
slanted through the window from a streetlight in the parking
lot.

Cassy and Beau were sound asleep: Cassy on her side
and Beau on his back. As was normal for her, Cassy had
been moving at regular intervals, first on one side, then the
other. Beau, on the other hand, had not moved at all. He'd

been motionlessly sleeping on his back just as he had that afternoon in the student overnight ward.

At exactly two-ten Beau's closed eyes began to glow, as did the radium dial of an old windup alarm clock Cassy had inherited from her grandmother. After a few minutes of gradually increasing intensity Beau's eyelids popped open. Both eyes were as dilated as his right eye had been that afternoon, and both eyes glowed as if they were light sources themselves.

After reaching a peak of luminosity they began to fade until the pupils were their usual black. Then the irises began to contract until they had assumed a more normal size. After a few blinks, Beau realized he was awake.

Slowly he sat up. Similar to the way he'd awakened in the hospital, he was momentarily disoriented. Sweeping his eyes around the room, he quickly pieced together where he was. Then he lifted his hands and studied them by flexing his fingers. His hands felt different, but he couldn't explain how. In fact, his whole body felt different in some inexplicable way.

Reaching over to Cassy he gently gave her shoulder a shake. She responded by rolling over onto her back. Her heavily lidded eyes regarded him. When she saw he was sitting up, she quickly did the same.

"What's the matter?" she asked huskily. "Are you all right?"

"Fine," Beau said. "Perfect."

"No cough?"

"Not yet. Throat feels fine too."

"Why'd you wake me? Can I get you something?"

"No, thanks," Beau said. "Actually I thought you'd like to see something. Come on!"

Beau got out of bed and came around to Cassy's side. He took her hand and helped her to her feet.

"You want to show me something now?" Cassy asked. She glanced at the clock.

"Right now," Beau said. He guided her into the living room and over to the slider that led to the balcony. When he motioned for her to step outside, she resisted.

"I can't go out," she said. "I'm naked."

"Come on," Beau said. "Nobody's going to see us. It's only going to take a moment, and if we don't go now we'll miss it."

Cassy debated with herself. In the half light she couldn't see Beau's expression, but he sounded sincere. The idea that this was some kind of prank had occurred to her.

"This better be interesting," Cassy warned as she finally stepped over the slider's track.

The night air had its usual chill, and Cassy hugged herself. Even so, everything erectile on the surface of her body popped up. She felt like one big goose pimple.

Beau stepped behind her and enveloped her in his arms to help control Cassy's shivering. They were standing at the railing facing a broad stretch of the sky. It was a cloudless, clear, moonless night.

"Okay, what am I supposed to be seeing?" she asked.

Beau pointed up toward the northern sky. "Look up there toward the Pleiades in the constellation of Taurus."

"What is this, an astronomy lesson?" Cassy questioned. "It's two-ten in the morning. Since when did you know anything about the constellations?"

"Watch!" Beau commanded.

"I'm watching," Cassy said. "What am I supposed to be seeing?"

At that moment there was a rain of meteors with extraordinarily long tails, all streaking from the same pinpoint of sky like a gigantic firework display.

"My God!" Cassy exclaimed. She held her breath until the rain of shooting stars faded. The spectacle was so impressive that she momentarily forgot the chill. "I've never seen anything like it. It was beautiful. Was that what they call a meteor shower?"

"I suppose," Beau said vaguely.

"Will there be more?" Cassy asked, her eyes still glued to the point of origin.

"Nope, that's it," Beau said. He let go of Cassy, then followed her back inside. He closed the slider.

Cassy sprinted back to the bed and dived in. When Beau

appeared she had the covers clutched around her neck and was shivering. She ordered him to get under the blanket to warm her up.

"Gladly," he said.

They snuggled for a moment and Cassy's shivering abated. Pulling back from where she had her face tucked into the crook of his neck, she tried to look into Beau's eyes, but they were lost in the gloom. "Thanks for getting me out there to see that meteor shower," she said. "At first I thought you were trying to play a joke on me. But I have one question: How did you know it was going to happen?"

"I can't remember," Beau said. "I guess I heard about it someplace."

"Did you read about it in the paper?" Cassy suggested.

"I don't think so," Beau said. He scratched his head. "I really don't remember."

Cassy shrugged. "Well, it doesn't matter. What matters is that we got to see it. How did you wake up?"

"I don't know," Beau said.

Cassy pushed away and turned on the bedside light. She studied Beau's face. He smiled under her scrutiny.

"Are you sure you feel all right?" she asked.

Beau smiled. "Yeah, I'm sure," he said. "I feel great."

6

IT WAS ONE OF THOSE CLOUDLESS, CRYSTALLINE MORNINGS
with the air so fresh it could almost be tasted. The most
distant mountains stood out with shocking clarity. The normally dry ground was covered with a cool layer of dew
that sparkled like so many diamonds.

Beau stood for a moment taking in the scene. It was as
if he'd seen it for the first time. He couldn't believe the
range of colors of the distant hills, and he questioned why
he'd not appreciated it before.

He was dressed casually in an Oxford shirt, jeans, and
loafers with no socks. He cleared his throat. His cough was
all but gone and his throat didn't hurt when he swallowed.

Pushing off from the entrance to his apartment building
he walked along the walkway, then up the driveway and
into the back parking area. In the sand lining the far periphery he found what he was looking for. Three black
mini-sculptures identical to the one he'd found in Costa's
parking lot the morning before. He scooped them up, dusted
them off, and slipped them into separate pockets.

With his mission accomplished, he turned and retraced
his steps.

Inside the apartment the alarm went off next to Cassy's
head. The alarm was on her side of the bed because Beau

had a bad habit of turning it off so quickly that neither of them truly woke up.

Cassy's hand snaked out from beneath the covers and hit the dream bar. The alarm fell silent for ten luscious minutes. Rolling onto her back, her hand extended toward Beau to give him a shove, the first of many. Beau was not a morning person.

Cassy's exploring hand found empty, cool sheets. The searching arc was extended. Still nothing. Cassy opened her eyes and looked over at Beau, but he was not there!

Surprised by this unexpected turn of events, Cassy sat up and listened for any tell-tale noise from the bathroom. The house was silent. Beau never got up before she did. Suddenly she was worried that his illness had returned.

After slipping on her robe, Cassy padded out into the living room. She was about to call out his name when she saw him over by their fish tank. He was bending down, studying the fish. He was so intent he'd not heard her. While she watched he placed his right index finger against the glass. Somehow his finger concentrated the fluorescent aquarium light so that the tip of his finger glowed.

Mesmerized by this scene, Cassy just stood there continuing to watch. Soon all the fish flocked to the point where Beau's finger touched the glass. When he moved the finger laterally, the fish all dutifully followed.

"How are you doing that?" Cassy asked.

Surprised by Cassy's presence, Beau stood up, letting his hand fall to his side. At the same instant the fish dispersed to the far ends of the tank.

"I didn't hear you come into the room," Beau said with a pleasant smile.

"Obviously," Cassy said. "What were you doing to attract the fish that way?"

"Damned if I know," Beau said. "Maybe they thought I was going to feed them." He came over to Cassy and draped his arms on her shoulders. His smile was radiant. "You look wonderful this morning."

"Oh, yeah, sure," Cassy said jokingly. She tussled her thick hair, then patted it into place. "There, now I'm ready for the Miss America Pageant.'' She looked up into Beau's eyes. They were a particularly effulgent blue, and the whites were whiter than white.

"You are the one who looks wonderful," Cassy said.

"I feel wonderful," Beau said. He bent down to kiss Cassy on the lips, but she ducked out from beneath his arms.

"Hold on," she said. "This beauty contestant has yet to brush her teeth. I wouldn't want to be disqualified on account of morning breath."

"Not a chance," Beau said with a lascivious smile.

Cassy cocked her head to one side. "You're feeling chipper today," she remarked.

"As I said, I feel great," Beau said.

"That was sure a short course of the flu," Cassy said. "I'd say you made a remarkable recovery."

"I guess I have you to thank for hauling me over to the medical center," Beau said. "That's where things took a turn for the better."

"But the doctor and the nurse didn't do anything," Cassy said. "They admitted so themselves."

Beau shrugged. "Then it's a new strain of a rapid flu. I'm certainly not going to complain about its short course."

"Me neither," Cassy said, starting for the bathroom. "Why don't you make coffee while I take a shower."

"Coffee is already made," Beau said. "I'll bring you a cup."

"Aren't we being efficient," Cassy called on her way through the bedroom.

"Nothing but five-star service in this hotel," Beau said.

Cassy continued to marvel at Beau's quick turnaround. Remembering how he looked when she'd climbed into the car in front of the Anna C. Scott school, she never would have suspected it. She turned on the shower and adjusted the temperature. When it was to her liking, she climbed in. The first order of business was her hair. She washed it every day.

No sooner had she gotten her scalp full of shampoo when she heard knocking on the outside of the shower door.

Without opening her eyes, she told Beau to leave her coffee mug on the back of the sink.

Sticking her head under the jet of water, she began to rinse. The next thing she knew was that Beau was in the shower with her.

She opened her eyes with disbelief. Beau was standing right in front of her in the shower fully clothed. He even still had on his loafers.

"What on earth are you doing?" Cassy sputtered. She had to laugh. It was such an unexpected, zany thing for him to do.

Beau didn't say anything. Instead he reached out and hungrily drew Cassy's wet, naked body to him while his lips sought hers. It was a deep, sensual, carnal kiss.

Cassy managed to come up for air, laughing at the absurdity of what they were doing. Beau laughed as well as the water flattened his hair against his forehead.

"You're crazy," Cassy commented. Her hair was still full of soap suds.

"Crazy for you is more accurate," Beau said. He started to fumble with his belt.

Cassy helped by undoing the buttons of his soaked shirt and peeling it from his muscular shoulders. The situation might have been unconventional, especially for the normally neat and compulsive Beau, but for Cassy it was a turn-on. It was so wonderfully spontaneous, and Beau's eagerness added additional spice.

Later, in the midst of their passion, Cassy began to appreciate something else. Not only were they making love in a unique circumstance, but they were making love in an atypical way. Beau was touching her differently. She wasn't able to explain it exactly, but it was marvelous, and she loved it. It had something to do with Beau being more gentle and sensitive than usual even in the midst of his overwhelming ardor.

REACHING HIS HANDS OVER HIS HEAD, PITT STRETCHED. HE looked at the clock on the ER desk. It was almost seven-thirty and soon his marathon twenty-four-hour shift would be over. He was already fantasizing how good his bed was going to feel when he slid his tired body between the sheets. The idea of the exercise was to give him an idea of what it's like being a resident, when shifts of thirty-six hours are commonplace.

"You should go down to the room where they found that poor guy from housekeeping," Cheryl Watkins said. Cheryl was one of the day staff nurses who'd recently come on duty.

"How come?" Pitt asked. He remembered the patient very well. The patient had been rushed into the ER a little after midnight by someone from housekeeping. The ER doctors had started resuscitation, but had stopped after quickly realizing the patient's body temperature was about the same as room temperature.

Deciding the man was dead had been easy. The hard part was deciding what had killed him other than the apparent seizures he'd had. There'd been a curious bloodless hole through his hand that one of the doctors thought might have been caused by electricity. Yet the history said he'd been found in a room without any access to a high voltage.

Another doctor noticed the patient had particularly dense cataracts. That was strange because cataracts had not been noted on the man's annual employment physical, and his co-workers denied he had any visual handicap. So that suggested the man had suffered sudden cataracts, which the doctors dismissed. They'd never heard of such a thing even when a powerful jolt of electricity was involved.

Confusion about the proximate cause of death lead to wild speculation and even some bets. The only thing that was certain was that no one knew for sure, and the body was sent to the medical examiner's office for the final word.

"I'm not going to tell you why you should see the room," Cheryl said. "Because if I did, you'd say I was pulling your leg. Suffice it to say that it's weird."

"Gimme a hint," Pitt said. He was so tired that the idea of walking all the way over to the hospital proper did not engender a lot of enthusiasm unless it was for something truly unique.

"You have to see for yourself," Cheryl insisted before she headed off to a meeting.

Pitt tapped a pencil against his forehead while he debated. The idea of the circumstance being weird intrigued him. Calling after Cheryl, he asked her where the room was located.

"In the student overnight ward," Cheryl called back over her shoulder. "You can't miss it because there's a ton of people there trying to figure out what happened."

Curiosity overcame Pitt's fatigue. If there were a lot of people involved maybe he should make the effort. He heaved himself to his feet and dragged his tired body down the corridor. At least the student overnight ward was close. While he walked he vaguely thought that if it were truly weird maybe Cassy and Beau would like to hear about it, since they'd just been there the previous afternoon.

As he rounded the final corner that lead to the student infirmary, Pitt could see a small crowd of people milling about. As he came up to the room his curiosity mounted because whatever the situation was, it involved the same room that Beau had occupied.

"What's going on?" Pitt whispered to one of his classmates who also worked in the hospital on a work-study program. Her name was Carol Grossman.

"You tell me," Carol said. "When I got a chance to see I suggested that perhaps Salvador Dali had stopped by, but nobody laughed."

Pitt gave her a quizzical look, but she didn't elaborate. He pushed on, literally. There were so many people he had to worm his way through. Unfortunately in the process he was a bit too aggressive and managed to jostle one of the doctors enough to cause her coffee to slosh out of her cup. When the doctor angrily turned around to glare at Pitt, Pitt caught his breath. Of all the staff, it had to be Dr. Sheila Miller!

"Damn it," Sheila snapped, shaking the hot coffee from the back of her hand. She was in her long white coat. Several fresh coffee stains graced the cuff of her right sleeve.

"I'm terribly sorry," Pitt managed.

Sheila raised her green eyes to Pitt's. She appeared particularly severe with her blond hair pulled tightly back from her face in a compact bun. Her cheeks were flushed with irritation.

"Mr. Henderson!" she snapped. "I hope to God you don't have your sights on a specialty requiring coordination, like eye surgery."

"It was an accident," Pitt pleaded.

"Yeah, that's what people said about World War I," Sheila said. "And think of the consequences! You're the ER clerk. What in God's name are you doing forcing your way in here."

Pitt frantically searched his mind for some reasonable explanation beyond simple curiosity. Simultaneously, his eyes swept the room, hoping to see something that might offer a suggestion. Instead what he saw stunned him.

The first thing that caught his eye was that the shape of the head of the bed was distorted as if it had been heated to the melting point and pulled toward the window. The night table looked the same. In fact as his eyes completed their circuit of the room, he noticed that most of the furniture and fixtures had been twisted out of shape as if they had been made of taffy. The windowpanes, meanwhile, appeared to have melted, with the glass forming stalactite-like formations that hung down from the muntins.

"What on earth happened in here?" Pitt asked.

Sheila spoke through clenched teeth: "Answering that question is why these professionals are standing here talking. Now get back to the ER desk!"

"I'm on my way," Pitt said quickly.

After one more quick glance at the strange transformation of the room, he retreated back through the crowd. He couldn't help but wonder what kind of damage he'd done to his career by pissing off the Dragon Lady.

"I'M SORRY FOR THE INTERRUPTION," SHEILA SAID. SHE was talking with Detective Lieutenant Jesse Kemper and his partner Vince Garbon.

"No problem," Jesse said. "I wasn't making a lot of

sense anyway. I mean, this is a pretty strange situation, but
I don't think it's a crime scene. My gut reaction tells me
this was not a homicide. Maybe you should get some science experts in here to tell us if a bolt of lightning could
have come in through this window.''

"But there wasn't a thunderstorm," Sheila complained.

"I know," Jesse said philosophically. He spread his
hands like a supplicant. "But you said your engineers ruled
out building power. It sure looks like the guy got electro-
cuted, and if he did, maybe it was lightning.''

"I can't buy it," Sheila said. "I'm not a forensic pathologist, but I seem to remember that when lightning
strikes an individual, it doesn't make a hole. It grounds,
usually coming out the feet, even occasionally blowing the
shoes off. There's no evidence of a ground in here. This is
more like some powerful laser beam.''

"Hey, there you go," Jesse said. "I never thought of
that. Don't you have laser beams here in the hospital?
Maybe somebody shot one in through the window.''

"We've certainly got lasers in the hospital," Sheila admitted. "But nothing that could make the kind of hole we
saw in Mr. Arnold's hand. Plus I can't imagine a laser
being responsible for these strange distortions that we see
with the furniture.''

"Well, I'm plumb out of my league here," Jesse said.
"If the autopsy suggests we got a corpus delecti and a
homicide, we'll get involved. Otherwise I think you have
to get the science guys over here.''

"We've put in a call to the physics department at the
university," Sheila said.

"I think that's the best idea," Jesse said. "Meanwhile,
here's my card." He stepped over to Sheila and gave her
the business card. He also gave one to Richard Halprin,
president of the University Medical Center, and Wayne
Maritinez, head of hospital security. "Any of you can call
me anytime. I'm interested, really. It's been a strange couple of nights. There's been more weird stuff happening than
in all the previous thirty years I've been on the force. Is it
a full moon or what?''

• • •

AT THE VERY END OF THE SHOW, THE MUSIC REACHED A
crescendo, and with a final clap of cymbals, the dome of
the planetarium went dark. Then the general lights came
on. Instantly the auditorium erupted in a smattering of applause, a few whistles, and a babble of excited voices. Most
of the seats were occupied by elementary school kids on a
field trip. Except for teachers and chaperones, Cassy and
Beau were the only adults.

"That was really fun," Cassy said. "I'd forgotten what
a planetarium show was like. The last time I'd seen one
was in Miss Korth's fourth-grade class."

"I liked it too," Beau said with enthusiasm. "It's fas-
cinating seeing what the galaxy looks like from the point
of view of Earth."

Cassy blinked and stared at Beau. All morning long he
seemed to have a penchant to pop off with a curious non
sequitur.

"Come on," Beau said, oblivious to Cassy's mild per-
plexity. He stood up. "Let's try to get out of here ahead
of these screaming kids."

Hand in hand they exited the auditorium and strolled out
onto the expansive lawn that separated the planetarium and
the natural history museum. From a pushcart vendor they
purchased hot dogs smothered with chili and onions. On a
seat in the shade of a large tree they sat down to enjoy their
lunch.

"I'd also forgotten how much fun playing hooky can
be," Cassy said in between bites of hot dog. "It's lucky
that I wasn't scheduled for student teaching today. I mean,
skipping class is one thing, but skipping student teaching
is something else entirely. I wouldn't have been able to
come."

"I'm glad it worked out," Beau said.

"I was surprised when you suggested it," Cassy said.
"Isn't this the first time you've ever skipped class?"

"Yup," Beau said.

Cassy laughed. "What is this, a new Beau? First you act
like an amorous animal and jump into the shower with your

clothes on and now you've willingly missed three classes.
But don't get me wrong, I'm not complaining.''

"It's all your fault," Beau said. He put down his hot
dog and pulled Cassy to him and enveloped her in a play-
fully sexy embrace. "You're irresistible." He tried to kiss
her, but Cassy got her hand up and parried the move.

"Wait a sec," she laughed. "I've got chili all over my
face."

"All the more spice," Beau joked.

Cassy wiped her face with her napkin. "What's gotten
into you?"

Beau didn't answer. Instead he gave Cassy a long, wonderful kiss. Just like in the shower, the impulsiveness of
the gesture was another distinct turn-on for her.

"Wow, you are transmogrifying into a world-class Ca-
sanova," Cassy said as she sat back, took a breath, and
tried to collect herself. The fact that she could be turned on
so easily in public in the middle of the day surprised her.

Beau happily went back to his hot dog. As he chewed
he raised his hand to block out the sun while he looked in
the sun's direction.

"How far did they say Earth is from the sun?" he asked.

"Jeez, I don't know," Cassy said. Having experienced
the stirring of desire, it was hard to change the subject,
especially to something as specific as astronomical dis-
tances. "Ninety-something million miles."

"Oh, yeah," Beau said. "Ninety-three. That means it
would take just a little over eight minutes for the effect of
a solar flare to reach here."

"Excuse me?" Cassy asked. There was another one of
his non sequiturs. She didn't even know what a solar flare
was.

"Look," Beau said excitedly, pointing up into the western sky. "You can see the moon even though it's day-
light."

Cassy shielded her eyes and followed the line of Beau's
pointing finger. Sure enough, she could just barely make
out the gossamer image of the moon. She looked back at
Beau. He was enjoying himself immensely in an endearing,

almost childlike way. His enthusiasm was infectious, and she couldn't help enjoying herself as well.

"What made you want to come to the planetarium today?" Cassy asked.

Beau shrugged. "Just pure interest," he said. "A chance to learn a little more about this beautiful planet. Let's head over to the museum next. You up for that?"

"Why not?" Cassy exclaimed.

JONATHAN CARRIED HIS LUNCH OUTSIDE. ON SUCH A DAY he hated to be in the crowded cafeteria, especially since he'd not seen Candee in there. Skirting the flagpole in the central quad, he headed over to the bleachers alongside the baseball diamond. He knew that was one of Candee's favorite places to get away from the crowd. As he approached he could see that his efforts were to be rewarded. Candee was sitting on the top row.

They waved to each other, and Jonathan started up. There was a slight breeze, and it was snapping the edges of Candee's skirt, revealing tantalizing glimpses of her thighs. Jonathan tried not to make it obvious that he was watching.

"Hi," Candee said.

"Hi," Jonathan answered. He sat down next to her and extracted one of his peanut butter and banana sandwiches.

"Ugh," Candee said. "I can't believe you can eat that stuff."

Jonathan studied his sandwich before taking a bite. "I like it," he said.

"What did Tim say about his radio?" Candee asked.

"He's still pissed," Jonathan said. "But at least he doesn't think it was our fault anymore. The same thing happened to a friend of his brother's."

"Can we still get the car?" Candee asked.

"I'm afraid not," Jonathan said.

"What are we going to do?" Candee asked.

"I don't know," Jonathan said. "I wish to hell my parents weren't so tight-assed about our family car. They treat me like I'm twelve. The only time I can drive the thing is when they are along."

"At least your parents let you get your license," Candee complained. "Mine are making me wait until I'm eighteen."

"That's criminal," Jonathan said. "If they tried that with me, I think I'd run away. But what good is my license without wheels? It's so frustrating my parents won't give me more credit than they do. I mean, I do have a brain. I'm getting good grades, I don't do drugs."

Candee rolled her eyes.

"I don't consider that pot we tried drugs," Jonathan said. "And how many times did we do it: twice!"

"Hey, look," Candee said. She pointed at the receiving dock about seventy-five feet away where trucks made deliveries. It was on the basement level and was approached by a ramp cut into the ground just behind the backstop of the baseball diamond.

"Isn't that Mr. Partridge with the school nurse?" Candee asked.

"It sure is," Jonathan said. "And he doesn't look so good. Look at the way Miss Golden is holding him up. And listen to the old windbag cough."

At that moment an aged Lincoln Town Car pulled around the side of the building and descended the ramp. Behind the wheel Candee and Jonathan recognized Mrs. Partridge, whom the kids in the school called Miss Piggy. Mrs. Partridge seemed to be coughing as much as Mr. Partridge.

"What a pair," Jonathan commented.

While Jonathan and Candee watched, Miss Golden managed to get the sagging Mr. Partridge down a half flight of cement steps and into the car. Mrs. Partridge didn't get out.

"He looks sicker than a dog," Candee said.

"Miss Piggy looks worse," Jonathan said.

The car backed up, turned, and accelerated up the ramp. Halfway up it scraped lightly against the concrete wall. The grating sound made Jonathan wince.

"So much for the paint job," he said.

"WHAT IN GOD'S NAME ARE YOU DOING BACK HERE?" Cheryl Watkins demanded. She was sitting at the ER desk as Pitt Henderson dragged himself through the swinging doors. He looked exhausted with dark circles under his eyes.

"I couldn't sleep," he said. "So I thought I might as well come back and try to salvage what I could of my medical career."

"What on earth are you talking about?" Cheryl asked.

"This morning when I went over to see that room you suggested, I committed a disastrous faux pas."

"Like what?" Cheryl questioned. She could see he was troubled, and she was concerned. Pitt was well liked in the unit.

"I accidentally bumped into the Dragon Lady and spilled her coffee over her and her white coat," Pitt said. "And let me tell you, she was royally pissed. She demanded to know what I was doing there and stupid me couldn't think of a reason."

"Uh oh!" Cheryl commiserated. "Dr. Miller is not fond of getting her white coat dirty, especially early in the morning."

"As we all know!" Pitt said. "She was pretty blunt. Anyway I thought maybe by coming back I could at least impress her with my dedication."

"Can't hurt, although it is above and beyond the call of duty," Cheryl said. "On the other hand, we can always use the help, and I'll make sure our fearless leader hears about it. Meanwhile, why don't you check in a couple of the more routine cases. We had a bad traffic accident an hour ago so we're way behind, and the RNs are all tied up."

Pleased to get a task, especially one that he enjoyed, Pitt grabbed the top clipboard and headed for the patient waiting area. The patient's name was Sandra Evans, aged four.

Pitt called out the name. From the multitude of people impatiently waiting on the hard plastic chairs in the crowded room, a mother and daughter stood up. The woman was in her early thirties and rather bedraggled. The child was darling with tightly curled blond hair, but appeared sick and dirty. She was dressed in soiled pajamas and a tiny robe.

Leading the way, Pitt took them back to an examination bay. He lifted the child up onto the table. Her blue eyes were glassy and her skin pale and moist. She was sick enough not to be overconcerned about the ER environment.

"Are you the doctor?" the mother asked. Pitt appeared much too young.

"The clerk," Pitt announced. Having worked in the ER long enough and having checked in enough prescreened patients Pitt was not self-conscious about his status.

"What's the trouble, sweetheart?" Pitt asked as he wrapped a child's blood pressure cuff around Sandra's arm and inflated it.

"I got a spider," Sandra said.

"She means a bug," the mother interjected. "She can't get that straight. It's the flu or something. It hit her this morning with coughing and sneezing. I tell you, it's always something with kids."

The blood pressure was fine. As Pitt undid the cuff he noted a colorful Band-Aid on Sandra's right palm.

"Looks like you got a booboo too," Pitt said. He got the body temperature instrument and was about to get a reading.

"A rock bit me in the yard," Sandra said.

"Sandra, I told you not to fib," Mrs. Evans said. It was obvious the mother was at the limit of her patience.

"I'm not fibbing," Sandra said indignantly.

Mrs. Evans made an expression as if to say, "What can I do?"

"Have a lot of rocks bitten you?" Pitt teased. He got a reading. The child had a temperature of 103° Fahrenheit. He wrote it and the blood pressure on the chart.

"Just one," Sandra said. "A black one."

"Guess we have to be careful with black rocks," Pitt said. He then instructed the mother to watch the child carefully until the doctor came in.

Pitt headed back to the desk and slipped the chart into the rack where it would be picked up by the next available doctor. He was about to go behind the desk when the swinging doors that led to the outside burst open.

"Help me," cried a man who was carrying a seizing woman. He staggered a few feet into the ER and threatened to collapse himself.

Pitt was the first person to reach the man's side. Without a second's hesitation he relieved the man of his burden by taking the woman into his own arms. It was difficult to hold her because she was still locked in the throes of a seizure.

By then Cheryl Watkins had come around from behind the desk along with several of the ER residents. Even Dr. Sheila Miller had dashed out of her office at the cries for help.

"Into the trauma bay," Dr. Miller commanded.

Without waiting for a gurney, Pitt carried the twitching woman back into the depths of the ER. With the help of Sheila, who'd positioned herself on the other side of the examination table, Pitt put the patient down. As he did so his eyes met Sheila's for the second time that day. No words were spoken but on this occasion a completely different message was conveyed.

Pitt backed up. Nurses and doctors jumped into the breach. Pitt stood there and watched, wishing he were at a stage in his training where he could participate.

The medical team which Sheila commanded quickly terminated the seizure. But then while they were beginning the evaluation of what caused the seizure, the patient had another, even more violent one.

"Why is she doing this?" the husband moaned. Everyone had forgotten he'd followed the group inside. One of the nurses went over to him and motioned for him to leave. "She's got diabetes, but she's never had a seizure. This shouldn't be happening. I mean, all she got was a cough. She's a young woman. Something is wrong, I know it."

A few minutes after the husband had been led out to the waiting room, Sheila's head snapped up so she could see the cardiac monitor. A sudden change in the sound of the beats had caught her attention.

"Uh oh," she said. "Something's going on here, and I don't like it."

The regular heartbeat had become erratic. Before anybody could react, the monitor's alarm went off. The patient was fibrillating.

"Code red ER!" blared out of the intercom system. More ER doctors flew into the cubicle in response to the cardiac arrest call. Pitt backed up even further so as not to interfere. He found the episode both stimulating and frightening. He wondered if he could ever learn enough to participate capably in such a situation.

The team worked tirelessly but to no avail. Eventually Sheila straightened up and ran her forearm across her sweaty brow.

"OK, that's it," she said reluctantly. "We've lost her." For the previous thirty minutes the monitor had traced a monotonous straight line.

The team hung their heads in dejection.

THE OLD SPRING-LOADED SCALE SQUEAKED AS DR. CURTIS Lapree allowed Charlie Arnold's liver to slosh into its basin. The needle jumped up the scale.

"Well, that's normal," Curtis said.

"Did you expect it to be abnormal?" Jesse Kemper asked. He and Detective Vince Garbon had stopped by to observe the autopsy on the dead University Medical Center housekeeping employee. Both policemen were dressed in disposable contamination suits.

Neither Jesse nor Vince were at all intimidated or sickened by the autopsy. They'd witnessed a hundred or so over the years, especially Jesse, who was eleven years older than Vinnie.

"Nope," Curtis said. "The liver looked normal, felt normal, so I expected it to weigh normal."

"Getting any ideas what killed this poor chap?" Jesse asked.

"Nope," Curtis said. "Looks like it's going to be just another one of those mysteries."

"Don't tell me that," Jesse said petulantly. "I'm counting on you to tell me if this was a homicide or accident."

"Calm down, Lieutenant," Curtis said with a laugh.

"I'm just pulling your leg. You should know by now that the dissection part of the autopsy is just the beginning. In this case I expect the microscopic is going to be more important. I mean on gross, I don't know what to make of the hole in the hand. Look at it!"

Curtis held up Charlie Arnold's hand. "The damn hole is a perfect circle."

"Could it be a bullet wound?" Jesse asked.

"You can answer your own question," Curtis said. "With all the bullet wounds you've seen."

"True, it doesn't look like a bullet wound," Jesse said.

"It sure as hell doesn't," Curtis said. "It would have had to be a bullet going the speed of light and hotter than the interior of the sun. Look at how everything got cauterized at the margins. And what happened to the missing tissue and bone? You said there was no blood or tissue at the scene."

"Nothing," Jesse said. "I mean no gore. There was melted glass and melted furniture, but no blood and no tissue."

"What do you mean, melted furniture?" Curtis asked. He wiped his hands on his apron after removing the liver from the scale.

Jesse described the room, to Curtis's utter fascination. "I'll be damned," Curtis said.

"Do you have any ideas?" Jesse asked.

"Sorta," Curtis admitted. "But you're not going to like it. I don't like it either. It's crazy."

"Try me," Jesse said.

"First let me show you something," Curtis said. He went to a side table and brought back a pair of retractors. Putting them inside the deceased's upper and lower lips, he exposed the teeth. The dead man assumed a horrid, grimacing expression.

"Oh, gross," Vinnie said. "You're going to give me nightmares."

"Okay, Doc," Jesse said. "What am I supposed to be looking at other than lousy dental work? Looks like the guy never brushed his teeth."

"Look at the enamel of the front teeth," Curtis said.

"I'm looking," Jesse said. "Looks a little messed up."

"That's it," Curtis said. He withdrew the retractors and returned them to the nearby table.

"Enough of this pussyfootin' around," Jesse said. "What's on your mind?"

"The only thing I can think of that can do that to tooth enamel is acute radiation poisoning," Curtis said.

Jesse's face fell.

"I told you you weren't going to like it," Curtis said.

"Jesse's very close to retirement," Vince said. "It's not nice to tease him like this."

"I'm serious," Curtis said. "It's the only thing that relates all the findings, like the hole in the hand and the changes in the enamel. Even the cataracts that weren't seen on his last yearly physical."

"So what happened to this poor slob?" Jesse asked.

"I know it's going to sound crazy," Curtis warned. "But the only way I can relate all the findings so far is to hypothesize that someone dropped a red-hot pellet of plutonium in his hand that burned through and gave him an enormous dose of radiation in the process. I mean a whopping dose."

"That's absurd," Jesse said.

"I told you you weren't going to like it," Curtis admitted.

"There was no plutonium at the scene," Jesse said. "Did you check if the body were radioactive?"

"I did, actually," Curtis said. "For personal safety concerns."

"And?"

"It's not," Curtis said. "Otherwise I wouldn't be up to my elbows into it."

Jesse shook his head. "This is getting worse instead of better," he said. "Plutonium, shit! That would be some kind of national emergency. Guess I'd better get someone over to that hospital and make sure there's no hot spots. Can I use a phone?"

"Be my guest," Curtis said agreeably.

A sudden burst of coughing got everyone's attention. It was Michael Schonhoff, a mortuary tech, who was over at the sink washing the entrails. The coughing went on for several minutes.

"Jeez, Mike," Curtis said. "You're sounding worse. And pardon my expression, but you look like death warmed over."

"Sorry, Dr. Lapree," Mike said. "I guess I got the flu. I've been trying to ignore it, but now I'm starting to get chills."

"Clock out early," Curtis said. "Get yourself home and in bed, take some aspirin, and drink some tea."

"I want to finish up here," Mike said. "Then I want to lable the specimen bottles."

"Forget it," Curtis said. "I'll have someone else finish up."

"Okay," Mike said. Despite his protestations to the contrary, he was happy to be relieved.

7

"WHAT I KEEP ASKING MYSELF IS WHY WE NEVER COME down here," Beau said. "This is beautiful." He, Cassy, and Pitt were strolling along the pedestrian mall in the city center eating ice cream after a dinner of pasta and white wine.

Five years previously the downtown had looked like a ghost town, with most of the people and restaurants having fled out to suburbia. But like a lot of other American cities, there'd been a reawakening. A few tasteful renovations had started a self-fulfilling prophecy. Now the entire downtown was a feast for the eyes as well as the palate. Crowds milled about, enjoying the spectacle.

"You guys really skipped school today?" Pitt questioned. He was impressed and incredulous.

"Why not," Beau said. "We went to the planetarium, the natural history museum, the art museum, and the zoo. We learned a lot, more than if we'd gone to class."

"That's an interesting rationalization," Pitt said. "I hope you get a bunch of questions about the zoo on your next exams."

"Ah, you're just jealous," Beau said, cuffing the top of Pitt's head.

"Maybe so," Pitt admitted. He stepped out of Beau's

reach. "I put in thirty hours in the ER since yesterday morning."

"Thirty hours?" Cassy questioned. "Really?"

"Honest," Pitt said. He then told them the story of the room where Beau had spent the afternoon and about spilling the coffee on Dr. Sheila Miller, the woman in charge of the entire emergency department.

Both Beau and Cassy were entranced, especially about the condition of the room and the death of the housekeeper. Beau asked the most questions, but Pitt had few answers. "They're waiting for the autopsy results," Pitt added. "Everybody's hoping then there will be some answers. Right now no one has any idea of what happened."

"Sounds horrid," Cassy said, making an expression of disgust. "A hole burned through his hand. Gads, I could never be a doctor. No way."

"I got a question for you, Beau," Pitt said after they'd walked a few moments in silence. "How did Cassy manage to talk you into this day of culture?"

"Hey, wait a sec!" Cassy interrupted. "This day wasn't my idea. It was Beau's."

"Get outta here," Pitt said skeptically. "You expect me to believe that . . . Mr. Type A who never misses a day of school."

"Ask him!" Cassy challenged.

Beau just laughed.

Cassy, intent on making her point that she'd not been to blame for the frivolous day and despite the crowded sidewalk, had turned and was walking backward so as to confront Pitt. "Come on, ask him," she urged.

Suddenly Cassy collided with a pedestrian coming in the opposite direction who wasn't paying much attention either. Both were mildly jolted but certainly unhurt.

Cassy immediately apologized as did the individual whom she'd hit. But then she did a double take. It was Mr. Partridge, the dour principal of the Anna C. Scott school.

Ed did a similar double take.

"Wait a second," he said as a smile spread across his

face. "I know you. You're Miss Winthrope, the charming student teacher assigned to Mrs. Edelman."

Cassy felt her face flush. Instantly she was aware that she'd possibly blundered into a minor catastrophe. But Mr. Partridge was the picture of gentility. "Such a nice surprise," he was saying. "Here, I'd like you to meet my bride, Clara Partridge."

Cassy dutifully shook hands with Mr. Partridge's wife and suppressed a smile. She was well aware of what the students called the woman.

"And here is a new friend of ours," Mr. Partridge said. He put his arm around his male companion. "I'd like you to meet Michael Schonhoff. He's one of those dedicated civil servants who labors at our medical examiner's office."

Everyone shook hands through their introductions. Beau was particularly interested in Michael Schonhoff, and they fell into their own conversation while Ed Partridge directed his attention to Cassy. "I've certainly been getting some good feedback on your student teaching," he said. "And I was impressed how well you were handling that class yesterday when Mrs. Edelman was delayed."

Cassy didn't know how to respond to these unexpected compliments. She also didn't know how to respond to Mr. Partridge's blatantly lewd inspection. Several times his eyes traveled up and down her body. After the first traverse she thought she could have been overreacting, but after the third time, she knew his behavior was deliberate.

Eventually the two groups said good-bye and went their separate ways.

"Who the hell is Ed Partridge?" Pitt asked as soon as they were out of earshot.

"He's the principal of the high school where I'm student teaching," Cassy said. She shook her head.

"He obviously is impressed with you," Pitt said.

"Did you catch the way he was looking at me?" Cassy asked.

"How could I miss it?" Pitt said. "I was embarrassed for him, especially with his tub of a wife standing right there. What'd you think, Beau?"

"I didn't catch it," Beau said. "I was talking with Michael."

"He's never acted like that before," Cassy said. "In fact he's usually a conservative sourpuss."

"Hey, guys, there's another ice cream place across the street," Beau said enthusiastically. "I'm going to have another. Anybody else?"

Both Cassy and Pitt shook their heads.

"I'll be right back," Beau said. He sprinted across the mall to wait in the ice cream concession line.

"You believe me about this day of playing hooky being Beau's idea?" Cassy questioned.

"If you say so," Pitt said. "But I'm sure you can understand my reaction. It is a little out of character."

"That's an understatement," Cassy said.

They watched while Beau flirted with a couple of attractive co-eds. Even from where they were standing they could hear Beau's characteristic laugh.

"He acts as loose as a goose," Pitt commented.

"That's one way to put it," Cassy said. "We've had a ball today, there's no doubt. But his behavior is starting to make me a little uneasy."

"How so?" Pitt questioned.

Cassy let out a short, mirthless laugh. "He's being too nice. I know that sounds crazy and maybe a little cynical, but he's just not acting normal. He's not acting like Beau normally acts. Skipping classes is just one thing."

"What else?" Pitt asked.

"Well, it's a little personal," Cassy said.

"Hey, I'm a friend," Pitt said encouragingly. At the same time his mouth went dry. He wasn't sure he wanted to hear anything too personal. As much as he tried to deny it, his feelings for Cassy weren't entirely platonic.

"Sexually he's been different," Cassy said haltingly. "This morning he . . ."

Cassy stopped in midsentence.

"He what?" Pitt asked.

"I can't believe I'm telling you this," Cassy said. She

was abashed. "Let's just say there's something different about him."

"Has it just been today?" Pitt asked.

"Last night and today," Cassy said. She considered telling about Beau dragging her out naked onto the balcony in the middle of the night to see the meteor shower but changed her mind.

"All of us have days when we just feel more alive," Pitt said. "You know, when food tastes better and sex . . . seems better." He shrugged. Now he was the embarrassed one.

"Maybe," Cassy said without conviction. "But what I'm wondering is whether his behavior could have something to do with that fleeting flu he had. I've never seen him so sick even though he got over it so quickly. Maybe it scared him. You know, like he thought he was going to die or something. Does that sound reasonable?"

Pitt shook his head. "I didn't think he was that sick."

"Do you have any other ideas?" Cassy asked.

"To be honest I'm a little too tired to think creatively," Pitt said.

"If you . . ." Cassy began, but she stopped. "Look what Beau's doing now!"

Pitt glanced at Beau. He had met up again with Ed Partridge, Mrs. Partridge, and their friend Michael. The foursome were deep in conversation.

"What on earth could he be talking with them for?" Cassy asked.

"Well, whatever it is they all seem to be in agreement," Pitt said. "They're all nodding their heads."

BEAU LOOKED AT THE CLOCK ON THE DASHBOARD OF HIS 4×4. It was two-thirty in the morning. He was with Michael Schonhoff, and they were parked in the loading dock of the medical examiner's office next to one of the mortuary vans.

"So you think this is the best time?" Beau asked.

"Absolutely," Michael said. "The cleaning crew will be

upstairs by now." He opened the passenger door and started to get out.

"You don't need me?" Beau asked.

"I'll be fine," Michael said. "Why don't you wait here. There'll be less explaining to do if I run into security."

"What are the chances of running into security?"

"Small," Michael admitted.

"Then I'm coming," Beau said. He climbed from the car.

"Suit yourself," Michael said agreeably.

Together they advanced to the door. Michael used his keys, and within seconds they were inside.

Without a word, Michael waved for Beau to follow him. Somewhere in the distance a radio could be heard. It was tuned to an all-night talk show.

The route lead through an antechamber, down a small ramp, and into the body holding room. The walls were lined with refrigerator compartments.

Michael knew precisely which compartment to open. The click of the door mechanism was loud in the silence. The body slid out effortlessly on a stainless steel tray.

Charlie Arnold's remains were in a clear plastic body bag. His face was ghostly white.

Intimately familiar with the surroundings, Michael produced a gurney. With Beau's help he got the body onto the gurney and closed the refrigerated compartment.

After a quick check to make sure the anteroom was still vacant, they wheeled the body up the ramp and out the door. It took only a moment to transfer it to the back of the 4×4.

While Beau climbed back into his car, Michael returned the gurney. Soon he was back to the car, and they left.

"That was easy," Beau said.

"I told you it'd be no problem," Michael said.

They drove east out into the desert. Leaving the main road, they took a dirt track until they were in uncontested wilderness.

"This looks okay to me," Beau said.

"I'd say it was perfect," Michael said.

Beau stopped the car. Together they lifted the body out of the car and carried it a hundred feet into the wilderness. They laid it on a ledge of sandstone. Above them stretched the moonless vault of the night sky with its millions of stars.

"Ready?" Beau questioned.

Michael stepped back a few paces. "Ready," he said.

Beau pulled out one of the black discs he'd retrieved that morning and put it on top of the body. Almost immediately it began to glow, and the intensity rapidly increased.

"We'd better get back," Beau said.

They moved about fifty feet away. By now the black disc's glow had reached the point that a corona was beginning to form, and as it did so Charlie Arnold's body also began to glow. The red glow of the disc changed to white and the corona expanded to envelop the body as well.

The whooshing sound started and with it a wind that pulled first leaves, then small stones, and finally larger rocks toward the body. The sound became instantly deafening, like the noise of an enormous jet engine. Beau and Michael hung on to each other to keep from being pulled off their feet.

The sound cut off with such suddenness that it caused a shock wave that jolted both men. The black disc, the body, and a number of stones, leaves, sticks, and other debris were gone. The rock where the body had been was hot, its surface twisted into a spiral.

"That should cause quite a stir," Beau said.

"Indeed," Michael said. "And keep them busy for a time."

8

"YOU'RE NOT GOING TO TELL ME WHERE YOU WENT LAST night?" Cassy asked petulantly. She had her hand on the door handle and was about to alight from the car. Beau had pulled into the horseshoe drive in front of the Anna C. Scott school.

"I already told you: just a drive," Beau said. "What's the big deal?"

"You've never gone for a drive in the middle of the night," Cassy said. "Why didn't you wake me and tell me you were going?"

"You were sleeping too soundly," Beau said. "I didn't want to disturb you."

"Didn't you think about me waking up and worrying about you?" Cassy asked.

"I'm sorry," Beau said. He reached over and patted her arm. "I guess I should have awakened you. At the time it seemed better to let you sleep."

"You'll wake me if it ever happens again?" Cassy asked.

"I promise," Beau said. "Jeez, you're making such a big deal out of this."

"It scared me," Cassy said. "I even called the hospital to make sure you weren't there. And the police station too, just to make sure there wasn't an accident.''

"All right already," Beau said. "You made your point."

Cassy got out of the van, then leaned back through the window. "But why a drive at two o'clock in the morning? Why not a walk, or if you couldn't sleep, why not watch a little TV? Or better yet, read."

"We're not going over this again," Beau said with conviction but not anger. "Okay?"

"Okay," Cassy said reluctantly. At least she'd gotten an apology and Beau seemed reasonably remorseful.

"See you at three," Beau said.

They waved as Beau pulled away from the curb. When he got to the corner, he didn't look back. If he had he would have seen that Cassy had not moved from the spot where she'd gotten out of the car. She watched him turn the corner, heading away from the university. She shook her head. Beau's strange behavior had not improved.

Beau was whistling softly to himself, blithely unaware of Cassy's concerns as he drove through the downtown. He had a mission and was preoccupied, but not too preoccupied to appreciate how many pedestrians and other drivers were coughing and sneezing, particularly when he stopped for traffic lights. In the very center of town it was as if almost every other person were suffering symptoms of an upper respiratory infection. On top of that many of them were pale and perspiring.

Reaching the outskirts of the city on the side of town opposite the university, Beau turned off Main Street onto Goodwin Place. On his right was the animal shelter, and he pulled through the open chain-link gate. He parked next to the administration building. It was constructed of painted cement block with aluminum jalousie windows.

From behind the building Beau could hear continuous barking. Inside Beau confronted a secretary, told her what he wanted, and was asked to sit in a small waiting area. Beau could have read while he waited, but instead he listened intently to the barking, even the intermittent meow of some cats. He thought it was a strange way to communicate.

"My name is Tad Secolow," a man said, interrupting Beau's thoughts. "I understand you are looking for a dog."

"That's right," Beau said, getting to his feet.

"You've come to the right place," Tad said. "We've got just about any breed you might be looking for. The fact that you are willing to give a home to a full-grown dog gives you a larger selection than if you were intent on a puppy. Do you have an idea of the breed?"

"Nope," Beau said. "But I'll know what I want when I see it."

"Excuse me?" Tad said.

"I said I'll recognize which animal I want when I spot it," Beau repeated.

"Do you want to look at photos first?" Tad asked. "We have pictures of all the dogs that are available."

"I'd prefer to see the animals themselves," Beau said.

"Okay," Tad said agreeably. He escorted Beau past the secretary and through the rear of the building that was filled with animal cages. It had a mild barnyard smell that competed with a cloying odor of deodorant. Tad explained that the dogs housed inside were being treated by the vet who came every other day. Most of these dogs weren't barking. Some looked ill.

The back yard of the shelter had rows of chain-link cages. Down the center were two long runs enclosed with chain-link fences. The floor of the whole complex was concrete. Coils of hose were stacked against the back of the building.

Tad led Beau down the first aisle. The dogs barked wildly at the sight of them. Tad maintained a running commentary on the pluses of each breed they passed. He paused longest at a cage that housed a standard poodle. It was a silver-gray color with dark, pleading eyes. It seemed to understand the urgency of its plight.

Beau shook his head, and they moved on.

While Tad was discussing the good qualities of a black Lab, Beau stopped and gazed in at a large, powerful, fawn-colored dog who returned his stare with mild curiosity.

"How about this one?" Beau asked.

Tad raised his eyebrows when he saw which dog Beau was referring to. "That's a beautiful animal," he said. "But he's big and very strong. Are you interested in a dog that large?"

"What's the breed?" Beau asked.

"Bullmastiff," Tad said. "People are generally afraid of them because of their size, and this guy probably could take your arm off if he were so inclined. But he seems to have a good disposition. The word 'mastiff' actually comes from a Latin word that means 'tame.' "

"How come this dog is here?" Beau asked.

"I'll be honest with you," Tad said. "The previous owners had an unexpected child. They were afraid of the dog's reaction and didn't want to take a chance. The dog loves to hunt small game."

"Open the door," Beau suggested. "Let's see if we get along."

"Let me get a choke collar," Tad said. He went back and disappeared inside the building.

Beau bent down and opened a small feeding door. The dog got up from where he was sitting against the back of the cage and came over to smell Beau's hand. His tail wagged tentatively.

Reaching into his pocket Beau pulled out another of his black discs. Holding it between his thumb and index finger with the index finger on the top of the dome, he pressed it against the dog's shoulder. Almost immediately the dog let out a muffled yelp and took a step back. He tilted his head questioningly.

Beau pocketed the disc just as Tad reappeared with the leash.

"Did he yelp?" Tad asked as he joined Beau.

"I guess I was scratching him too hard," Beau said.

Tad opened the door to the cage. For a moment the dog hesitated, looking back and forth between the two humans.

"Come on, big boy," Tad said. "For the size of you, you shouldn't be so hesitant."

"What's his name?" Beau asked.

"King," Tad said. "Actually it's King Arthur. But that's

going a bit far. Can you imagine trying to yell 'King Arthur' out your back door?''

"King's a good name," Beau said.

Tad got the collar on King and led him out of the cage. Beau reached out to pet him, but King hung back.

"Come on, King!" Tad complained. "Here's your big chance. Don't blow it."

"It's okay," Beau said. "I like him. I think he's perfect."

"Does that mean you'll take him?" Tad asked.

"Absolutely," Beau said. He took the leash, then squatted down and gave King a few pats on the head. King's tail slowly rose and then began to wag.

"I DON'T HAVE MUCH TIME," CASSY SAID TO PITT. THEY were walking down the corridor from the emergency room, heading toward the student overnight ward. "I've only got an hour between classes."

"This will only take a minute," Pitt said. "I just hope we are not too late."

They arrived at the room that Beau had occupied. Unfortunately for the moment they couldn't enter. Two workmen were struggling to carry out the twisted, disassembled bed.

"Look at the headboard," Pitt said.

"Weird," Cassey said. "It does look like it melted."

As soon as they could they stepped inside. Additional workmen were busy removing other warped fixtures including the metal supports for the suspended ceiling. Someone else was reglazing the window.

"Do they have any idea of what happened yet?" Cassy asked.

"Not a clue," Pitt said. "After the autopsy there was a short-lived scare about radiation, but the room and the general area was exhaustively checked and there wasn't any."

"Do you think there is any connection between all this and the way Beau has been acting?" Cassy asked.

"That's why I wanted you to see this," Pitt said. "I can't imagine how, but after you told me he'd been acting differently, I started thinking. After all, he did occupy this room the afternoon before all this happened.''

"It is strange," Cassy said. She walked over to look at the twisted arm that previously held the TV. It was as bizarre as the head of the bed. Just as she was about to rejoin Pitt, her eyes happened to meet those of the man replacing the glass.

The workman stared at Cassy for a beat, then eyed her body lasciviously, much the same way Mr. Partridge had leered at her the night before.

Cassy stepped over to Pitt and tugged at his sleeve. He was looking up at the institutional clock on the wall. He'd noticed that the hands had fallen off.

"Let's get out of here," Cassy said. She made a beeline for the door.

Out in the hall Pitt caught up to her. "Hey, slow down," he said.

Cassy slowed. "Did you see the way that man at the window looked at me?" she demanded.

"No, I didn't," Pitt said. "What did he do?"

"He was like Partridge last night," Cassy said. "What is it with these men? It's as if they are reverting to adolescent behavior."

"Aren't construction workers famous for that?" Pitt asked.

"It was more than the proverbial cat-whistle and 'hey baby,' " Cassy said. "This was more like visual rape. Maybe I can't explain it to you. But a woman would know what I'm talking about. It's unpleasant, even frightening."

"You want me to go back in there and confront him?" Pitt asked.

Cassy shot him an "are you crazy" look. "Don't be silly," she said.

They got back to the ER.

"Well, I got to get to school," Cassy said. "Thanks for inviting me over here, although seeing that room has hardly made me feel any better. I don't know what to make of all this."

"I'll tell you what," Pitt said. "Today is the day Beau

and I play our three-on-three basketball. It will give me an
opportunity to ask him what's up.''

"Don't mention that I said anything about sex," Cassy
said.

"Of course not," Pitt said. "I'll use the playing hooky
to start things off. Then I'll tell him straight out that last
night at dinner and when we were walking around, he
wasn't the Beau I know. I mean the difference is subtle,
but it's real.''

"You'll let me know what he says?" Cassy asked.

"Absolutely," Pitt said.

THE SQUAD ROOM AT POLICE HEADQUARTERS WAS ALWAYS
busy, especially around noon. But Jesse Kemper was accustomed to the bustle and could easily ignore it. His desk
was in the back, against the glass wall that separated the
captain's office from the main room.

Jesse was reading the preliminary autopsy report that Dr.
Curtis Lapree had sent over. Jesse didn't like it one bit.

"Doc is still sticking to the idea of radiation poisoning,"
Jesse called out to Vince, who was at the coffee machine.
Vince drank on average fifteen cups a day.

"Did you let him know there was no radiation at the
scene?" Vince asked.

"Of course I told him," Jesse said irritably. He tossed
the single-page report on the desk and picked up the photo
of Charlie Arnold that showed the hole through his hand.
Jesse scratched the top of his head where his hair was thinning while he studied the picture. It was one of the strangest
things he'd ever seen.

Vince came over to Jesse's desk. His teaspoon clanked
against the side of his cup as he stirred.

"This has to be the weirdest damn case," Jesse complained. "I keep seeing in my mind's eye the appearance
of that room and ask how.''

"Any news from that doctor lady about the science types
she was going to have examine the scene?" Vince asked.

"Yeah," Jesse said. "She called and said that no one
had any bright ideas. She did say that one of the physicists

discovered the metal in the room was magnetized.''

"So what does that mean?" Vince asked.

"Not much to me," Jesse admitted. "I called Doc Lapree and told him. His response was that lightning can do that.''

"But everybody agrees there wasn't any lightning," Vince said.

"Exactly," Jesse said. "So we're back to square one."

Jesse's phone rang. He ignored it, so Vince picked it up.

Jesse rotated himself around in his swivel chair, tossing the photo of Charlie's hand over his shoulder in the process. It landed back on the desk amid the rest of the clutter. Jesse was exasperated. He still didn't know if he were dealing with a crime or an act of nature. Absently he heard Vince talking on the phone, saying "yeah" over and over. Vince concluded by saying: "Okay, I'll tell him. Thanks for calling, Doc."

Before Jesse could spin back around his eye caught two uniformed officers coming out of the captain's office. What had attracted his attention was that both of them looked terrible, almost as pale as Charlie Arnold in the photo Jesse'd just thrown over his shoulder. The officers were coughing and sneezing like they had the plague.

Jesse was something of a hypochondriac and it irritated him that people were inconsiderate enough to be spreading their germs all over creation. As far as Jesse was concerned they should have stayed the hell home.

A muffled "oww!" emanated from inside the captain's office and diverted Jesse's attention from the two sick officers. Through the window Jesse could see the captain sucking on his finger. In his other hand he was gingerly holding a black disc.

"Jesse, you listening or what?" Vince demanded.

Jesse spun around. "I'm sorry, what were you saying?"

"I said that was Doc Lapree on the phone," Vince said. "There's been a further complication on the Charlie Arnold case. The body disappeared.''

"You're joking," Jesse said.

"Nope," Vince said. "Doc said he'd decided to go back

and take a bone marrow sample, and when he opened up the refrigerator where Charlie Arnold's body had been placed, it was gone.''

"Holy crap," Jesse voiced. He hauled himself to his feet. "We better go down there. This is getting too bizarre."

PITT CHANGED INTO HIS BASKETBALL GEAR AND USED HIS bike to travel from the dorm to the courts. He and Beau played frequently in the intramural three-on-three league. The competition was always good. A lot of the players could have played intercollegiate had they had the motivation.

As was his custom, Pitt arrived early in order to practice his shooting. He felt it took him longer than others to warm up. To his surprise Beau was already there.

Beau was dressed to play but was off to the side, behind a chain-link fence, conversing intently with two men and a woman. What was surprising was that the people appeared professional and in their middle to late thirties. All three were dressed in business suits. One of the men was carrying a fancy leather briefcase.

Pitt picked up a ball and began shooting. If Beau noticed him he didn't give any indication. After a few minutes something else about the situation seemed surprising to Pitt. Beau was doing all the talking! The others were simply listening, occasionally responding with nods of agreement.

The other players began to arrive including Tony Ciccone who made up the third person on Pitt and Beau's team. It was only after everyone had arrived including the opposition team and had warmed up that Beau wound up his conversation with the three businesspeople and joined Pitt. Pitt was now doing some stretching exercises.

"Hey, man, good to see you," Beau said. "I was afraid after that marathon you put in at the ER you weren't going to make it today."

Pitt straightened up and lifted a basketball in the process. "The way you were feeling the day before yesterday, you should be surprised you're here," he said.

Beau laughed. "Seems like ages ago. Now I feel terrific.

In fact, I've never felt better, and we're going to cream these pansies."

The other three players were continuing to warm up down at the other basket. Tony was tightening the laces of his high-tops.

"I wouldn't be too cocky," Pitt said, squinting against the sun. "See the muscle-bound guy in the purple shorts? Believe it or not, his name is Rocko. He's a ball-breaker and a good shot to boot."

"No problem," Beau said. He snatched the ball away from Pitt and let it sail toward the basket. It went through the goal with a snapping sound having hit nothing but net.

Pitt was impressed. They were standing a good thirty feet away.

"Best of all, we have a cheering section," Beau said. Putting the tip of his thumb and index fingers together and puckering up his mouth, he let loose with a shrill whistle. About a hundred feet away an enormous light-brown dog got up from where he'd been lying in the shade and sauntered over. He collapsed at the edge of the tarmac of the court and lowered his head on his front paws.

Beau squatted down and gave him a series of pats on the top of the head. The tail wagged briefly then went limp.

"Whose dog?" Pitt asked. "If you can call it a dog. It looks more like a small pony."

"He's mine," Beau said. "His name is King."

"You got a dog?" Pitt asked incredulously.

"Yup," Beau said. "I felt like some canine companionship, so I went out to the pound this morning, and there he was, waiting for me."

"A week ago you said you didn't think it was fair to have big dogs in the city," Pitt said.

"I changed my mind," Beau said. "The moment I saw him I knew he was the dog of my dreams."

"Does Cassy know?"

"Not yet," Beau said. He scratched King enthusiastically behind his ears. "Won't she be surprised?"

"That's an understatement," Pitt said, rolling his eyes. "Especially a dog that size. But what's the matter with him? Is he sick? He seems lethargic and his eyes are red.''

"Ah, he's just having trouble adjusting," Beau said. "He's just been let out of his cage. I've only had him a few hours."

"He's salivating," Pitt said. "You don't think he has rabies, do you?"

"Not a chance," Beau said. "Of that I'm certain." Beau cupped the dog's large head in his hands. "Come on, King. You should be feeling better by now. We need you to cheer us on."

Beau got to his feet, still gazing at his new companion. "He might be lethargic, but he's a good-looking dog, don't you agree?"

"I suppose," Pitt said. "But listen, Beau. Getting a dog, much less a huge one like this, is an awfully impulsive act, and knowing you the way I do, I'd have to say very unexpected. In fact, from my perspective you've been doing a number of unexpected things lately. I'm concerned, and I think we should have a talk."

"Talk about what?"

"About you," Pitt said. "The way you've been acting, like not going to class. It seems like ever since you had the flu . . ."

Before Pitt could finish Rocko had come up behind Pitt and given him a friendly slap on the shoulder that sent Pitt staggering forward several steps.

"Are you dorks going to play or forfeit?" Rocko jeered. "Pauli, Duff, and I have been ready to take you guys to the cleaners for the last half hour."

"I think we better talk later," Beau whispered to Pitt. "The natives are getting restless."

The game commenced. As Pitt guessed, Rocko dominated the play with his bulldozer tactics. To Pitt's chagrin the burden of covering him had fallen on his shoulders since Rocko had selected to guard Pitt. Every time Rocko got the ball he made it a point to crash right into Pitt before dropping back to put in a jump shot.

Halfway through the game with Rocko et al in the lead,

Pitt called a foul after Rocko purposefully elbowed him in the gut in order to get a rebound.

"What?" Rocko demanded angrily. He threw the ball forcibly against the ground so that it bounced some ten feet into the air. "Is the little chicken-shit going to call an offensive foul? No way. Our ball! No way I'm going to honor a call like that."

"It's my call," Pitt persisted. "I say you fouled me. In fact, it's the second time you pulled the same cheap trick."

Rocko stepped over to Pitt and purposefully butted him with his chest. Pitt took a step backward.

"Cheap trick, huh?" Rocko snarled. "All right, tough guy, talk is cheap. Let's see the crybaby take a swing. Come on! I got my arms at my side."

Pitt knew better than to get into a fight with Rocko. Others had tried only to end up with chipped front teeth or black eyes.

"Excuse me," Beau said congenially. He stepped between Pitt and Rocko. "I don't think this issue is worth any hard feelings. I tell you what. We'll give up the ball, but we're going to change who guards whom. I think I'll take a turn guarding you, Rocko, and you can guard me."

Rocko gave a short laugh as he looked Beau up and down. Although they were both about six feet, Rocko outweighed Beau by more than fifteen pounds.

"You don't mind, do you?" Beau asked Pitt.

"Hell no," Pitt said.

With that settled, the game resumed. Rocko's thin-lipped, hard face had settled into a slight smile of anticipation. The next time he got the ball, he charged directly at Beau with his heavy thighs pumping.

With uncanny coordination, Beau managed to step out of the way at the instant Rocko expected contact. The result was almost comical. Expecting the collision, Rocko had his torso way out in front of his center of gravity. When no contact occurred, he sprawled on the pavement.

Everyone, even Pitt, winced, as Rocko skidded across the asphalt. He suffered several large abrasions that were liberally sprinkled with embedded gravel.

Beau was at the downed man's side instantly with an extended hand.

"Sorry, Rocko," Beau said. "Let me help you up."

Rocko glared up at Beau. He ignored the gesture for help and got to his feet under his own power.

"Oww," Beau said with a sympathetic wince. "You got some nasty scrapes there. I think we'd better call the game so you can go over to the infirmary and have them cleaned."

"Hell with you," Rocko said. "Give me the ball. We'll finish the game."

"It's up to you," Beau said. "But it's our ball. You lost it with your little tumble."

Pitt had watched this interchange with growing concern. Beau didn't seem to realize what kind of bully Rocko truly was, and Beau was taunting him. Pitt was afraid the afternoon would end with trouble.

As play resumed Rocko continued to try to use his strong-man tactics, but on each occasion, Beau was able to avoid contact. Rocko fell several more times, which clearly irritated him, and the angrier he got, the more easily Beau was able to deal with him.

Offensively Beau turned into a dynamo. Given the ball he could score at will despite Rocko's efforts to restrain him. On several drives, Beau had gone around Rocko with such a sudden burst of speed, Rocko was left in the dust with a confused expression. By the time Beau put in the final basket to win the game, Rocko's face was suffused with an angry blush.

"Hey, thanks for letting us win," Beau said to Rocko. He stuck out his hand but Rocko ignored it. Rocko and his fellow teammates slunk off to the sideline to towel off.

Beau, Pitt, and Tony walked back to where King was lying in the grass. King seemed even more lethargic than before the game.

"I told you King was going to help," Beau said.

Tony broke out some cold drinks. Pitt was particularly glad to get some fluid, and despite his panting, downed a can in record time. Tony handed him another.

Pitt was about to start on his second drink when he noticed that Beau was casually staring off at a couple of attractive co-eds coming along the track. They were wearing skimpy running gear.

"Great legs," Beau said.

That was when Pitt noticed that Beau was not out of breath like he and Tony were. In fact Beau wasn't even sweating and had yet to take a drink.

Beau caught Pitt staring at him out of the corner of his eye. "Something the matter?" Beau asked.

"You're not sucking air like we are," Pitt said.

"I guess I was loafing out there, letting you guys do all the work."

"Uh oh," Tony said. "Here comes the Sherman tank."

Both Beau and Pitt turned to see Rocko sauntering across the court in their direction.

"Don't taunt him," Pitt whispered forcibly.

"Who, me?" Beau asked innocently.

"We want a rematch," Rocko growled when he reached the group.

"I've had it for today," Pitt said. "I'm through."

"Me too," Tony said.

"I guess that's that," Beau said with a smile. "It wouldn't be quite fair if I played all three of you guys."

Rocko stared at Beau for a beat. "You're mighty arrogant for a little prig."

"I didn't say I'd win," Beau said. "Although I'm sure it would be close, especially the way you guys were playing toward the end of that last game."

"Man, you're looking for it," Rocko snarled.

"I'd rather you didn't raise your voice," Beau said. "My dog's sleeping right next to you, and he's feeling a bit under the weather."

Rocko glanced down at King, then back up at Beau. "I couldn't care a twit about your bag of turd of a dog."

"Wait a sec," Beau said. He got to his feet. "I'm a little confused. Are you calling my new dog a 'bag of turd'?"

"Worse than that," Rocko said. "I think he's a f—"

With hand speed that shocked everyone, Beau reached

out and grabbed Rocko by the throat. Rocko reacted quickly as well, clenching his left hand into a tight fist and unleashing a powerful left hook.

Beau saw the blow coming but ignored it. It struck him on the side of his face, just in front of his right ear. The sound was a solid "thunk" that made Pitt wince.

Rocko felt a stab of pain from his knuckles after hitting up against Beau's cheekbone. The punch had been a hefty one and right on target yet Beau's facial expression didn't change. It was as if he'd not felt the blow.

Rocko was shocked by the seeming ineffectiveness of what heretofore had been his best weapon. People never expected a powerful left hook to be the first contact in a fight. It had always worked for Rocko, and more often than not, finished the fight. But with Beau it was different. The only change in Beau's appearance after the punch was that his pupils dilated. Rocko even thought they began to glow.

The other problem Rocko was experiencing was lack of oxygen. His face got redder and his eyes began to bulge. He tried to twist out of Beau's grasp but couldn't. It was as if he were being held by a pair of iron tongs.

"Excuse me," Beau said calmly. "I think you owe my dog an apology."

Rocko grabbed Beau's arm with both hands but still couldn't break Beau's hold around his neck. All Rocko could do was gurgle.

"I can't hear you," Beau said.

Pitt, who moments before had been worried about Beau, was now concerned about Rocko. The man's face was turning blue.

"He can't breathe," Pitt offered.

"You're right," Beau said. He let go of Rocko's neck and grabbed a handful of hair instead. Exerting an upward force, he was able to bring Rocko up onto his tiptoes. Rocko was still clutching Beau's arm with both hands but was unable to free himself.

"I'm waiting for the apology," Beau said. He increased the tension on Rocko's hair.

"I'm sorry about your dog," Rocko managed.

"Don't tell me," Beau said calmly. "Tell the dog."

Pitt was speechless. For a second it almost appeared as if Beau had lifted Rocko off his feet.

"I'm sorry, dog," Rocko squeaked.

"His name is King," Beau said.

"I'm sorry, King," Rocko echoed.

Beau released his hold. Rocko's hands shot to the top of his head. His scalp was burning. With a look that was a combination of anger, pain, and humiliation, Rocko slunk away to join his shocked teammates.

Beau brushed off his hands. "Ugh," he said. "I wonder what kind of goop he uses in his hair."

Pitt and Tony were as shocked as Rocko's teammates and were staring at Beau with their mouths hanging open. Beau noticed their expressions after reaching down for the end of King's leash.

"What is it with you guys?" Beau asked.

"How did you do that?" Pitt asked.

"What are you talking about?" Beau asked.

"How were you able to handle Rocko so easily?" Pitt asked.

Beau tapped the side of his head. "With intelligence," he said. "Poor Rocko uses only brawn. Brawn can be useful but its power pales compared to intelligence. It's why humans dominate this planet. In terms of natural selection, there's nothing that comes close."

All the sudden Beau looked off across the grass toward the library. "Uh oh," he said. "Looks like I'm going to have to leave you guys."

Pitt followed his line of sight. About a hundred yards off and coming in their direction was another group of businessmen types. This time there were six: four men and two women. All were carrying briefcases.

Beau turned back to his teammates. "Great game, guys," he said. He stuck up his hand and high-fived with both. Then he turned to Pitt. "We'll have to have that conversation you suggested another time."

Responding to a tug, King got reluctantly to his feet and

followed his master out across the grass to the impromptu conference.

Pitt looked at Tony. Tony shrugged. "I never knew Beau was so strong," he said.

"HOW THE HELL CAN A BODY DISAPPEAR?" JESSE ASKED Dr. Curtis Lapree. "I mean, has it ever happened before?" Jesse and Vince had ridden over to the morgue and were standing on either side of the empty refrigeration compartment where Charlie Arnold's body had been.

"Unfortunately it has happened before," Dr. Lapree admitted. "Not often, thank God, but it has happened. The last time was a little over a year ago. It was the body of a young woman, a suicide case."

"Was the body ever recovered?" Jesse asked.

"No," Dr. Lapree said.

"Was it reported to us?" Jesse asked.

"I don't know, to be truthful," Dr. Lapree said. "It was handled by the commissioner of health, who dealt directly with the commissioner of the police. It was an embarrassment all around and hence was kept as quiet as possible."

"What have you done on this case?" Jesse asked.

"The same thing," Dr. Lapree said. "I've turned it over to the head medical examiner, who's turned it over to the commissioner of health. Before you do anything you'd better check with your bosses. I probably shouldn't have even told you."

"I understand," Jesse said. "And I'll respect your confidence. But have you any suspicions of why someone would steal the body?"

"As a forensic pathologist I know more than most people that the world is full of weird people," Dr. Lapree said. "There are people out there who like dead bodies."

"You think that was the motivation in this instance?" Jesse asked.

"I haven't the slightest idea," Dr. Lapree admitted.

"We're concerned that the disappearance of the body adds weight to the idea that the man's death was a homicide," Jesse said.

"Like the perpetrator didn't want to leave a trail," Vince added.

"I understand," Dr. Lapree said. "But the problem with that line of thinking is that I'd already done the autopsy."

"Yeah, but you were coming back for more tissue," Jesse said.

"True," Dr. Lapree said. "I'd failed to take a sample of bone marrow. But that was just to add more weight to my acute radiation theory."

"If the reason the body was taken was to keep you from getting this final sample, then it sounds as if it were an inside job," Jesse said.

"We are aware of that," Dr. Lapree said. "We're in the process of reviewing everyone who had access to the body."

Jesse sighed. "What a case," he moaned. "The idea of retiring is sounding better and better."

"You'll let us know if you learn anything," Vince said.

"Absolutely," Dr. Lapree said.

JONATHAN CLOSED AND LOCKED HIS GYM LOCKER. FOR that semester he'd pulled gym as the last period of the day, and he hated it. He much preferred to have gym sometime in the middle of the day as an oasis between academic subjects.

Leaving the gym wing by the side door he started out across the quad. In the distance he could see a group of kids grouped around the flagpole. As he approached he could hear them cheering. When he got to the base of the flagpole he saw what was going on. A ninth grader, who Jonathan vaguely knew, was in the process of shinnying to the top. His name was Jason Holbrook. Jonathan knew him because he'd played on the freshman basketball team.

"What's happening?" Jonathan asked one of his classmates who was standing off to the side. His name was Jeff.

"Ricky Javetz and crowd have found some new ninth-grader to harass," Jeff said. "The kid's got to touch the eagle on top or he's not going to be allowed in the gang."

Jonathan shielded his eyes from the bright afternoon sun.

"That pole's damn high," he said. "Must be fifty, sixty feet or more."

"And it's pretty skinny at the top," Jeff said. "I'm glad I'm not up there."

Jonathan looked around. He was surprised that no teachers had materialized to put a stop to this ridiculous situation. Just then he saw Cassy Winthrope emerge from the north wing. Jonathan elbowed Jeff. "Here comes that sexy student teacher."

Jeff turned to look. Cassy was dressed as usual in a loose-fitting simple cotton dress. As the sun angled through it, the boys could see a silhouette of Cassy's body, including a distinct outline of her high-cut panties.

"Wow," Jeff said. "What a piece of ass."

Mesmerized, the boys watched Cassy melt into the crowd then reappear at the base of the flagpole. She tossed some books she was carrying onto the ground, cupped her hands, and shouted up to Jason to come down.

The crowd hissed at Cassy's interference.

Almost three-quarters of the way to the eagle, Jason hesitated. The pole was beginning to wobble. It seemed higher than he'd expected.

Cassy looked around. The throng of students had closed in. Most of them were seniors and significantly larger than herself. It went through her mind that teachers were assaulted on a daily basis in schools across the United States.

Cassy looked back up the flagpole. From its base the wobbling was apparent.

"Did you hear me," Cassy called again, ignoring the crowd. She had her hands on her hips. "Get down here this instant!"

Cassy felt a hand grab her arm. She jumped. Surprisingly she found herself staring into Mr. Ed Partridge's leering, smiling face. "Miss Winthrope, you're looking delightful today."

Cassy peeled Ed's fingers from her arm. "We've got a student three-quarters of the way up the flagpole," she said.

"I've noticed," Ed said. He chuckled as he tilted his

head back and gazed up at the now scared student. "I bet he can make it."

"I hardly think this kind of activity should be condoned," Cassy said in spite of herself.

"Ah, why not?" Ed said. Then cupping his hands he called up to Jason. "Come on, boy, don't fink out now. You're almost there."

Jason looked up. He had another twenty feet or so to go. Hearing the crowd urging him on, he recommenced climbing. The problem was that his hands were perspiring and moist. With each shinny, he slid back half of the gained distance.

"Mr. Partridge," Cassy began. "This isn't . . ."

"Calm down, Miss Winthrope," Ed said. "We have to let our students express themselves. Besides, it's entertaining to see if a prepubescent boy like Jason up there is capable of accomplishing this kind of feat."

Cassy looked up. The wobbling had increased. She shuddered to think of what would happen if the boy fell.

But Jason didn't fall. Benefiting from the crowd's support, he managed to get to the top, touch the eagle, and begin the descent. When he reached the ground, Mr. Partridge was the first to congratulate him.

"Well done, lad," Ed said, giving Jason a pat on the back. "I didn't think you had it in you." Mr. Partridge then looked out over the crowd. "Okay, everybody, time to break it up."

Cassy didn't leave immediately. She watched as Mr. Partridge herded many of the students toward the central wing while maintaining an animated conversation. Cassy was confused. Encouraging such an act seemed irresponsible and certainly out of character for Mr. Partridge.

"I believe these are your books," a voice said.

Cassy turned to see Jonathan Sellers extending her texts to her. She took them and thanked him.

"No problem," he said. He looked off at the fading image of Mr. Partridge. "He's become a different man all of a sudden," Jonathan said, mirroring Cassy's thoughts.

"Just like my parents," another voice said.

Jonathan turned to see Candee. He'd been unaware that she'd been in the crowd from the beginning. Stumbling over his words, he introduced her to Cassy, and as he did so, he noticed her eyes had a red-rimmed, sleepless appearance.

"Are you okay?" Jonathan asked.

Candee nodded. "I'm all right, but I didn't sleep much last night." She stole a self-conscious glance at Cassy, concerned about talking in front of a stranger. At the same time she had a strong urge to unburden herself. As an only child she'd not spoken with anyone, and she was troubled.

"How come you couldn't sleep?" Jonathan asked.

"Because my parents have been acting very strange," Candee said. "It's like I don't know them. They've changed."

"What do you mean 'changed'?" Cassy asked, thinking immediately of Beau.

"They're different," Candee said. "I don't know how to explain it. They're different. Like old Mr. Partridge."

"How long have you noticed this?" Cassy asked. She was amazed; what was happening to people?

"It's been just the last day or so," Candee said.

9

4:15 P.M.

"DO YOU WANT PHENYTOIN?" DR. DRAPER YELLED AT DR.
Sheila Miller. Dr. Draper was one of the senior residents
in the emergency medicine program at the University Medical Center.

"No!" Sheila snapped. "I don't want to take any
chances on causing an arrhythmia. Give me ten milligrams
of Valium IV now that we have the airway secured."

The city ambulance had called earlier to report that they
were bringing in a forty-two-year-old diabetic who was in
the throes of a major seizure. Considering what had happened with the seizing, diabetic woman the day before, the
whole ER team, including Dr. Sheila Miller, had turned out
for this new emergency.

Upon arrival the man had been taken directly into one
of the bays where his airway had been given top priority.
Then stat blood work had been drawn. Concurrently monitors were attached followed by a bolus of IV glucose.

Since the seizing had continued, more medication was
necessary. That was when Sheila decided on the Valium.

"Valium given," Ron Severide said. Ron was one of the
evening RNs.

Sheila was watching the monitor. Remembering what

had happened with the woman the day before, she did not want this patient to arrest.

"What's the patient's name?" Sheila asked. By that time the patient had been in the ER for ten minutes.

"Louis Devereau," Ron said.

"Any other medical history besides the diabetes?" Sheila asked. "Any cardiac history?"

"None that we're aware of," Dr. Draper said.

"Good," Sheila said. She began to calm down. So did the patient. After a few more jerks, the seizing stopped.

"Looking good," Ron said.

No sooner had this positive assessment escaped from Ron's lips than the patient starting convulsing again.

"That's amazing," Dr. Draper said. "He's seizing in the face of both the Valium and the glucose. What's going on here?"

Sheila didn't respond. She was too busy watching the cardiac monitor. There'd been a couple of ectopic beats. She was about to order some lidocaine when the patient arrested.

"Don't do this," Sheila cried as she joined the others in a resuscitation effort.

In a fashion eerily similar to the experience with the woman the day before, Louis Devereau went from fibrillation to flatline no matter what the ER team did. To their great chagrin they had to admit defeat once again, and the patient was pronounced dead.

Feeling anger at the inadequacy of their effort, Sheila snapped her gloves off her hands and threw them forcibly into the appropriate container. Dr. Draper did the same. Together they walked back toward the main desk.

"Get on the phone with the medical examiner," Sheila said. "Make sure you convey to him the necessity of trying to figure out what caused this death. This can't go on. These were both relatively young patients."

"They both were insulin-dependent," Dr. Draper said. "And both had had long-term diabetes."

They reached the expansive ER desk. There was a lot of activity.

"So when has middle-aged diabetes become a fatal illness?" Sheila asked.

"Good point," Dr. Draper said.

Sheila glanced into the waiting room, and her eyebrows lifted. There were so many patients that there was standing room only. Ten minutes previously there'd been the normal number for that time of day. She turned to ask one of the clerks sitting behind the desk if there was some explanation for the sudden crowd and found herself looking at Pitt Henderson.

"Don't you ever go home?" she asked. "Cheryl Watkins told me you were back here hours after a twenty-four-hour shift."

"I'm here to learn," Pitt said. It was a planned retort. He'd seen her approach the desk.

"Well, good grief, don't burn out," Sheila said. "You haven't even started medical school yet."

"I just heard that the diabetic who'd just come in passed away," Pitt said. "That must be very hard for you to deal with."

Sheila looked down at this college senior. He was surprising her. Only the morning before he'd irritated her by sloshing her coffee all over her arm in a room where he had no business being. Now he was being uncharacteristically sensitive for a college-aged male. He was also attractive, with his coal-black hair and dark, liquid eyes. In a fleeting instant, she wondered how she would respond if he were twenty years older.

"I have something here that you will want to see," Pitt said. He handed her a printout from the lab.

Sheila took the sheet and glanced at it. "What is this?" she asked.

"It's the blood work on that diabetic who died yesterday," Pitt said. "I thought you might be particularly interested because all the values are entirely normal. Even the blood sugar."

Sheila scanned the list. Pitt was right.

"It will be interesting to see what today's patient's values are," Pitt said. "From the reading I've done, I can't

think of any reason the first patient should have had a seizure."

Sheila was now impressed. None of the other college
students who'd come through on the clerking program had
shown such a degree of interest. "I'll count on you to get
me the blood work on today's patient," she said.

"My pleasure," Pitt said.

"Meanwhile," Sheila said, "do you have any idea why
there are so many people in the waiting room?"

"I think so," Pitt said. "It's probably because most of
the people delayed coming in until after work. They're all
complaining of the flu. Checking through the records from
yesterday and today, we've been seeing more and more
people with the same symptoms. I think it's something that
you should look into."

"But it's flu season," Sheila said. She was even more
impressed. Pitt was actually thinking.

"It might be flu season, but this outbreak seems unique,"
Pitt said. "I checked with the lab, and they have yet to
have a positive test for influenza."

"Sometimes they have to grow the influenza virus in
tissue culture before they get a positive test. That can take
a few days."

"Yeah, I read that," Pitt said. "But in this instance I
think it's strange because all these patients have had a lot
of respiratory symptoms, so the virus should be there in a
high titer. At least that's what it said in the text I was
reading."

"I have to say I'm impressed with your initiative,"
Sheila said.

"Well, the situation worries me," Pitt said. "What if it
is a new strain, maybe a new illness? My best friend got it
a couple of days ago, and he was really sick, but only for
a number of hours. That doesn't sound like regular old flu
to me. Besides, after he'd recovered he hasn't been himself.
I mean he's been healthy, but he's been acting strange."

"How do you mean strange?" Sheila asked. She began
to consider the possibility of viral encephalitis. It was a rare
complication of influenza.

"Like a different person," Pitt said. "Well, not totally different, just a little different. The same thing seems to have happened to the principal of the high school."

"You mean like a slight personality change?" Sheila asked.

"Yeah, I suppose you could say that," Pitt said. He was afraid to tell her about Beau's apparent increase in strength and speed and the fact that Beau had occupied the room that had become distorted; Pitt was afraid he'd lose all credibility. He was nervous about talking to Dr. Miller as it was and wouldn't have approached her on his own accord.

"And one other thing," Pitt said, thinking that he'd come this far and might as well let it all out. "I checked the chart of the diabetic woman who died yesterday. She had had flu symptoms before she got her seizure."

Sheila stared into Pitt's dark eyes while she pondered what he'd said. Suddenly she looked up and called out to Dr. Draper, asking him if Louis Devereau had had flu symptoms before he had his seizure.

"Yes, he did," Dr. Draper said. "Why do you ask?"

Sheila ignored Dr. Draper's question. Instead she looked down at Pitt. "About how many patients have we seen with this flu and how many are waiting?"

"Fifty-three," Pitt said. He held up a sheet of paper where he'd kept a tally.

"Jesus H. Christ," Sheila said. For a moment she stared off down the hall with unseeing eyes and chewed the inside of her cheek while she considered the options. Looking back at Pitt she said: "Come with me and bring that sheet of paper!"

Pitt struggled to catch up with Sheila who was moving as if on a power walk. "Where are we going?" Pitt asked as they entered the hospital proper.

"The president's office," Sheila said without elaboration.

Pitt squeezed onto the elevator with Dr. Miller. He tried to read her face but couldn't. He didn't have any idea why he was being taken to the administration. He worried it was for disciplinary purposes.

"I'd like to see Dr. Halprin immediately," Sheila said to the head administrative secretary. Her name was Mrs. Kapland.

"Dr. Halprin is tied up at present," Mrs. Kapland said with a friendly smile. "But I'll let him know you are here. Meanwhile can I get you coffee or perhaps a soft drink?"

"Tell him it's urgent," Sheila said.

They were kept waiting for twenty minutes after which the secretary escorted them into the administrator's office. Both Sheila and Pitt could tell that the man was not feeling well. He was pale and coughing almost continuously.

After Sheila and Pitt had taken chairs, Sheila concisely summarized what Pitt had told her and suggested that the hospital take appropriate action.

"Hold on," Dr. Halprin said between coughs. "Fifty cases of flu during flu season is not a reason to scare the community. Hell, I got the bug myself, and it isn't so bad, although if I had the choice, I suppose I'd be home in bed."

"That's fifty-plus cases at this hospital alone," Sheila said.

"Yes, but we are the major hospital in the community," Halprin said. "We see the most of everything."

"I've had two deaths of previously well-controlled diabetics who've possibly died of this illness," Sheila said.

"Influenza can do that," Dr. Halprin commented. "Unfortunately we all know it can be a nasty illness for the aged and the infirm."

"Mr. Henderson knows of two people who've had the illness and who have demonstrated personality changes as an aftermath. One of those people is his best friend."

"Marked personality change?" Halprin asked.

"Not marked," Pitt admitted. "But definite."

"Give me an example," Dr. Halprin asked while he blew his nose loudly.

Pitt related Beau's sudden carefree attitude and the fact that he'd skipped a whole day of classes to go to museums and the zoo.

Dr. Halprin lowered his tissue and eyed Pitt. He had to smile. "Excuse me, but that hardly sounds earth-shaking."

"You'd have to know Beau to realize how surprising it is," Pitt said.

"Well, we've had some experience with this illness right here in this office," Dr. Halprin said. "Not only do I have it today but both of my secretaries had it yesterday." He bent over and pressed his intercom button. He asked both secretaries to come into his office.

Mrs. Kapland appeared immediately and was followed by a younger woman. Her name was Nancy Casado.

"Dr. Miller is concerned about this flu bug that's going around," Dr. Halprin said. "Perhaps you two could set her mind at ease."

The two women looked at each other, unsure of who should speak. As the more senior employee Mrs. Kapland started.

"It came on sudden, and I felt terrible," she said. "But four or five hours later I was on the mend. Now I feel wonderful. Better than I have in months."

"It was pretty much the same for me," Nancy Casado said. "It started with a cough and sore throat. I'm sure I had a fever although I never took my temperature so I don't know how high it went."

"Do either of you think the other's personality has changed since your recovery?" Dr. Halprin asked.

Both women giggled and covered their mouths with their hands. They looked at each other conspiratorially.

"What's so funny?" Dr. Halprin asked.

"It's just a private joke," Mrs. Kapland said. "But to answer your question, neither of us feel our personalities have changed. Do you think so, Dr. Halprin?"

"Me?" Dr. Halprin questioned. "I don't think I have time to notice such things, but no, I don't think either one of you has changed."

"Do you know others who have been ill?" Sheila asked the women.

"Many," they said in unison.

"Have you noticed a change in anyone's personality?" Sheila asked.

"Not me," Mrs. Kapland said.

"Nor I," Nancy Casado said.

Dr. Halprin spread his hands out, palm up. "I don't think we have a problem here," he said. "But thanks for coming over." He smiled.

"Well, it's your call," Sheila said. She stood up.

Pitt did the same, and he nodded to the president and the secretaries. As his eyes met Nancy Casado's, he noticed that she was looking at him in a curiously provocative way. Her lips were slightly parted and the tip of her tongue played within the shadows. As soon as she could see he was looking at her, she let her eyes roam up and down his body.

Pitt quickly turned and followed Dr. Miller out of the president's office. He felt uncomfortable. All at once he had an appreciation of what Cassy had been trying to tell him that morning after their visit to the room Beau had occupied in the student overnight ward.

BALANCING HER BOOKS, PURSE, AND SOME TAKE-OUT CHI-nese food, Cassy managed to get her key in the door and the door open. Entering, she kicked the door closed.

"Beau, are you home yet?" she called as she unburdened herself on the small table next to the door.

A deep, threatening growl made the hairs on the back of Cassy's neck stand straight up. The growl had been very close. In fact it sounded as if it had been right behind her. Slowly she raised her eyes to the decorative mirror above the entrance table. Just to the left of her image was the image of a huge light-brown bull mastiff with its enormous canines bared.

Ever so slowly so as not to upset the already perturbed animal, Cassy rotated to face it. Its eyes were like black marbles. It was a fearsome creature that stood taller than her waist.

Beau, munching an apple, appeared in the kitchen door-way. "Whoa, King! It's okay. This is Cassy."

The dog stopped growling and turned toward Beau and cocked his head to the side.

"It's Cassy," Beau repeated. "She lives here too."

Beau pushed off the doorjamb, gave King a pat and told him "good boy" before giving Cassy a solid kiss on the lips. "Welcome, lover," Beau said breezily. "We've been missing you. Where have you been?"

Beau moved over to the couch and draped himself over the arm.

Cassy hadn't moved a muscle. Nor had the dog except for his brief look at Beau. He wasn't growling any longer, but he'd continued to fix her with his baleful stare.

"What do you mean, where have I been?" Cassy asked. "You were supposed to pick me up. I waited for half an hour."

"Oh yeah," Beau said. "Sorry about that. I had an important meeting and there was no way to get in touch with you. You told me yourself you could get a ride easy enough."

"Yes, when it's planned," Cassy said. "By the time I realized you weren't coming, everyone I knew had left. I had to call a cab."

"Jeez!" Beau said. "I'm sorry. Really I am. There's just a lot going on all the sudden. How about I take you out to dinner tonight to your favorite place, the Bistro?"

"We were just out last night," Cassy said. "Don't you have work to do? I brought home some Chinese food."

"Well, whatever you want, sweetie," Beau said. "I feel badly about leaving you in the lurch this afternoon, so I'd like to make it up to you."

"Just the fact that you're willing to apologize goes a long way," Cassy said. She then looked down at the immobile dog.

"What's the story with this beast?" she asked. "Are you minding it for someone?"

"Nope," Beau said. "He's my dog. His name is King."

"You're joking," Cassy said.

"Hardly," Beau said. He hauled himself from the arm of the couch and stepped over to King. He scratched him roughly behind the ears. King responded with tail wagging and licking Beau's hand with his enormous tongue. "I figured we could use the protection."

"Protection from what?" Cassy asked. She was dumbstruck.

"Just in general," Beau said vaguely. "A dog like this has olfactory and auditory senses far better than ours."

"Don't you think we should have discussed this decision?" Cassy asked. Her fear was turning to anger.

"We can discuss it now," Beau said innocently.

"Good grief!" Cassy voiced angrily. She picked up the Chinese take-out and walked into the kitchen. She took the containers out of the bag and got plates from the cupboard, making sure the door banged against its hinges. From the drawer next to the dishwasher she got flatware and noisily set the table.

Beau appeared at the door. "There's no need to get upset," he said.

"Oh yeah?" Cassy questioned as tears unwillingly welled up. "That's easy for you to say. I'm not the one acting weird, like going out in the middle of the night and coming home with a dog the size of a buffalo."

Beau stepped into the kitchen and tried to put his arms around Cassy. She pushed him away and ran into the bedroom. She was sobbing now.

Beau came in behind her and put his arms around her, and she didn't resist. For a moment he didn't say anything and let her cry. Finally he turned her around and looked into her eyes, and she into his.

"Okay," he said. "I'm sorry about the dog too. I should have talked to you about the idea, but my mind has been so overwhelmed. I've got so many things going on right now. I've heard back from the Nite people. I'll be going out there to meet them."

"When did you hear from them?" Cassy asked, wiping her eyes. She knew how much Beau was counting on getting a job with Cipher Software. Maybe there was an explanation for his odd behavior.

"I heard from them today," Beau said. "It's all so promising."

"When will you go?" Cassy said.

"Tomorrow," Beau said.

"Tomorrow!" Cassy repeated. Things were happening too quickly. It was an emotional overload. "Weren't you going to tell me?"

"Of course I was going to tell you," Beau said.

"And you really want a dog?" Cassy asked. "What will you do with him when you go visit the Nite people?"

"I'll take him," Beau said without hesitation.

"You'll take him on an interview trip?"

"Why not? He's a wonderful animal."

Cassy digested this surprising information. From her perspective it seemed inappropriate to say the least. Having a dog seemed incompatible with their lifestyle.

"Who's going to walk him when you're in class? And feed him. Having a dog is a lot of responsibility."

"I know, I know," Beau intoned, raising his hands as if to surrender. "I promise to take care of him. I'll take him out, feed him, pick up after him, and punish him if he chews any of your shoes."

Cassy smiled in spite of herself. Beau sounded like the cliché of the small boy pleading with his mother to get a dog while the mother knows full well who will end up assuming the burden of taking care of the pet.

"I got him from the pound," Beau said. "I'm sure you'll like him, but if you don't, we'll take him back. We'll consider the whole thing an experiment. After a week we'll decide."

"Really?" Cassy asked.

"Absolutely," Beau said. "Let me get him so you can meet him properly. He's a great dog."

Cassy nodded, and Beau left the room. Cassy took a deep breath. So much seemed to be happening. Heading for the bathroom to wash her face, Cassy noticed that Beau's computer was running some weird, rapid program. Cassy hesitated and looked at the monitor. Data in the form of text and graphics was appearing and disappearing from the screen at bewildering speed. Then she noticed something else. Sitting in front of Beau's infrared port was the curious black object that Beau had found a few days previously in the parking lot of Costa's Diner. Cassy had forgotten it, and remembering that the men had said it was heavy, she reached for it.

"Here's the monster," Beau called, diverting Cassy's attention. Following Beau's commands, King was happy to bound over to Cassy and lick her hand.

"What a rough tongue," Cassy said.

"He's a great dog," Beau said, beaming.

Cassy patted King's flank. "He is solid," she said. "How much does he weigh?" She was wondering how many cans of dog food he'd need each day.

"I'd guess about one-twenty-five," Beau said.

Cassy scratched King behind the ear, then nodded toward Beau's computer. "What's going on with your PC? It looks like it's running out of control."

"It's just downloading some data off the Internet," Beau said. He stepped over to the machine. "I guess I could turn off the monitor."

"You're going to print all that?" Cassy said. "You'll have to get a lot more paper than we have."

Beau switched off the monitor but made certain the light on the hard drive kept up its rapid blinking.

"So what's it going to be?" Beau said, straightening up. "The Chinese take-out or the Bistro. It's your call."

BEAU'S EYES SNAPPED OPEN SIMULTANEOUSLY WITH King's. Pushing up on one elbow Beau glanced across Cassy's sleeping form to see the time. It was 2:30 A.M.

Being careful to keep the bedsprings from squeaking, Beau eased his legs from beneath the covers and stood up. He patted King's head before slipping on his clothes. Then he moved over to his computer. A moment earlier the red light on his hard drive had finally stopped blinking.

He picked up the black disc and slipped it into his pocket. Using a notepad next to his computer he scribbled: "Gone for a walk. Be right back. Beau."

After placing the note on his pillow, he and King silently left the apartment.

Beau exited the building and walked around to the parking lot. King stayed at his side without a leash. It was

another gorgeous night with the broad stripe of the Milky
Way galaxy arching directly overhead. There was no moon,
and the stars appeared more dazzling as a consequence.

Toward the rear of the parking lot Beau found an area
devoid of cars. Taking the black disc from his pocket, he
placed it on the asphalt. Almost the moment it left his hand,
it began to glow. By the time Beau and King were fifty
feet away it had begun to form its corona and was beginning to turn from red to white-hot.

CASSY HAD BEEN SLEEPING RESTLESSLY ALL NIGHT WITH
anxiety-filled dreams. She had no idea what had awakened
her, but all at once she found herself staring at the ceiling.
It was being progressively illuminated by an unusual light.

Cassy sat up. The whole room had a peculiar, mounting
glow, and it was apparent that it was streaming in through
the window. As she began to slip out of bed to investigate,
she noticed Beau was absent just as he'd been the night
before. This time, however, she could see that there was a
note.

Taking the note with her, Cassy padded across the floor
to the window and looked out. She saw the source of the
glow immediately. It was a white ball of light which was
rapidly increasing its intensity so that the surrounding cars
were casting dark shadows.

In the next instant the light disappeared as if it had been
suddenly snuffed out. It gave Cassy the impression it had
imploded. An instant later she heard a loud whooshing
sound that ended equally abruptly.

Having no idea of what she'd just seen, Candy wondered
if she should call the police. While debating with herself,
she started to turn back into the room when movement out
in the parking lot caught her attention. Refocusing her eyes,
she saw a man and a dog. Almost immediately she recognized Beau and King.

Certain he must have seen the ball of light, she was about
to yell down to him when she saw other figures emerge out
of the shadows. To her surprise thirty or forty people mystically appeared.

There were a few streetlights bordering the parking area, so Cassy could just make out some of the faces. At first she didn't recognize anyone. But then she saw two people she thought she knew. She thought she saw Mr. and Mrs. Partridge!

Cassy forced herself to blink several times. Was she really awake or was this a dream? A shudder passed through her. It was terrifying to be confused about her sense of reality. It gave her an immediate appreciation of the horror of psychiatric illness.

Looking again Cassy saw that the people had all congregated in the center of the parking lot. It was as if they were having a clandestine meeting. She thought briefly about putting on her clothes and going out to see what it was all about, but she had to admit to herself that she was frightened. The whole situation was surreal.

Then suddenly she had the sense that King had spotted her at the window. The dog's head had turned in her direction, and his eyes glowed like a cat's eyes when a light is shined in them. A bark from King made all the people look up, including Beau.

Cassy stepped back from the window in shocked surprise. All the people's eyes were glowing like King's. It gave her a shiver, and again she had to wonder if she were dreaming.

She stumbled back to her bed in the darkness and turned on the light. She read the note, hoping there might be some explanation, but it was completely generic. She put the note on the night table and wondered what she should do. Should she call the police? If she did, what would she say? Would they laugh at her? Or if they came would it turn out to be a big embarrassment if there were some reasonable explanation.

All at once she thought of Pitt. Snapping up the phone, she started to dial. But she didn't finish. She remembered it was three o'clock in the morning. What could he do or say? Cassy replaced the receiver and sighed.

Cassy decided she'd just have to wait for Beau to return. She had no idea what was going on, but she was going to find out. She'd confront Beau and demand that he tell her.

Having made a decision, even a passive one, Cassy felt a little less anxious. She leaned back against her pillow and tucked her hands behind her head. She tried not to think about what she'd just seen. Instead she made a conscious effort to relax by concentrating on her breathing.

Cassy heard the front door to the apartment squeak, and she sat bolt upright. She'd been asleep which made her wonder if she been dreaming after all. But a glance at the bedside table revealed Beau's note, and the fact that the light was on told her it had not been a dream.

Beau and King appeared at the doorway with Beau carrying his shoes. He was trying to be quiet.

"You're still awake," Beau said. He sounded disappointed.

"Waiting for you," Cassy said.

"I trust you got my note?" Beau asked. He tossed his shoes into the closet and started peeling off his clothes.

"I did," Cassy said. "I appreciated it." Cassy struggled with herself. She wanted to ask her questions but she felt a reluctance. The whole situation was like a nightmare.

"Good," Beau said. He disappeared into the bathroom.

"What was going on out there?" Cassy called out, marshalling her courage.

"We went for a walk like the note says," Beau called back.

"Who were all those people?" Cassy called.

Beau appeared in the doorway toweling off his face.

"Just a bunch of people out walking like me," Beau said.

"The Partridges?" Cassy questioned sarcastically.

"Yeah, they were there," Beau said. "Nice people. Very enthusiastic."

"What were you talking about?" Cassy asked. "I saw you from the window. It was like a meeting."

"I know you saw us," Beau said. "We weren't hiding or anything. We were just talking, mostly about the environment."

A sardonic half laugh escaped from Cassy. Under the

circumstances she couldn't believe Beau would make such a ridiculous statement. "Yeah, sure," she intoned. "Three o'clock in the morning there's a neighborhood meeting on the environment."

Beau came over to the bed and sat on the edge. His expression was one of deep concern.

"Cassy, what is the matter?" he asked. "You're so upset again."

"Of course I'm upset," Cassy yelled.

"Calm down, dear, please," Beau said.

"Oh, come on, Beau. What do you take me for? What's going on with you?"

"Nothing," Beau said. "I feel wonderful, things are going great."

"Don't you realize how strange you've been acting?"

"I don't know what you are talking about," Beau said. "Maybe my value system is shifting, but hell, I'm young, I'm in college, I'm supposed to be learning."

"You haven't been yourself," Cassy persisted.

"Of course I have," Beau said. "I'm Beau Eric Stark. The same guy I was last week and the week before that. I was born in Brookline, Mass., to Tami and Ralph Stark. I have a sister named Jeanine, and I . . ."

"Stop it, Beau!" Cassy cried. "I know your history isn't different, it's your behavior. Can't you tell?"

Beau shrugged his shoulders. "I can't. I'm sorry, but I'm the same person I've always been."

Cassy let out a sigh of exasperation. "Well, you're not, and I'm not the only person who's noticed it. So has your friend Pitt."

"Pitt?" Beau questioned. "Well, now that you mention it, he did say something about me doing some unexpected things."

"Exactly," Cassy said. "That's just what I'm talking about. Listen! I want you to see somebody professional. In fact we'll both go. How's that?" Cassy let out another short sarcastic laugh. "Hell, maybe it's me."

"Okay," Beau said agreeably.

"You'll see someone?" Cassy said. She'd expected an argument.

"If it will make you feel better, I'll see someone," Beau said. "But of course it will have to wait until I get back from meeting with the Nite people, and I don't know exactly when that will be."

"I thought you'd just be going for the day," Cassy said.

"It will be longer than that," Beau said. "But exactly how long I won't know until I get there."

10

NANCY SELLERS WORKED AT HOME AS MUCH AS SHE could. With her computer networked into the mainframe at Serotec Pharmaceuticals and with a superb group of technicians in her lab, she got more work done at home than in her office. The main reason was that the physical separation shielded her from the myriad administrative headaches involved in running a large research lab. The second reason was the tranquility of the silent house fostered her creativity.

Accustomed to absolute silence, the sound of the front door banging closed at ten minutes before ten got Nancy's attention immediately. Pessimistically thinking it could only be bad news, she exited from the program she was working on, and walked out of her home office.

She stopped at the balustrade in the hall and looked down into the front hall. Jonathan came into her line of sight.

"Why aren't you at school?" Nancy called down. Already she'd made a mental assessment of his health. He seemed to be walking okay, and his color was good.

Jonathan stopped at the foot of the stairs and looked up. "We need to talk with you."

"What do you mean, we?" Nancy asked. But no sooner had the question left her lips than she saw a young woman come up behind her son and tilt her head back.

"This is Candee Taylor, Mom," Jonathan said.

Nancy's mouth went dry. What she saw was a pixielike face on top of a well-developed female body. Her first thought was that she was pregnant. Being the mother of a teenager was like a high-wire act: disaster was always lurking around the corner.

"I'll be right down," Nancy said. "I'll meet you in the kitchen."

Nancy made a quick detour into the bathroom, more to get her emotions in check than to attend to her appearance. She'd been worried about Jonathan getting into this kind of a problem for the last year as his interest in girls skyrocketed, and he'd become uncommunicative and secretive.

When Nancy thought she was prepared, she met the kids in the kitchen. They had helped themselves to coffee that she kept on the stove. Nancy poured herself a cup and sat on one of the bar stools along the central island. The kids were sitting in the banquette.

"Okay," Nancy said, prepared for the worst. "Shoot."

Jonathan spoke first since Candee was obviously nervous. He described how Candee's parents were acting out of character. He said that he'd gone over there yesterday afternoon and had witnessed it himself.

"This is what you wanted to talk to me about?" Nancy asked. "About Candee's parents."

"Yes," Jonathan said. "You see, Candee's mom works at Serotec Pharmaceuticals in the accounting department."

"That must be Joy Taylor," Nancy said. She tried to keep the relief she felt out of her voice. "I've talked with her many times."

"That's what we thought," Jonathan said. "We were hoping you might be willing to talk with her because Candee is really worried."

"How is Mrs. Taylor acting that's so strange?" Nancy asked.

"It's both my mother and my father," Candee said.

"I can tell you from my perspective," Jonathan said. "Up until yesterday they didn't want me around. No way.

Then yesterday they were so friendly I couldn't believe it. They even invited me to stay overnight.''

"Why would they think you'd want to stay overnight?'' Nancy asked.

Jonathan and Candee exchanged glances. Both blushed.

"You mean they were suggesting you two sleep together?'' she asked.

"Well, they didn't say that exactly,'' Jonathan said. "But we kinda got that idea.''

"I'll be happy to say something,'' Nancy said, and she meant it. She was appalled.

"It's not only the way they are acting,'' Candee said. "It's like they are different people. A few days ago they had like zero friends. Now all the sudden they're having people over . . . at all hours of the day and night to talk about the rain forests and pollution and things like that. People I swear they've never even met before who wander around the house. I've got to lock my bedroom door.''

Nancy put her coffee cup down. She felt embarrassed about her initial suspicions. She looked at Candee, and instead of a seductress, she saw a frightened child. The image twanged the cords of her maternal instincts.

"I'll be happy to talk with your mother,'' Nancy repeated. "And you're welcome to stay here if you'd like in our guest room. But I'll be straight with you two. No fooling around, and I think you know what I mean.''

"WHAT WILL IT BE?'' MARJORIE STEPHANOPOLIS ASKED. Both Cassy and Pitt noticed her radiant smile. "Beautiful day, wouldn't you say.''

Cassy and Pitt exchanged glances of amazement. This was the first time Marjorie had ever tried to have a conversation with them. They were in one of the booths at Costa's Diner for lunch.

"I'll have a hamburger, fries, and a Coke,'' Cassy said.

"Me too,'' Pitt said.

Marjorie collected the menus. "I'll have your orders out as soon as I can,'' she said. "I hope you enjoy your lunch.''

"At least someone is enjoying the day,'' Pitt said as he

watched Marjorie disappear back into the kitchen. "In the three and a half years I've been coming here, that's the most I've ever heard her say."

"You never eat hamburgers and fries," Cassy said.

"Nor do you," Pitt reminded her.

"It was the first thing that came to my mind," Cassy said. "I'm just so weirded out. And I'm telling you the truth about last night. I wasn't hallucinating."

"But you told me yourself you wondered if you were awake or were dreaming," Pitt reminded her.

"I convinced myself I was awake," Cassy said angrily.

"All right, calm down," Pitt said. He glanced around. Several people in the diner were glaring at them.

Cassy leaned across the table and whispered: "When they all looked up at me, including the dog, their eyes were glowing."

"Aw, Cassy, come on," Pitt said.

"I'm telling you the truth!" she snapped.

Pitt hazarded another look around the room. Even more people were eyeing them now. Clearly Cassy's voice was disturbing people.

"Keep your voice down!" Pitt whispered forcibly.

"Okay," Cassy said. She too could appreciate the stares they were getting.

"When I asked Beau what he was out there talking about at three o'clock in the morning, he told me, 'The environment,' " Cassy said.

"I don't know whether to laugh or cry," Pitt said. "Do you think he was trying to be funny?"

"No, not at all," Cassy said with conviction.

"But the idea of meeting out in the parking lot in the middle of the night to talk about the environment is absurd."

"So is the fact that their eyes were glowing," Cassy said. "But you haven't told me what Beau said when you spoke with him yesterday."

"I didn't get a chance," Pitt said. He then told Cassy everything that happened at the game and after it. Cassy listened with great interest, especially the part about Beau meeting the well-dressed business types on the athletic field.

"Do you have any idea what they were talking about?" Cassy asked.

"Not a clue," Pitt said.

"Could they have been from Cipher Software?" Cassy asked. She kept hoping for a reasonable explanation for everything that had been happening.

"I don't know," Pitt said. "Why would you ask that?" Before Cassy could answer, Pitt noticed Marjorie standing off to the side holding two Cokes. The moment he saw her she came over and placed the drinks on the table.

"Your food will be right out," she said cheerfully.

After Marjorie had again disappeared Pitt said: "I must be getting paranoid. I could have sworn she was standing there listening to us."

"Why would she do that?" Cassy asked.

"Beats me," Pitt said. "Tell me, did Beau go to his classes today?"

"No, he's flown off to Cipher Software," Cassy said. "That's why I asked you about them. He said he'd heard from them yesterday. I assumed they phoned but maybe they came in person. At any rate he's off for an interview."

"When will he be back?"

"He didn't know."

"Well, maybe that's good," Pitt said. "Maybe by the time he gets back he'll be back to normal."

Marjorie reappeared carrying the food. With a flourish she placed their orders before them and even gave their dishes a little spin to orient them perfectly as if Costa's were a fine restaurant.

"Enjoy!" Marjorie said happily before disappearing back into the kitchen.

"It's not just Beau who's been acting differently," Cassy said. "It's Ed Partridge and his wife, and I've heard of others. I think whatever it is, it's spreading. In fact I think it has something to do with the flu that's been going around."

"Amen!" Pitt said. "I have the same feeling. In fact I

said as much yesterday to the head of the emergency room.''

"And what was the reaction?" Cassy asked.

"Better than I anticipated," Pitt said. "The head of the ER is a rather hard-nosed no-nonsense woman by the name of Dr. Sheila Miller, yet she was willing to listen to me, and even took me over to talk with the president of the hospital."

"What was his response?" Cassy asked.

"He wasn't impressed," Pitt said. "But the man had the flu symptoms while we were talking with him."

"Is something wrong with your food?" Marjorie asked. She'd reappeared at the tableside.

"It's fine," Cassy said with exasperation at the interruption.

"But you haven't touched it," Marjorie said. "If there is a problem I can get you something else."

"We're okay!" Pitt snapped.

"Well, just call if you need me." She hurried off.

"She's going to drive me bananas," Cassy said. "I think I preferred her sullen."

All at once the same idea occurred to Cassy and Pitt.

"Oh my God!" Cassy said. "Do you think she's had the flu?"

"I wonder!" Pitt said with equal concern. "Obviously she's acting very out of character."

"We've got to do something," Cassy said. "Who should we go to? Do you have any ideas?"

"Not really," Pitt said. "Except maybe go back to Dr. Miller. She was at least receptive. I'd like to tell her there are other people with personality changes. I'd only mentioned Beau."

"Would you mind if I came along?" Cassy asked.

"Not at all," Pitt said. "In fact I'd prefer it. But let's do it right away."

"I'm game," Cassy said.

Pitt vainly scanned the room for Marjorie to get the check. When he didn't see her, he sighed with exasperation. It was frustrating that after pestering them for the whole meal, the moment he wanted her, she was nowhere to be seen.

"Marjorie is behind you," Cassy said. She pointed over Pitt's shoulder. "She's at the cash register having an animated chat with Costa."

Pitt twisted in his seat. The moment he did so, Marjorie and Costa both turned their heads in his direction and locked their eyes on his. There was an intensity in their gaze that gave Pitt a chill.

Pitt swung around to face Cassy. "Let's get the hell out of here," he said. "I must be getting paranoid again. I don't know why I'm so sure about this, but Marjorie and Costa were talking about us."

BEAU HAD NEVER BEEN TO SANTA FE BEFORE, BUT HE'D heard good things about it and had been looking forward to his visit. He wasn't disappointed: he liked the town immediately.

He had arrived on schedule at the modest airport and had been picked up by a stretch Jeep Cherokee! Beau had never seen such a vehicle before, and at first he'd thought it was comical. But after riding in it, he was willing to believe it might be superior to a normal limousine because of its height. Of course he had to admit to himself that he hadn't had much experience with limousines of any sort.

As attractive as Beau found Santa Fe in general, it was only a harbinger of the beauty of the grounds of Cipher Software. After they had passed through a security gate Beau thought the facility had more of a resemblance to a posh resort than to a business establishment. Lush, rolling green lawns stretched between widely dispersed, well proportioned, modern buildings. Dense conifer forests and reflecting pools completed the picture.

Beau was dropped off at the central facility which, like the other buildings, was constructed of granite and gold-tinted glass. Several people who Beau had already met greeted him and told him that Mr. Randy Nite was waiting for him in his office.

As Beau and his escorts rose up in a glass-enclosed el-

evator through a plant-filled atrium, Beau was asked
whether he was hungry or thirsty. Beau told them that he
was fine.

Randy Nite's office was huge, occupying most of the
west wing of the third and top floor of the building. About
fifty feet square, it was bounded on three sides with floor-
to-ceiling glass. Randy's desk stood in the center of this
expansive space. It was made of a four-inch-thick slab of
black and gold marble.

Randy was on the phone when Beau was ushered in, but
he stood up immediately and waved Beau over to take a
starkly modern black leather chair. He motioned to Beau
that he'd be just a few minutes longer. Their job done, the
escorts silently withdrew.

Beau had seen photos of Randy innumerable times as
well as having seen him on TV. In person he appeared just
as young and boyish, with a shock of red hair and a crop
of pleasing freckles sprinkled across a wide, healthy-
looking face. His gray-green eyes had a hint of merriment.
He was about Beau's height but not as muscular although
he appeared fit.

"The new software will be shipping next month," Randy
was saying, "and the advertising blitz is poised to begin
next week. It's a dynamite campaign. Things couldn't look
any better. It's going to take the world by storm. Trust
me!"

Randy hung up and smiled broadly. He was dressed casually in a blue blazer, acid-washed jeans, and tennis shoes.
It was no accident that Beau was dressed in a similar fashion.

"Welcome," Randy said. He extended his hand, and
Beau shook it. "I must say that my team has never recommended someone as highly as they have recommended
you. Over the last forty-eight hours I've heard nonstop
praise. It intrigues me. How has a college senior been able
to manage such successful PR?"

"I suppose it's a combination of luck, interest, and old-
fashioned hard work," Beau said.

Randy smiled. "Well put," he said. "I've also heard

you'd like to start out, not in the mail room, but as my personal assistant.''

"Everybody has to start someplace," Beau said.

Randy laughed heartily. "I like that," he said. "Confidence and a sense of humor. Kinda reminds me of myself when I started. Come on! Let me show you around.''

"THE EMERGENCY ROOM LOOKS CROWDED," CASSY SAID.

"I've never seen it like this," Pitt said.

They were walking across the parking lot toward the ER dock. Several ambulances were there with their lights blinking. Cars were parked haphazardly, and the hospital security was trying to straighten things out. The dock itself was full of people overflowing from the waiting room.

Climbing the stairs Pitt and Cassy had to literally push their way through to the main desk. Pitt saw Cheryl Watkins and called out to her: "What on earth is going on?"

"We've been inundated with the flu," Cheryl said. She sneezed herself, then coughed. "Unfortunately the staff hasn't been immune."

"Is Dr. Miller here?" Pitt asked.

"She's working along with everyone else," Cheryl said.

"Hang here," Pitt told Casey. "I'll see if I can find her."

"Try to be quick," Cassy said. "I've never liked hospitals."

Pitt got himself a white coat and pinned his hospital ID to the breast pocket. Then he started searching through the bays. He found Dr. Miller with an elderly woman who wanted to be admitted to the hospital. The woman was in a wheelchair ready to go home.

"I'm sorry," Dr. Miller said. She finished writing on the ER sheet and slipped its clipboard into a pocket in the back of the wheel chair. "Your flu symptoms don't warrant an admission. All you need is bed rest, analgesic, and fluids. Your husband will be in here in a moment to take you home."

"But I don't want to go home," the woman complained. "I want to stay in the hospital. My husband frightens me. He's not the same. He's someone else."

At that moment the husband appeared. He'd been brought back to retrieve his wife by one of the orderlies. Although as elderly as his wife, he appeared far more spry and mentally alert.

"No, no, please," the woman moaned when she saw him. She tried to grasp Dr. Miller's sleeve as the husband quickly rolled her out of the bay and toward the exit. "Calm down, dear," the man was saying soothingly. "You don't want to be a bother to these good doctors."

In the process of slipping off her latex examining gloves, Sheila caught sight of Pitt. "Well, you were certainly right about this flu being on the increase. And did you hear the little exchange I just had?"

Pitt nodded. "Sounds suspiciously like there might have been a personality change on the part of the husband."

"My thought as well," Sheila said as she threw away the gloves. "But of course older people can be prone to disorientation."

"I know you are busy," Pitt said, "but could you spare a minute? A friend and I would like to talk with you. We don't know who else to go to."

Sheila agreed immediately despite the chaos in the ER. Pitt's opinions the day before were appearing to be prophetic. She was now convinced this flu was different; for one thing an influenza virus had yet to be isolated.

She took Pitt and Cassy back to her office. As soon as the door closed it was like an island of tranquility in the middle of a storm. Sheila sat down. She was exhausted.

Cassy told the whole story of Beau's transformation after his illness. Although she felt self-conscious about certain parts, she left nothing out. She even related what had happened the previous night, including the strange ball of light, the clandestine meeting, and the fact that everyone's eyes glowed.

When Cassy was finished, Sheila didn't say anything at first. She'd been absently doodling with a pencil. Finally she looked up. "Under normal circumstances with a story like this I'd send you over to psychiatry and let them deal with you. But these are not normal circumstances. I don't know what to think about all this, but we should establish what facts we can. Now, Beau came down with his illness three days ago.''

Cassy and Pitt nodded in unison.

"I should see him," Sheila said. "Do you think he'd be willing to come in and be examined?''

"He said he would," Cassy said. "I asked him specifically about seeing someone professional.''

"Could you get him in here today?'' Sheila asked.

Cassy shook her head. "He's in Santa Fe.''

"When will he be back?''

Cassy felt a wave of emotion. "I don't know," she managed. "He wouldn't tell me.''

"THIS IS ONE OF MY FAVORITE LOCATIONS IN THE COMpound or the Zone as we like to call it,'' Randy said. He pulled the electric golf cart to a halt and climbed out. Beau got out his side and followed the software mogul up a small grassy knoll. When they reached the top the view was spectacular.

In front of them was a crystalline lake populated with wild ducks. The backdrop was virgin woodland silhouetted against the Rocky Mountains.

"What do you think?'' Randy said proudly.

"It's awe-inspiring," Beau said. "It shows what concern for the environment can do, and it provides a ray of hope. It's such an unbelievable tragedy for an intelligent species like human beings to have done the damage they have to this gorgeous planet. Pollution, political strife, racial divisiveness, overpopulation, mismanagement of the gene pool . . .''

Randy had been nodding in agreement until the very last statement. He cast a quick look in Beau's direction, but Beau was dreamily staring off at the distant mountains. Randy wondered what Beau meant by "mismanagement of the gene pool.'' But before he could ask, Beau continued: "These negative forces have to be controlled, and they can be. I firmly believe there are adequate resources to reverse the harm done to the planet. All it will take is a great visionary man to carry the torch, someone who knows the problems, has the power, and is not afraid to lead."

A smile of acknowledgment spread involuntarily across Randy's face. Beau caught it out of the corner of his eye. The smile alone told Beau that he had Randy exactly where he wanted him.

"These certainly are visionary ideas for a college senior," Randy said. "But do you really think that human nature, such as it is, can be controlled enough to make it happen?"

"I've realized that human nature is a stumbling block," Beau admitted. "But with the financial resources and world community connections that you have amassed with Cipher Software, I think the obstacles can be overcome."

"It's good to have a vision," Randy said. Although he considered Beau overly idealistic, he was nonetheless impressed. But he wasn't impressed enough to start Beau out as his personal assistant. Beau would start in the mail room and work his way up like all his assistants.

"What is that over there on that pile of gravel?" Beau asked.

"Where?" Randy asked.

Beau walked over and bent down. He pretended to pick up one of his black discs that he'd actually pulled out of his pocket. Cradling it in his palm, he returned to Randy, and held it out.

"I don't know what it is," Randy said. "But I've seen some of my assistants with them over the last couple of days. What is it made of?"

"I can't tell," Beau said. "But it's heavy, so maybe it's metal. But take it. Maybe you can tell me."

Randy took the object and tested its weight. "A dense little thing," he remarked. "And what a smooth surface. And look at these symmetrically arranged bumps around the periphery.

"Owwww!" Randy cried. He dropped the disc to grab his finger. A drop of blood rapidly formed.

"The damn thing stung me!"

"That's odd," Beau said. "Let me see."

• • •

"THERE HAVE BEEN OTHER PEOPLE WHO HAVE SHOWN PER-
sonality changes," Cassy told Sheila. "For instance, the
principal where I'm student teaching has been acting totally
different since his flu episode. I've also heard of others but
haven't seen them in person."

"Frankly it is this mental status change that has me the
most concerned," Sheila said.

Cassy, Pitt, and Sheila were on their way to Dr. Halprin's
office. Armed with new information, Sheila was confident
the president of the medical center would have a different
response than he'd had the day before. But when they arrived, they were in for a disappointment.

"I'm sorry but Dr. Halprin called this morning to say he
was going to take some time off," Mrs. Kapland told them.

"I've never known Dr. Halprin to miss a day at the hospital," Sheila said. "Did he give a reason?"

"He said he and his wife needed to spend some quality
time together," Mrs. Kapland said. "But he will be calling
in. Would you like to leave a message?"

"We'll be back," Sheila said.

Sheila spun on her heels. Cassy and Pitt hurried after
her. They caught up to her at the elevator.

"What now?" Pitt asked.

"It's time someone made a phone call to the people who
should be looking into this problem," she said. "Halprin's
taking a day off for personal reasons is too weird."

"I HATE SUICIDES," VINCE SAID AS HE TURNED RIGHT ON
Main. Up ahead was a gaggle of squad cars and emergency
vehicles. Crime-scene tape held back a throng of onlookers.
It was late afternoon and just getting dark.

"More than homicides?" Jesse asked.

"Yeah," Vince said. "In homicides the victim doesn't
have any choice. Suicides are just the opposite. I can't
imagine what it's like to kill yourself. It gives me the
creeps."

"You're weird," Jesse said. For him it was just the other
way around. It was the innocence of the homicide victim

that disturbed him. Jesse couldn't conjure up the same sympathy for a suicide. He figured that if someone wanted to do himself in, it was his business. The real problem was making sure the suicide was a suicide and not a homicide in disguise.

Vince parked as close to the scene as he could. On the sidewalk a yellow tarp covered the deceased's remains. The only gore visible was a trail of blood that ran to the curb.

The detectives climbed out of their car and looked up. On a ledge six stories up they saw several crime-scene boys nosing around.

Vince sneezed violently twice in a row.

"Bless you," Jesse said reflexly.

Jesse approached a uniformed officer standing near the crowd barrier.

"Who's in charge here?" Jesse asked.

"Actually, the captain," the officer said.

"Captain Hernandez is here?" Jesse asked with surprise.

"Yup, upstairs," the officer said.

Jesse and Vince exchanged confused glances as they headed toward the entrance. The captain rarely ventured out to scenes.

The building belonged to Serotec Pharmaceuticals. It housed their administrative and research offices. Their manufacturing division was outside the town.

In the elevator Vince started to cough. Jesse moved away as much as the small car would allow. "Jeez," Jesse complained. "What's the matter with you?"

"I don't know," Vince said. "Maybe I'm having an allergic reaction or something."

"Well, cover your mouth when you cough," Jesse said.

They reached the sixth floor. The front of the building was occupied by a research lab. There were several uniformed policemen loitering by an open window. Jesse asked where the captain was and the policemen pointed toward an office off to the side.

"I don't think you guys are going to be needed," Captain Hernandez said when he saw Jesse and Vince enter. "The whole episode is on tape."

Captain Hernandez introduced Jesse and Vince to the half-dozen Serotec personnel in the room as well as the crime-scene investigator who'd found the tape. His name was Tom Stockman.

"Roll that tape once more, Tom," Captain Hernandez said.

It was black-and-white security camera footage taken with a wide-angle lens. The sound had an echolike quality. It showed a short man in a white lab coat facing the camera. He'd backed himself against the window and appeared anxious. In front of him were a number of Serotec people, all in similar white coats. They were seen from the back since they were facing the short man. Jesse guessed they were the same people who were now in the office.

"His name was Sergei Kalinov," Captain Hernandez said. "All of a sudden he started screaming for everyone to leave him alone. That was earlier in the tape. Plainly you can see that no one is touching him or even threatening him."

"He just flipped out," one of the Serotec employees said. "We didn't know what to do."

Sergei then began to sob, saying he knew he was infected and that he couldn't stand it.

One of the Serotec employees was then seen moving forward toward Sergei.

"That's the head tech, Mario Palumbo," Captain Hernandez said. "He's trying to calm Sergei. It's hard to hear his voice because he's speaking so softly."

"I was only telling him that we wanted to help," Mario said defensively.

Suddenly Sergei turned and made a dash for the window. He struggled to get it open. His frantic haste suggested he feared interference. But none of the people present including Mario tried to restrain him.

Once Sergei had the window open, he climbed out on the ledge. With one last glance back at the camera, he leaped off into space.

"Aw, man . . ." Vince voiced and looked away.

Even Jesse felt an unpleasant sinking feeling in his gut

having watched this terrified little man kill himself. As the tape continued, Jesse watched as several of the Serotec people, including Mario, walked over to the window and looked down. But they weren't acting as if they were horrified. It was more like they were curious.

Then to Jesse's surprise they closed the window and went back to work.

Tom turned off the tape. Jesse glanced at the Serotec workers. Since they had just watched the harrowing sequence again he would have expected some reaction. There wasn't any. They were all eerily detached from the whole affair.

Tom ejected the tape and was about to slip it into an evidence bag with an attached custody slip when Captain Hernandez took it.

"I'll take care of this," the captain said.

"But that's not . . ."

"I'll take care of it," the captain repeated authoritatively.

"Okay," Tom said agreeably, even though he knew it was not accepted policy.

Jesse watched his captain walk out of the room with the tape in his hand. He looked at Tom.

"He's the captain," Tom said defensively.

Vince coughed explosively directly behind Jesse. Jesse turned and gave him a dirty look. "Jeez," he said. "You're going to get us all sick if you don't cover your mouth."

"Sorry," Vince said. "All of a sudden I feel terrible. Is it cold in here?"

"No it's not cold," Jesse said.

"Shit, I must have a fever," Vince said.

"MAYBE WE SHOULD JUST GO OUT AND GET SOME MEXI-can food," Pitt said.

"No, I want to cook," Cassy said. "It always calms me down."

They were walking beneath the bare lightbulbs strung on wires over the European-style outdoor market. The main commodities were fresh produce and fruit brought directly from outlying farms. But there were other stalls as well that sold everything from fish to antiques and objets d'art. It was a colorful, festive environment and popular. At that time in the early evening it was crowded with shoppers.

"Well, what do you want to make?" Pitt asked.

"Pasta," Cassy said. "Pasta primavera."

Pitt held the bag while Cassy made her selections. She was particularly choosy about the tomatoes.

"I don't know what I'm going to do when he does come back," Cassy said. "The way I feel right now, I don't even want to see him. At least not until I'm sure he's back to normal. This whole episode is frightening me more and more."

"I have access to an apartment," Pitt said.

"Really?" Cassy asked.

"It's over near Costa's," Pitt said. "The owner is a second cousin or something like that. He teaches in the chemistry department but is on a semester sabbatical in France. I go in to feed his fish and water his plants. He'd invited me to stay, but it was too much trouble to move at the time."

"You don't think he'd mind if I stayed there?" Cassy asked.

"Nope," Pitt said. "It's a big place. Three bedrooms. I'd stay too if you wanted."

"Do you think I'm overreacting?" Cassy asked.

"Not at all," Pitt said. "After his little demonstration at basketball I'm a bit leery of him myself."

"God! I can't believe we're talking this way about Beau," Cassy said with emotion.

Instinctively Pitt reached out and put his arms around Cassy. Just as instinctively she did the same. They clung to each other, momentarily oblivious to the other shoppers who swirled about them. After several moments Cassy glanced up into Pitt's dark eyes. Both felt a fleeting sense of what might have been. Then, suddenly embarrassed, they released each other and quickly went back to selecting tomatoes.

With their groceries purchased, including a bottle of dry Italian wine, they headed back to the car. The route took them through the flea market section. Pitt suddenly stopped in front of one of the stalls.

"Holy crap!" he exclaimed.

"What?" Cassy demanded. She was ready to flee. As keyed up as she was she expected the worst.

"Look!" Pitt said, pointing toward the stall's display.

Cassy's eyes swept over a bewildering collection of junk that a sign proclaimed to be antiques. There were mostly small items like ashtrays and ceramic animals, but there were a few larger things like plaster garden statues and bedside lamps. There were also several glass boxes of old, cheap costume jewelry.

"What am I supposed to be noticing?" Cassy asked impatiently.

"On the top of the shelf," Pitt said. "In between the beer mug and the pair of bookends."

They moved over to the stall. Cassy now saw what had caught Pitt's eye. "Isn't that interesting," she commented. Lined up in a perfect row were six of the black disc objects like the one Beau had found in the parking lot of Costa's Diner.

Cassy reached out to pick one up, but Pitt grabbed her hand. "Don't touch it!" he said.

"I wasn't going to hurt it," Cassy said. "I just wanted to see how heavy it was."

"I was worried about it hurting you!" Pitt said. "Not vice versa. Beau's stung him somehow. Or at least Beau thought so. What a coincidence seeing these things. I'd forgotten all about Beau's." He bent over and examined one of the discs more closely. He remembered that he and Beau had not been able to decide its composition.

"I saw the one Beau found just last night," Cassy said. "It was sitting in front of his computer when he was downloading a bunch of data from the Internet."

Pitt tried to get the attention of the owner to inquire about the discs, but he was busy with another customer.

While they were eyeing the discs and waiting for the stall keeper to be free, a heavyset man and woman pushed ahead of them.

"Here's some more of those black stones that Gertrude was talking about last night," the woman said.

The man grunted.

"Gertrude said she found four of them in her back yard," the woman said. She then added with a laugh: "She thought they might be valuable until she found out that people had been finding them all over."

The woman picked one of them up. "Wow, it's heavy," she said. She closed her fingers around it. "And it feels cold."

She was about to hand it to her friend when she cried, "Ahhh!" and irritably tossed it back onto the shelf. Unfortunately it skidded off and dropped less than a foot into the bowl of an ashtray. The ashtray shattered into a million pieces.

The sound of the breaking glass brought over the proprietor. Seeing what had happened, he demanded payment for the lost ashtray.

"I ain't paying nothing," the woman said indignantly. "That little black thingamajig cut my finger." Defiantly she held up her wounded middle finger. The gesture incensed the owner who mistook its motivation as obscene.

While the woman and the owner argued, Pitt and Cassy looked at each other for confirmation about what they'd seen in the gathering gloom. When the woman had held up her finger it had appeared to have a faint blue iridescence!

"What could have caused it?" Cassy whispered.

"You're asking me?" Pitt questioned. "I'm not even sure it happened. It was only for an instant."

"But we both saw it," Cassy said.

It took another twenty minutes for the owner and the woman to come to an agreement. After the woman and her friend had left, Pitt asked the owner about the black discs.

"What do you want to know?" the man said morosely. He'd only gotten half the value of the ashtray.

"Do you know what they are?" Cassy asked.

"I haven't the slightest idea."

"How much do you sell them for?"

"In the beginning I got as much as ten dollars," the man said. "But that was a day or so ago. Now they're coming out of the woodwork, and the market's been flooded. But I'll tell you what. These happen to be exceptional quality. I'll sell you all six for ten dollars."

"Have any of these discs injured anyone else?" Pitt asked.

"Well, one of them stung me too," he said. He shrugged. "But it was nothing: just a pinprick. Yet I couldn't figure out how it happened." He picked up one of the discs. "I mean they're as smooth as a baby's bottom."

Pitt took Cassy's arm and began to lead her away. The man called after them. "Hey, how about eight dollars."

Pitt ignored him. Instead he told Cassy about the little girl in the ER who had been scolded by her mother for saying that a black rock had bitten her.

"Do you think it had been one of those discs?" Cassy asked.

"That's what I'm wondering," Pitt said. "Because she had the flu. That's why she was in the ER."

"Are you suggesting the black disc had something to do with her getting the flu?"

"I know it sounds crazy," Pitt said. "But that was the sequence with Beau. He got stung, then hours later he got sick."

11

"WHEN DID YOU HEAR ABOUT THIS RANDY NITE NEWS conference?" Cassy asked.

"This morning when I was watching the *Today* show," Pitt said. "The news anchor said NBC was going to be carrying it live."

"And they mentioned Beau's name?"

"That was the astounding thing," Pitt said. "I mean, he only went out there for an interview, and now he's part of a news conference. That's big-time weird."

Cassy and Pitt were in the doctors' lounge in the ER watching a thirteen-inch TV. Sheila Miller had called Pitt early and told him to be there and to bring Cassy. The room was called the doctors' lounge but was used by all the ER personnel for moments of relaxation and for those who brought paper bag lunches.

"What are we here for?" Cassy asked. "I hate to miss class."

"She didn't say," Pitt said, "but my guess is that she's gone over Dr. Halprin's head somehow and wants us to talk with whomever she's contacted."

"Are we going to mention about last evening?" Cassy asked.

Pitt held up his hand to quiet Cassy. The TV anchor was

announcing that Randy Nite had entered the room. A moment later Randy's familiar boyish face filled the screen.

Before he began speaking, he turned to the side and coughed. Returning to the microphones he apologized in advance for his voice and said: "I'm just getting over a bout of the flu, so bear with me."

"Uh oh," Pitt said. "He's had it too."

"Now then," Randy said. "Good morning, everyone. For those of you who don't know me, my name is Randy Nite, and I'm a software salesman."

Discreet laughter could be heard from the onscreen audience. While Randy paused the anchor complimented Randy's humorous modesty; he was one of the world's richest men, and there were few people in the industrialized nations who didn't know of Randy Nite.

"I have called a news conference today to announce that I am starting a new venture . . . truly the most exciting, most important undertaking of my life."

An excited murmur erupted from the TV audience. They had expected big news, and it sounded as if they weren't to be disappointed.

"This new venture," Randy continued, "will be called the Institute for a New Beginning, and it will be backed by all the combined resources of Cipher Software. To describe this bold new venture, I would like to introduce a young man of tremendous vision. Ladies and gentlemen, please welcome my new personal assistant, Mr. Beau Stark."

Cassy and Pitt glanced at each other with mouths agape. "I don't believe this," Cassy said.

Beau bounded onto the speaker's platform amid applause. He was dressed in a designer suit with his dark hair slicked back from his forehead. He exuded a politician's confidence.

"Thank you all for coming," Beau boomed with a charming smile. His blue eyes sparkled like sapphires in the midst of his tanned face. "The Institute for a New Beginning is aptly named. We will be seeking the best and the brightest in the fields of science, medicine, engineering, and architecture. Our aim will be to reverse the negative

trends that our planet has been experiencing. We can end
pollution! We can end social and political strife! We can
create a world suitable for a new humankind! We can and
we will!''

The reporters present at the news conference erupted in
a frenzy of questions. Beau held out his hands to quiet
them.

"We will not be entertaining questions today. The purpose of this meeting was merely to make the announcement. One week from today we will hold another news
conference in which our agenda will be spelled out in detail. Thank you all for coming.''

Despite questions shouted from the news media, Beau
stepped from the speakers' platform, embraced Randy Nite,
and then the two of them, arm in arm, disappeared from
view.

The announcer then tried to fill the gap caused by the
precipitous end to the news conference. He began specu-
lating on exactly what the specific goals of the new institute
would be and what Randy Nite meant when he said that
the venture would be backed by all the combined resources
of Cipher Software. He pointed out that those resources
were substantial, more than the GNP of many countries.

"My God! Pitt," Cassy said. "What's going on with
Beau?''

"My guess is that his interview went okay," Pitt said,
trying to be funny.

"This isn't a laughing matter," Cassy said. "I'm getting
more and more scared. What are we going to tell Dr. Miller?''

"For the moment I think we've told her enough," Pitt
said.

"Come on!" Cassy complained. "We have to tell her
about what we saw last night and about the little black
discs. We have to . . .''

"Cassy, hold on," Pitt said, taking her by the shoulders.
"Think for a second how this is going to sound to her.
She's our one chance to get someone important to take

notice of what's going on. I don't think we should push it.''

"But all she knows right now is that there's this strange flu,'' Cassy said.

"That's exactly my point,'' Pitt said. "We've got her attention about the flu and that it seems to cause personality changes. I'm worried if we start talking about far-out stuff like the flu being spread by tiny black discs, or even worse, seeing a fleeting blue light in someone's finger after it had been stung by a black disc, they'll not listen to us. She already threatened to send us to psychiatry.''

"But we saw the blue light,'' Cassy said.

"We think we saw it,'' Pitt said. "Look, we have to get people involved first. Once they've investigated this flu and know something strange is going on, then we tell them everything.''

The door opened and Sheila stuck in her head. "The man I want you two to talk with just arrived,'' she said. "But he was hungry, and I sent him down to the cafeteria. Let's move into my office so that we'll be prepared for him when he gets back.''

Cassy and Pitt got to their feet and followed Sheila.

"ALL RIGHT, YOU TWO,'' NANCY SELLERS SAID TO JONA-than and Candee. "I want you to wait here in the van while I go in and talk to Candee's mom. Sound reasonable?''

Both Jonathan and Candee nodded.

"I really appreciate this, Mrs. Sellers,'' Candee said.

"You don't have to thank me,'' Nancy said. "Just the fact that your parents were too busy to talk on the phone last night when I called and chose not to call back tells me something is seriously wrong. I mean they didn't even know you stayed over.''

Nancy alighted from the van, waved to the kids, and started out toward the front entrance of Serotec Pharma-ceuticals. She could still see the stain on the sidewalk where poor Mr. Kalinov had impacted the concrete. She hadn't known the man well since he was a relatively new em-ployee and was in the biochemistry department, but the news had saddened her. She knew he had a family with two teenage daughters.

Entering the building, Nancy wondered what to expect. After the death the day before she was unsure how the whole establishment would be functioning. A memorial service was scheduled for that afternoon. But she immediately sensed that everything was already back to routine.

The accounting department was on the fourth floor, and as she rode up in the crowded elevator, she overheard normal conversation. There was even laughter. At first it made Nancy feel relieved that people had taken the episode in stride. But when the whole car burst into laughter about a comment Nancy hadn't heard well enough to understand, she began to feel uncomfortable. The joviality seemed disrespectful.

Nancy found Joy Taylor with ease. As one of the more senior people she had her own office. When Nancy walked through the open door, Joy was busy at her computer terminal. As Nancy had remembered, she was a mousy person about Nancy's size although much thinner. Nancy guessed that Candee took after her father.

"Excuse me," Nancy called out.

Joy looked up. Her pinched features registered momentary irritation at being disturbed. Then her expression warmed and she smiled.

"Hello," Joy said. "How have you been?"

"Just fine," Nancy said. "I wasn't sure you'd remember me. I'm Nancy Sellers. My son Jonathan and your daughter Candee are classmates."

"Of course I remember you," Joy said.

"Terrible tragedy yesterday," Nancy said while she thought about how to bring up the issues she wanted to discuss.

"Yes and no," Joy said. "Certainly for the family, but I happen to know that Mr. Kalinov had serious kidney disease."

"Oh?" Nancy questioned. The comment confused her.

"Oh yes," Joy said. "He'd been on weekly dialysis for

years. There was talk of a transplant. It was bad genes. His brother had the same problem.''

"I hadn't heard about his medical problems," Nancy said.

"Is there something I can help you with?" Joy asked.

"Yes, there is," Nancy said, taking a seat. "Well, it's more that I wanted to talk with you. I'm sure it's not serious, but I felt I should at least mention it to you. I'd want you to do the same for me if Jonathan had come to you.''

"Candee came to you?" Joy asked. "About what?"

"She's upset," Nancy said. "And frankly, so am I."

Nancy noticed a slight hardening of Joy's features.

"What did Candee say she was upset about?" Joy asked.

"She feels that things have changed at home," Nancy said. "For one thing she said that you and your husband are suddenly doing a lot of entertaining. It's made her feel insecure. Apparently some people have even wandered into her bedroom."

"We have been entertaining," Joy said. "Both my husband and I have recently become very active in environmental causes. It requires work and sacrifice, but we're willing to do both. Perhaps you'd like to come to our meeting tonight.''

"Thanks, but some other time," Nancy said.

"Just let me know when," Joy said. "But now I've got to get back to work.''

"Just a moment longer," Nancy said. The conversation was going poorly. Joy was not being receptive despite Nancy's diplomatic efforts. It was time for more candor. "My son and your daughter also got the impression that you were encouraging them to sleep together. I'd like you to know that I don't agree with this at all. In fact I'm adamantly against it.''

"But they are healthy and their genes are well matched," Joy said.

Nancy struggled to remain calm. She'd never heard such a ridiculous statement. Nancy could not understand Joy's casual attitude about such an issue, especially with the burgeoning problem of teen pregnancy. Just as aggravating was

Joy's equanimity in the face of Nancy's obvious agitation.

"Jonathan and Candee do make a cute couple," Nancy forced herself to say. "But they are only seventeen and hardly ready for the responsibilities of adult life."

"If that is how you feel I will be happy to respect it," Joy said. "But my husband and I feel that there are a lot more pressing issues, like the destruction of the rain forest."

Nancy had had enough. It was plain to her that she was not going to have a rational conversation with Joy Taylor. She stood up. "Thank you for your time," she said stiffly. "My only recommendation is that perhaps you might pay a little more attention to your daughter's state of mind. She is upset."

Nancy turned to leave.

"Just a moment," Joy said.

Nancy hesitated.

"You seem to be extremely anxious," Joy said. "I think I can help you." She pulled out the top drawer of her desk and gingerly lifted out a black disc. Placing it in the palm of her hand, she extended it toward Nancy. "Here's a little present for you."

Nancy was already convinced that Joy Taylor was more than a little eccentric, and this unsolicited proffering of a talisman just added to the impression. Nancy leaned over to take a closer look. She had no idea what the strange object was.

"Take it," Joy encouraged.

Out of curiosity Nancy reached for the object. But then she thought better of it and withdrew her hand. "Thank you," she said, "but I think I should just leave."

"Take it," Joy urged. "It will change your life."

"I like my life as it is," Nancy said. Then she turned and walked out of Joy's office. As she descended in the elevator she marveled over the conversation she'd just had. It wasn't anything like she'd expected. And now she had to worry about what she was going to tell Candee. Jonathan, of course, was a different story. She'd tell him to stay the hell away from the Taylor residence.

• • •

THE DOOR TO DR. MILLER'S OFFICE OPENED AND BOTH PITT and Cassy got to their feet. A balding yet relatively youthful man walked into the room ahead of Dr. Miller. He was dressed in a nondescript, wrinkled gray suit. Rimless glasses were perched on the end of a broad nose.

"This is Dr. Clyde Horn," Sheila said to Cassy and Pitt. "He's an epidemiological investigative officer from the Centers for Disease Control in Atlanta. He works specifically for the influenza branch."

Clyde was introduced to Pitt and Cassy in turn.

"You two are the youngest-looking residents I think I've ever seen," Clyde commented.

"I'm not a resident," Pitt said. "In fact I'm only starting medical school in the fall."

"And I'm a student teacher," Cassy said.

"Oh, I see," Clyde said, but he was obviously confused.

"Pitt and Cassy are here to put the problem in a personal perspective," Sheila said as she motioned for Clyde to take a seat.

They all sat down.

Sheila then made a presentation of the influenza cases that they had been seeing in the emergency room. She had some charts and graphs which she showed to Clyde. The most impressive was the one that showed the rapid increase in the number of cases over the previous three days. The second most impressive dealt with the number of deaths of people with the same symptoms associated with various chronic disease like diabetes, cancer, kidney problems, rheumatoid arthritis, and liver ailments.

"Have you been able to determine the strain?" Clyde asked. "When you spoke with me on the phone, that had yet to be done."

"It still isn't done," Sheila said. "In fact we still haven't isolated the virus."

"That's curious," Clyde said.

"The only thing we have consistently seen is marked elevation of lymphokines in the blood," Sheila said. She handed Clyde another chart.

"Oh my, these are high titers," Clyde said. "And you said the symptoms are all typical flu."

"Yes," Sheila said. "Just more intense than usual, and generally localizing in the upper respiratory tract. We've seen no pneumonia."

"It certainly has stimulated the immune systems," Clyde said as he continued to study the lymphokine chart.

"The course of the illness is quite short," Sheila said. "In contrast to normal influenza, it reaches a peak in only hours, like five or six. Within twelve hours the patients are apparently well."

"Even better than they were before the illness," Pitt said.

Clyde wrinkled his forehead. "Better?" he questioned.

Sheila nodded. "It is true," she said. "Once recovered the patients exhibit a kind of euphoria with increased energy levels. The disturbing aspect is that many also behave as if they have had a personality change. And that is why Pitt and Cassy are here. They have a mutual friend who they insist is acting like a different person subsequent to his recovery. His case may be particularly important because he might have been the first person to get this particular illness."

"Have there been any neurological workups done?" Clyde asked.

"Indeed," Sheila said. "On a number of patients. But everything was normal including cerebrospinal fluid."

"What about the friend, whatever his name," Clyde said.

"His name is Beau," Cassy said.

"He has not be examined neurologically," Sheila said. "That was planned, but for the moment he's unavailable."

"In what ways is Beau's personality different?" Clyde asked.

"In just about every way," Cassy said. "Prior to his flu he'd never missed a class. After recovery he hasn't gone to any. And he's been waking up at night and going outside to meet strange people. When I asked him what he'd been talking to these people about, he said the environment."

"Is he oriented to time, place, and person?" Clyde asked.

"Most definitely," Pitt said. "His mind seems particularly sharp. He also seems to be significantly stronger."

"Physically?" Clyde asked.

Pitt nodded.

"Personality change after a bout of flu is uncommon," Clyde said while absently scratching the top of his bald pate. "This flu is unique in other ways as well. I've never heard of such a short course. Strange! Do you know if the other hospitals in the area have been seeing the same problem?"

"We don't know," Sheila said. "But finding that out is much easier for the CDC to do."

A loud rap on the door got Sheila out of her chair. Having left specific instructions not to be disturbed, she was concerned a medical emergency had arrived. But instead it was Dr. Halprin. Behind him stood Richard Wainwright, the chief lab tech who had helped draw up the charts Sheila had been presenting. Richard was red-faced and nervously shifting his weight from one foot to the other.

"Hello, Dr. Miller," Dr. Halprin said cheerfully. He had completely recovered from his illness and was now the picture of health. "Richard just informed me that we have an official visitor."

Dr. Halprin pushed into the room and introduced himself as the hospital president to Clyde. Richard self-consciously remained by the door.

"I'm afraid you've been called here under less than forthright pretenses," Dr. Halprin said to Clyde. He smiled graciously. "As Chief Executive Officer any requests for CDC assistance has to come through my office. That's stated in our bylaws. This is, of course, unless it is a reportable illness. But influenza is not."

"I'm terribly sorry," Clyde said. He stood up. "It had been my impression we'd received a legitimate request and all was in order. I don't mean to interfere."

"No problem," Dr. Halprin said. "Just a minor misunderstanding. The fact of the matter is we don't need the services of the CDC. But come to my office, and we can straighten it all out.'' He put his arm around Clyde's shoulders and urged him toward the door.

Sheila rolled her eyes in frustration. Cassy, already distraught and sensing they were about to lose a significant opportunity, stepped in front of the door, barring egress. "Please, Dr. Horn," she said. "You must listen to us. There is something happening in this city. People are changing with this illness. It's spreading.''

"Cassy!" Sheila called out sharply.

"It's true," Cassy persisted. "Don't listen to Dr. Halprin. He's had this flu himself. He's one of them!"

"Cassy, that's enough!" Sheila said. She grabbed Cassy and dragged her aside.

"I'm sorry about this, Clyde," Dr. Halprin said soothingly. "May I call you Clyde?"

"Certainly," Clyde said, nervously looking over his shoulder as if he expected to be attacked.

"As you can see this minor problem has caused significant emotional upset," Dr. Halprin continued as he motioned for Clyde to precede him into the hall. "Unfortunately it has clouded objectivity. But we'll discuss it in my office, and we can make arrangements to get you back to the airport. I've even got something I want you to take back to Atlanta for me. Something I think that will interest the CDC.''

Sheila closed the door behind the departing figures and leaned against it. "Cassy, I don't think that was wise."

"I'm sorry," Cassy said. "I couldn't help myself.''

"It's because of Beau," Pitt explained to Sheila. "He and Cassy are engaged."

"You don't have to apologize," Sheila said. "I felt equally frustrated. The problem is: now we are back to square one."

THE ESTATE WAS MAGNIFICENT. ALTHOUGH IT HAD BEEN whittled down to less than five acres over the years, the central house was still standing and in fine condition. It was built in the early nineteen-hundreds in a French château style. The stone was a local granite.

"I like it," Beau said. He spun in the middle of the expansive ballroom with his arms outstretched. King sat near the door as if he feared he was going to be left in the mansion by himself. Randy and a realtor by the name of Helen Bryer were standing off to the side.

"It is four point six acres," Ms. Bryer told Randy. "It is not a lot of land for the size of this house, but it is immediately adjacent to your own holdings at Cipher, so the effective land would be much more."

Beau strolled over to the massive windows and let the sunlight cascade over him. The view was stupendous. With a reflecting pool in the foreground it reminded him of the view from the knoll on the Cipher property.

"I heard your announcement this morning," Ms. Bryer said. "I must tell you, Mr. Nite, I think your Institute for a New Beginning sounds wonderful. Humankind will be grateful."

"New humankind," Randy said.

"Yes, right," Ms. Bryer said. "A new humankind awakened to the needs of the environment. I think something like this has been a long, long time in coming."

"You have no idea how long," Beau called out from where he was standing at the window. Then he strolled over to Randy and Ms. Bryer. "This house is perfect for the institute. We'll take it!"

"Excuse me?" Ms. Bryer said, even though she'd clearly heard Beau. She cleared her throat. She glanced at Randy for confirmation. Randy nodded. Beau smiled and wandered out of the room. King followed.

"Well, this's wonderful!" Ms. Bryer said excitedly when she'd found her voice. "It's a gorgeous property. But don't you want to know how much the seller is asking?"

"Call my lawyers," Randy said. He handed Ms. Bryer a card. "Let them draw up the papers." Randy then left the room looking for Beau.

"Of course, Mr. Nite," Ms. Bryer said. She blinked. Her voice echoed in the now empty ballroom. She smiled to herself. It had been the strangest sale she'd ever made, but what a commission!

THE RAIN SOUNDED LIKE GRAINS OF SAND AS IT PUMMELED the window off to the right of Jesse's desk. Peals of thunder added to the atmosphere. Jesse liked lightning storms. It reminded him of summertime during his childhood back in Detroit.

It was late afternoon and under normal circumstances Jesse would have been ready to head home. Unfortunately Vince Garbon had called in sick that morning, and Jesse had to do work for two. With another hour of paperwork to go, Jesse picked up his empty coffee mug and pushed back from his desk. From years of experience he knew that one more cup wouldn't keep him up that night, and it would help him get through the rest of the day.

On his way to the communal pot, Jesse was struck by how many of his fellow officers were coughing, sneezing, or sniffling. On top of that were all the guys out sick, like Vince. Something was going around, and Jesse considered it a blessing that he'd not been stricken.

On his way back to his desk, Jesse happened to glance through the glass divider into the captain's office. To his surprise the captain was standing at the window facing into the squad room with his hands behind his back and a contented smile glued to his face. When he caught Jesse's eye he waved and flashed a toothy grin.

Jesse waved back. But as he sat down, he wondered what was up with the captain. First of all, he rarely stayed this late unless there was some special ops, and second of all he was always in a bad mood by the afternoon. Jesse had never seen him smile after twelve.

After getting himself comfortable once again and with his pen in his hand poised above one of the innumerable forms, Jesse hazarded another glance into the captain's office. To his surprise the captain was still in the same spot sporting the same smile. Like a voyeur, Jesse stared at the captain for a beat and tried to divine what on earth the captain was smiling about. It wasn't a humorous smile. It was more a smile of satisfaction.

With a bewildered shake of his head, Jesse refocused his attention to the stack of forms in front of him. He detested paperwork, but it had to be done.

A half hour later, with several of the forms completed, Jesse again got up from his desk. This time it was nature calling. As usual the coffee had gone right through him.

Heading for the men's room at the end of the hall, he glanced into the captain's office and was relieved to see it was empty. Inside the lavatory Jesse didn't dally. He did his thing and got the hell out because there were a half dozen guys in there coughing and sneezing and blowing their noses.

En route back to his desk Jesse passed by the drinking fountain to wet his whistle. That took him by the property booking desk, where he was spotted by Sergeant Alfred Kinsella through the wire mesh of his cage.

"Hey, Jesse!" Alfred called out. "What's up?"

"Not much," Jesse answered. "How's that blood problem of yours?"

"No change," Alfred said. He cleared his throat. "I still have to go in for a transfusion now and then."

Jesse nodded. He had given blood just like most of the guys on the force for Alfred's benefit. Jesse felt sorry for Alfred. He couldn't comprehend what it would be like to have a serious illness the doctors couldn't even diagnose.

"Want to see something bizarre?" Alfred asked. He cleared his throat again and then coughed forcibly several times. He put a hand to his chest.

"You okay?" Jesse asked.

"Yeah, I suppose," Alfred said. "But I've been feeling a little punk over the last hour or so."

"You and everyone else," Jesse said. "What do you have that's bizarre?"

"These little guys," Alfred said.

Jesse moved over to the chest-height counter of the property lockup. He saw that Alfred had a row of black discs in front of him, each about an inch and a half in diameter.

"What are they?" Jesse asked.

"I haven't the foggiest idea," Alfred said. "In fact I was hoping you might be able to tell me."

"Where'd they come from?"

"You know the rash of first-time offenders being brought in the last couple of nights and booked for crazy stuff like lewd behavior or having mass meetings in public spaces without permits."

Jesse nodded. Everybody had been talking about it, and Jesse himself had seen some strange behavior lately.

"Every last one of those people had been carrying one of these black miniature frisbees."

Jesse got his face close to the wire mesh so he could get a better look. The black discs appeared like container tops. There were about twenty of them.

"What are they made of?" Jesse asked.

"Damned if I know, but they are heavy for their size," Alfred said. He sneezed several times and blew his nose.

"Let me see one," Jesse said. He reached through the opening of the wire mesh cage with the intention of picking one of them up. Alfred grabbed his arm.

"Careful!" he warned. "They look perfectly smooth but they can sting. It's kinda spooky because I've not been able to find a sharp edge. Yet I've been stuck several times already. Feels like a bee sting."

Taking Alfred's advice, Jesse took a ballpoint pen from his pocket and used it to push around one of the discs. To his surprise it was not easy. They were indeed heavy. It was particularly hard to get one of them to flip over. Jesse gave up.

"Well, you're on your own," Jesse said. "I don't have any idea what they are."

"Thanks for looking at them," Alfred said in between coughs.

"You sound like you've gotten worse just while I've been standing here," Jesse said. "Maybe you'd better go home."

"I'll stick it out," Alfred said. "I just came on duty at five."

Jesse headed for his desk planning on staying another

half hour tops, but he didn't get far. Behind him he heard a fit of coughing and then a crash.

Turning around Jesse saw that Alfred had disappeared from view. Running back to the counter he could hear thumps like someone kicking the cabinets. Pulling himself over the counter Jesse looked down. There on the floor was Alfred with his back arched and his body quivering. He was having a convulsion.

"Hey everybody!" Jesse shouted. "We got a man down in property booking."

Jesse went over the top of the booking desk head first, knocking most of the clutter on its surface to the floor, including the twenty or so black discs. Intent on the convulsing figure of Alfred, Jesse didn't notice that all of the discs landed lightly and right side up.

The first thing Jesse did was get Alfred's keys and plop them on the counter so others could unlock the cage door. Although Jesse had a key, most people didn't. Next he forced a pad of paper between Alfred's tightly clenched jaws. He was about to unbutton the top button of his shirt when he saw something that startled him. A foam was oozing out of Alfred's eyes!

Shocked by this spectacle, Jesse straightened up. He'd never seen anything like it. It was like bubble bath.

Within seconds Jesse was joined by other officers. All were equally amazed at the burgeoning froth.

"What the hell is that foam?" one of the officers asked.

"Who the hell cares," Jesse said, breaking the trance. "Let's get an ambulance. Now!"

THERE WAS A LOUD CLAP OF THUNDER SIMULTANEOUS with the gurney as it slammed through the main ER doors of the University Medical Center. It was being pushed by two burly EMTs. A few steps behind was Jesse Kemper. On the gurney Alfred Kinsella was still convulsing. His face was blue, and foam was still bubbling from his eyes like two bottles of disturbed champagne.

Sheila, Pitt, and Cassy emerged from Sheila's office where they'd been most of the day collating all the flu

cases, including all the cases seen that day. Sheila had heard
the commotion and had responded immediately. She'd been
forewarned by the head nurse that a strange case was on
its way. The EMTs had called ahead as they'd left the police headquarters.

Intercepting the gurney, Sheila glanced at Alfred. Seeing
the foam, she directed the EMTs to take the patient into the
bay reserved for contaminated cases. She'd never seen anything like it and wasn't about to take any chances. As the
gurney was quickly pushed away, Sheila got the head
nurse's attention and told her to page a neurologist stat.

Jesse grabbed Sheila's arm. "Remember me? I'm Detective Lieutenant Jesse Kemper. What's wrong with Officer Kinsella?"

Sheila pulled away. "That's what we would like to find
out. Pitt, come on with me; this will be a trial by fire. Cassy,
take Lieutenant Kemper into my office. The waiting room
is too crowded."

Cassy and Jesse watched Sheila and Pitt run down the
hall after the gurney.

"I'm glad I'm not a doctor," Jesse said.

"You and me both," Cassy said. Then she pointed toward Sheila's office. "Come on! I'll show you where you
can wait."

The wait was not long. Within a half hour Sheila and
Pitt appeared at the door. Their expressions were funereal.
It wasn't hard to guess the outcome.

"No luck?" Cassy asked.

Pitt shook his head.

"He never regained consciousness," Sheila said.

"Was it the same flu?" Cassy asked.

"Probably; his lymphokines were very high," Pitt said.

"What the hell are lymphokines?" Jesse asked. "Is that
what killed him?"

"Lymphokines are part of the body's defense against
invasion," Sheila said. "They are a response, not a cause
of disease. But tell me, did Mr. Kinsella have any chronic
disease like diabetes?"

"He didn't have diabetes," Jesse said. "But he had a

serious problem with his blood. He had to have transfusions every so often.''

"I have a question," Cassy said suddenly. "Do you know if Sergeant Kinsella had ever mentioned anything about a black disc about this big." Cassy made a circle about an inch and a half in diameter with her thumbs and forefingers.

"Cassy!" Pitt moaned.

"Quiet!" Cassy said to Pitt. "At this point we don't have much to lose and a lot to gain."

"What's this about a black disc?" Sheila asked.

Pitt rolled his eyes. "Here we go," he said to no one in particular.

"You mean a black disc that's flat on the bottom but has a dome on the top and little nubbin-like bumps around the edge."

"Exactly," Cassy said.

"Yeah, he showed me a bunch of them just before he had his convulsion."

Cassy cast a triumphant look at Pitt whose expression had gone from exasperation to intense interest in the matter of seconds.

"Did he say anything about being stung by one of these discs?" Pitt asked.

"Yeah, a number of times," Jesse said. "He said it was kinda spooky since he couldn't find a sharp edge. And you know something, now that I think about it, I remember the police chief, Captain Hernandez, getting stung by one."

"Somebody better fill me in on these black discs," Sheila said.

"We found one four days ago," Cassy said. "Well, actually it was Beau who found it. He picked it up from the gravel in a parking lot."

"I was there when he found it," Pitt said. "We had no idea what it was. I thought it might have fallen out from beneath Beau's car."

"After just a few minutes Beau said it stung him," Cassy said. "Then a number of hours later Beau came down with his flu.''

"We had really forgotten about the disc, to tell the truth," Pitt said. "But then here in the emergency room I was checking in a little girl with the flu who said that a black rock had bitten her."

"But it was an episode just last night that really got us thinking," Cassy said. She went on to describe the incident at the market. She even described the faint blue glow that she and Pitt thought they'd seen.

When Cassy was finished there was a silence.

Sheila finally blew out through pursed lips. "Well, this all sounds crazy, and as I said before, under normal circumstances I'd call in a psychiatry consult for you two. But at this point I'm willing to explore just about anything."

"Tell me," Jesse said. "Does Beau recognize that he's acting differently?"

"He says he doesn't," Cassy said. "But I find it hard to believe. He's doing things he's never done before."

"I agree," Pitt said. "A week ago he was adamantly against large dogs in the city. Suddenly he gets one."

"Yeah, and without discussing it with me," Cassy said. "And we live together. But why do you ask?"

"It would be an important point if the people who are affected are purposefully dissembling," Sheila said. "We'll have to be discreet. But let's get us one of these black discs."

"We can go back to the market," Pitt said.

"I might be able to get one out of property booking," Jesse said.

"Well, try both," Sheila said. She took out a couple of business cards and wrote her home number on the backs. She gave one to Jesse and one to Pitt and Cassy. "Whoever gets one of these discs first, give me a call. But, as I said, let's be discreet about this. It sounds to me that this is the type of thing that could cause a panic if there's any truth to it."

Just before they broke up, Pitt gave both Sheila and Jesse the number of his cousin's apartment. He said that he and Cassy would be staying there. Cassy gave him a questioning look but didn't contradict him.

• • •

"WHICH WAY DO YOU THINK THE STALL WAS THAT HAD the discs?" Pitt asked. They had entered the outdoor market about the same time as the evening before. It was a large area, about the size of two city blocks, and with all the tiny stalls it was like a maze.

"I remember where we got the produce," Cassy said. "Why don't we go there first and follow our trail?"

"Good idea," Pitt said.

They found the stand, where they'd bought tomatoes, with comparative ease.

"What did we do after the tomatoes?" Pitt asked.

"We got the fruit," Cassy said. "It was in that direction." She pointed over Pitt's shoulder.

After they found the fruit stall they both remembered the route into the flea market section. A few minutes later they were standing in front of the booth they sought. Unfortunately it was empty.

"Excuse me," Cassy called to the proprietor of the next stand. "Could you tell me where the man is that runs this empty stall?"

"He's sick," the man said. "I talked with him this morning. He's got the flu like most of us have."

"Thanks," Cassy said. Then to Pitt she whispered: "What do we do now?"

"Hope that Lieutenant Kemper has better luck," Pitt said.

JESSE HAD DRIVEN BACK TO POLICE HEADQUARTERS DIrectly from the hospital, but he'd hesitated before going in. The news of Kinsella's death had undoubtedly reached the station, and people were going to be upset. It hardly seemed to be the time to be nosing around in Kinsella's cage, especially if the captain was still hanging around. After listening to Cassy and Pitt he'd been reminded of how weird the captain had been acting of late.

So Jesse had driven home. He lived a mile away from headquarters in a small house that was big enough for one person. He'd been living by himself since his wife died of breast cancer eight years previously. They'd had two children but both of them preferred the excitement of Detroit.

Jesse made himself a simple dinner. After a few hours passed he began to entertain the idea of going back to the station, but he knew it would raise a few eyebrows since it was not usual for him to be there unless something out of the ordinary was going on. While he was trying to think up some sort of an explanation, he wondered if Cassy and Pitt had already gotten one of the discs. If they had, there was no need for him to make the effort.

Looking through the scraps of paper in his pocket, he located the kid's telephone number. He placed the call. Pitt answered.

"We bombed," Pitt said. "The guy who had the discs is sick. We asked at other stalls and were told the market had become so flooded, they couldn't sell them. So no one is carrying them anymore."

"Damn," Jesse said.

"You weren't able to get one either?" Pitt asked.

"I haven't tried yet," Jesse admitted. Suddenly an idea occurred to him. "Hey, would there be any chance of you two coming with me to the station? Maybe it sounds funny but if I walk in there by myself, everybody's going to be wondering what I'm doing. If I come in acting like I'm in the process of investigating something, there won't be a problem."

"It's okay by me," Pitt said. "Hang on, let me ask Cassy."

Jesse toyed with the phone cord. Pitt came right back on the line. "She's ready to do anything that might help," Pitt said. "Where should we meet?"

"I'll come and pick you up," Jesse said. "But it will be after midnight. I want the evening gang to have gone home. It will be easier during the graveyard shift. There's a lot less personnel involved." The more Jesse thought about the idea the better it sounded.

• • •

IT WAS QUARTER PAST ONE WHEN JESSE PULLED INTO THE police headquarters' parking lot and came to a stop in his reserved spot. He killed the engine.

"Okay, guys," Jesse said. "Here's how this is going to play. We're going to walk in the front door. You'll have to go through the metal detector. Then we'll head directly for my desk. If anybody asks you what you're doing, just say you are with me. Okay?"

"Should I be scared about going in there?" Cassy asked. She never thought she'd be concerned about going to police headquarters.

"Nah, not in the slightest," Jesse assured her.

They climbed from the car and entered the station. While Pitt and Cassy were going through the metal detector they overheard the uniformed policeman at the front desk: "Yes, ma'am. We'll be there as soon as we can. We understand that raccoons can be unsettling. Unfortunately we're understaffed with the flu that's going around . . ."

A few minutes later they were sitting around Jesse's desk. The squad room was deserted. "This is better than I thought," Jesse said. "There's hardly anybody here."

"This would be the time to rob the bank," Pitt said.

"That's not funny," Cassy chastised.

"Okay, let's get up and go back to property booking," Jesse said. "Here's my Cross pen. If need be we'll pretend we're booking it in as if it belonged to you."

Pitt took the pen. All three got to their feet.

The property booking cage was locked up tight. Only the light from the hall shone through the wire mesh to illuminate the interior.

"All right, you guys wait here," Jesse said. He used his key to open the door. A quick glance around the floor told him that someone had picked up the discs and the other objects that he'd knocked off the counter when he'd vaulted over to help Alfred. "Damn," he voiced.

"Is there a problem?" Pitt asked.

"Somebody's picked up in here," Jesse said. "The discs must have been placed in envelopes, and there's a whole dad-blasted stack of them in here."

"What are you going to do?"

"Open them up," Jesse said. "There's no shortcut."

Jesse started. It took longer than he expected. He had to twist the clasps, open the envelope, and look inside.

"Can we help?" Pitt offered.

"Yeah, why not," Jesse said. "We'll be here all night."

The kids entered the cage and, following Jesse's lead, began opening envelopes.

"They got to be here someplace," Jesse said irritably.

They worked in silence. After about five minutes Jesse reached out and whispered, "Hold up!"

Slowly Jesse raised himself so he could see over the top of the counter. He'd heard what he thought were footsteps. What he saw made his heart skip a beat. He had to blink to make sure it wasn't an apparition. It wasn't. It was the captain and he was coming in their direction.

Jesse ducked back down. "Jesus," he whispered. "The captain is coming. Move back under the counter and don't move."

As soon as the kids were in position, Jesse stood up. Since there was still time he exited the property booking cage. Walking quickly, he intercepted the captain in the hall.

"The duty officer said you were here, Kemper," the captain said. "What the hell are you doing? It's almost two o'clock in the morning."

Jesse was tempted to turn the question around since it was a lot stranger for the captain to be there than it was for him. But Jesse held his tongue. Instead he said: "Just dealing with a problem involving a couple of kids."

"In the property booking cage?" the captain asked, looking over Jesse's shoulder.

"Yeah, I'm looking for a bit of evidence," Jesse said. But then to change the subject he added: "Terrible tragedy about Kinsella."

"Hardly," the captain said. "He had that chronic illness with his blood. Listen, Kemper, how are you feeling?"

"Me?" Jesse questioned. He was nonplussed by the captain's response concerning Kinsella.

"Of course you," the captain said. "Who else am I talking to."

"I'm fine," Jesse said. "Thank the Lord."

"Well, that's strange," the captain said. "Listen, stop by my office before you leave. I've got something for you."

"Sure thing, Captain," Jesse said.

The captain took another look over Jesse's shoulder before heading back to his office. Jesse watched him leave, perplexed at what was going through his mind.

When the captain had disappeared from view, Jesse hustled back inside the property booking cage. "Let's find one of those discs and get the hell out of here," he said.

Cassy and Pitt emerged from their hiding place in the knee space below the counter. All three went back to opening envelopes.

"Ah ha!" Jesse said as he peered into a particularly heavy one. "Finally!" He reached in to pull it out.

"Don't touch it," Cassy cried out.

"I was going to be careful," Jesse said.

"It happens quickly," Pitt said.

"All right, so I won't touch it," Jesse said. "I'll leave it in the envelope. Let me sign this custody chit and then let's get out of here."

A few minutes later they were back at Jesse's desk in the nearly empty squad room. Jesse glanced into the captain's office. The light was on, but the captain was nowhere to be seen.

"Let's take a look at this thing," Jesse said. He opened the clasp on the envelope and let the disc slide out onto his blotter.

"Looks innocent enough," Jesse commented. As he'd done earlier, he used a pen to push it around. "There's also no opening. How could it possibly sting someone?"

"Both times that I witnessed, the person had wrapped either their fingers or palm around the periphery," Pitt said.

"But if there's no opening it can't happen," Jesse said. "Maybe they're all not the same. Maybe some sting, some don't." He got out his reading glasses, which he detested for vanity reasons, put them on, and then leaned over to get a closer, magnified view. "It looks like polished onyx, only not as shiny." With the tip of his finger he touched the top of the dome.

"I wouldn't do that," Pitt warned.

"It feels cold," Jesse said, ignoring Pitt. "It's also very smooth." Gingerly he moved the very tip of his finger down from the apex of the dome toward the periphery with the intention of feeling the little bumps that lined the edge. The sound of a cabinet banging shut over at the duty officer's desk made him snatch his hand away.

"I guess I'm a little tense," Jesse explained.

"For good reason," Pitt said.

Ready to withdraw his hand at the slightest provocation, Jesse touched one of the little bumps. Nothing happened. Equally carefully he began to run the tip of his finger around the disc's periphery. He got about a quarter of the way around when an extraordinary thing happened. A millimeter-wide slit formed in the seamless surface of the disc's edge.

Jesse yanked his hand away in time to see a chrome-colored needle punch out through the slit a distance of several millimeters. From its tip sprang a single drop of yellowish fluid. In the next instant the needle withdrew and the slit vanished. The whole sequence lasted only a second.

Three pairs of startled eyes rose to regard each other.

"Did you see that?" Jesse asked. "Or am I crazy?"

"I saw it," Cassy said. "And there's proof. There's a wet spot on the blotter."

Nervously Jesse bent his head forward and, with his magnifiers, as he called his glasses, studied the area where the slit had formed. "There's nothing there, not even a seam."

"Wait a sec," Pitt said. "Don't get too close. That fluid must be infectious."

As a hypochondriac Jesse didn't need any more encouragement. He got out of his chair and backed several steps away. "What should we do?"

"We need some scissors and a container, preferably glass," Pitt said. "Plus some chlorine bleach."

"How about a coffee creamer jar?" Jesse suggested. "I don't know about the bleach, but I'll check the janitor's closet. The scissors are in the top drawer."

"A coffee creamer jar is fine," Pitt said. "How about latex gloves?"

"We got those too," Jesse said. "I'll be right back."

Jesse managed to find everything Pitt needed. With the scissors Pitt carefully cut out a circle of the blotter containing the wet dot and deposited it in the jar. The underside of the blotter didn't appear wet, but still he disinfected the area of the desk with the bleach. The gloves and the scissors went into a plastic bag.

"I think we should call Dr. Miller," Pitt said when he was finished.

"Now?" Jesse questioned. "It's after two in the morning."

"She's going to want to know about this right away," Pitt said. "It's my guess she'll want to start immediately trying to grow out whatever is in this sample."

"Okay, you call," Jesse said. "I've got to go in and see the captain. By the time I get back you can tell me if I'm taking you to the med center or home."

Jesse's mind was a jumble of disconnected thoughts as he headed for the captain's office. So much crazy stuff had happened in so short a time, particularly the crack appearing like magic in the black disc, that he felt numb. He was also exhausted since it was way past his bedtime. Nothing seemed real. Even the fact that he was heading in to see the captain after two in the morning.

The captain's office door was ajar. Jesse halted on the threshold. The captain was at his desk busily writing as if it were the middle of the day. Jesse had to admit to himself that the captain looked better than he had in a year despite the hour.

"Excuse me, Captain," Jesse called out. "You wanted to see me?"

"Come in," the captain said, waving Jesse over to the desk. He smiled. "Thanks for coming by. Tell me, how are you feeling now?"

"Pretty tired, sir," Jesse said.

"Not sick?"

"No, thank goodness," Jesse said.

"Get that problem taken care of with the two kids?"

"Still working on it," Jesse said.

"Well, I wanted to reward you for your hard work," the captain said. He opened the center drawer of his desk, reached in and pulled out one of the black discs!

Jesse's eyes widened in shocked surprise.

"I want you to have this symbol of a new beginning," the captain said. He had the disc in the palm of his hand, and he extended it toward Jesse.

Jesse felt a sense of panic. "Thank you, sir, but I can't accept that."

"Of course you can," the captain said. "It doesn't look like much, but it will change your life. Trust me."

"Oh, I believe you, sir," Jesse said. "I just don't deserve it."

"Nonsense," the captain said. "Take it, my man."

"No, thank you," Jesse said. "I'm really tired. I got to get some sleep."

"I'm ordering you to take it," the captain said. A distinct edge had appeared in his voice.

"Yes, sir," Jesse said. He reached forward with a quivering hand. In his mind's eye he saw the glistening chrome needle. At the same time he remembered that to stimulate the mechanism, he'd touched the edge of the disc. He also noticed that the captain was not touching the edge but rather palming the disc in his flattened hand.

"Take it, my friend," the captain urged.

Jesse flattened his own hand palm up and put it next to the captain's. The captain looked him in the eye. Jesse returned the stare and noticed the captain's pupils were widely dilated.

For a few moments it was a Mexican standoff. Finally the captain carefully insinuated his thumb beneath the disc and lifted it with his index finger on top of the dome. He was obviously avoiding the edge. Then he put it in Jesse's palm.

"Thanks, Chief," Jesse said. He avoided looking at the cursed thing and beat a hasty retreat.

"You'll be thanking me," the captain called out after him.

Jesse dashed out to his desk, terrified by the fear of being stung at any moment. But it didn't happen, and he was able to slide the disc out of his hand without incident. It clacked up against its colleague with a sound like two ivory billiard balls colliding.

"What on earth . . ." Pitt remarked.

"Don't ask!" Jesse said. "But I'll tell you one thing. The captain ain't on our side."

HOLDING THE COFFEE CREAMER JAR UP TO THE LIGHT, Sheila looked beneath the label at the scrap of blotter contained inside. "This might be the break we needed," she said. "But tell me again exactly what happened."

Cassy, Pitt, and Jesse all began speaking at once.

"Whoa!" Sheila said. "One at a time."

Cassy and Pitt deferred to Jesse. Jesse retold the episode with Cassy and Pitt adding bits of detail. When Jesse got to describing the part about the slit appearing in the disc, he opened his eyes widely and yanked back his hand in imitation of what he'd done at the time.

Sheila placed the jar on her desk and peered through the oculars of a binocular dissecting microscope. One of the black discs was positioned on the tray.

"This situation gets more and more bizarre," Sheila remarked. "I gotta tell you; the surface appears fault-free. I'd swear it was a solid chunk of whatever it is."

"It may look that way, but it isn't," Cassy said. "It's definitely mechanical. We all saw the slit."

"And the needle," Pitt added.

"Who would make something like this?" Jesse questioned.

"Who could make it?" Cassy asked.

The four people stared at each other. For a few minutes no one spoke. Cassy's rhetorical question was unsettling.

"Well, we won't be able to answer any questions until

we find out what's in the fluid that soaked into the blotter,'' Sheila said. ''The problem is I've got to do it myself. Richard, the head tech in the hospital lab, has already blabbed to the CEO about our CDC visitor. I can't trust the people in the lab.''

''We need to get other people involved,'' Cassy said.

''Yeah, like a virologist,'' Pitt said.

''Considering what happened with the man from the CDC, that's not going to be easy,'' Sheila said. ''It's hard to know who has had this flu and who hasn't.''

''Except when it's people we know well,'' Jesse said. ''I knew the captain was acting weird. I just didn't know why.''

''But we can't use the fear of not knowing who's been sick as an excuse to sit around and do nothing,'' Cassy said. ''We have to warn people who haven't been infected. I know a couple who could be a great help. She's a virologist and he's a physicist.''

''Sounds ideal provided they've not been stung,'' Sheila said.

''I think I can find out,'' Cassy said. ''Their son is a student in one of the classes I'm student teaching. He has an inkling that something strange is going on because his girlfriend's parents apparently were infected.''

''That might be a source of worry,'' Sheila said. ''From what Jesse has told us about the captain, I have a distinct and uncomfortable sense that the infected people feel evangelistic about their condition.''

''Amen,'' Jesse said. ''He was not to be denied. He was going to give me that black disc no matter what I said. He wanted me sick, no doubt.''

''I'll be wary,'' Cassy said, ''and as you said before, discreet.''

''Okay, give it a try,'' Sheila said. ''Meanwhile I'll run some preliminary tests on the fluid.''

''What are we going to do with the discs?'' Jesse asked.

''The question is more what are they going to do with us,'' Pitt said. He was looking at the one positioned under the microscope.

12

IT WAS A GLORIOUS MORNING WITH A CLOUDLESS, CRYS-
tal-blue sky. The distant saw-toothed purple mountains
looked like amethyst crystals bathed in a golden light.

At the gate of the estate an expectant crowd had formed.
There were people of all ages and from all walks of life,
from mechanics to rocket scientists, from housewives to
presidents of corporations, from high-school students to
university professors. Everyone was eager, happy, and
glowing with health. The atmosphere was festive.

Beau came out of the house with King at his side, descended the steps, walked fifty feet, then turned around.
What he saw pleased him greatly. Overnight a large banner
had been made that draped all the way across the front of
the building. It said: ''The Institute for a New Beginning
. . . Welcome!''

Beau's eyes swept around the grounds. He'd accomplished an extraordinary amount in twenty-four hours. He
was glad he no longer needed to sleep except for short
snatches. Otherwise it wouldn't have been possible.

In the shade of trees or walking through sun-dappled
meadows, Beau could see dozens of dogs of various breeds.
Most were large dogs, and none had leashes. Beau could
see that they were as alert as sentinels, and he was glad.

With a happy spring to his step, he returned to the porch to join Randy.

"This is it," Beau said. "We're ready to begin."

"What a day for the Earth," Randy replied.

"Let in the first group," Beau said. "We'll get them started in the ballroom."

Randy took out his cellular phone, dialed, and told one of his people to open the gate. A few moments later Randy and Beau could hear a cheer rise up into the crisp morning air. From where they were standing they couldn't see the front gate, but they could certainly hear the people shouting as they entered.

Buzzing with excitement, the crowd swarmed to the house and formed a spontaneous semicircle around the front porch.

Beau extended his hand like a Roman general and instantly the crowd went dead silent.

"Welcome!" Beau shouted. "This is the new beginning! You all bear witness that we share the same thoughts and vision. We all know what we must do. Let's do it!"

A cheer and applause erupted from the crowd. Beau turned to Randy, who beamed. He was applauding as well. Beau gestured for Randy, to enter the house and then followed him.

"What an electric moment," Randy said as they walked toward the ornate ballroom.

"It's like being one huge organism," Beau said with a nod of understanding.

The two men entered the vast, sun-drenched room and stood off to the side. The crowd followed at their heels, filling the room. Then, responding to an unseen, unspoken cue, they fell to dismantling the room.

CASSY BREATHED OUT A SILENT SIGH OF RELIEF WHEN SHE found herself facing Jonathan when the Sellerses' front door had been pulled open. Expecting the worst, she'd anticipated having to face Nancy Sellers right off the bat.

"Miss Winthrope!" Jonathan said with a mixture of surprise and delight.

"You recognized me away from the school," Cassy said. "I'm impressed."

"Of course I recognized you," Jonathan blurted. Consciously he had to resist letting his eyes wander below Cassy's neck. "Come in."

"Are your parents home?" Cassy asked.

"My mom is."

Cassy studied the boy's face. With his flaxen hair hanging down over his forehead and his self-consciously flitting eyes, he looked himself. His manner of dress was reassuring as well. He had on an oversized sweatshirt and a loose-fitting pair of Jams that were just barely hanging on to his buttocks.

"How's Candee?" Cassy asked.

"I haven't seen her since yesterday."

"What about her parents?" Cassy questioned.

Jonathan let out a little sardonic laugh. "They're gonzo. My mom had a talk with Candee's mom, and it was like zero."

"What about your mom?" Cassy asked. She tried to study Jonathan's eyes, but it was like trying to examine a Ping-Pong ball during a game.

"My mom is fine. Why?"

"A lot of people are acting strange lately. You know, like Candee's parents and Mr. Partridge."

"Yeah, I know," Jonathan said. "But not my mom."

"Your dad?"

"He's fine too."

"Good," Cassy said. "Now I'd like to take you up on your invitation to come in. I'm here to talk with your mom."

Jonathan closed the door behind Cassy and then bellowed at the top of his lungs that there was company. The sound echoed around the inside of the house, and Cassy jumped. Despite trying to act calm, she was as taut as a banjo wire.

"Can I get you some water or something?" Jonathan asked.

Before Cassy could respond Nancy Sellers appeared at

the balustrade on the second floor. She was dressed casually in acid-washed jeans and loose-fitting blouse.

"Who is it, Jonathan?" Nancy asked. She could see Cassy, but because of the way the sun was coming through the window into the stairwell, Cassy's face was lost in shadow.

Jonathan yelled up who it was and motioned for Cassy to follow him into the kitchen. No sooner had Cassy sat at a banquette than Nancy appeared.

"This is a surprise," Nancy said. "Can I offer you some coffee?"

"Sure," Cassy said. Cassy eyed the woman as she motioned for Jonathan to get a cup while she went to the stove to pick up the coffeepot. As far as Cassy could tell Nancy looked and acted the same as she did when Cassy had first met her.

Cassy was beginning to relax a degree when Nancy reached out to pour the coffee. On her index finger was a fresh Band-Aid, and Cassy felt her own pulse quicken. A wound of any sort on the hands was not what she wanted to see.

"To what do we owe this visit?" Nancy asked as she poured herself a half cup of the coffee.

Cassy stumbled over her words. "What happened to your finger?"

Nancy glanced at her Band-Aid as if it had just appeared. "Just a small cut," she said.

"From some kitchen implement?" Cassy asked.

Nancy studied Cassy's face. "Does it matter?" she asked.

"Well . . ." Cassy stammered. "Yes, it does. It matters a lot."

"Mom, Miss Winthrope is concerned about the people who are changing," Jonathan said, coming to Cassy's aid once again. "You know, like Candee's mom. I've already told her you talked with her and thought that she was out in left field."

"Jonathan!" Nancy snapped. "Your father and I agreed

we wouldn't discuss the Taylors outside the home. At least until . . ."

"I don't think it can wait," Cassy interrupted. Nancy's little outburst had encouraged her to trust that Nancy had not been infected. "People are rapidly changing all over the city, not just the Taylors. It might even be happening in other cities. We don't know. It's happening with an illness that resembles the flu, and as far as we can tell it is spread by little black discs that have the capability of stinging people on their hands."

Nancy stared at Cassy. "Are you taking about a black disc with kind of a hump in the middle, about four centimeters in diameter?"

"Exactly," Cassy said. "Have you seen any? Lots of people have them."

"Candee's mother tried to give me one," Nancy said. "Is that why you questioned my Band-Aid?"

Cassy nodded.

"It was a knife," Nancy said. "A recalcitrant bagel and a knife."

"I'm sorry to be so suspicious," Cassy said.

"I suppose it is understandable," Nancy said. "But why did you come here?"

"To enlist your help," Cassy said. "We have a group, a small group, who have been trying to figure out what's happening. But we need help. We have some fluid from one of the discs, and with you being a virologist, you'd know what to do with it. We're afraid to use the hospital lab because we think too many people in the hospital have been infected."

"You suspect a virus?" Nancy questioned.

Cassy shrugged. "I'm not a doctor, but the illness seems like the flu. We also don't know anything about the black discs. That's where we thought your husband might help. We don't know how the things work or even what they are made of."

"I'll have to discuss this with my husband," Nancy said. "How can I get in touch with you?"

Cassy gave the telephone number of Pitt's cousin's apart-

ment where she'd stayed the previous night. She also gave
her Dr. Sheila Miller's direct dial number.

"Okay," Nancy said. "I'll be back to you sometime
today."

Cassy stood up. "Thank you, and as I've said, we need
you. This problem is spreading like a plague."

THE STREET WAS DARK SAVE FOR THE WIDELY DISPERSED
street lights. From the distance two men approached, walking large German shepherds. Both the men and the dogs
acted as if they were patrolling the street. Their heads were
constantly turning from side to side as if they were searching and listening.

A dark sedan appeared and stopped. The window came
down and the pale face a of woman appeared within. The
two men stared at the woman but no one spoke. It was as
if they were having a conversation without the need for
words. After a few minutes the car window soundlessly
went back up and the car moved off.

The two men resumed their walk, and as the eyes of one
of the men passed by the line of Jonathan's sight, Jonathan
thought he saw a glow as if the eyes were reflecting an
unseen light source.

Jonathan reflexively pulled back from the window and
let the drape fall into place. He didn't know if the man in
the street had seen him or not.

After a moment Jonathan carefully parted the center of
the drapes with his finger, exposing only the barest crack.
Being in a dark room himself, Jonathan was not afraid of
light giving him away.

Jonathan brought his eye to the crack. Down in the street
he could see that the two men and dogs had continued
walking just as they had earlier. Jonathan breathed a sigh
of relief. They'd not spotted him.

Letting the curtain fall back into place, Jonathan left the
bathroom and went out into the living room to join the
others. He and his parents had come to the place where
Cassy and her friend Pitt were staying. It was a large three-
bedroom flat in a garden apartment complex. Jonathan

thought it was cool. There were a number of impressive aquariums and tropical plants.

Jonathan considered telling everyone what he'd just seen, but they were too preoccupied. At least everybody but his father. His father was standing away from the group with his elbow on the mantel. Jonathan recognized his expression. It was one of those condescending ones he'd assume whenever Jonathan asked him for help with math.

Jonathan had been introduced to the others. He'd seen the black policeman before and had been impressed by him. He'd come to the school the previous autumn for career day. Jonathan had never met Dr. Sheila Miller but was wary of her. Except for her blond hair she reminded him of the witch in the *Snow White* video his parents had made him watch when he was a kid. There wasn't anything feminine about her like there was about Cassy. The long fingernails didn't quite hack it, especially since they were painted a rather dark color.

Cassy's friend Pitt was an okay guy except Jonathan felt a twinge of jealousy because of Cassy. Jonathan didn't know if they were exactly dating, but it seemed like they were living there in the same apartment. Jonathan wished he had a physique like Pitt and maybe even black hair if that was what Cassy liked.

SHEILA CLEARED HER THROAT. "SO LET'S SUMMARIZE," she said. "What we're dealing with is an infectious agent that rapidly sickened guinea pigs, but the animals produced no detectable microorganisms, specifically no viruses. The illness is not airborne, otherwise we'd all be infected. At least I certainly would be, since I've been essentially living in the ER. It's been literally filled with infected people over the last couple of days who've been continuously coughing and sneezing."

"Have you inoculated any tissue cultures?" Nancy asked.

"No," Sheila said. "I don't think of myself as experienced enough for that type of work."

"So you believe the illness is only spread parenterally," Nancy said.

"Exactly," Sheila said. "By one of these black discs."

Both the discs were sitting in a topless Tupperware container resting on the coffee table. Nancy picked up a fork and began pushing them around so she could examine them. Then she tried to turn one of them over, but being unwilling to touch it with her finger to stabilize it, it seemed impossible. She gave up. "I can't imagine how these things could sting anything. They are so uniform."

"But they most certainly can," Cassy assured her. "We saw it happen."

"A slit opens up at the edge," Jesse said, taking the fork and pointing. "Then a chromelike needle shoots out."

"But I don't see where a slit could be," Nancy said.

Jesse shrugged. "It's got us buffaloed as well."

"The illness is unique," Sheila said, refocusing the discussion. "It basically resembles the flu symptomatically, but its incubation period is only a few hours after injection. Its course is also short and self-limited, again only a few hours except for people with chronic disease like diabetes. Unfortunately, for those people it is rapidly lethal."

"And people with blood disease," Jesse added in memory of Alfred Kinsella.

"True," Sheila agreed.

"And so far no influenza virus has been isolated from any of the victims," Pitt said.

"Also true," Sheila said. "And the most unique and one of the more disturbing aspect of this illness is that after recovery the victim's personality changes. They even profess to feel better generally than they had before the illnesss. And they start talking about environmental problems. Isn't that right, Cassy?"

Cassy nodded: "I discovered my fiancé out in the middle of the night having a conversation with strangers. When I asked him what he'd been talking about, he said the environment. At first I thought he was joking, but he wasn't."

"Joy Taylor told me she and her husband were having environmental meetings every night," Nancy said. "Then with me she brought up the issue about the destruction of the rain forests.''

"Just a minute!" Eugene said. "As a scientist all I'm hearing is hearsay and anecdotes. You people are getting way ahead of yourselves."

"That's not true," Cassy said. "We saw the disc open, and we saw the needle. We've even seen people get stung."

"That's not the point," Eugene said. "You don't have any scientific proof that the stinging caused the illness."

"We don't have a lot of proof but the guinea pigs did get sick," Sheila said. "That was for sure."

"You have to establish causality in a controlled circumstance," Eugene said. "That's the scientific method. Otherwise you can't talk about anything except in vague generalities. You need reproducible evidence."

"We got these black discs," Pitt said. "They are not figments of one's imagination."

Eugene pushed off the mantel and bent over to look at the two discs. "Let me understand you: you're trying to say that this solid little thing formed a slit where there is no seam or even microscopic evidence of a door or a flap."

"I know it sounds crazy," Jesse said. "I wouldn't have believed it either if we all hadn't seen it together. It was like it unzipped and then welded itself shut."

"I just thought of something else," Sheila said. "We had a strange episode in the hospital. A man from housekeeping died with an unexplained circular hole in his hand. The room where he'd been found was all strangely twisted out of shape. You remember, Jesse. You were there."

"Of course I remember," Jesse said. "There was some speculation about radiation, but we never found any."

"That was the room which my fiancé was in," Cassy said.

"If that episode is associated with this flu and these black discs, we've got a bigger problem than we think," Sheila said.

Everyone except Eugene, who'd gone back to leaning against the mantel, stared at the two black discs feeling skeptical about what their minds were telling them. Finally

Cassy spoke. "I'm sensing that we are all thinking the same thing but are afraid to say it. So I'm going to say it. Maybe these little black discs aren't from around here. Maybe these things are not from this planet."

After an initial impatient sigh from Eugene, Cassy's comments were greeted with total silence. The sounds of respiration and the ticking of a wall clock were the only interior noise. Outside a car horn honked in the distance.

"Come to think about it," Pitt said finally, "the night before Beau found one of these discs, my TV blew up. In fact a lot of us students lost TVs, radios, computers, all sorts of electronic equipment if the equipment happened to be on at the time."

"What time was that?" Sheila asked.

"Ten-fifteen," Pitt said.

"That's when my VCR exploded," Sheila said.

"It's also when my radio blew up," Jonathan said.

"What radio?" Nancy asked. It was the first time she'd heard of it.

"I mean Tim's car radio," Jonathan corrected himself.

"Do you think all those episodes could be related to these black discs?" Pitt asked.

"It's a thought," Nancy said. "Eugene, has that surge of powerful radio waves ever been explained?"

"No, it hasn't," Eugene admitted. "But I wouldn't use that fact to support some half-baked theory."

"I don't know," Nancy said. "I'd say that it makes it at least suspicious."

"Wow," Jonathan commented, "that would mean we're talking about an extraterrestrial virus. Cool!"

"Cool, nothing!" Nancy said. "It would be terrifying."

"Whoa, everybody," Sheila warned. "Let's not let our imaginations run away with themselves. If we start jumping to conclusions and talking about some Andromeda strain it's going to be a lot harder trying to elicit any help."

"This is just what I was trying to warn you about," Eugene said. "You are all beginning to sound like a group of paranormal nuts."

"Whether this illness comes from Earth or outer space,

it's here," Jesse said. "I don't think we should be arguing about it. I think we better start finding out what it is and what we can do about it. I don't think we should be wasting a lot of time, because if it is spreading as fast as we think it is, we could be too late."

"You are absolutely right," Sheila said.

"I'll isolate the virus if it's in the sample," Nancy said. "I can use my own lab. No one questions what I do. Once we have the virus we can present our case all the way to Washington and the Surgeon General."

"That's if the Surgeon General isn't already infected by the time we get the information," Cassy said.

"That's a sobering thought," Nancy said.

"Well, we have no choice," Sheila said. "Eugene is right in the sense that if we start calling around now without something more than hearsay and conjecture, no one is going to believe us."

"I'll start the isolation in the morning," Nancy said.

"Is there any chance I could help?" Pitt asked. "I'm a chem major, but I've taken microbiology and worked in the hospital lab."

"Sure," Nancy said. "I've noticed people acting strange at Serotec. I won't know whom to trust."

"I'd like to offer to help figure what these black discs are," Jesse said. "But I wouldn't know where to start."

"I'll take them into my lab," Eugene offered. "Even if it's just to prove to you alarmists that they are not from Andromeda, it will be worth my time."

"Don't touch the edge," Jesse warned.

"No need to worry," Eugene said. "We have the capability of manipulating them from a distance as if they were radioactive."

"It's too bad we just can't talk to one of these infected people directly," Jonathan said. "Heck, we could just ask them what's happening. Maybe they know."

"That would be dangerous," Sheila said. "There's reason to believe they are actively recruiting. They want the rest of us infected. They may even come to view us as an enemy."

"They're recruiting all right," Jesse said. "I think the police chief is actively searching out people on the squad who've yet to get the illness."

"It might be dangerous, but it might also be revealing," Cassy said. She stared off for the moment with unseeing eyes while her mind churned.

"Cassy!" Pitt said. "What are you thinking? I don't like that look on your face."

13

"THESE PEOPLE ARE WITH ME," NANCY SELLERS SAID. Nancy, Sheila, and Pitt were standing in front of the Serotec Pharmaceutical night security desk. The guard was fingering her ID. Nancy had already shown it at the gate before driving onto the parking area.

"You people have any picture IDs?" the security man asked Sheila and Pitt. Both produced driver's licenses which satisfied the man. The trio trooped to the elevator.

"Security is still on edge after the suicide," Nancy said.

The reason Nancy had them get there so early was to avoid the other workers. And it worked. As yet no one else had arrived, and the entire fourth floor was empty. The fourth floor was reserved entirely for biological research. There was even a small menagerie of experimental animals at one end.

Nancy unlocked her private lab, and they all entered. She locked the door behind them. She did not want any interruptions or questions.

"Okay!" Nancy said. "We are going to wear containment suits and everything will be done under a level three hood. Any questions?"

Neither Sheila nor Pitt had any.

Nancy led them into a side room which had changing

cubicles. She gave them appropriate-sized gear and let them change. She changed as well.

Meeting back in the main room Nancy said: "Now, let's have the samples."

Sheila produced the coffee-creamer jar containing the snippet of desk blotter. She also produced multiple blood samples from people who'd acquired the flu. The samples had been drawn at various stages of their illness.

"All right," Nancy said, rubbing her gloved hands together in anticipation. "First I'm going to show you how to inoculate a tissue culture."

"WHERE THE HELL DID YOU GET THIS THING?" CARL MA-ben asked his boss, Eugene Sellers. Carl was a Ph.D. candidate who also worked for the physics department.

With raised eyebrows Eugene glanced over at Jesse Kemper, whom he'd invited to watch the analysis of one of the black discs. Jesse told them that it had been taken from an individual who'd been arrested for lewd behavior.

Both Eugene and Carl expressed interest.

"I don't know the details," Jesse admitted.

Eugene's and Carl's faces fell.

"Well, I do know that the man had been arrested for making love in the park," Jesse said.

"My God! It's amazing the risks people take," Carl said. "It's dangerous just to walk in the park at night, much less make love."

"This wasn't at night," Jesse said. "It was at lunch-time."

"They must have been embarrassed," Eugene said.

"Quite the contrary," Jesse said. "They were irritated at being disturbed. They said that the police should be more concerned about the rising levels of carbon dioxide in the atmosphere and the resultant greenhouse effect."

Both Eugene and Carl laughed.

As soon as Jesse told the story it reminded him of the conversation the previous evening about the infected people's concerns about environmental issues. The possibility

that the noontime lovers were infected people had never
occurred to him.

Redirecting his attention to the task at hand, Carl said to
Eugene: "I don't think this is going to work." At that moment behind a darkly tinted glass screen they were blasting
one of the black discs with a high energy laser to knock
off some molecules. A gas chromatograph was poised to
analyze the resultant gas. Unfortunately the laser wasn't
doing the trick.

"All right, turn it off," Eugene said.

The bright beam of coherent light was instantly extin-
guished when the power was interrupted. The two scientists
gazed at the small disc.

"That's one hard surface," Carl said. "What do you
think it's composed of?"

"I don't know," Eugene admitted. "But I'm as sure as
hell going to find out. Whoever made it better have a patent
or I'm going to file one."

"What should we do next?" Carl asked.

"Let's use a diamond drill," Eugene said. "Then we'll
vaporize the shavings and let the gas chromatograph do the
work."

SLIPPING AN ANTACID TABLET INTO HER MOUTH, CASSY
emerged from the airline terminal building and waited her
turn in the taxi line. She'd been anxious from the moment
she'd awakened that morning, and the closer she got to
Santa Fe the worse it had become. She'd magnified the
problem by having coffee on the plane. Now her stomach
was in a knot.

"Where to, Miss?" the cab driver asked.

"Do you know anything about this Institute for a New
Beginning?" Cassy asked.

"For sure," the driver said. "It's brand new, yet it's the
destination of half my fares. Is that where you want to go?"

"Please," Cassy said. She sat back and blankly watched
the scenery roll by. Pitt had been adamantly against the idea
of Cassy visiting Beau, but once it had taken hold in
Cassy's mind, she couldn't let it go. Although she admitted

there might be some danger as Sheila predicted, in her heart she could not imagine Beau would ever harm her in any way.

"I have to drop you off here at the gate," the driver said when they had reached the edge of the institute's property. "They don't like car exhaust up near the house. But it isn't far. Only a couple of hundred yards."

Cassy paid the fare and got out. It was a pristine location. There was a white fence as if it were a horse farm. There was also a gate across the driveway, but it was ajar.

Two nicely dressed men about Cassy's age stood off to the side of the gate. They looked tanned and healthy. They were both smiling pleasantly, but as Cassy approached, their smiles didn't change. It was as if their faces were frozen in an expression of gaiety.

Even if the smiles seemed contrived, the two men were cordial. When Cassy said she was hoping to see Beau Stark, they replied that they understood perfectly. They directed her to walk to the house.

Mildly unnerved by this strange interaction, Cassy followed the twisting driveway through the trees. On either side beneath the shade of the trees she caught sight of an occasional large dog. Although every dog she saw turned to watch her, none of them bothered her.

When the shadows of the pines gave way to the sweeping lawns surrounding the mansion, Cassy was impressed despite her anxieties. The only thing that marred the gorgeous scene was the huge banner draped across the entrance.

The moment Cassy started up the front steps a woman appeared who was approximately Cassy's age. She sported a similar smile to the men at the gate. From inside the house Cassy heard sounds of construction.

"I'm here to see Beau Stark," Cassy said.

"Yes, I know," the woman said. "Please follow me."

The woman took Cassy back down the steps and around the enormous house.

"Beautiful home," Cassy commented to make conversation.

"Isn't it," the woman replied. "And to think this is just the beginning. We're all very excited."

The rear of the house was dominated by a large terrace complete with ivy-draped pergolas. Beyond the terrace was a swimming pool. At the edge of the pool was a large umbrella shading a table seating eight. Beau was at the head of the table. About twenty feet away lay King.

As Cassy approached she studied Beau. She had to admit that he looked wonderful. In fact he'd rarely looked so good. His thick hair had more than its usual shine and the skin of his face glowed as if he'd just emerged from a refreshing plunge into the sea. He was carefully dressed in a white billowy shirt. The rest of the people were dressed in suits and ties, including two women.

Several easels were set up to support large pads of paper. The exposed pages were covered with arcane schematics and incomprehensible equations. The table was strewn with papers with similar content. A half dozen laptops were open and humming.

Cassy had never felt more uncertain in her life. Her anxiety had gone up a notch the closer she got to Beau. She had no idea what she was going to say to him. It made it worse that she was interrupting a meeting with important-appearing people. They were all older than Beau and looked professional, like lawyers or doctors.

But before Cassy reached the table, Beau turned toward her, smiled broadly when he recognized her, and leaped to his feet. Without a word to the other people at the table, he ran to Cassy and took her hands. His blue eyes sparkled. For a second Cassy swooned. She felt as if she could have fallen into his huge black pupils.

"I'm so glad you've come," Beau said. "I've been so eager to talk with you."

Beau's words nudged Cassy from her momentary helplessness. "Why didn't you call?" she asked. It was a question she'd not dared ask herself until that moment.

"It's been so hectic," Beau explained. "I've been busy twenty-four hours a day. Believe me."

"I guess I'm lucky to get to see you," Cassy said. She glanced over at the group at the table who were patiently waiting. Same with King who'd raised himself to a sitting position. "You've become quite an important man now."

"There are responsibilities," Beau admitted. He led her a few yards farther away from the group and then pointed up at the house. His other hand still held hers.

"What do you think?" he asked proudly.

"I'm a bit overwhelmed," Cassy said. "I'm not sure what to think."

"What you see here is only the beginning. Only the tip of the iceberg. It's so exciting."

"Only the beginning of what?" Cassy asked. "What are you doing here?"

"We are going to make everything right," Beau said. "Remember me telling you over the last six months that I was going to play an important role in the world if I got a job with Randy Nite? Well, it's happening in a way that I never could have anticipated. Beau Stark, the boy from Brookline, is going to help lead the world to a new beginning."

Cassy looked directly into the depths of Beau's eyes. She knew he was in there. If only she could get to him behind this megalomania facade. Lowering her voice and not taking her eyes from his she said: "I know this isn't you talking, Beau. You are not doing this. Something . . . someone is controlling you."

Beau put his head back and laughed heartily. "Oh, Cassy," he remarked. "Always the skeptic! Believe me, no one is controlling me. I'm just Beau Stark. I'm still the same guy you love and who loves you."

"Beau, I do love you," Cassy said with sudden vehemence. "And I think you love me. For the sake of that love come back home with me. Come to the medical center. There is a doctor there who wants to examine you, to find out what's made you change. She thinks it started with that flu you had. Please fight this, whatever it is!"

Despite Cassy's vow to keep her emotions in check, they welled up anyway. Tears came and formed rivulets on her cheeks. She'd not meant to cry but was powerless to prevent it.

"I do love you," she managed.

Beau reached out and wiped the tears from the corners of Cassy's eyes. He regarded her in a truly loving way. He pulled her toward him and enveloped her with his arms, pressing his face against hers.

At first Cassy held back. But as she felt Beau clutching her she relented. She put her own arms around him and, closing her eyes, squeezed him tightly. She didn't want to let him go, ever.

"I do love you," Beau whispered. His lips were brushing her ear. "And I want you to join us. I want you to become one of us because you won't be able to stop us. No one will!"

Cassy stiffened. Hearing Beau's words was like having a knife driven into her heart. Her eyes popped open. With her face still pressed up against his she could see the blurry form of his ear. But what made her blood run cold was a small patch of skin behind his ear that was grayish-blue in color. Reflexively her hand came up and her fingers touched the area. It was rough, almost scaly in texture, and cold. Beau was mutating!

With a rush of revulsion, Cassy tried to extract herself from Beau's grasp, but he held her tightly. He was stronger than she remembered.

"You'll be joining us soon, Cassy," Beau whispered. He acted unaware of her struggles. "Why not let it be now? Please!"

Changing tactics, Cassy abandoned trying to push away from Beau. Instead she quickly ducked beneath his arms and collapsed on the ground. She was up immediately. Her love and concern had turned to terror. She took several steps backward. The only thing that kept her from bolting was the shock of seeing tears had formed in Beau's eyes.

"Please!" Beau pleaded. "Join us, my dearest."

Cassy tore herself away despite Beau's unexpected show of emotion and sprinted beneath the nearest pergola, heading for the end of the house.

The woman who'd met Cassy on the front porch when she had first arrived stepped forward. During Cassy and Beau's conversation she'd stood discreetly to the side. Now her eyes met Beau's, and she motioned toward Cassy's flee-ing figure.

Beau understood the meaning of the gesture. She was asking if she should send someone after Cassy. Beau hes-itated. He was struggling with himself. Finally he shook his head and turned back to the men and women waiting for him.

HAVING ALREADY FOUND MOST OF THE THINGS ON THE shopping list already, Jonathan rewarded himself by load-ing up with Coke and then strolling up the aisle with all the potato chips. He selected a few of his favorite types and was nearing the meat department when his cart prac-tically ran into Candee's.

"My God, Candee!" Jonathan blurted. "Where have you been? I've called twenty times."

"Jonathan," Candee said happily. "I'm so glad to see you. I've missed you."

"You have?" Jonathan asked. He couldn't help notice how fantastic Candee looked. She was wearing a miniskirt over a tank top body suit. Every curve of her tight, lithe body was there to see and appreciate.

"Oh yes," Candee said. "I've been thinking about you lots."

"How come you haven't been at school?" Jonathan asked. "I looked for you."

"I've been looking for you as well," Candee said.

Jonathan managed to coax his eyes to travel northward to Candee's elfin face. When he did he noticed her smile. There was something abnormal about it even though he couldn't put his finger on what it was.

"I wanted to tell you that I was wrong about my par-ents," Candee said. "Totally wrong."

Before Jonathan could respond to this shocking reversal, both of Candee's parents rounded the end of the aisle and came up behind Candee. Her father, Stan, put his hands on Candee's shoulders and beamed.

"Now this is one cute chick, wouldn't you say?" Stan

said proudly. "And as an added inducement, there's good, healthy genes in these ovaries."

Candee glanced up into her father's face and gave him an adoring look.

Jonathan averted his eyes. He thought he might puke. These people belonged in a zoo.

"We've missed you at the house," Candee's mother, Joy, said. "Why don't you come over tonight. Us adults will be having a get-together, but it doesn't mean you two youths can't spend some quality time together."

"Yes, well, that sounds great," Jonathan said. He felt a mild degree of panic since Joy had moved to his side, hemming him in against the shelving. Candee and Stan were blocking his way forward.

"Can we count on you?" Joy asked.

Jonathan let his eyes streak past Candee's face. She was still smiling that same smile, and Jonathan realized what it was that was abnormal about it. It was fake. It was the kind of smile people made when they tell themselves to smile. It wasn't a reflection of inner emotion.

"I got a lot of homework tonight," Jonathan said. He started to back up his shopping cart.

Joy gazed into Jonathan's cart. "You certainly are a busy little shopper. Are you having a meeting at your house as well? Perhaps we should all come over there."

"No, no," Jonathan said nervously. "Nobody's coming over. Nothing like that at all. I'm just picking up some TV munchies." Jonathan wondered if these people somehow knew about their little group.

Another glance at their fake smiles gave Jonathan a shiver of fear and propelled him to "make tracks." Abruptly he yanked his cart backward, turned it around, yelled that he had to be going, and rapidly headed toward the check-out lanes. As he walked he could feel the Taylor family's eyes on his back.

"THIS IS THE STREET," PITT SAID. HE WAS DIRECTING Nancy to his cousin's apartment where they'd all agreed to meet once again. Sheila was in the backseat of the minivan clutching a sheaf of papers.

It was already dark and the streetlamps were lit. As they approached the proper garden apartment complex, Nancy slowed.

"Seems to be a lot of people out tonight," Nancy said.

"You're right," Pitt said. "Looks like noontime in the city center rather than evening in the suburbs."

"I can understand the ones with dogs," Sheila said. "But what are these other people doing? Are they just walking aimlessly?"

"It's weird," Pitt admitted. "No one seems to be talking to anyone, yet they are all smiling."

"So they are," Sheila said.

"What should I do?" Nancy asked. They were almost to their destination.

"Drive around the block," Sheila suggested. "Let's see if they notice us."

Nancy took the suggestion. As they came back to where they'd started, none of the many pedestrians appeared to look in their direction.

"Let's go in," Sheila said.

Nancy parked. They all alighted quickly. Pitt let the women go ahead. By the time he got to the common entry door, the women were already heading up the interior stairway. Pitt looked back out to the street. He'd had the distinct feeling as he'd come up the path that he was being watched, but as he scanned the area, none of the people were looking in his direction.

Cassy opened the door in response to Pitt's knock. Pitt's face brightened. He was relieved to see her. "How'd the trip go?" he asked.

"Not so good," Cassy admitted.

"Did you see Beau?"

"Yes, I saw him," Cassy said. "But I'd rather not talk about it now."

"Okay," Pitt said supportively. He was concerned. He could tell Cassy was truly troubled. He followed her into the living room.

"I'm glad you all are finally here," Eugene said. His blue chambray shirt was open at the neck and his knitted tie was loosened. His dark eyes darted from person to person. He was wired: a far cry from his bored condescension the evening before.

Sitting around the coffee table were Jesse, Nancy, and Sheila. On the table was the Tupperware container with the two black discs along with an assortment of potato chips from Jonathan's shopping foray. Jonathan was at the window intermittently peeking out. Pitt and Cassy took chairs.

"You know there's a shitload of people wandering around outside," Jonathan said.

"Jonathan, watch your language," Nancy scolded.

"We saw them," Sheila said. "They ignored us."

"Can I have everyone's attention," Eugene said. "I've had an interesting day to say the least. Carl and I threw everything we had at this black disc. It is incredibly hard."

"Who's Carl?" Sheila asked.

"My Ph.D. assistant," Eugene said.

"I thought we agreed to keep all this among ourselves," Sheila said. "At least until we know what we're dealing with."

"Carl's fine," Eugene said. "But you're right. Maybe I should have been working by myself. I have to admit I was skeptical about all this, but I'm not now."

"What did you find?" Sheila asked.

"The disc is not made of any natural material," Eugene said. "It's a polymer of sorts. Actually more like a ceramic, but not a true ceramic because there's a metallic component."

"It's even got diamond in it," Jesse said.

Eugene nodded. "Diamond, silicon, and a type of metal that we have yet to identify."

"What are you saying?" Cassy asked.

"We're saying that it's made of a substance that our current capabilities could not possibly duplicate."

"So say it in English," Jonathan voiced. "It's extraterrestrial, that's what it is."

The reality of the confirmation stunned everyone, even

though everyone except Eugene had expected as much.

"Well, we've made some progress today as well," Sheila said. She looked at Nancy.

"We've tentatively located a virus," Nancy said.

"An alien virus?" Eugene asked, turning pale.

"Yes and no," Sheila said.

"Come on!" Eugene complained. "Stop teasing us. What are you suggesting?"

"From my initial investigations," Nancy said, "and I have to emphasize initial, there is a virus involved, but it hasn't come in these black discs. At least not now. The virus has been here a long time: a long, long time, because it's in every organism I tested today. My guess is that it is in every earthly organism with a genome large enough to house it."

"So it didn't come in these little spaceships?" Jonathan asked. He sounded disappointed.

"If it's not a virus, what's in the infectious fluid?" Eugene asked.

"It's a protein," Nancy said. "Something like a prion. You know, like what causes Mad Cow disease. But not exactly the same because this protein reacts with the viral DNA. In fact that's how I found the virus so easily. I used the protein as a probe."

"What we think is the protein unmasks the virus," Sheila said.

"So the flulike syndrome is the body reacting with this protein," Eugene said.

"That's my guess," Nancy said. "The protein is antigenic and causes a kind of overcharged immunological insult. That's why the lymphokines are produced in such abundance, and it's the lymphokines that are actually responsible for the symptoms."

"Once unmasked what is this virus doing?" Eugene asked.

"That's a question that's going to take some work," Nancy admitted. "But our impression is that unlike a normal virus which only takes over a single cell, this virus is capable of taking over an entire organism, particularly the brain. So just calling it a virus is misleading. Pitt had a good suggestion. He called it a mega-virus.''

Pitt blushed. "It just came to me," he explained.

"This mega-virus has apparently been around way before humans evolved," Sheila said. "Nancy found it in a highly conserved segment of DNA.''

"A segment that researchers have ignored," Nancy said. "It's one of those noncoding segments, or so people thought. And it's big. It's hundreds of thousands of base pairs long.''

"So this mega-virus has been just waiting," Cassy said.

"That's our thought," Nancy said. "Perhaps some alien viral race or maybe an alien race capable of packaging itself in a viral form for space travel visited the Earth eons ago when life was just evolving. They planted themselves in the DNA like sentinels that waited to see what kind of life might develop. I suppose they could be intermittently awakened with these little spaceships. All they need is the enabling protein.''

"And now we've finally evolved into something that they want to inhabit," Eugene said. "Maybe that's what that blast of radio waves was the other night. Maybe these discs can communicate back to wherever they come from.''

"Wait a sec," Jonathan said. "You mean that this alien virus is already inside me, like in hibernation?''

"That's what we believe," Sheila said, "provided our initial impressions are correct. The virus's potential to express itself is in our genomes, sort of like an oncogene has the power to express itself as a cancer. We already know that bits and pieces of regular viruses are nestled into our DNA. This just happens to be a humongus piece.''

For a few minutes the room was dominated by an awed silence. Pitt took a potato chip. His chewing sounds seemed abnormally loud. He glanced at the others when he became aware they were staring at him. "Sorry," he said.

"I have a feeling that these so called mega-viruses are not content just to take over," Cassy said suddenly. "I'm afraid they have the power to cause organisms to mutate.''

All eyes turned to Cassy.

"How do you know that?" Sheila asked.

"Because I went to see my fiancé, Beau Stark, today," Cassy admitted.

"I hardly think that was wise," Sheila said angrily.

"I had to," Cassy said. "I had to try to talk to him and get him to come back and be examined."

"Did you tell him about us?" Sheila demanded.

Cassy shook her head. Thinking about her visit, she fought against tears.

Pitt got out of his chair and sat on the arm of Cassy's. He put his arm around her shoulders.

"What made you think about mutation?" Nancy asked. "Do you mean somatic mutation, like his body changing?"

"Yes," Cassy said. She reached up and took hold of Pitt's hand. "The skin behind his ear has changed. It's not human skin. It's like something I've never felt."

This new revelation brought another period of silence. Now the threat seemed even greater. There was a monster lurking in everyone.

"We have to try to do something about this," Jesse said. "We have to do it now!"

"I agree," Sheila said. "We don't have a lot of data but we have some."

"We've got the protein," Nancy said. "Even if we don't know much about it yet."

"And we have the discs with the preliminary analysis of their composition," Eugene added.

"The only problem is we don't know who is infected and who isn't," Sheila said.

"We'll have to take that chance," Cassy said.

Nancy agreed. "We don't have any choice. Let's put all our data together in a more or less formal report. I want to have something in hand. A good place to do it is in my office at Serotec. We won't be bothered, and we'll have access to word processing, printers, and copiers. What do you all say?"

"I say time's a'wasting," Jesse remarked and got up from the couch.

Eugene put the Tupperware container with the two black

discs into a knapsack that also contained printouts of the various tests he'd run. He slung it over his shoulder and followed the others outside.

Everybody squeezed into the Sellerses' minivan. Nancy drove. As they pulled away from the curb, Jonathan looked out the back window. A few of the many pedestrians were watching them but most ignored them.

Within an hour the entire group was hard at work. They divided the task up according to abilities. Cassy and Pitt were busy typing on computer terminals with Jonathan's technical assistance. Nancy and Eugene were making copies of their test results. Sheila was collating the patients' charts of hundreds of flu cases. Jesse was on the telephone.

"I think you should be the one to speak," Nancy told Sheila. "You're the medical doctor."

"No doubt about it," Eugene said. "You'll be much more convincing. We can back you up by providing details as needed."

"That's a lot of responsibility," Sheila said.

Jesse hung up the phone. "There's a red-eye to Atlanta that leaves in an hour and ten minutes. I booked three seats. I assumed that just Sheila, Nancy, and Eugene were going."

Nancy looked over at Jonathan. "Maybe Eugene or I should stay here," she said.

"Mom!" Jonathan whined. "I'll be fine."

"I think it is important that both you people come," Sheila said. "You're the ones who have done the tests."

"Jonathan can stay with us," Cassy said.

Jonathan's face brightened.

SEVERAL CARS PULLED UP TO THE FRONT OF THE SEROTEC building. Pedestrians stopped their wanderings and walked over. They helped open the doors. From the first car emerged Captain Hernandez. His driver got out on the other side. It was Vince Garbon. From the car behind emerged plainclothes officers as well as Candee and her parents.

The pedestrians stood in front of the captain and pointed up to the lights in the fourth-floor windows. They told the captain that all the "unchanged" were up there. The captain nodded, then waved to the others to follow him. En masse they entered the building.

CASSY HAD FINISHED HER TYPING AND WAS WAITING BY the printer as it spewed out the pages. Jonathan moved over so he was standing next to her.

"I still don't understand why Atlanta," Jonathan said. "Why not just go to the the health authorities here?"

"Because we don't know whose side the local health people are on," Cassy said. "The problem is here in this city, and we can't risk spilling all we know to somebody who might be one of them."

"But how do you know it's not happening in Atlanta?" Jonathan asked.

"We don't know," Cassy admitted. "At this stage we're just hoping."

"Besides," Pitt said, overhearing, "the CDC is the best bet for handling this kind of problem. It's a national organization. If need be they could quarantine this city or even the whole state. And perhaps most critical of all, they can get the word out. This whole affair has happened so fast here that the media hasn't even picked up on it."

"Either that or the people who control the media are all infected," Cassy said.

Cassy got her pages together and joined them with Pitt's. As she was stapling them together the lights flickered.

"What the hell was that?" Jesse asked. He was tense like everyone else.

For a moment no one moved. Then the lights went out. The only illumination came from computer screens that had backup battery power sources.

"Don't panic," Nancy said. "The building has its own generators."

Jonathan went to the window. He cranked it open and stuck his head out. Below he could see light coming from lower floors. He relayed this disturbing information to the others.

"I don't like this," Jesse said.

The faint but high-pitched whine of the elevator permeated the room. The elevator was coming up.

"Let's get out of here!" Jesse yelled.

Frantically the group threw together all their papers and packed them into a leather briefcase before racing from the room. In the darkened hall they could see from the floor indicator that the elevator was almost there.

With Nancy silently beckoning to show the way, they ran the length of the corridor and burst through the door into the stairwell. They started down but almost immediately heard a door opening three floors below them on the ground level.

Jesse, who was now in the lead, made a snap decision and detoured into the corridor of the third floor. Everyone followed.

They dashed to the stairwell at the opposite end. Jesse held up until Sheila brought up the rear. As Jesse was about to open the door, he caught a glimpse through the door's window of someone coming up the stairs. Quickly he ducked down and motioned frantically for the others to do the same. They all heard the heavy footfalls of several people charging up the stairs, heading to the fourth floor.

The moment Jesse thought he heard the stairwell door above close, he pulled open the door in front of him. He looked up. Satisfied the stairwell was now empty, he motioned for the others to follow him down to the ground level.

They regrouped in front of a door that said it was armed and was restricted for emergency use only.

"Everybody here?" Jesse whispered.

"We're all here," Eugene said.

"We get in that van and we're out of here," Jesse said. "I'll drive. Let me have the keys."

Nancy gladly passed them to him.

"Okay, go!" Jesse said. He burst through the door, setting off the alarm. The others followed closely at his heels. They ran half bent over. Within a few seconds they were inside the car, and Jesse had the engine roaring.

"Hang on," he warned. He gunned the engine. With a

screech of tires they rocketed out of the parking lot. Jesse didn't bother to stop at the security gate. The van hit the black-and-white wooden bar and snapped it cleanly off.

Jonathan turned and looked out the rear window. Glancing up at the darkened windows of the fourth floor, he saw several pairs of glowing eyes. They appeared like cats' eyes reflecting the beam of a headlight.

Jesse drove rapidly but purposefully within the speed limit. He'd passed a few squad cars and didn't want to attract their attention.

At a traffic light everyone began to calm down enough to discuss who it could have been that had tried to corner them in the Serotec building. No one had any idea. Nor did anyone know who would have tipped them off. Nancy questioned whether the night security man might be one of "them."

At the next light, Pitt happened to glance over at the car alongside them. When the driver turned to look at Pitt, his face immediately reflected recognition. Pitt saw him reach for his cellular phone.

"This sounds crazy," Pitt said. "But I think the guy next to us recognizes us."

Jesse responded by ignoring the red light. He surged forward between cars, then turned off the main street. They bumped down a back alley.

"Aren't we going the opposite direction from the airport?" Sheila asked.

"Don't worry," Jesse said. "As the expression goes, I know this city like the back of my hand."

They made a few more surprising turns down small, out-of-the-way streets. Then to everyone's surprise they sped up an entrance to the freeway that no one in the car besides Jesse knew existed.

They drove the rest of the way to the airport in silence. It was becoming clear to everyone the extent of the conspiracy and that they could not let down their guard.

Jesse drove up to the departure level of the airport and pulled to a halt at terminal C. Everyone piled out of the van.

"We can take care of ourselves from here," Sheila said, grabbing the briefcase containing the hastily assembled report. "Why don't the rest of you get back home to safety?"

"We're going to see you three off," Jesse said. "I want to make sure there is no more trouble."

"What about the van?" Pitt asked. "Do you want me to stay here with it?"

"No," Jesse said. "I want all of us inside."

The interior of the terminal at that hour was all but deserted. A cleaning crew was polishing the expansive terrazzo floor. The Delta counter was the only one occupied. The monitors said that the Atlanta flight was on time.

"All you people head out to the gate," Jesse said. "I'll get the tickets. Just be sure to have your picture IDs handy."

The group hurried across the terminal and approached airport security. There were a few other passengers who were waiting their turn to put their carry-on baggage into the X-ray detector.

"Where are the black discs?" Cassy whispered to Pitt.

"Eugene has them in his knapsack," Pitt answered.

At that moment Eugene dropped the knapsack on the conveyer, and it disappeared inside the machine. He stepped through the metal detector.

"What if they set off an alarm?" Cassy said.

"I'm more worried that the security personnel might be one of 'them' and recognize the image on X-ray," Pitt said.

Both Pitt and Cassy held their breath as the woman security guard halted the machine. Her eyes were glued to the X-ray image. It seemed like a full minute before the woman restarted the conveyer belt. Cassy sighed in relief. She and Pitt stepped through the metal detector and caught up with the others.

They all avoided locking eyes with any of the other passengers as they walked out the concourse. It was nerve-racking not knowing who was infected and who wasn't. As if reading everybody's mind, Jonathan said: "I think you can tell who they are by either their smiles or their eyes."

"What do you mean?" Nancy asked.

"It's either a fake smile or their eyes glow," Jonathan said. "Of course you can only see the eyes in the dark."

"I think you are right, Jonathan," Cassy said. She'd witnessed both.

They arrived at the gate. The plane was already mostly boarded. They moved to the side to wait for Jesse.

"See that woman over there?" Jonathan said while pointing. "Look at that stupid grin. I bet five bucks she's one of them."

"Jonathan!" Nancy whispered forcibly. "Don't be so obvious."

VINCE GARBON PULLED THE UNMARKED POLICE CAR OVER to the curb, directly behind the Sellerses' minivan.

"Obviously they are here," Captain Hernandez said as he got out of the car. A second car pulled up behind the first. Candee, her parents, and the other plainclothes officers emerged.

Like iron filings being drawn to a magnet, a number of infected airport workers immediately drew around the captain and his group.

"Gate 5, terminal C," one these people said to the captain. "Flight 917 for Atlanta."

"Let's go," Captain Hernandez said. He stepped through the automatic door into the terminal and waved for the others to follow him.

"NOW WHERE'S JESSE?" SHEILA ASKED. SHE LOOKED FOR him back along the concourse toward the main terminal. "I don't want to miss this flight."

"Eugene," Nancy whispered to her husband. "With all that's going on, I'm having second thoughts about leaving Jonathan. Maybe one of us should stay here."

"I'll watch out for him," Jesse said. He'd come up behind the group in time to hear Nancy's comment. "You do your thing in Atlanta. He'll be fine."

"How did you get here?" Sheila asked.

Jesse pointed toward an unmarked, locked door just behind them. "I've been to the airport so many times investigating various crimes that I know the place better than my own basement.''

He handed tickets to Nancy, Eugene, and Sheila. Nancy gave her son one last hug. Jonathan remained stiff with his arms at his side.

"You be careful, hear me?" Nancy said, trying vainly to look Jonathan in the eye.

"Mom!" Jonathan complained.

"Let's go," Sheila said. "It's last call."

With Sheila in the lead and Nancy bringing up the rear to give her son a final wave, the three checked in at the gate, showed their picture ID's then disappeared down the jetway. A few minutes later the jetway pulled back from the plane and the plane taxied out into the night.

Jesse turned from the window with a sigh of relief. "They're off, thank God," he said. "But now we . . .''

Jesse didn't get to finish his sentence because he saw Captain Hernandez and Vince Garbon leading a large pack of people. They were walking quickly down the center of the concourse, heading directly toward gate 5.

Cassy saw the cloud descend over Jesse's face and started to ask what was wrong. But Jesse didn't give her a chance. Roughly he herded the group back against the unmarked door.

"What's going on?" Pitt demanded.

Jesse ignored him and quickly punched in the combination on the keypad next to the doorknob. The door opened. "Go!" he commanded.

Cassy was first through the door followed by Jonathan and then Pitt. Jesse pulled the door shut behind himself.

"Come on!" he whispered harshly. He rapidly descended a flight of metal stairs, and ran along a corridor until he came to a door to the outside. On a series of pegs next to the door were yellow rain ponchos with hoods. Quickly he tossed one to each of the others and told them to put them on, including the hoods.

Everyone complied. Cassy asked who he'd seen.

"The chief of police," Jesse said. "And I know for sure he's one of them.''

Once again typing the combination onto a keypad, Jesse opened the door to the outside. The group stepped out onto the tarmac. They were directly below the jetway for gate 5.

"See that luggage train over there?" Jesse said as he pointed. It was a tractor-like vehicle hitched to a string of five baggage carts. It was parked about fifty feet away. "We are going to walk over there real casual like. The problem is we'll be visible from the windows above. Once there you all are going to climb into one of the baggage cars. Then, God willing, we'll ride back to terminal A, not C."

"But our car is at terminal C," Pitt said.

"We're leaving the car," Jesse said.

"We are?" Jonathan asked. He was shocked. It was his parents' car.

"Damn right we are," Jesse said. "Let's go!"

They got to the baggage cart without incident. Everyone was tempted to look up into the windows, but no one did.

Jesse started the engine while the others climbed aboard. They were thankful for Jesse's decisive authority. Everyone breathed a sigh of relief as the baggage train twisted around like a snake and then headed for terminal A.

They passed a few airline workers, but no one challenged Jesse's performance. They arrived at terminal A baggage claim without incident. There, they again benefited from Jesse's knowledge of the airport layout and procedure. Within minutes they were outside on the arrival level waiting for the airport bus.

"We'll take the bus back to the city center," Jesse said. "I can get my car from there."

"What about my parents' van?" Jonathan asked.

"I'll take care of it tomorrow," Jesse said.

The sound of a huge jet thundered overhead, making conversation momentarily impossible.

"That must have been them," Jonathan said as soon as he could be heard above the din.

"Now if they can only find receptive people at the CDC," Pitt said.

"They have to," Cassy said. "It could be our only chance."

BEAU WAS OCCUPYING THE MASTER SUITE AT THE château. There were French doors over a balcony that looked down on the terrace and the swimming pool. The doors were ajar and a soft night breeze rustled the papers on the desk. Randy Nite and a few of his more senior people were there, going over the work that had been accomplished that day.

"I'm really pleased," Randy said.

"So am I," Beau said. "Things couldn't be going better." He ran his hand through his hair and his fingers touched the area of altered skin behind his right ear. He scratched it, and it felt good.

The phone rang and one of Randy's assistants answered. After a quick conversation he handed the phone to Beau.

"Captain Hernandez," Beau said happily. "Good of you to call."

Randy tried to hear what the captain was saying, but he couldn't.

"So they are on their way to the CDC in Atlanta," Beau said. "I'm glad you called to let us know, but I assure you there won't be a problem."

Beau disconnected but did not hang up the receiver. Instead he dialed another number with a 404 area code. When the call was answered Beau said: "Dr. Clyde Horn, this is Beau Stark. That group of people I told you about today is on their way to Atlanta as we speak. I imagine they'll be at the CDC tomorrow so handle them as we discussed."

Beau replaced the receiver.

"Do you expect any trouble?" Randy asked.

Beau smiled. "Of course not. Don't be silly."

"Are you sure you should have let that Cassy Winthrope leave today?" Randy asked.

"Goodness, you are a worrywart tonight," Beau said. "But yes, I'm sure. She's been rather special to me, and I decided I didn't want to force her. I want her to embrace the cause voluntarily."

"I don't understand why you care," Randy said.

"I'm not sure why I do either," Beau admitted. "But enough of this talk. Come outside! It's almost time."

Beau and Randy stepped out onto the balcony. After a glance up at the night sky, Beau stuck his head back inside the room and asked one of the assistants to go down and turn off the underwater lights in the pool.

A few minutes later the pool lights went out. The effect was dramatic. The stars were much more intense, especially those in the galactic core of the Milky Way.

"How much longer?" Randy asked.

"Two seconds," Beau said.

No sooner had the words escaped from Beau's lips that the sky lit up with a profusion of shooting stars. Literally thousands of them rained down like a gigantic firework display.

"Beautiful, isn't it?" Beau said.

"Marvelous," Randy said.

"It's the final wave," Beau said. "The final wave!"

14

"I'VE NEVER SEEN ANYTHING LIKE THIS," JESSE SAID. "You know what I'm saying. I mean, how long does it take three young people to get themselves together to go out for breakfast?"

"It's Cassy's fault," Pitt said. "She was in the bathroom for eight years."

"That's untrue," Cassy said, taking immediate umbrage. "I didn't take as long as Jonathan here. Besides, I had to wash my hair."

"I didn't take long," Jonathan said.

"You most certainly did," Cassy said.

"All right, enough already," Jesse shouted. Then in a more moderate tone he added: "I've just forgotten what it's like having kids around."

They had stayed the night at Pitt's second cousin's apartment, thinking it was the safest place. It had worked out fine with Pitt and Jonathan sharing a bedroom. The only minor problem had been the single bathroom.

"Where should we eat?" Jesse asked.

"We usually eat at Costa's," Cassy said. "But I think the waitress there is an infected person."

"There's going to be infected people no matter where we go," Jesse said. "Let's go to Costa's. I don't want to go anyplace where I might run into any of my fellow officers.''

It was a beautiful morning as they emerged into the sunlight. Jesse had them wait by the front door a few minutes while he went out to reconnoiter his car. When he saw no evidence of it having been tampered with, he waved them over. They piled in.

"I got to stop for gas," Jesse informed them as he pulled out into the street.

"There's still a lot of people walking around," Jonathan said. "Just like last night. And they all have that weird shit-eating grin."

"Foul language is no longer cool," Cassy admonished.

"Jeez, you sound like my mother," Jonathan said.

They drove into a gas station. Jesse got out to pump the gas. Pitt got out to keep him company.

"Have you been noticing what I have?" Jesse asked when the tank was almost full. The gas station was very busy at that time in the morning.

"Are you referring to the fact that everybody seems to have the flu?" Pitt commented.

"That's exactly what I'm referring to," Jesse said. Most everyone they saw was either coughing, sneezing, or looking pale.

A few blocks away from the diner, Jesse pulled over to the curb at a newsstand and asked Pitt to get a paper. Pitt got out and waited his turn. Like the gas station, the newsstand was busy. As Pitt got closer to the stacks of papers, he noticed that each was being held down with a black disc!

Pitt asked the proprietor about his paperweights.

"Cute little things, ain't they?" he said.

"Where did you get them?" Pitt asked.

"They were all over my yard this morning," the man said.

Pitt ducked back into the car with the paper and told the others about the black discs.

"Wonderful!" Jesse said sarcastically. He glanced at the headlines: *Mild Flu Spreading*. "As if we didn't know that already," he added.

Cassy took the paper in the back seat and read the article as Jesse drove on to Costa's.

"It says the illness is miserable but short," Cassy said. "At least for healthy people. For people with chronic diseases, it advises them to seek medical attention at the first sign of symptoms."

"A lot of good that's going to do them," Pitt commented.

Once inside Costa's they took a booth toward the front. Pitt and Cassy were on the lookout for Marjorie. They didn't see her. When a boy about Jonathan's age came over to take their order, Cassy asked about the waitress.

"She went to Santa Fe," the boy said. "A lot of our staff went there. That's why I'm working. I'm Stephanos, Costa's son."

After Stephanos disappeared back into the kitchen, Cassy told the others about what she'd seen in Santa Fe. "They're all working at this castlelike house," she added.

"What are they doing?" Jesse asked.

Cassy shrugged. "I asked; it was a natural question. But Beau just gave me platitudes and generalities about a new beginning and making everything right, whatever the hell that meant."

"I thought foul language wasn't cool," Jonathan said.

"You're right," Cassy said. "I'm sorry."

Pitt glanced at his watch for the tenth time since they'd been in the diner. "It shouldn't be too long now before they arrive at the CDC."

"They might be waiting for the place to open," Cassy said. "By now they've been in Atlanta for several hours. With the time difference maybe the CDC doesn't open for another hour or so."

A family of four in the next booth started to cough and sneeze almost simultaneously. The flu symptoms progressed rapidly. Pitt looked over and recognized the pale, feverish appearance, particularly of the father. "I wish I could warn them," he said.

"What would you tell them?" Cassy asked. "That they have an alien monster inside that's now been activated and that by tomorrow they won't be themselves?''

"You're right," Pitt said. "At this stage there's not much that can be said. Prevention is key.''

"That's why we've gone to the CDC," Cassy said. "Prevention is what they are about. We just have to keep our fingers crossed that they'll take the threat seriously before it is too late.''

DR. WILTON MARCHAND LEANED BACK IN HIS HIGH-BACKED desk chair and folded his hands over his expansive abdomen. He'd never followed any of his own organization's recommendations concerning diet and exercise. He looked more like a successful brewery proprietor of the late nineteenth century than the director of the Centers for Disease Control.

Dr. Marchand had hastily called together some of his department heads for an impromptu meeting. Attending were Dr. Isabel Sanchez, head of the Influenza branch; Dr. Delbert Black, head of Special Pathogens; Dr. Patrick Delbanco, head of virology; and Dr. Hamar Eggans, head of epidemiology. Dr. Marchand would have liked to have included others, but they were either out of town or tied up with other commitments.

"Thank you," Dr. Marchand said to Sheila who'd just finished an impassioned presentation of the entire problem. Dr. Marchand gazed at his branch heads who were looking over each other's shoulders, busily reading the single copy of the report that Sheila had handed them prior to her presentation.

Sheila glanced at Eugene and Nancy who were sitting to her immediate right. The room had gone silent. Nancy nodded to Sheila to convey that she thought Sheila had done an excellent job. Eugene shrugged and raised his eyebrows in response to the silence. He was silently asking the question of how this collection of CDC brass could be taking this information with such apparent composure.

"Excuse me," Eugene said a minute or so later, unable to bear the prolonged silence. "As a physicist, I have to emphasize to you people that these black discs are made of a material that could not have been made on Earth.''

Dr. Marchand picked up the Tupperware container on his desk and with lidded eyes gazed in at the two objects.

"And they are definitely manufactured," Eugene continued. "They are not natural. In other words, it would have to be from an advanced culture . . . an alien culture!" It was the first time the trio had used the word "alien." They had implied as much but had avoided being so explicit.

Dr. Marchand smiled to indicate that he understood Eugene's point. He extended the Tupperware container out toward Dr. Black who took it and peered within.

"Quite heavy," Dr. Black commented before handing the container on to Dr. Delbanco.

"And you say that there are many such objects in your city," Dr. Marchand said.

Sheila threw up her hands in exasperation and got to her feet. She couldn't sit a moment longer. "There could be thousands," she said. "But that's not the point. The point that we are making is that we are in the beginning of an epidemic stemming from a provirus in our genomes. In fact, it's in every higher animal's genome that we've tested, suggesting it's been there for maybe a billion years. And the scariest part is that it has to be extraterrestrial in origin."

"Every element, every atom, and every particle of our bodies are 'extraterrestrial,' " Dr. Black said sternly. "Our entire makeup has been forged in the supernova of dying stars."

"That may be," Eugene said. "But we are talking about a life form. Not mere atoms."

"Exactly," Sheila said. "A viruslike organism that has been lying dormant in the genomes of Earth creatures, including human beings."

"Which you purport was transported to Earth in these miniature spaceships in the Tupperware container," Dr. Marchand said wearily.

Sheila rubbed her face to get herself under control. She knew she was exhausted and emotionally drained. Like Nancy and Eugene she'd not slept a wink all night. "I know it sounds implausible," she said, deliberately speaking slowly. "But it is happening. These black discs have the capability of injecting a fluid into living organisms. We were lucky to obtain a drop of the fluid from which we have isolated a protein that we believe functions like a prion."

"A prion only carries one of the spongiform encephalopathies," Dr. Delbanco said with a broad smile. "I doubt your protein is a prion."

"I said, 'Like a prion!'" Sheila added venomously. "I didn't say it was a prion."

"The protein reacts with the particular segment of DNA that was previously considered noncoding," Nancy said. She could see that Sheila was getting angry. "Perhaps it is better to say it's functioning more like a promoter."

"Perhaps we could take a short break," Sheila said. "I know I could use a little coffee."

"Of course," Dr. Marchand said. "How thoughtless of me."

BEAU GAVE KING AN EXUBERANT SCRATCHING BEHIND HIS ears as he gazed out over the lawns in front of the institute. From the wrought-iron balcony off the library, he and King could see a long stretch of the driveway before it disappeared into the trees. It was clogged with new converts patiently making their way to the château. A few waved up to Beau, and he waved back.

Letting his eyes roam the rest of the grounds, Beau could see his canine friends were reliably on duty. Beau was pleased. He did not want interruptions.

Turning back into the house, Beau descended to the first floor and entered the ballroom. It was jammed with energetically toiling people. Now that the space was almost completely gutted, it looked far different than it had just the day before.

The people working in the room were a remarkably diverse group from all walks of life and of all ages. Yet they were working together like a synchronized swim team. From Beau's perspective it was a sight to behold and the picture of efficiency. No one had to give orders. Like the individual cells of a multicelled organism, each person had in their mind the blueprints of the entire project.

Beau saw Randy Nite laboring happily at a makeshift workbench set up in the center of the room. Randy's team was particularly disparate, with ages ranging from a man in his eighties to a girl less than ten. They were working on banks of sophisticated electronic equipment. Each person wore lighted magnifying headgear reminiscent of a retinal surgeon.

Beau strolled over.

"Hey, Beau!" Randy said cheerfully, catching sight of him. "Great day, huh!"

"Perfect," Beau answered with equal enthusiasm. "Sorry to interrupt, but I'm going to need you this afternoon. Your lawyers are coming by with more papers for you to sign. I'm having the remainder of your assets signed over to the institute."

"No problem," Randy said. He wiped some plaster dust from his brow. "Sometimes I think we should move these electronics away from all this demolition."

"Probably would have been a good idea," Beau admitted. "But the demolition is almost over now."

"The other problem is that these instruments don't have the sophistication we're going to need."

"We'll just use what we can of theirs," Beau said. "We knew there would be problems with their degree of precision. But what we don't have, we'll have to develop ourselves."

"All right," Randy said, although he was less than convinced.

"Come on, Randy," Beau said. "Relax! Everything is going to work out fine."

"Well, at least they're making fantastic progress with the space," Randy said. His eyes roamed the room. "It certainly looks different now. The realtor told me it had been a re-creation of the ballroom of a famous French palace."

"It will serve a far greater purpose once we've finished it," Beau said. He gave Randy a friendly slap on the back.

"Don't let me keep you. I'll see you later when the lawyers get here."

STEPHANOS PICKED UP THE SOILED DISHES FROM IN FRONT of Cassy, Pitt, Jonathan, and Jesse. Jesse asked for another "hit" of coffee. Stephanos went back behind the counter for the coffee pot.

"Did you hear him cough just before he got to our table?" Cassy asked.

Pitt nodded. "He's coming down with it. No doubt about it. But I'm not surprised. Last time we were in here we thought his father was infected."

"Hell with the coffee," Jesse said. "This place is starting to give me the creeps. Let's get."

The group got to their feet. Jesse threw down a tip. "This is my treat," he said. He picked up the check and headed for the cash register by the door.

"What do you think Beau is doing right now?" Pitt asked, as the group followed behind Jesse.

"I don't want to think about it," Cassy said.

"I just can't believe that my best friend is the leader of all this," Pitt said.

"He's not the leader!" Cassy snapped. "He's not Beau any longer. He's being controlled by the virus."

"You're right," Pitt said quickly. He knew he was touching a sore point for Cassy.

"Once the CDC is involved," Cassy said, "do you think they could come up with a cure, like a vaccine?"

"A vaccine is used to prevent an illness," Pitt said. "Not cure it."

Cassy stopped and with eyes that reflected a hint of desperation, looked up into Pitt's face. "You don't think they could come up with a cure?"

"Well, there are antiviral drugs," Pitt said, trying to sound hopeful. "I mean it's possible."

"Oh, Pitt, I hope so," Cassy said, near tears.

Pitt inwardly gulped. There was a nasty part of him that celebrated Beau's departure from the scene because of Pitt's feelings for Cassy. Yet he could see how bad she felt.

Reaching out he took her in his arms and hugged her. She hugged him back.

"Hey, guys, take a gander at this," Jesse said, while blindly tapping Pitt on the shoulder. Jesse's eyes were glued to a tiny TV set behind the cash register.

Pitt and Cassy let go of each other. Jonathan crowded in from behind. The TV was tuned to CNN and an instant news break was coming on.

"This is just in to CNN," the announcer said. "There was an unprecedented meteor shower last night seen halfway around the world from the extreme western part of Europe all the way to Hawaii. Astronomers believe it was worldwide but could not be seen in the rest of the world because of sunlight. The cause is unknown since the phenomenon has caught astronomers totally unaware. We will bring more to you about this breaking news as soon as it is available."

"Could that have something to do with you-know-what?" Jonathan asked.

"Maybe more of the black discs?" Jesse suggested. "It must be."

"My God!" Pitt exclaimed. "If it is, then it's now involving the whole world."

"It will be unstoppable," Cassy said. She shook her head.

"Something the matter, folks?" Costa, the owner, asked. It was Jesse's turn at the register. Jesse'd originally lined up behind several other customers.

"Nope," Pitt said quickly. "It was a great breakfast."

Jesse paid the bill, and the group walked outside.

"Did you see his smile?" Jonathan questioned. "Did you see how fake it was? He's one of the infected. I'll bet five bucks."

"You'll have to bet with someone else," Pitt said. "We already knew he was one of them."

AFTER A SHORT BREAK THAT SHEILA AND NANCY HAD USED to go into the ladies' room and wash their faces, the trio returned to Dr. Marchand's office. Sheila was still exasperated so Nancy spoke.

"We understand that what we are saying is largely anecdotal and that our report is weak in actual data," Nancy said. "But the fact is that we are three professionals with impeccable credentials who are here because we are concerned. This event is truly happening."

"We certainly are not questioning your motives," Dr. Marchand said. "Just your conclusions. Since we had already dispatched an epidemiological investigative officer to the scene we are understandably dubious. We have his report here." Dr. Marchand raised a single-page memorandum. "It was his feeling that you people were experiencing an outbreak of a mild form of influenza. He described extensive consultation with the CEO of your hospital, Dr. Halprin."

"His visit occurred before we realized what we were dealing with," Sheila said. "Besides, Dr. Halprin had already been a victim of the illness. We tried to make that very clear to your EIS officer."

"Your report is very sketchy," Dr. Eggans said to Sheila, slapping it down onto the edge of Dr. Marchand's desk after he'd read it from cover to cover. "There's too much supposition and very little substance. However . . ."

Sheila had to restrain herself from getting up and angrily walking out. She couldn't believe how these passive intellectual midgets had risen to their current positions within the CDC bureaucracy.

"However," Dr. Eggans repeated, running a hand pensively through his full beard, "it's still compelling enough that I'd like to go and investigate on site."

Sheila turned to Nancy. She wasn't sure she'd heard correctly. Nancy flashed a thumbs up sign.

"Have you circulated this report to any other government agencies?" Dr. Marchand asked. He picked it up from his desk and idly thumbed through it.

"No!" Sheila said emphatically. "We all thought the CDC was the best place to start."

"It hasn't been sent to the State Department or the Surgeon General?"

"No one," Nancy affirmed.

"Did you try to determine the amino acid sequence of the protein?" Dr. Delbanco asked.

"Not yet," Nancy said. "But that will be easy to do."

"Have you determined if the virus is able to be isolated from the patients after they have recovered?" Dr. Delbanco asked.

"What about the nature of the reaction between the protein and DNA?" the willowy Dr. Sanchez asked.

Nancy smiled and held up her hands. She was pleased with the sudden interest. "Slow down," she said. "I can only handle one question at a time."

The queries came fast and furious. Nancy did her best to answer them, and Eugene helped when he could. Sheila initially was as pleased as Nancy, but after ten minutes had passed and the questions were becoming more and more hypothetical, she began to sense that something was wrong.

Sheila took a deep breath. Maybe she was just too tired. Maybe these questions were reasonable from such research-oriented professionals. The problem was that she expected action, not intellectualization. At that point they were busily questioning Nancy how she even came up with the idea of using the protein as a DNA probe.

Sheila let her eyes wander around the room. The walls were decorated with the usual profusion of professional diplomas, licenses, and academic awards. There were pictures of Dr. Marchand with the President and other politicians. Suddenly Sheila's eyes stopped at a door that was open about a foot. Beyond the door she saw the face of Dr. Clyde Horn. She recognized him instantly partially due to his shiny bald pate.

As Sheila's eyes locked onto Dr. Horn's his face twisted into a great smile. Sheila blinked, and when she opened her eyes, Dr. Horn was gone. Sheila closed her eyes again. Was she hallucinating from exhaustion and tension? She wasn't sure, but the image of Dr. Horn's face brought back the memory of him leaving her office with Dr. Halprin. As clearly as if it had been an hour previously, she could hear Dr. Halprin saying: "I've even got something I want you to take back to Atlanta for me. Something I think that will interest the CDC."

Sheila's eyes blinked open. With sudden clairvoyance and absolute certitude she knew what Dr. Halprin had been referring to: a black disc. Sheila glanced at the CDC people in the room and it dawned on her with equivalent certitude that they were all infected. Instead of being interested in the epidemic in order to contain it, they were grilling Nancy and Eugene to find out how they had learned what they had.

Sheila stood up. She grabbed Nancy's arm and tugged. "Come on, Nancy. Time for us to get some rest."

Nancy pulled her arm free. She was surprised at the interruption. "We're finally making some progress here," she forcibly whispered.

"Eugene, we need a few hours of sleep," Sheila said. "You must understand even if Nancy doesn't."

"Is there something wrong, Dr. Miller?" Dr. Marchand asked.

"Not at all," Sheila said. "I just realized that we're exhausted, and that we shouldn't be taking your time until we've had some rest. We'll make a lot more sense after a little sleep. There's a Sheraton nearby. It will be best for everyone."

Sheila stepped up to Marchand's desk and reached for the report that she and the Sellerses had brought. Dr. Marchand put his hand on it. "If you don't mind, we'd like to peruse this while you're resting."

"That's fine," Sheila said agreeably. She backed away and tugged on Nancy's arm again.

"Sheila, I think . . ."· Nancy began but her eyes met Sheila's. She could see Sheila's intensity and resolve. Nancy stood up. It dawned on her Sheila knew something she didn't.

"Why don't we say we'll be back after lunch," Sheila offered. "Say between one and two o'clock."

"I think that will work for us," Dr. Marchand said. He

looked at his department heads, and they all nodded.

Eugene crossed his legs. He'd not seen the unspoken communication between his wife and Sheila. "Maybe I'll stay here," he said.

"You are coming with us," Nancy said to Eugene, yanking him to his feet. Then she smiled at her hosts. They smiled back.

Sheila led the way out of Dr. Marchand's office. They passed through the secretarial area and down the pale, institutional green corridor.

At the elevators Eugene started to complain, but Nancy told him to stay quiet.

"At least until we get into the rental car," Sheila whispered.

They boarded the elevator and smiled at the occupants. They all smiled back and commented on how nice the weather was.

By the time they got to the car and climbed in, Eugene was mildly irritated.

"What's wrong with you women?" he said as he put the key in the ignition. "It took us an hour to get them interested and then poof, we have to go rest. This is crazy."

"They are all infected," Sheila said. "Every last one of them."

"Are you sure?" Eugene asked. He was aghast.

"Absolutely," Sheila said. "Not a doubt in my mind."

"I assume we're not going to the Sheraton," Nancy said.

"Hell no!" Sheila said. "Let's get to the airport. We're back to square one."

THE REPORTERS HAD GATHERED AT THE GATE·OF THE INstitute. Although they had not been invited, Beau had anticipated their coming, he just didn't know which day. When the young men at the gate had informed Beau they were there, Beau told the gatekeepers to hold them back for fifteen minutes to give Beau a chance to walk out to where the driveway entered the trees. Beau did not want any reporters in the ballroom, at least not yet.

When Beau confronted the group he was mildly surprised by the number. He'd expected ten or fifteen people. Instead there were around fifty. They were equally divided between newspaper, magazine, and TV. There were about ten TV cameras. Everyone had microphones.

"So here you see the new Institute for a New Beginning," Beau said, gesturing toward the château with a sweep of his hand.

"We understand that you are doing a lot of renovation in the building," a journalist said.

"I wouldn't say a lot," Beau said. "But yes, we are making a few changes to suit our needs."

"Can we see the interior?" a journalist asked.

"Not today," Beau said. "It would be too disruptive for the work that is being done."

"So we've come all the way out here for nothing," a journalist commented.

"I hardly think that is the case," Beau said. "You certainly can see that the institute is a reality and not a mere figment of imagination."

"Is it true that all the assets of Cipher Software are now controlled by the Institute for a New Beginning?"

"Most," Beau said vaguely. "Perhaps you should direct that question to Mr. Randy Nite."

"We'd like to," a journalist said. "But he's not been available. I've been trying around the clock to get an appointment to interview him."

"I know he's busy," Beau said. "He has committed himself wholeheartedly to the goals of the institute. But I think I could convince him to talk to you people in the near future."

"What is this 'new beginning,'" a particularly skeptical journalist demanded.

"Exactly that," Beau said. "It is born out of the need to take seriously the stewardship of this planet. Human beings have been doing a terrible job up until now as witnessed by pollution, destruction of ecosystems, constant strife, and warfare. The situation necessitates a change, or, if you will, a new beginning, and the institute will be the agent for that change.''

The skeptical reporter smiled wryly. ''Such practiced rhetoric,'' he commented. ''It certainly sounds highfalutin, maybe even true, at least the part about the mess humans have made of the world. But the idea of an institute accomplishing this out here in an isolated mansion is ludicrous. This whole operation with all these brainwashed people strikes me more as a cult than anything else.''

Beau fixed the skeptical reporter with his eyes and his pupils dilated maximally. He walked toward the man, oblivious to the people who were blocking his path. Most stepped aside, a few Beau pushed. He didn't shove them hard but rather eased them out of the way.

Beau reached the reporter who defiantly returned Beau's stare. The whole group of journalists went silent as they watched the confrontation. Beau resisted the temptation to reach out, grab the individual, and demand he show proper respect. Instead Beau decided he would bring this contumacious individual back to the institute and infect him.

But then Beau thought it might be easier to infect them all. He'd just give them each a parting gift of a black disc.

''Excuse me, Beau!'' an attractive young woman called who'd just arrived. Her name was Veronica Paterson. She'd run down from the chateau and was out of breath. She was clothed in an alluring one-piece spandex outfit that appeared as if it had been sprayed on her lithe and shapely body. The male reporters in particular were intrigued.

She pulled Beau away from the group so she could tell him in private that there was an important telephone call for him up at the institute.

''Do you think you can handle these reporters?'' Beau asked her.

''Most certainly,'' Veronica said.

''They are not to go inside,'' Beau said.

''Of course not,'' Veronica said.

''And they're to leave with gifts,'' Beau said. ''Give them all black discs. Tell them that it is our emblem.''

Veronica smiled. ''I like that,'' she said.

"Excuse me, everybody!" Beau called out to the crowd of reporters. "I must leave unexpectedly, but I'm sure I will be seeing each of you again. Miss Paterson will be available for your remaining questions. She will also be handing out small parting gifts for you to take as souvenirs from your day at the institute."

A babble of questions bubbled forth in response to Beau's announcement. Beau merely smiled and moved off. He clapped his hands, and King came bounding to his side. While Beau had been speaking with the reporters he'd had King keep his distance.

A sharp whistle from Beau brought a number of the other dogs from around the grounds. Beau snapped his fingers and pointed toward the group of journalists. The newly summoned dogs quickly moved to positions ringing the reporters and patiently sat on their haunches.

Upon reaching the house, Beau went directly up to the library. He dialed Dr. Marchand's direct number and the line was immediately answered.

"They have left," Dr. Marchand said. "But it was an unexpected ruse. They informed us they were going to the Sheraton, but they did not."

"Do you have their report?" Beau asked.

"Of course," Dr. Marchand said.

"Destroy it," Beau said.

"What do you want us to do about them?" Dr. Marchand asked. "Should we stop them?"

"By all means," Beau said. "You shouldn't ask a question to which you already know the answer."

Marchand laughed. "You are right," he said. "It's just this weird human trait about trying to be diplomatic."

MID-MORNING ATLANTA TRAFFIC WASN'T BAD COMPARED with rush hour, but it was a lot more than Eugene was accustomed to.

"Everybody seems so aggressive here," Eugene complained.

"You're doing fine, dear," Nancy said, although she

hadn't appreciated how close Eugene had come to another car at the previous intersection.

Sheila was busy looking out the back window.

"Anybody following us?" Eugene asked, glancing at Sheila in the rearview mirror.

"I don't think so," Sheila said. "I guess they bought the story about getting some rest. After all, it was reasonable. But what worries me is that now they know that we know! Maybe I should say 'it' knows."

"You make it sound like a single entity," Eugene said.

"All the infected people have a way of working together," Sheila said. "It's spooky. It's like viruses themselves, all working for the collective good. Or like an ant colony where each individual seems to know what everyone else is doing and what they should be doing as a consequence."

"That suggests there is networking among the infected people," Eugene said. "Maybe the alien form is a composite of a number of different organisms. If that were the case, it would be a different dimension of organization than we're accustomed to. Hey, maybe it needs a finite number of infected organisms to reach a critical mass."

"The physicist is getting far too theoretical for me," Sheila said. "And keep your eye on the road! We just came too close to that red car next to us."

"But one thing is for sure," Nancy said. "Whatever the level of organization, we have to remember that we are dealing with a life form. That means that self-preservation will be high on its list."

"And self-preservation depends on recognizing and destroying enemies," Sheila said. "Like us!"

"That's a comforting thought," Nancy said with a shiver.

"Where should we go when we get to the airport?" Eugene asked.

"I'm open to suggestions," Sheila said. "We still have to get to someone or some organization who can do something."

Sheila did a double take when she glanced at the face of

the driver in the red car that had been cruising alongside them. It was now pulling ahead.

"My God!" Sheila said.

Nancy's head snapped around. "What's the matter?"

"The driver of the red car," Sheila yelled. "It's the bearded guy: the epidemiologist from the CDC. What's his name?"

"Hamar Eggans," Nancy said. She spun back around and looked. "You're right. It is him. Do you think he's seen us?"

At that moment the red car swerved directly in front of Eugene. He cursed. The bumpers had missed by millimeters.

"There's a black car on our left," Nancy cried. "I think it is Delbanco."

"Oh no! They are on the right too," Sheila shouted. "Dr. Black is in a white car. They have us penned in."

"What should I do?" Eugene yelled in panic. "Is there anybody behind us?"

"There are cars," Sheila said, twisting around in her seat. "But I don't see anyone I recognize."

The moment the words left Sheila's lips, Eugene jammed on the brakes. The tiny four-cylinder rental car shuddered and jackknifed from side to side. Its tires screeched in protest against the pavement, as did the tires of the cars behind.

Eugene did not stop completely, but still the car behind thumped into them. But he had accomplished what he'd wanted to do. The three CDC cars had sped ahead before belatedly putting on their brakes. That gave Eugene the opportunity to turn left across traffic. Nancy screamed as she saw oncoming cars bearing down on her side of the vehicle.

Eugene stomped on the accelerator to avoid a collision and shot into the mouth of a narrow alley. It was filled with trash and several trash barrels. Its width was just adequate for the small car so that all the garbage, cardboard boxes, and barrels were met head on in a flurry of flying debris.

Nancy and Sheila hung on for dear life.

"My God, Eugene!" Nancy shouted as they hit a par-

ticularly large barrel that flipped up to bounce off the roof
of the car. In the process it shattered the sun roof.

Eugene fought the steering wheel to keep the car going
straight despite the rubbish and the containers. Still the car
caromed repeatedly off the cement walls with an agonizing
scraping sound akin to fingernails on a giant blackboard.

Toward the rear of the alley the way was clear, and Eugene hazarded a glance in the rearview mirror. To his horror he could see the front of the red car just entering the
narrow byway.

"Eugene, look out!" Nancy cried, pointing ahead.

Eugene took his gaze away from the rearview mirror in
time to see a cyclone fence rushing toward them. Deciding
there was little choice, he yelled for the women to hold on
and pushed the accelerator to the floor.

The tiny car gained speed. Both Eugene and Nancy were
roughly thrown against their seat belts while Sheila
bounced off the back of the front seat.

Despite trailing segments of the fence the tiny car sped
out into a field churning up plumes of dust. It jackknifed
several more times, but on each occasion Eugene was able
to steer into the skid to keep the car from rolling over.

The vacant lot was about a hundred yards square and
treeless. Ahead Eugene could see a rise stubbled with scrag-
gly vegetation. Beyond the rise was a busy part of the city.
Over the crest of the hill the tops of vehicles caught in
stop-and-go traffic were visible.

With his mouth dry and forearms aching, Eugene cast
another look behind. The red car was attempting to maneuver through the hole in the chain-link fence. The white car
was immediately behind it.

Eugene's hastily conceived plan was to rocket over the
hill and melt into the traffic. But the terrain had other ideas.
The earth was particularly soft, and as the small car's front
wheels hit the base of the hill, they dug in. The car spun
to the left and lurched to a halt in a cloud of dust. All three
of the occupants were severely jolted.

Eugene was the first to recover. He reached out to touch
his wife. She responded as if waking from a bad dream.

He turned to look at Sheila. She was dazed but okay.

Eugene undid his seat belt and got out on shaky legs and looked toward the chain-link fence. The red car was apparently hung up in the ragged opening: the sound of its tires spinning could be heard across the field.

"Come on!" Eugene called to the women. "We have a chance. Let's get over this hill and melt into the city."

The women emerged on the passenger side of the car. As they did so Eugene nervously glanced back at the red car in time to see the bearded man get out.

"Come on, hurry!" Eugene urged the women. Expecting the bearded man to come running in their direction, Eugene was surprised to see him retrieve something from the car. When he held it aloft, Eugene thought it suspiciously like the Tupperware container they'd brought with them to Atlanta.

Confused by this gesture, Eugene continued to watch while Nancy and Sheila helped each other up the hill. A few seconds later Eugene found himself staring at one of the black discs. To his utter shock it was hovering in midair right in front of his face.

"Come on, Eugene!" Nancy called from near the summit of the rise. "What are you waiting for?"

"It's a black disc," Eugene yelled back.

Eugene noticed that the disc was rotating rapidly. The individual bumps that lined the edge now appeared like a tiny ridge.

The black disc moved closer to Eugene. His skin tingled.

"Eugene!" Nancy called urgently.

Eugene took a step back but did not take his eyes off the disc in front of him, which was now turning red and radiating heat. Slipping off his jacket and rolling it, Eugene swatted at the disc in an attempt to knock it from the air. But it didn't happen. Instead the disc burned a hole through the jacket so quickly, Eugene felt no resistance whatsoever. It had been like a knife through room-temperature butter.

"Eugene!" Nancy shouted. "Come on!"

As a physicist, Eugene was mystified, especially when a corona began to form around the disc and the color began to turn from red to white. The tingling sensation he felt on his skin increased.

The corona rapidly expanded into a glaring ball of light so bright that the image of the disc contained in it was no longer visible.

Nancy could now see what was occupying Eugene's attention. She was about to call out to him again when she saw the bright ball of light suddenly expand to engulf her husband. Eugene's instant scream was immediately choked off and replaced by a whooshing sound. This noise grew deafening, but only for an instant; then it was cut off with such suddenness that Nancy and Sheila felt a concussive force like a silent explosion.

Eugene was gone. The rental car was left as a curiously twisted hulk as if it had been melted and pulled toward the point where Eugene had been standing.

Nancy started to run back down the hill, but Sheila grabbed her.

"No!" Sheila yelled. "We can't." There was now another ball of light forming next to the wreck of the car.

"Eugene!" Nancy cried desperately. Tears had burst forth.

"He's gone," Sheila said. "We have to get out of here."

The second ball of light was now expanding to envelop the car.

Sheila grabbed Nancy's arm and pulled her off the top of the hill toward the busy city. Ahead of them was heavy traffic and, even better, thousands of pedestrians. Behind them they heard the strange whooshing sound again and another concussion.

"What on earth was that?" Nancy asked through tears.

"I believe they thought we were in the car," Sheila said. "And if I had to guess, I'd say we just witnessed the creation of a couple of miniature black holes."

"WHY HAVEN'T WE HEARD FROM THEM?" JONATHAN asked. He'd become progressively more worried as the day drew to a close. Now that it was dark, his concerns magnified. "I mean, it's even later in Atlanta."

Jonathan, Jesse, Cassy, and Pitt were in Jesse's car cruising along Jonathan's street. They'd passed his house several times already. Jesse was nervous about making this visit, but he'd relented when Jonathan insisted he needed some more clothes and his laptop. He also wanted to make sure his parents hadn't called and left some kind of message on his computer.

"Your parents and Dr. Miller are probably terribly busy," Cassy said. But her heart wasn't in the explanation. She herself was worried.

"What do you think, Jesse?" Pitt asked as they came to Jonathan's house for the third time. "Do you think it's safe?"

"It looks clear to me," Jesse said. "I don't see anything that looks like a stakeout. All right, let's do it, but we'll make it fast."

They pulled into the driveway and killed the headlights. At Jesse's insistence, they waited for another few minutes to see if there were any changes in the neighboring homes or vehicles parked on the street. All seemed peaceful.

"Okay," Jesse said. "Let's go."

They went in the front door, and Jonathan disappeared upstairs to his room. Jesse turned on the TV in the kitchen and found cold beer in the refrigerator. He offered one to Cassy and Pitt. Pitt accepted. The TV was tuned to CNN.

"This just in," the reporter announced. "A few moments ago the White House canceled the multinational summit on terrorism, saying that the President has come down with the flu. Presidential press secretary Arnold Lerstein said that the meeting probably would have gone on as scheduled without the President except that, by coincidence, most of the other world leaders seemed to be suffering from the same illness. The President's personal physician made the statement that he is convinced the President has the same 'short' flu that has been decimating Washington over the last few days and should resume normal duties in the morning."

Pitt shook his head in dismay. "It's taking over our whole civilization the same way a central nervous system virus takes over a host. It's going for the brain.''

"We need a vaccine," Cassy said.

"We needed it yesterday," Jesse said.

The phone startled everyone. Cassy and Pitt looked at Jesse to see if they should answer it. Before Jesse could respond, Jonathan answered it upstairs.

Jesse charged up the stairs with Cassy and Pitt at his heels. He ducked into Jonathan's room.

"Hold on," Jonathan said into the phone, seeing the others. He told everyone that it was Dr. Miller.

"Put her on the speakerphone," Jesse suggested.

Jonathan pushed the button.

"We are all here," Jesse said. "You're on a speakerphone. How did you fare?"

"Miserably," Sheila admitted. "They led us on. It took several hours before I realized that they were all infected. The only thing they were interested in was how we'd found out what was going on.''

"Christ!" Jesse mumbled. "Was it hard to get away? Did they try to detain you?"

"Not initially," Sheila said. "We told them we were just going to a motel to get some sleep. They must have followed us because they intercepted us on our way to the airport.''

"Was there trouble?" Jesse asked.

"There was," Sheila admitted. "I'm sorry to say we lost Eugene.''

The group looked at each other. Everyone had a different interpretation of what "lost" meant. Jesse was the only one who knew for certain.

"Have you looked for him?" Jonathan asked.

"It was like the hospital room," Sheila said. "If you know what I mean.''

"What hospital room?" Jonathan asked. He was getting panicky.

Cassy put her arm around Jonathan's shoulder.

"Where are you?" Jesse asked.

"At the Atlanta airport," Sheila said. "Nancy is in kind of a bad way as you might guess, but we're coping. We've decided to come home, but we need someone to call up and prepay some tickets for us. We're afraid to use our credit cards.''

''I'll do that right away,'' Jesse said. ''We'll see you as soon as you get back.''

Jesse hung up and dialed the airline ticket office. While he was making the arrangements, Jonathan asked Cassy directly if something had happened to his father.

Cassy nodded. ''I'm afraid so,'' she said. ''But I don't know what. You'll have to wait until your mother comes back to find out more.''

Jesse hung up the phone and looked at Jonathan. He tried to think of something kind to say, but before he was able he heard the sound of skidding tires. From the front window came an intermittant flash of colored lights.

Running to the window Jesse parted the curtains. Outside in the street behind his car was a city police cruiser with its lights flashing. The uniformed occupants were just in the process of getting out, along with Vince Garbon. All had German shepherds on short leashes.

Other police department vehicles appeared, some marked, some not, including a paddy wagon. All pulled to a stop in front of the Sellers house and unloaded.

''What is it?'' Pitt asked.

''The police,'' Jesse said. ''They must have been watching the place. I even see my old partner or what's left of him.''

''Are they coming here?'' Cassy asked.

''I'm afraid so,'' Jesse said. ''Kill all the lights.''

The group frantically raced around the house and turned out the few lights they had turned on. They ended up in the darkened kitchen. Flashlight beams from outside stabbed through windows. It was an eerie image.

''They must know we are here,'' Cassy said.

''What are we going to do?'' Pitt asked.

''I don't think there's much we can do,'' Jesse said.

''This house has a hidden exit,'' Jonathan said. ''It's through the basement. I used it to sneak out at night.''

''What are we waiting for?'' Jesse said. ''Let's go!''

Jonathan led the way, carrying his laptop. They moved slowly and silently, avoiding the flashlight beams that came in through the kitchen bay window. Once they got to the cellar stairs and had closed the door, they felt a bit less vulnerable. But it was difficult going because of the absolute darkness. They were not willing to put on any light because the cellar had several small windows.

They moved in single file. They all hung onto each other to avoid getting lost. Jonathan led them to the back wall of the basement. Once there he opened a massive door that rumbled on its hinges. Cool air flowed out over their ankles.

"In case you are wondering what this is," Jonathan said, "it's a bomb shelter that was built back in the fifties. My parents use it as a wine cellar."

They all entered and Jonathan told whoever was last to close the door. It settled into its jamb with a solid thump.

As soon as the door was closed, Jonathan switched on a light. They were in a cement passageway lined with wood shelving. A few cases of wine were haphazardly scattered about.

"This way," Jonathan said.

They came to another door. Beyond the second door was a step down into a room twelve feet square with bunk beds and an entire wall of cupboards. There was also a well head and a tiny bathroom.

A second chamber had a kitchen. Beyond the kitchen was another solid door. This door lead to another corridor that eventually led outside to a dry river bed behind the Sellerses' house.

"Well, I'll be!" Jesse commented. "Just like the escape route from an old medieval castle. I love it."

15

"NANCY," SHEILA CALLED GENTLY. "WE'RE HERE."

Nancy's eyes popped open, and she awoke with a start. "What time is it?" she asked, orienting herself to place and person.

Sheila told her.

"I feel awful," Nancy said.

"You and me both," Sheila said.

They had spent the night on the move in the Hartsfield Atlanta International Airport, constantly afraid they would be recognized. Boarding their flight in the wee hours of the morning had been a relief of sorts. Neither had slept for forty hours. Once airborne they had fallen into a deep sleep.

"What am I going to say to my son?" Nancy asked, not really expecting an answer. Every time she thought about the fiery disappearance of her husband, tears came to her eyes.

The women gathered their things and made their way off the plane. They were paranoid of everyone and were sure people were staring at them. When they emerged from the jetway, Nancy saw Jonathan and rushed to him. They hugged silently for several minutes while Sheila greeted Jesse, Pitt, and Cassy.

"Okay, let's move out," Jesse said, tapping the silently grieving mother and child.

They walked in a group toward the terminal. The whole time Jesse's head was a swivel as he constantly evaluated the people around them. He was pleased that no one was paying any attention to them, particularly airport security.

Fifteen minutes later they were in Jesse's personal van heading for town. Sheila and Nancy described in detail their disastrous trip. In a shaky voice Nancy managed to explain Eugene's last moments. The tragedy was greeted with silence.

"We have to decide where to go," Jesse said.

"Our house will be the most comfortable," Nancy said. "It's not elegant but there's a lot of room."

"I don't think that will be wise," Jesse said. He then told Nancy and Sheila what had happened the evening before.

Nancy felt outraged. "I know it's selfish of me to be so upset about a house considering everything that is going on," she said. "But it's my home."

"Where did you all stay last night?" Sheila asked.

"At my cousin's apartment," Pitt said. "The problem is it's only got three bedrooms and one bath."

"Under the circumstances, convenience is a luxury we can't afford," Sheila said.

"This morning on the *Today* show a bunch of health officials told everyone that the flu that was going around was nothing to worry about," Cassy said.

"They were probably from the CDC," Sheila said. "Those bastards."

"What bugs me is that the media hasn't said one word about all the black discs," Pitt said. "Why hasn't the presence of the discs been questioned, especially after so many of them appeared?"

"They're a harmless-appearing curiosity," Jesse said. "People have certainly been talking about them, but it was never considered newsworthy. Unfortunately there's no reason to make a connection between the discs and the flu until it is too late."

"We're going to have to figure out a way to start warning people," Cassy said. "We can't wait any longer."

"Cassy's right," Pitt said. "It's time for us to go public any way we can: TV, radio, newspapers, everything. The public has to know."

"Screw the public," Sheila said. "It's the medical-scientific community we've got to get involved. Pretty soon there won't be anybody left with the skills necessary to figure out a way to stop this thing."

"I think the kids are right," Jesse said. "We tried the CDC and bombed. We got to find some media people who are not infected and just blast this thing around the world. Problem is, I don't know any media people except for a few slimy crime reporters."

"No, Sheila's right . . ." Nancy began.

Jonathan tuned out. He was crushed about his father's fate. As a teenager the concept of death was totally unreal. To a large degree he couldn't accept what he'd been told.

Jonathan's attention drifted from the bickering inside the car to the appearance of the city. There were plenty of people out and about. It seemed from the beginning the streets were always full of people wandering no matter what time of day or night. And everybody was sporting a stupid fake smile.

Jonathan noticed something else as they passed through the downtown. The people were all busily interacting and helping each other. Whether it was a passerby aiding a workman unload his tools or a child helping an older person with a parcel, the people were working together. To Jonathan the city resembled a beehive.

Inside the car the argument reached a crescendo with Sheila raising her voice to drown out Pitt.

"Shut up!" Jonathan cried.

To Jonathan's surprise his outburst worked. Everyone looked at him, even Jesse, who was driving.

"This arguing is stupid," Jonathan said. "We have to work together." He tilted his head to the outside. "They certainly are."

Chastised by a teenager, everyone took his suggestion

and looked out at the scene around them. They saw what he meant and were sobered.

"It's scary," Cassy said. "They're like automatons."

Jesse turned onto the street where Pitt's cousin's apartment was located. He started to brake when he saw two cars he was certain were unmarked police cars. From his perspective he was sure that they were staking the place out. It was as if they had signs on their car proclaiming it.

"Here's the apartment complex," Pitt said when he noticed Jesse was about to pass by.

"We're not stopping," Jesse said. He pointed to the right. "See those two stripped-down, late-model Fords. Those are plainclothes officers. I'm sure of it."

Cassy stared at the men.

"Don't look!" Jesse warned. "We don't want to attract their attention."

Jesse kept driving.

"We could go to my apartment," Sheila suggested. "But it's a one-bedroom, and it's high-rise."

"I got a better place," Jesse said. "In fact, it is perfect."

TRAVELING IN A CARAVAN OF TWO OF RANDY NITE'S PERsonal Mercedeses, Beau and a group of close aides drove from the institute to the Donaldson Observatory built on top of Jackson Mountain. The view from the site was spectacular, especially on such a clear day.

The observatory itself was as impressive as the location. It was a huge hemispheric dome set directly on top of the rocky pinnacle of the mountain. It was painted a glistening white that was blinding in the bright sunlight. Its dome shutter was closed to protect the enormous reflective telescope housed within.

As soon as the first car came to a stop, Beau hopped out along with Alexander Dalton. Alexander had been a lawyer in his previous life. Veronica Paterson got out from the driver's side of the car. She was still dressed in her skintight spandex outfit. Beau had changed his clothes to a dark print, long-sleeved shirt. He had the collar turned up and the cuffs buttoned at his wrists.

"I hope this equipment is worth this effort," Beau said.

"My understanding is that it is the latest model," Alexander said. He was a tall, thin man with particularly long, spidery fingers. He was currently functioning as one of Beau's closest aides.

The second Mercedes pulled up and a team of technicians got out. They were all carrying their tools.

"Hello, Beau Stark," a voice called.

Everyone turned to see a white-haired man nearly eighty years old standing at an open door at the base of the observatory. His face was creased and creviced like a piece of dried fruit from the intensity of the high-altitude sun.

Beau walked over to the man and shook hands. Then he introduced Veronica and Alexander to Dr. Carlton Hoffman. Beau told his aides that they were meeting the reigning king of American astronomy.

"You're too kind," Carlton said. "Come on in and get started."

Beau waved for his whole team to enter the observatory. They trooped in without a word.

"Do you need anything?" Carlton asked.

"I think we brought the tools we need," Beau said.

The technicians immediately set to work dismantling the giant telescope.

"I'm particularly interested in the prime focus observing capsule," Beau called out to one of the men who had climbed up into the interchangeable end assembly.

Beau turned to Carlton. "Of course you know you're welcome at the institute any time you'd like to come," he said.

"That's kind of you," Carlton said. "I'll be there, especially once you are ready."

"It's not going to be too long," Beau said.

"Stop!" a voice yelled. The sound echoed around inside the domed observatory. The dismantling came to a grinding halt. "What's going on in here? Who are you people?"

All eyes turned to the air lock door. Standing in front of it was a small, mousy man. He coughed violently but continued to fiercely eye the workers who'd taken apart portions of the telescope.

"Fenton, we're over here," Carlton called out to the man. "Everything is okay. There's someone I want you to meet."

The newly arrived individual's name was Fenton Tyler. His position was Assistant Astronomer, and as such, he was the heir apparent of Carlton Hoffman. Fenton cast a quick glance in Carlton's direction, but then quickly looked back at the workers lest they unscrew another single bolt.

"Please, Fenton," Carlton said. "Come over here."

Reluctantly Fenton moved sideways, continuing to keep his beloved telescope in view. As he approached Beau and the others, it was apparent he was sick.

"He has the flu," Carlton whispered to Beau. "I didn't expect him to come over."

Beau nodded knowingly. "I understand," he said.

Fenton reached his boss's side. He was pale and feverish. He sneezed violently. Carlton introduced him to Beau and explained that Beau was borrowing portions of the telescope.

"Borrowing?" Fenton repeated. He was totally confused. "I don't understand."

Carlton put his hand on Fenton's shoulder. "Of course you don't understand," he said. "But you will. I promise you that you will and sooner than you imagine."

"Okay!" Beau called out while clapping his hands loudly. "Back to work, everyone. Let's get it done."

Despite Carlton's comments, Fenton was aghast at the destruction he was witnessing and voiced his confusion. Carlton drew him aside to try to explain it.

"I'm glad Dr. Hoffman was here," Alexander said.

Beau nodded. But he was no longer thinking about the interruption. He was thinking about Cassy.

"Tell me, Alexander," Beau said. "Have you been able to locate that woman I asked you about?"

"Cassy Winthrope," Alexander said. He knew instantly to whom Beau was referring. "She's not been located. Obviously she's not one of us yet."

"Hmm," Beau said pensively. "I never should have let her out of my sight when she made her surprise visit. I don't know what came over me. I supposed it was some vestigial romantic human trait. It's embarrassing. At any rate, find her."

"We'll find her," Alexander said. "No doubt."

THE LAST MILE WAS ROUGH GOING, BUT JESSE'S VAN MANaged to navigate the ruts in the poorly maintained dirt road.

"The cabin is just around the next bend," Jesse said.

"Thank God!" Sheila complained.

Finally the van lurched to a stop. In front of them was a log cabin nestled into a stand of gigantic virgin pines. Sunlight slanted down through the needles in startlingly bright shafts of light.

"Where are we?" Sheila questioned. "Timbuktu?"

"Hardly," Jesse laughed. "It's got electricity, telephone, TV, running water, and a flush toilet."

"You make it sound like a Four Seasons Hotel," Sheila said.

"I think it's beautiful," Cassy said.

"Come on," Jesse said. "Let me show you the inside and the lake that's out back."

They climbed stiffly from the car, especially Sheila and Nancy. All grabbed the meager belongings they had with them. Jonathan carried his laptop.

The air was clean and crisp and smelled of pine needles. The fresh breeze made a slight sighing noise as it passed through the tall evergreen trees. The sound of birds was everywhere.

"How'd you happen to buy this cabin?" Pitt asked as they mounted the front porch. The posts and balustrade were tree trunks. The deck was rough-hewn planks of pine.

"We bought this place mostly for the fishing," Jesse explained. "Annie was the fisherman, not me. After she passed on I couldn't get myself to sell it. Not that I come here that often, especially over the last couple of years."

Jesse wrestled open the front door, and everybody went inside. It smelled mildly musty. The interior was dominated by a huge fieldstone fireplace that went all the way to the peak of the cathedral ceiling. There was a galleylike kitchen to the right, with a hand pump over a soapstone sink. To the left were two bedrooms. The door to the bathroom was to the right of the fireplace.

"I think it is charming," Nancy said.

"Well, it's certainly remote," Sheila said.

"I can't imagine we could have found a better place," Cassy said.

"Let's air it out," Jesse said.

For the next half hour they made the cabin as comfortable as possible. En route from the city they had stopped at a supermarket and loaded up with groceries. The men carried them in from the van and the women put them away.

Jesse insisted on making a fire even though it wasn't cold. "It'll take the dampness out of the place," he explained. "And come evening, you'll be glad it's going. It gets cold here at night, even this time of year."

Finally they all collapsed on the gingham couches and captain's chairs that were grouped around the fireplace. Pitt was using Jonathan's computer.

"We should be safe here," Jonathan said. He'd opened a pack of potato chips and was crunching away.

"For a while," Jesse said. "No one at the station knew about this place to the best of my knowledge. But we ain't here for a vacation. What are we going to do about what's going on out in the world?"

"How fast can this flu spread to everyone?" Cassy asked.

"How fast?" Sheila questioned. "I think we've had ample demonstration."

"With an incubation period of only a few hours," Pitt said, "combined with it being a short illness and the infected people wanting to infect others, it spreads like wildfire." He was typing away on the laptop as he spoke. "I could do some reasonably accurate modeling if I had some idea of how many of the black discs have landed on Earth.

But even with a low-ball, rough estimate, things don't look so good.''

Pitt turned around the computer screen for the others to see. It was a pie graph with a wedge in red. ''This is only after a few days,'' he said.

''We're talking about millions and millions of people,'' Jesse said.

''Considering both how well the infected work together and their evangelistic attitude, it's going to be billions before too long,'' Pitt said.

''What about animals?'' Jonathan asked.

Pitt sighed. ''I never gave that much thought,'' he said. ''But sure. Any organism that has the virus in its genome.''

''Yeah,'' Cassy said pensively. ''Beau must have infected that huge dog of his. I thought it acted weird right from the start.''

''So these aliens take over other organisms' bodies,'' Jonathan said.

''Analogous to the way a normal virus takes over individual cells,'' Nancy said. ''Remember, that's why Pitt called it a mega-virus.''

Everybody was glad to hear Nancy's voice. She'd been silent for hours.

''Viruses are parasites,'' Nancy continued. ''They need a host organism. Alone, they are incapable of doing anything.''

''Damn right they need hosts,'' Sheila said. ''Especially this alien breed. There's no way a microscopic virus built those spacecraft.''

''True!'' Cassy said. ''This alien virus must have infected some other species somewhere in the universe which had the knowledge, size, and capability of building those discs for them.''

''I wouldn't be too sure,'' Nancy said. ''They possibly could have done it themselves. Remember, I suggested that the aliens might be able to package themselves or part of their knowledge into viral form to withstand intergalactic space travel. In that case their normal form could be quite different than viral.

"Eugene, before he disappeared, was hypothesizing that perhaps the alien consciousness could be achieved by a finite number of infected humans working in consonance."

"You all are getting way ahead of me," Jesse commented.

"Anyhow," Jonathan said, "maybe these aliens control millions of life forms around the galaxy."

"And now they view humans as a comfortable home in which to live and grow," Cassy said. "But why now? What's so special now?"

"I'd guess it is just random," Pitt said. "Maybe they've been checking every few million years. They send a single probe to Earth to see what life form has evolved."

"Awakening the sleeping virus," Nancy said.

"The virus takes control of that single host," Sheila said. "And the host observes the lay of the land, so to speak, and reports back home."

"Well, if that's what happened," Jesse said, "the report must have been mighty good because we're knee-deep in those probes now."

Cassy nodded. "It makes sense," she said. "And Beau might have been that first host."

"Possibly," Sheila said. "But if this scenario is correct, then it could have been anyone anyplace."

"Thinking back to everything that has happened," Cassy said more to Pitt than the others, "Beau had to have been the first. And you know something? If it hadn't been for Beau we'd be like everyone else out there, completely unaware of what is going on."

"Or we'd already be one of them," Jesse said.

These sobering thoughts quieted everyone. For a few minutes the only sounds were the crackling of the fire and the chirping of the birds outside the open windows.

"Hey!" Jonathan said, breaking the silence. "What are we going to do about it, just sit here?"

"Hell, no!" Pitt said. "We'll do something. Let's get started fighting back."

"I agree," Cassy said. "It's our responsibility. After all,

it's possible that we know more about this calamity right now than anyone else in the world."

"We need an antibody," Sheila said. "An antibody and maybe a vaccine for either the virus or the enabling protein. Or maybe one of the antiviral drugs. Nancy, what do you think?"

"No harm in trying," she said. "But we'll need equipment and luck."

"Of course we'll need equipment," Sheila said. "We can set up a lab right here. We'll need tissue cultures, incubators, microscopes, centrifuges. But it's all available. We just have to get it up here."

"Make a list," Jesse said. "I can probably get most of it."

"I'll have to get into my lab," Nancy said.

"Me too," Sheila said. "We need some of the blood samples from the flu victims. And we have to have the fluid sample from the disc."

"Let's do an abstract of that report we made for the CDC," Cassy said, "and disseminate it."

"Yeah," Pitt said, catching on to Cassy's line of thinking. "We'll put it out on the Internet!"

"Hey, great idea," Jonathan said.

"Let's start by sending it to all the top virology labs," Sheila said.

"Absolutely," Nancy said. "And the research-oriented pharmaceutical houses. All of those sources can't be infected yet. We're bound to get someone to listen to us."

"I can set up a network of 'ghosts,' " Jonathan said. "Or false Internet links. As long as I keep changing them, nobody will ever be able to trace us."

For a beat the group regarded each other. They were a bit giddy and at the same time overwhelmed with the enormity and difficulty of what they were about to undertake. Each had their own assessment of the chances of success, but no matter what the appraisal was, they were all in agreement they had to do something. At that point doing nothing would have been psychologically more difficult.

•   •   •

THE SUN HAD JUST SET WHEN NANCY, SHEILA, AND JESSE trooped out to the van and climbed in. Cassy, Jonathan, and Pitt stood on the porch, waved, and told them to be careful.

After Sheila and Nancy had taken a much-needed nap, it had been decided to make a foraging raid into the city for laboratory equipment. It had also been decided that the kids would remain behind to provide room in the van. At first the kids had objected, particularly Jonathan, but after much discussion they had agreed it was best.

As soon as the van had vanished from sight, Jonathan disappeared back inside. Cassy and Pitt took a brief walk. They skirted the cabin and descended through the pines to the lake. They came to a short dock, and they strolled out to its end. Standing there they silently marveled at the natural beauty of the surroundings. Night was fast approaching, painting the distant hills with deep purples and dark silver blues.

"Standing here in the middle of this splendid nature makes the whole affair seem like a bad dream," Pitt said. "Like it can't be happening."

"I know what you mean," Cassy said. "At the same time, knowing it is happening and that all humans are at risk, I feel connected in a way I've never felt before. I mean, we're all related. I've never felt like all humans are a big family until now. And to think of what we have done to each other." Cassy visibly shivered at the thought.

Pitt reached out and enveloped her in his arms. It was a gesture to comfort her and keep her warm. As Jesse had promised the temperature had dropped the moment the sun had gone down.

"The threat of losing your identity also makes you look at your life," Cassy said. "It's hard for me to let go of Beau, but I have to. I'm afraid the Beau I knew is no longer around. It's as if he died."

"Maybe we'll develop an antibody," Pitt said. He looked down at Cassy and wanted so much to kiss her, but he didn't dare.

"Oh, yeah, sure," Cassy said scornfully. "And Santa Claus is going to visit us tomorrow."

"Come on, Cassy!" Pitt said, giving her a little shake. "Don't give up."

"Who said anything about giving up," Cassy said. "I'm just trying to deal with reality the best I can. I still love the old Beau, and probably always will. But I've been slowly realizing something else."

"What is that?" Pitt asked innocently.

"I'm realizing that I've always loved you too," Cassy said. "I don't mean to embarrass you, but back when you and I were dating off and on, I didn't think you really cared for me in a serious way, that you purposefully kept things casual. So I didn't question my own feelings. But over the last couple of days I've been getting a different impression of what your feelings might have been, and that maybe I was wrong back then."

A smile erupted from the depths of Pitt's soul and rose up to spread across his face like the rising sun. "I can assure you," he said. "If you thought I didn't care for you, you were absolutely, totally, incontrovertibly wrong."

Pitt and Cassy silently regarded each other in the gathering gloom. They were both experiencing an unexpected exhilaration despite the situation. It was a magical moment until it was shattered by a high-pitched shout.

"Hey, you guys, get your asses up here," Jonathan screamed. "Come and see this!"

Fearing the worst, Pitt and Cassy raced up to the cabin. Just within the few minutes they'd been at the lake, it had gotten considerably darker beneath the lofty pines, and they tripped over the roots. Rushing into the cabin they found Jonathan watching the TV with one leg casually draped over the arm of the sofa. He was eating potato chips mechanically.

"Listen," Jonathan mumbled, pointing to the TV.

". . . everyone agrees that the President is more vibrant and energetic than ever before. To quote a White House staffer, 'He's a changed man.' "

The announcer then had a fit of coughing. She apologized, then continued: "Meanwhile, this curious flu continues to sweep through the nation's capital. High-ranking cabinet officers, as well as most of the key members of both houses of Congress, have all been felled by this swiftly moving illness. Of course the entire country mourns the death of Senator Pierson Cranmore. As a known diabetic he had been an inspiration to others afflicted with chronic illness.''

Jonathan clicked the mute button on the remote. ''Sounds like they control most of the government,'' he said.

''I think we already conceded as much,'' Cassy said. ''What about the abstract we did this afternoon? I thought you were going to get it ready to put it out on the Internet.''

''I did,'' Jonathan said. He put his finger on the laptop which was sitting on the coffee table and pushed it around so Cassy could see the screen. The phone line was connected to its side. ''All ready,'' he added.

''Well, then put it out there,'' Cassy said.

Jonathan hit the proper button, and the first description and warning of what was happening to the world zoomed out over the vast electronic superhighway. Word was now on the Internet.

16

BEAU WAS SITTING IN FRONT OF A GROUP OF TV MONITORS that he'd had installed in the library. The heavy velvet drapes were drawn across the arched windows to make viewing easier. Veronica stood behind him and massaged his shoulders.

Beau's fingers lightly danced across the control panel and the monitors all came to life. He raised the sound on the top one on the left. It was NBC covering a news conference by the Presidential Press Secretary, Arnold Lerstein.

"There is no need to panic. That is the word from both the President and the Surgeon General, Dr. Alice Lyons. The flu has definitely reached epidemic proportions, but it is a brief illness with no negative side effects. In fact, most people report increased vigor after the illness. Only those people with chronic illness should . . ."

Beau switched the sound to the next monitor. The interviewee was obviously British. He was saying: ". . . over the British Isles. If you or someone you love begins to show symptoms, do not panic. Bed rest, tea, and attention to the fever is recommended."

Beau switched from one monitor to another in rapid succession. The message was similar whether in Russian, Chi-

nese, or Spanish, or any of the other forty-some-odd
languages represented.

"That's all reassuring," Beau commented. "The infestation is proceeding as planned."

Veronica nodded and continued her massage.

Beau switched to the monitor for the camcorder at the
front gate of the institute. It was a wide-angle shot that
included a gang of approximately fifty protesters attempting
to heckle the augmented group of young guards. A number
of the institute's dogs were in the background.

"My wife is in there," a protester yelled. "I demand to
see her. You've no right to keep her."

The smiles on the gatekeepers remained fixed.

"My two sons," another protester screamed. "They're
in there. I know it! I want to talk with them. I want to make
sure they are okay."

At the same time this group was yelling and screaming,
there was a steady stream of calm, smiling people entering
through the gate. These were all infected people who'd
been summoned for service at the institute, and they were
wordlessly recognized by the gatekeepers.

The fact that some people were being allowed entrance
without question further inflamed the protesters. They had
been ignored since their arrival. Without warning they
stormed the gate en masse.

A melee erupted with a lot of yelling and shoving. Even
a few fists were thrown. But it was the dogs who quickly
determined the outcome. They came charging in from the
periphery and attacked. Their vicious snarling and tearing
at the legs of the protesters quickly eroded the group's collectively inspired courage. The protesters fell back.

Beau switched off the monitors. He bent his head over
onto his chest so Veronica could get at the muscles at the
base of his neck. He'd only had one hour of sleep instead
of the two he needed.

"You should be pleased," she said. "Everything is going so well."

"I am," Beau responded. Then he changed the subject:

"Is Alexander Dalton in the ballroom? Did you see him when you went down there?"

"The answer is yes to both questions," Veronica said. "It's as you wish. He would never contravene your order."

"Then I should go to the ballroom," Beau said. He straightened his neck and stood. A short whistle brought King instantly to his feet. Together they descended the central stairs.

The level of activity in the vast room had increased. Many more workers were involved than the previous day. The support beams of the ceiling were now totally exposed, as were the studs of the walls. The huge chandeliers as well as the massive decorative corniches were all gone. The enormous arched windows were almost completely sealed over. In the center of the room a complicated electronic structure was rising. It was being constructed with all the pirated parts from the observatory, various electronic concerns, and the nearby university physics department.

Observing all the coordinated activity for such great purpose brought a particularly broad smile to Beau's lips. He couldn't help recalling that the room had once been used for something as frivolous as dancing.

Alexander saw Beau standing at the ballroom's entrance and joined him immediately. "Looks good, wouldn't you say?"

"It looks tremendous," Beau said.

"I've got some other good news," Alexander said. "We're effecting immediate closure of most of the highest polluting factories around the Great Lakes. This should be completed within the week."

"What about Eastern Europe?" Beau asked. "They are the ones that have been troubling me the most."

"Same situation," Alexander said. "Particularly Romania. They'll be closed this week."

"Excellent," Beau said.

Randy Nite saw Beau speaking with Alexander and hastened over.

"What do you think?" Randy said, while proudly eyeing the emerging central structure.

"It's coming along well," Beau said. "But I'd appreciate a little more speed."

"I'll need more help then," Randy said.

"Whatever you need," Beau said. "We must be ready for the Arrival."

Randy flashed a smile of appreciation before rushing back to his project.

Beau turned to Alexander. "What about Cassy Winthrope?" he asked. There was a sudden edge to his voice.

"She's not been accounted for as yet," Alexander said.

"How can that be?" Beau asked.

"It is a mystery," Alexander said. "The police and the university officials have been exemplarily cooperative. She'll turn up. Maybe even at the gate on her own accord. I wouldn't worry about it if I were you."

Beau lashed out with his right hand, seizing Alexander's forearm in a powerful grip that immediately cut off circulation to Alexander's hand.

Shocked by this overtly hostile gesture, Alexander looked down at the hand that was holding him. It wasn't a human hand. The fingers were long and wrapped around Alexander like minature boa constrictors.

"This request of mine to find this girl is not an idle whim," Beau said. He regarded Alexander with eyes that were almost all pupil. "I want the girl now."

Alexander raised his eyes to meet Beau's. He knew enough not to struggle.

"We shall make it a top priority," Alexander said.

JESSE HAD CUT PINE BOUGHS IN THE NEARBY FOREST, AND after parking the van alongside the shed, had covered it with the branches. From the outside the cabin looked completely deserted save for the wisps of smoke rising from the stone chimney.

In marked contrast to the placid exterior, the interior had been transformed into a crowded workstation. Taking up a lion's share of floor space was the makeshift biological laboratory.

Nancy was in charge in that arena with Sheila working

closely with her. Everyone suspected that Nancy was re-directing her powerful grief over Eugene's death to the task of finding a way to stop the alien virus. She was a woman possessed.

Pitt was busy with a PC. He was attempting to do more accurate modeling with information that had become avail-able on the TV. The media had finally picked up the story about the black discs, but not in regard to the flu epidemic. The stories were presented more as a way to stimulate the public's interest in going out and finding them.

Jesse recognized that his input was more in logistics, particularly the practical aspects such as food and keeping the fire going. Presently he was busy putting the finishing touches on one of his specialties: chili.

Cassy and Jonathan were sitting at the communal eating table with the laptop. To Jonathan's delight there'd been a distinct role reversal: now he was the teacher. Also to Jon-athan's delight, Cassy had on one of her thin cotton dresses. Since it was apparent she had no bra, Jonathan found it excruciatingly difficult to concentrate.

"So what do I do?" Cassy asked.

"What?" Jonathan asked as if waking up from sleep.

"Am I boring you?" Cassy asked.

"No," Jonathan said hastily.

"I'm asking if I change these last three letters in the URL?" Cassy said. She was intent on the LCD screen and oblivious to the effect the physical aspects of her femininity were having on Jonathan. She'd just come in from a swim and her nipples were sticking out like marbles.

"Right . . . uh, yeah," Jonathan said. "Dot G O V. Then . . ."

"Then backslash, 6 0 6, capital R, small g, backslash," Cassy said. "Then I hit Enter."

Cassy looked up at Jonathan and noticed he was blush-ing.

"Is there something the matter?" Cassy asked.

"Nope," Jonathan said.

"Well, then should I do it?" Cassy asked.

Jonathan nodded, and Cassy hit Enter. Almost simultaneously the printer activated and began spewing out printed pages.

"Voilà," Jonathan said. "We're into our mailbox without anybody being able to trace us."

Cassy smiled and gave Jonathan a friendly poke. "You are one fine teacher."

Jonathan blushed anew and averted his eyes. He busied himself by getting the pages out of the printer. Cassy got up and moved over to Pitt.

"Soup's on in three minutes," Jesse called out. No one responded. "I know, I know," he added. "Everybody's too busy, but you gotta eat. It will be on the table for whomever is interested."

Cassy rested her hands on Pitt's shoulders and looked at his computer screen. He had another pie graph, and now the red was larger than the blue.

"Is this where you think we stand now?" Cassy asked.

Pitt reached up and grasped one of Cassy's hands and gave it a squeeze. "Afraid so," he said. "If the data I got from the TV is reasonable or even if it is low, the projections suggest that sixty-eight percent of the world's population is now infected."

Jonathan tapped Nancy on the back. "Sorry to bother you, Mom," he said. "Here's the latest off the Web."

"Anything from the group up in Winnipeg about the protein amino-acid sequence?" Sheila asked.

"Yeah," Jonathan said. He shuffled the pages and pulled out the one from Winnipeg. He handed it to Sheila who stopped what she was doing to read it.

"I've also connected with a new group in Trondhiem, Norway," Jonathan said. "They're working in a hidden lab beneath the gym in the local university."

"Did you send them our original data?" Nancy asked.

"Yup," Jonathan said. "Just like with the others."

"Hey, they've made some progress," Sheila said. "We now have the entire amino acid sequence of the protein. That means we can start making our own."

"Here's what the Norway people sent," Jonathan said. He started to hand the sheet to Nancy, but Sheila reached over and took it instead. She read it rapidly, then crumpled it. "We've already determined all that," she said. "What a waste of time."

"They've been working in total isolation," Cassy said in their defense, having heard Sheila's remark.

"Anything from the group in France?" Pitt asked.

"A lot," Jonathan said. He separated the French pages from the rest and handed them to Pitt. "Seems that the infestation is still progressing slower there than anyplace else."

"Must be the red wine," Sheila said with a laugh.

"That might be an important point," Nancy said. "If it continues and is not just a random blip on the bell curve and if we can figure out why, it might be useful."

"Here's the bad news," Jonathan said, holding up a sheet of paper. "People with diabetes, hemophilia, cancer, you name it, are dying in record numbers all over the world."

"It's as if the virus is consciously cleaning the gene pool," Sheila said.

Jesse carried the pot of chili to the table and told Pitt to move the PC. As he waited to put the food down he asked Jonathan how many research centers he was in touch with around the world the previous day.

"A hundred and six," Jonathan said.

"And how many today?" Jesse asked.

"Ninety-three," Jonathan said.

"Wow!" Jesse said, putting down the chili. He headed back to the kitchen for dishes and flatware. "That's rapid attrition."

"Well, three of them might still have been okay," Jonathan said. "But they were asking too many questions about who we are and where we are so I cut them off."

"As the saying goes, 'Better to be safe than sorry,' " Pitt said.

"It's still rapid attrition," Jesse said.

"What about the man calling himself Dr. M?" Sheila asked. "Anything from him?"

"A bunch of stuff," Jonathan said.

"Who's Dr. M?" Jesse asked.

"He was the first to respond to our letter on the Internet," Cassy explained. "He responded in the first hour. We think he is in Arizona, but we have no idea where."

"He's given us a lot of important data," Nancy said.

"Enough so he's made me a tad suspicious," Pitt said.

"Come on, everyone," Jesse said. "This chili is going to get cold."

"I'm suspicious of everyone," Sheila said. She walked over to the table and took her usual seat at the end. "But if someone is coming up with useful info, I'll take it."

"As long as contacting him doesn't jeopardize our location," Pitt said.

"Obviously that's a given," Sheila said condescendingly. She took the pages from Dr. M that Jonathan held out for her. Holding them in front of herself, she started reading while shoveling chili into her mouth with her free hand. She acted like a high-school student cramming for exams.

Everyone else sat down at the table in a more civilized manner and spread napkins on their laps.

"Jesse, you've outdone yourself," Cassy said after her first mouthful.

"Compliments are freely accepted," Jesse said.

They ate for a few minutes in silence until Nancy cleared her throat. "I hate to bring this up," she said. "But we're running out of basic lab supplies. We aren't going to be able to continue working much longer unless we make another run into the city. I know it is dangerous, but I'm afraid we have little choice."

"No problem," Jesse said. "Just make out a list. I'll manage it somehow. It's important that you and Sheila keep working. Besides, we need more food."

"I'll go too," Cassy said.

"Not without me you won't," Pitt said.

"And me too," Jonathan said.

"You are staying here," Nancy said to Jonathan.

"Come on, Mom!" Jonathan said. "I can't be coddled. I'm as much a part of this as anybody else."

"If you are going, I'm going too," Nancy said. "Besides, either I or Sheila should go. We're the only ones who know what we need."

"Oh my God!" Sheila said suddenly.

"What's the matter?" Cassy demanded.

"This Doc M guy," Sheila said. "Yesterday he asked us what we had on the sedimentation rate for that section of DNA which we knew contained the virus."

"We sent him our estimate, didn't we?" Nancy asked.

"I sent exactly what you gave me," Jonathan said. "Even the part about our centrifuge not being able to reach such an RPM."

"Well, apparently he has access to one that can," Sheila said.

"Let me see," Nancy said to Sheila. She took the page and read it. "My gosh, we're closer to isolating the virus than we thought."

"Exactly," Sheila said. "Isolating the virus is not an antibody or a vaccine, but it is an important step. Maybe the single largest step."

"WHAT TIME IS IT?" JESSE ASKED.

"Ten-thirty," Pitt said, holding his watch up to his face to see the dial. It was dark beneath the trees on the bluff overlooking the university campus. Jesse, Pitt, Cassy, Nancy, and Jonathan were sitting in the van. They had arrived a half hour earlier, but Jesse had insisted they wait. He didn't want anyone going into the medical center until the eleven o'clock shift change. He was counting on the general confusion at that time to facilitate getting what they needed and getting it out of there.

"We'll start at ten forty-five," Jesse said.

From their vantage point they could see that a number of the university asphalt parking lots had been dug up. Lights were strung across some of the open areas created and infected people were busy planting vegetables.

"They certainly are well organized," Jesse said. "Look at the way they work together without any conversation."

"But where are the cars going to park?" Pitt asked.

"That's taking environmentalism to an extreme."

"Maybe they intend not to have cars," Cassy said. "After all, cars are major polluters."

"They do seem to be cleaning up the city," Nancy said. "You have to give them credit for that."

"They're probably cleaning up the whole planet," Cassy said. "In a curious way it's making us look bad. I guess it takes an outsider to appreciate what we've always taken for granted."

"Stop it," Jesse said. "You're starting to sound as if you are on their side."

"It's almost time," Pitt said. "Now here's what I think. Jonathan and I should go into the medical lab in the hospital. I know my way around in there, and Jonathan knows computers. Between the two of us, we'll be able to decide what we need and carry it."

"I think I should stay with Jonathan," Nancy said.

"Mom!" Jonathan moaned. "You have to go to a pharmacy, and you don't need me there. Pitt needs me."

"It's true," Pitt said.

"Cassy and I will go with Nancy," Jesse said. "We'll use the pharmacy in the supermarket, so while she's getting the drugs she needs, we'll load up on groceries."

"All right," Pitt said. "We'll meet back here in thirty minutes."

"Better say forty-five," Jesse said. "We got a little farther to walk."

"Okay," Pitt said. "It's time. Let's go!"

They climbed out of the van. Nancy gave Jonathan a quick hug. Pitt grabbed Cassy's arm.

"Be careful," Pitt said.

"You too," Cassy said.

"Remember, everybody," Jonathan said. "Put a big shit-eating grin on your face and hold it. It's what all of them do."

"Jonathan!" Nancy admonished.

They are about to move off when Cassy grabbed Pitt's arm. When he turned, she gave him a kiss on the lips. Then

Cassy ran after Nancy and Jesse while Pitt caught up with Jonathan. They all moved off into the night.

THE PICTURE WAS ONE OF CASSY TAKEN SIX MONTHS PRE-viously. It had been shot in an alpinelike meadow with wildflowers forming a natural bed. Cassy was lying down with her thick hair splayed out around her head like a dark halo. She was impishly smiling at the camera.

Beau's wrinkled, rubberlike hand reached out. The long snakelike fingers wrapped around the framed photo and lifted it and drew it closer to his eyes. Their inherent glow served to illuminate the picture so Beau could more clearly make out Cassy's features. He was sitting in the upstairs library with the lights off. Even the bank of monitors was off. The only light was an anemic moonbeam that slanted through the windows.

Beau became aware that someone had entered the room behind him.

"Can I turn on the light?" Alexander asked.

"If you must," Beau said.

Illumination filled the room. Beau's eyes narrowed.

"Is there something wrong, Beau?" Alexander asked before he saw the photo in Beau's hands.

Beau didn't answer.

"If you don't mind me saying," Alexander said, "you shouldn't be obsessing on an individual like this. It is not our way. It is against the collective good."

"I've tried to resist," Beau admitted. "But I can't help it."

Beau slammed the framed photo face down on the table. The glass shattered.

"As my DNA replicates it is supposed to supplant the human DNA, yet the wiring in my brain continues to evoke these human emotions."

"I've felt something of what you speak," Alexander admitted. "But my former mate had a genetic flaw, and she did not pass the awakening stage. I suppose that made it easier."

"This emotionalism is a frightful weakness," Beau admitted. "Our kind has never come up against a species with such interpersonal bonds. There is no precedent to guide me."

Beau's snakelike fingers inserted themselves beneath the broken picture frame. A shard of glass cut him and his finger emitted a green foam.

"You've injured yourself," Alexander said.

"It's nothing," Beau protested. He lifted the broken frame and gazed at the image. "I must know where she is. We have to infect her. Once it's done, then I will be satisfied."

"The word is out," Alexander insisted. "As soon as she is spotted we will be informed."

"She must be in hiding," Beau lamented. "It's driving me mad. I can't concentrate."

"About the Gateway . . ." Alexander began but Beau cut him off.

"I need you to find Cassy Winthrope," Beau said. "Don't talk to me about the Gateway!"

"MY GOD! LOOK AT THIS PLACE!" JESSE SAID.

They were standing in the parking lot in front of Jefferson's Supermarket. There were a few abandoned cars with their doors ajar as if the occupants had suddenly run for their lives.

Several of the huge plate-glass windows fronting the store were broken and the shattered glass was scattered about the sidewalk. The interior was illuminated only with night lights, but it was adequate to see that the store had been partially looted.

"What happened?" Cassy questioned. It looked like a scene from a third-world country locked in a civil war.

"I can't imagine," Nancy commented.

"Perhaps the few uninfected people panicked," Jesse said. "Maybe law enforcement as we knew it no longer exists."

"What should we do?" Cassy asked.

"What we came here for," Jesse said. "Hell, this makes

it easier. I thought I was going to have to break into the place.''

The group moved forward tentatively and looked into the store through one of the broken floor-to-ceiling windows. It was eerily quiet.

''It's a mess, but it doesn't look like much of the merchandise has been taken,'' Nancy said. ''It appears that whoever did this was mostly interested in the cash registers.''

From where they were standing they could see that the cash drawers on all the registers were open.

''Stupid people!'' Jesse commented. ''If civil authority breaks down, paper money is going to be worth only what it's printed on.''

Jesse took one last look around the empty parking lot. He didn't see a soul. ''I wonder why there is no one around here?'' he asked. ''They all seem to be walking around the rest of the city. But let's not look a gift horse in the mouth. Let's do it.''

They stepped through the broken window and headed up the central aisle toward the pharmacy, which was located in the back. The walking was difficult in the half light since the floor was covered with scattered cans, bottles, and boxes of food stuff that had been knocked from the shelves.

The pharmacy section was divided from the rest of the store by a wire mesh grate that rolled out of the ceiling and locked to the floor. Whoever had ransacked the grocery section had also been into the pharmacy. A rough hole was cut in the grate with a pair of chain cutters that were still on the floor.

Jesse held the jagged edges of the hole apart so Nancy could squeeze through. She quickly reconnoitered behind the pharmacy desk.

''What's it look like?'' Jesse asked from outside the grate.

''The narcotics are gone,'' Nancy said, ''but that's no problem. The antiviral drugs are here and so are the antibiotics. Give me about ten minutes and I'll have what I need.''

Jesse turned to Cassy. "Let's you and I get those provisions," he said.

Cassy and Jesse went back to the front of the store and got bags. Then they started down the appropriate aisles. Cassy selected the items while Jesse played porter.

They were in the middle of the pasta section when Jesse slipped on fluid spilled from a broken bottle. The fluid had made the vinyl floor as slippery as ice.

Cassy managed to grab his arm to help keep him upright. Even after he regained his balance, his feet continued to slide around, forcing him to walk with his legs wide apart. It was like a comedy routine.

Cassy bent over and looked at the bottle. "No wonder," she said. "It's olive oil. So be careful!"

"Careful is my middle name," Jesse said. "How do you think I lasted thirty years as a cop?" He smiled and shook his head. "Funny, I'd been hoping for one big last hurrah before retiring. But I got to tell you, this episode is a lot more than I bargained for."

"It's a lot more than any of us bargained for," Cassy added.

They rounded the corner and entered the aisle with all the cereals. Cassy had to push through an enormous pile of boxes which included some large cardboard containers. All all at once she sucked in her breath as if shocked. Jesse was at her side in an instant.

"What's the matter?" he demanded.

Cassy pointed. In the middle of what had been a crude hut constructed from the boxes was the cherubic face of a young boy. He was no more than five years old. His skin was smudged and his clothing disheveled.

"Good Lord!" Jesse blurted out. "What's he doing in here?"

Cassy instinctively bent down to pick the child up. Jesse grabbed her arm.

"Hold on," Jesse said. "We don't know anything about him."

Cassy made a motion to free her arm, but Jesse held firm.

"He's only a child," Cassy said. "He's terrified."

"But we don't know . . ." Jesse began.

"We can't just leave him here," Cassy said.

Reluctantly Jesse let go of Cassy's arm. Cassy bent over and extracted the child from his house of cereal boxes. The boy instinctively clung to Cassy, burying his face in the crook of her neck.

"What's your name?" Cassy asked the child while gently patting his back. She was surprised by the strength with which he held her.

Cassy and Jesse exchanged glances. They were both thinking the same thing: How was this unexpected event going to impact their already desperate situation?

"Come on, now," Cassy said to the child. "Everything is going to be okay. You're safe, but we need to know your name so we can talk to you."

Slowly the child leaned back.

Cassy smiled warmly at the boy and was about to reassure him again when she noticed the child was smiling as if ecstatic. And even more shocking were his eyes. His pupils were enormous, and they glowed as if illuminated from within.

Feeling an instinctive wave of revulsion Cassy bent over to put the child down. She tried to maintain hold of his arm, but he was unexpectedly strong and twisted from her grip and scurried away toward the front of the store.

"Hey!" Jesse called out. "Come back here!" Jesse started after the boy.

"He's infected," Cassy yelled.

"I know," Jesse said. "That's why I don't want him to get away."

Running down the aisle in the half light was not easy for Jesse. The soles of his shoes still had traces of olive oil, making traction difficult. On top of that were all the cans, bottles, and boxes of scattered merchandise.

The boy seemed to have no problem navigating the obstacles and reached the front of the store well before Jesse. Positioning himself before one of the broken windows, he raised his chubby hand and opened his fingers. A black disc immediately levitated off his palm and disappeared out into the night.

Jesse reached the boy out of breath from all the slipping and sliding he'd been doing. He was also limping slightly from a bruise on his hip. He'd taken a fall near one of the cash registers and had collided with a can of tomato soup.

"Okay, son," Jesse said, trying to catch his breath as he turned the boy around. "What's the story. Why are you in here?"

Sporting the same exaggerated smile the child gazed up into Jesse's face. He didn't say a word.

"Come on, boy," Jesse said. "I'm not asking much."

Cassy came up behind Jesse and looked over his shoulder.

"What did he do?" she asked.

"Nothing as far as I can tell," Jesse said. "He just ran up here and stopped. But I wish he'd wipe that smile off his face. I feel like he's mocking us."

Both Cassy and Jesse saw the headlights at the same moment. A vehicle had turned into the supermarket's parking lot and was coming toward them.

"Oh no!" Jesse said. "Just what we didn't want: company."

It was immediately apparent that the vehicle was coming at a high rate of speed. Both Cassy and Jesse instinctively took several steps backward. A screech of tires against the asphalt heralded the car's sudden halt directly in front of the store. The high beams flooded the interior with blinding light. Both Cassy and Jesse held up their hands to shield their eyes. The child ran toward the light and disappeared in its glare.

"Get Nancy and get out the back of the store!" Jesse forcibly whispered.

"What about you?" Cassy asked.

"I'll keep them company," Jesse said. "If I'm not back at the rendezvous location in fifteen minutes, leave without me. I'll find another vehicle to get back."

"Are you sure?" Cassy questioned. She did not like the idea of leaving without Jesse.

"Of course I'm sure," Jesse snapped. "Now get!"

Cassy's eyes had adjusted enough so that she could just make out indistinct figures climbing down from either side of the vehicle. The headlights' intensity still precluded seeing any details.

Cassy turned and fled back into the depths of the store. Halfway up the aisle, she turned momentarily to see Jesse stepping out through the broken window, heading directly into the blinding light.

Cassy ran as best she could and purposefully collided with the grate separating the pharmacy section from the market. Gripping it with her hands she noisily shook it and called out for Nancy. Nancy's head popped up from behind the pharmacy desk. Nancy immediately saw the light coming from the front of the store.

"What's going on?" she demanded.

Cassy was breathless. "Trouble," she said. "We got to get out of here."

"Okay," Nancy said. "I've got everything anyway." She came from behind the counter and tried to push through the hole in the mesh. The cut ends of the wires had other ideas, and she was snagged.

"Here, take this," Nancy said, handing her sack of drugs to Cassy. Using both hands she tried to extract herself. She found it was not easy.

The light coming from the front of the store was suddenly dramatically augmented. At the same time a whooshing sound commenced and rapidly increased. When it reached earsplitting levels it cut off with such suddenness that its concussive effect knocked some teetering merchandise off shelving.

"Oh no!" Nancy moaned.

"What?" Cassy demanded.

"That was the sound when Eugene was consumed," Nancy said. "Where's Jesse?"

"Come on!" Cassy yelled. "We have to get out of here."

She put down the parcel Nancy had given her and tried to pull back the edges of the wire mesh. Flashlight beams began sweeping around the inside of the store.

"Go!" Nancy cried. "Take the package and run!"

"Not without you," Cassy said, struggling with the stiff wire.

"All right," Nancy said. "You hold this side, and I'll push the other." Working together they were at last able to free Nancy.

Nancy grabbed the bag of drugs and together they began to run along the back of the store. They didn't have a specific destination. They were merely counting on the store having a back entrance. Instead all they found was an interminable frozen food bin.

Reaching the far corner, they turned into the first aisle and headed forward. They thought that by running along the periphery of the building they'd eventually find a door. But they didn't get far. Ahead a shadowy group of people rounded the corner. Most were carrying flashlights.

A simultaneous whimper of fear escaped from both Cassy's and Nancy's lips. What made the group particularly frightening was their eyes. They glowed in the dim light of the store like distant galaxies in a night sky.

Cassy and Nancy simultaneously reversed directions only to be confronted by a second group coming from behind. Huddling together they waited as the two groups closed in on them. When the people were close enough for the women to see their features, it was obvious they were equally divided between male and female, elderly and young. What they had in common was their glowing eyes and their plastic smiles.

For a few moments nothing happened except the infected people completely surrounded the women and pressed in on them. Cassy and Nancy were back to back with their hands clasped over their mouths. Nancy had dropped her bag of drugs.

Terrified at being touched, Cassy screamed when one of the infected people suddenly lunged for her and grabbed her wrist.

"Cassy Winthrope, I presume," the man said with a

short laugh. "This is indeed a pleasure. You have been
missed."

PITT DRUMMED HIS FINGERS ON THE STEERING WHEEL OF
Jesse's van. Jonathan fidgeted in the passenger seat. Both
were anxious.

"How long as it been now?" Jonathan asked.

"They are twenty-five minutes late," Pitt said.

"What are we going to do?"

"I don't know," Pitt said. "If anybody was going to
have trouble I thought it would have been us."

"As long as we kept smiling, nobody seemed to care
what the hell we did," Jonathan said.

"Stay here!" Pitt said suddenly. "I got to check on that
supermarket. If I'm not back here in fifteen minutes, drive
back to the cabin."

"But how will you get back?" Jonathan whined.

"There's plenty of deserted vehicles around," Pitt said.
"That won't be the problem."

"But . . ."

"Just do it," Pitt snapped. He climbed out of the van
and quickly descended the bluff. He emerged from the trees
on a deserted street and set out toward the supermarket. He
estimated he had about six blocks before he'd have to turn
for the final block.

Ahead an individual came out of a building and turned
in Pitt's direction. Pitt could see his eyes glowing. Suppressing an urge to flee Pitt coaxed his face into a broad
smile just as he and Jonathan had done in the medical center. Having already smiled so much his facial muscles were
sore.

Pitt found it was nerve-racking to walk directly at the
changed person. He had to concentrate not only on the
smile but also in keeping his eyes directly ahead. He and
Jonathan had learned the hard way that any eye contact was
viewed suspiciously.

The man passed without incident, and Pitt breathed a
sigh of relief. What a way to live, he mused sadly. How
long could they survive this cat and mouse game?

Pitt rounded the corner and approached the supermarket. The first thing he saw was a group of cars parked directly in front of the store. What worried him was the fact that their lights were on. As he got closer he could hear their engines were running as well.

Reaching the edge of the parking lot, Pitt saw a tight group of people emerge from the store and begin to climb into the cars. Soon the sound of slamming car doors reached him.

Pitt dashed ahead and ducked into the shadowy doorway of a building at the edge of the entrance to the supermarket's parking lot. Almost immediately the cars began moving and turned in his direction. As they gathered speed they formed into a single line. Pitt pressed himself back into his hiding place as the lights of the leading car swept across the front of him.

Moments later the first of the six cars passed within twenty feet of Pitt. It hesitated momentarily before turning out into the street, giving Pitt a fleeting look at the smiling faces of infected occupants.

Each car in turn passed. As the last car hesitated, Pitt caught his breath. A shiver of abject horror passed down his spine. Seated in the backseat was Cassy!

Unable to restrain himself and without considering the consequences, Pitt took a step forward as if he'd planned on racing to the car and yanking open the door. The low-level ambient light washed over him, and at that moment Cassy glanced in his direction.

For the briefest fraction of a second their eyes met. Pitt urged himself forward, but Cassy shook her head and the moment passed. The car lurched forward and quickly accelerated off into the night.

Pitt staggered back against the darkened door. He was furious with himself for not having done anything. Yet deep down he knew it would have been hopeless. All he could see when he closed his eyes was the image of Cassy's face framed in the car window.

17

THE DAZZLING DESERT NIGHT SKY THAT HAD BEEN AWASH
with stars was fast fading to shades of pinkish blue as the
promise of another day brightened the eastern sky. Dawn
was coming.

Beau had been on the terrace off the master bedroom
enjoying the night air since he'd heard the good news. Now
he was impatiently waiting for the last few minutes to pass.
He knew the meeting was imminent since he'd seen the car
come along the driveway and disappear from view in front
of the mansion.

Beau heard footfalls through the bedroom and the sound
of the latch on the French doors opening. But he didn't turn
around. He kept his eyes rooted at the place on the horizon
where the sun was about to appear for a new day, a new
beginning.

"You have company," Alexander said. Then he withdrew and closed the doors behind him.

Beau watched the first golden rays of sun sparkle forth.
He felt a curious stirring in his body that in one sense he
understood but in another sense he found mysterious and
threatening.

"Hello, Cassy," Beau said, breaking the silence. Slowly
he turned around. He was dressed in a dark velvet robe.

Cassy lifted her hands to shield the rays of the sun which silhouetted Beau's face. She couldn't see his features.

"Is that you, Beau?" she asked.

"Of course it is I," Beau said. He moved forward.

Suddenly Cassy could see him clearly and she caught her breath. He'd mutated further. The small patch of skin behind his ear she'd inadvertently seen on her previous visit had spread to the front of his neck up to the line of his jaw. Some fingers of it had even spread up onto his cheeks in a serpiginous margin. His scalp was a patchwork quilt of thinning hair and alien skin. His mouth, although still smiling, was now pinched and thin-lipped, and his teeth had receded and yellowed. His eyes were black holes with no irises, and they blinked continuously, with the lower lid rising up rather than vice versa.

Cassy shrank back in utter horror.

"Don't be afraid," Beau said. He moved up to her and placed his arms around her.

Cassy stiffened. Beau's fingers felt like snakes as they wrapped around portions of her body. And there was an indescribable feral odor.

"Please, Cassy, don't be afraid," Beau said. "It's only me, Beau."

Cassy didn't respond. She had to struggle against an almost irresistible urge to scream.

Beau leaned back, forcing her to again look into his transmogrified face.

"I've missed you so much," Beau said.

With a sudden, unexpected burst of energy, Cassy screamed and pushed herself free. The move caught Beau completely by surprise. "How could you say you missed me?" Cassy cried. "You're not Beau any longer."

"But I am," Beau said soothingly. "I will always be Beau. But I'm also something more. I am a mixture of my former human self and a species almost as ancient as the galaxy itself."

Cassy warily eyed Beau. One part of her told her to flee, another part was paralyzed by the horror of it all.

"You will be part of the new life as well," Beau said.

"Everyone will be a part, at least those who are not harboring some terrible genetic flaw. I just had the honor of being the first, but it was a random event. It could have been you or anyone else."

"So, am I talking with Beau now?" Cassy asked. "Or am I talking with the virus's consciousness through the medium of Beau?"

"The answer, as I've already said, is both," Beau said patiently. "But the alien consciousness increases with every person changed. The alien consciousness is a composite of all the infected humans just like a human brain is a composite of its individual cells."

Beau reached out tentatively to avoid frightening Cassy any more than she already was. Compressing his snakelike fingers into a fist of sorts he stroked her cheek.

Cassy had to steel herself against the revulsion she felt to allow this creature to caress her.

"I must make a confession," Beau said. "At first I tried not to think about you. Initially it was easy because of the work that had to be done. But you kept creeping back into my thoughts and made me comprehend the beguiling power of human emotion. It is a weakness unique in the galaxy.

"The human in me loves you, Cassy, and I'm excited about the prospect of being able to give you many worlds. I long for you to want to be one of us."

"THEY ARE NOT COMING," SHEILA SAID. "AS PAINFUL AS that reality is, I'm afraid we're going to have to accept it." She stood up and stretched. It had been a sleepless night.

Through the cabin's windows the early morning sun could be seen bathing the tops of the trees on the western shore of the lake. The surface of the lake was covered with a mist that the rising sun would quickly dissipate.

"And if that's reality," Sheila added, "then we have to get our asses out of here before we have uninvited visitors."

Neither Pitt nor Jonathan responded. They were sitting on opposing couches, slouched forward with their chins cradled in their hands and elbows resting on their knees.

Their expressions were a mixture of exhaustion, disbelief, and grief.

"Well, we don't have time to take everything," Sheila was saying. "But I think we should take all the data and the tissue cultures that we hope are producing some virions."

"What about my mom?" Jonathan said. "And Cassy and Jesse? What if they come back here looking for us?"

"We've been over this," Sheila said. "Let's not make it more difficult than it already is."

"I don't think we should leave either," Pitt said. Although he'd given up hope about Cassy, he still thought Nancy and Jesse might appear.

"Listen, you two," Sheila said. "Two hours ago you agreed we'd wait until dawn. Now it's dawn. The longer we wait the more chance there is that we will be caught."

"But where will we go?" Pitt asked.

"I'm afraid we'll have to play it by ear," Sheila said. "Come on, let's start getting things ready."

Pitt pushed himself off the couch and stood up. He looked at Sheila, and his expression mirrored his great pain. She softened, stepped over to the couch, and gave him a hug.

Jonathan got up with sudden resolve and went over to his laptop. Flipping it open he began rapidly typing. After sending his message, he stared blankly at the screen. Within minutes an answer came back.

"Hey," he called out to Sheila and Pitt. "I just contacted Dr. M. He's changed his mind. He's willing to meet us. What do you say?"

"I'm naturally skeptical," Sheila admitted. "The idea of putting our lives into the hands of somebody we only know as Doc M sounds absurd. But then again, he's been sending us intriguing data."

"It's not as if we have a lot of choices," Jonathan said.

"Let me see his latest message," Pitt said. He moved over to Jonathan and read over his shoulder. Finishing, he glanced up at Sheila. "I think we should take the chance. I can't imagine he's not legitimate. Hell, Dr. M has been as scared about us as we've been about him.''

"It's better than just going out on the road and wandering around," Jonathan said. "Besides, he's obviously connected to the Internet. That means we can leave a message here, so if my mom or the others come back they'll at least be able to contact us."

"All right, you two," Sheila said, relenting. "I suppose it is a compromise. We'll meet this Dr. M, but it means getting the hell out of here, so let's get cracking."

"CASSY, I KNOW IT IS HARD FOR YOU," BEAU SAID. "I don't look at myself in the mirror any more. But you have to get beyond that."

Cassy was leaning on the balustrade, looking out over the halcyon view of the institute's grounds. The sun had come up and the morning dew was just about gone. Out in the driveway there was a steady single-file stream of infected people who were arriving from around the globe.

"We are building an amazing environment here," Beau said. "And it is about to spread around the world. It's truly a new beginning."

"I was partial to our old world," Cassy said.

"You can't mean that," Beau said. "Not with all the problems there were. Humans had steered the Earth into a collison course with self-destruction, especially over the last half century. And that shouldn't be, because the Earth is an amazing place. There are innumerable planets in the galaxy but few as warm and wet and as inviting as this one."

Cassy closed her eyes. She was exhausted and needed sleep, yet some of the things Beau was saying did make a modicum of sense. She forced herself to try to think. "When did the virus first come to Earth?" she asked.

"The very first invasion?" Beau asked. "About three billion Earth years ago. It was back when conditions on Earth had reached a point where life was evolving at a fairly rapid clip. An explorer ship released the virions into the primordial seas, and they incorporated into the evolving DNA."

"And this is the first time that a probe ship has returned?" Cassy asked.

"Heavens no," Beau said. "Every hundred million Earth years or so, a probe would return to reawaken the virus and see what form of life had evolved."

"And the virus consciousness didn't remain?" Cassy asked.

"The virus itself remained," Beau said. "But you are right, the consciousness was allowed to lapse. The organisms were always so inconvenient."

"When was the last stopover?" Cassy asked.

"Just about a hundred million Earth years ago," Beau said. "It was a disastrous visit. The Earth had become completely infested with large, reptilian creatures who preyed on each other cannibalistically."

"You mean dinosaurs?" Cassy asked.

"Yes, I believe that is what you have labeled them," Beau said. "But whatever the name, it was a totally unacceptable situation for consciousness. So the infestation was terminated. However, genetic adjustments were made so that the reptilians would die out to allow other species to evolve."

"Like human beings," Cassy suggested.

"Exactly," Beau said. "These are wonderfully versatile bodies and reasonably sized brains. The downside is the emotions."

Cassy let out a short laugh in spite of herself. The concept of an alien culture capable of ranging around the galaxy having trouble with human emotion was preposterous.

"It's true," Beau said. "Primacy of the emotions translates to an exaggerated importance of the individual, which is contrary to the collective good. From my dual perspective it is amazing humans have accomplished as much as they have. In a species in which each individual is striving to maximize his circumstance above and beyond basic needs, war and strife are inevitable. Peace becomes the aberration."

"How many other species in the galaxy has the virus taken over?" Cassy asked.

"Thousands," Beau said. "Whenever we find a suitable envelope."

Cassy continued to stare out into the distance. She didn't want to look at Beau because his appearance was so disturbing that it made it difficult to think, and she wanted to think. She couldn't help but believe that the more she knew the better chance she had of avoiding infection and staying herself. And she was learning a lot. The longer she'd talked with Beau the less she was hearing the human side and the more she was hearing the alien side.

"Where do you come from?" Cassy asked suddenly.

"Where is our home planet?" Beau repeated as if he'd not heard her question. He hesitated, trying to draw upon the collective information available to him. But the answer wasn't forthcoming. "I guess I don't know. I don't even know what our original physical form was. Strange! The question has never come up."

"Does it ever occur to the virus that it is somehow wrong to take over an organism that already has a consciousness?" Cassy asked.

"Not when we are offering something far better," Beau said.

"How can you be so sure?" Cassy asked.

"Simple," Beau said. "I refer back to your history. Look at what you have done to each other and to this planet during your short reign as the dominant creature."

Cassy nodded. Again there was some sense in what she was hearing.

"Come with me, Cassy," Beau said. "There is something I want to show you." Beau went to the door leading to the bedroom and opened it.

Cassy made herself turn around. She steeled herself against Beau's appearance, which she found almost as shocking as when she'd first seen him. He was holding the door for her. He gestured and said, "It's downstairs."

They descended the main stairs. In contrast with the tranquility upstairs, the first floor was filled with busy, smiling people. No one paid any attention to Beau and Cassy. He took her to the ballroom where the level of the activity was almost frantic. It was difficult to comprehend how so many people could work together.

The floor, walls, and ceiling of the enormous room were covered with a maze of wiring. In the middle of the space was a huge structure that appeared to Cassy to be of an otherworldly design and purpose. At its core was a huge steel cylinder that looked vaguely reminiscent of a very large MRI machine. Steel girders angled off in various directions. This superstructure supported what looked to Cassy like equipment for the storage and transmission of high-voltage electricity. A command control center was off to the side, containing a bewildering number of monitors, dials, and switches.

At first Beau didn't speak. He just allowed Cassy to be overwhelmed by the scene.

"It is nearly finished," Beau said finally.

"What is it?" Cassy asked.

"It is what we call a Gateway," Beau said. "It is a formal connection to other worlds that we have infested."

"What do you mean, connection?" Cassy asked. "Is this some communication device?"

"No," Beau said. "Transportation, not communication."

Cassy swallowed. Her throat had gone dry. "You mean other species from other planets that you, I mean, the virus has infected. They will be able to come here. To Earth!"

"And we there," Beau said triumphantly. "The Earth will henceforth be linked to these other worlds. Its isolation is over. It will truly become part of the galaxy."

Cassy felt suddenly weak. The horror of the Earth being invaded by countless alien creatures was now added to the personal fear she had for herself. Combining this with the frantic swirl of nightmarish activity around her and her physical, emotional, and mental exhaustion, Cassy swooned. The room begin to spin and darken, and she fainted.

When she came to, Cassy had no idea how long she'd been unconscious. The first thing she was aware of was a slight nauseousness, but it quickly passed after a shiver.

The next thing she sensed was that her right hand was balled into a fist and held firmly.

Cassy's eyes blinked open. She was on the floor in the busy ballroom looking up at a portion of the futuristic, jury-rigged contraption that was allegedly capable of transporting alien creatures to Earth.

"You're going to be okay," Beau said.

Cassy shuddered. It was the cliché that was always told to the patient no matter what the prospective prognosis. Cassy let her eyes fall toward Beau. He was kneeling next to her, clutching her fist closed. That was when Cassy realized there was something in her palm, something heavy and cold.

"No," Cassy cried. She tried to pull her hand free, but Beau would not let it go.

"Please, Beau," Cassy cried.

"Don't be afraid," Beau said soothingly. "You will be content."

"Beau, if you love me don't do this," Cassy said.

"Cassy, calm down," Beau said. "I do love you."

"If you have any control over your actions, let go of my hand," Cassy said. "I want to be myself."

"You will be," Beau said assuringly. "And much more. I do have control. I'm doing what I want. I want the power that has been given me, and I want you."

"Ahhh!" Cassy cried.

Beau immediately let go of her hand. Cassy sat up and with an exclamation of disgust threw the black disc away from herself. It skidded on a small patch of floor before thumping into a bundle of wires.

Cassy grabbed her injured hand with the other and looked at the slowly enlarging drop of blood at the base of her index finger. She'd been stung, and the crushing realization of what that meant caused her to collapse back onto the floor. A single tear rolled out from beneath each eyelid and ran off on either side of her face. She was now one of them.

18

THE GAS STATION LOOKED LIKE A MOVIE SET IN THE NINE-teen-thirties or the cover of an old *Saturday Evening Post* magazine. There were two old skinny gas pumps that resembled miniature skyscrapers with art deco round tops. In the middle of the tops an image of a red Pegasus still could be discerned despite the peeling paint.

The building behind the pumps was of the same vintage. It defied belief it was still standing. Over the last half century the sand blowing in off the desert had scoured the clapboards of any vestige of paint. The only thing that was reasonably intact was the old asphalt shingle roof. The screen door minus its screens blew back and forth in the hot breeze: a standing tribute to the longevity of its hardware.

Pitt pulled the van over to the side of the road opposite the dilapidated station so that they could look at it.

"What a Godforsaken place," Sheila commented, wiping the sweat out of her eyes. The desert sun was just beginning to give evidence of its noonday power.

They were on an essentially abandoned two-lane road that at one time had been a major route across the Arizona desert. But the interstate twenty miles to the south had changed that. Now cars rarely ventured along this rutted tarmac, as evidenced by the encroaching wisps of sand.

"This is where he said he'd meet us," Jonathan said. "And it is exactly as he described it, screen door and all."

"Well, where is he?" Pitt asked. He ran his eyes around the distant horizon. Except for a few lonely mesas in the distance, there was nothing but flat desert in every direction. The only movement visible was that of clumps of tumbleweed.

"Maybe we should just sit and wait," Jonathan suggested. He was finding it difficult to keep his eyes open from lack of sleep.

"There's no cover out here whatsoever," Pitt said. "It gives me the willies."

"Maybe we should look inside the broken-down station house," Sheila said.

Pitt restarted the van, pulled across the road, and parked between the ancient gas pumps and the dilapidated building. They all eyed the structure with unease. There was something about it that was spooky, particularly with the screen door opening and closing repeatedly. Now that they were close enough they could hear the aged hinges squeaking. The small paned windows, which were surprisingly intact, were too filthy to see through.

"Let's take a look inside," Sheila said.

Hesitantly they climbed out of the van and warily approached the porch. There were two old rocking chairs whose cane seats had long ago rotted out. Next to the door was the rusting hulk of an old-style, ice-cooled Coke dispenser. The sliding lid was open and the interior was filled with all manner of debris.

Pitt propped open the screen door and tried the interior door. It was unlocked. He pushed it open.

"You guys coming or what?" Pitt asked.

"After you," Sheila said.

Pitt stepped inside followed by Jonathan and then Sheila. They stopped just over the threshold and glanced around. With the dirty windows the light was meager. There was a metal desk to the right with a calendar behind it. The year was 1938. The floor was littered with dirt, sand, broken bottles, old newspaper, empty oil cans, and old car parts. Cobwebs hung like Spanish moss from portions of the ceiling joists. To the left was a doorway. The paneled door was partially ajar.

"Looks like nobody's been in here for a long time," Pitt said. "You think this supposed meeting was some kind of setup?"

"I don't think so," Jonathan said. "Maybe he's waiting for us in the desert, watching us to make sure we're okay."

"Where could he be watching us from?" Pitt asked. "It's as flat as a pancake outside." He walked over to the partially opened door and pushed it open all the way. Its hinges protested loudly. The second room was even darker than the first, with only one small window. The walls were lined with shelving, suggesting it had been a storeroom.

"Well, I'm not sure it makes a hell of a lot of difference if we find him or not," Sheila said dejectedly. She nudged some of the trash on the floor with her foot. "I was holding out hope that since he was giving us some interesting information, he had access to a lab or something. Needless to say we're not going to be able to do any work in a place like this. I think we'd better move on."

"Let's wait a little while," Jonathan said. "I'm sure this guy is legit."

"He told us he'd be here when we got here," Sheila reminded Jonathan. "He either lied to us or . . ."

"Or what?" Pitt asked.

"Or they got to him," Sheila said. "By now he could be one of them."

"That's a happy thought," Pitt said.

"We have to deal with reality," Sheila said.

"Wait a second," Pitt said. "Did you hear that?"

"What?" Sheila asked. "The screen door?"

"No, it was something else," Pitt said. "A scraping noise."

Jonathan reached up and felt the top of his head. "Something's fallen on me. Dust or something." He looked up. "Uh oh, there's someone up there."

Everyone looked up. Only now did they appreciate that

there was no ceiling. Above the rafters it was darker than
below in the room. But now that their eyes had adjusted to
the low level of illumination they could just make out a
figure in the attic space, standing on the joists.

Pitt reached down and snatched up a tire iron from the
debris on the floor.

"Drop it," a raspy voice called down. With surprising
speed the figure dropped out of the attic by swinging down
on one hand. In his other hand he held an impressive Colt
.45. He studied his visitors with a steady eye. He was a
man in his early sixties with ruddy skin, curly gray hair,
and a wiry frame.

"Drop the club," the man repeated.

Pitt abandoned the tire iron by tossing noisily onto the
floor and held up his hands.

"I'm Jumpin Jack Flash," Jonathan said excitedly while
repeatedly tapping his chest. "It was my name on the Internet. Are you Dr. M?"

"I might be," the man said.

"My real name is Jonathan. Jonathan Sellers."

"I'm Dr. Sheila Miller."

"And I'm Pitt Henderson."

"Were you checking us out?" Jonathan asked. "Is that
why you were hiding up in the rafters?"

"Maybe," the man said. Then he motioned for his three
guests to move into the storeroom.

Pitt was hesitant. "We're friends. Really we are. We're
normal people."

"Get!" the man said while extending the pistol toward
Pitt's face.

Pitt had never seen a .45 before, particularly not from
the point of view of looking directly down the dark, threatening barrel.

"I'm going," Pitt said.

"All of you," the man said.

Reluctantly everyone crowded into the dark storeroom.

"Turn around and face me," the man said.

Fearful about what was going to happen, everyone did
as he was told. With throats that had gone completely dry

they eyed this sinewy man who'd literally dropped in on them. The man returned their stare. There was a moment of silence.

"I know what you are doing," Pitt said. "You're checking our eyes. You're looking to see if our eyes glow!"

The man nodded finally. "You're right," he said. "And I'm pleased to report, they don't shine at all. Good!" He holstered his .45. "My name's McCay. Dr. Harlan McCay. And I guess we'll be working together. I'm glad to see you people, really I am."

With great relief Pitt and Jonathan shadowed the man out into the sunlight where they shook hands enthusiastically. Sheila followed but seemed irritated over the initial reception. She complained that he'd terrified her.

"Sorry," Harlan said. "I didn't mean to scare you, but being careful is a product of the times. But that's all behind us now. Let's get you over to where you'll be working. I'm afraid we don't have a lot of time if we're going to have any effect whatsoever."

"You have a lab or someplace to work?" Sheila questioned. Her mood brightened.

"Yeah," Harlan said. "I got a little lab. But we need to drive a ways. It'll take about twenty minutes." He opened the van's slider and climbed in. Pitt got behind the wheel. Sheila took the front passenger seat, and Jonathan joined Harlan.

Pitt started the van. "Where to?" he asked.

"Straight on," Harlan said. "I'll let you know when to turn."

"Were you in private practice before all this trouble?" Sheila asked as the van pulled out into the road.

"Yes and no," Harlan said. "The first part of my professional life was spent at UCLA in an academic position. I was trained in internal medicine with a subspecialty in immunology. But about five years ago I realized I was burned out, so I came out here and started a general practice in a little town called Paswell. It's just a blip on the map. I worked a lot with Native Americans on the surrounding reservations."

"Immunology!" Sheila commented. She was impressed. "No wonder you were sending us such interesting stuff."

"I could say the same to you," Harlan said. "What's your training?"

"Unfortunately mostly emergency medicine," Sheila admitted. "I did do an internal medicine residency, though."

"Emergency medicine!" Harlan commented. "Then I'm even more impressed with the sophistication of your data. I thought I was communicating with a fellow immunologist."

"I'm afraid I can't take the credit," Sheila said. "Jonathan's mother was with us then, and she was a virologist. She did most of the work."

"Sounds like I shouldn't be asking where she is now," Harlan said.

"We don't know where she is," Jonathan said quickly. "She went to a pharmacy last night to get some drugs and didn't come back."

"I'm sorry," Harlan said.

"She'll contact me on the Internet," Jonathan said, not about to give up hope.

They drove for a few minutes in silence. No one wanted to contradict Jonathan.

"Are we heading for Paswell now?" Sheila asked. The idea of being in a town had a lot of appeal. She wanted a shower and a bed.

"Heavens no," Harlan said. "Everybody's infected there."

"How did you manage to avoid being infected yourself?" Pitt asked.

"Dumb luck at first," Harlan said. "I happened to be with a friend at the moment he got stung by one of those black discs, so I avoided them like the plague. Then when I got an inkling of what was happening and that there wasn't anything I could do, I took to the desert. I've been out here ever since."

"How does being out here in the desert account for the data you were requesting and sending?" Sheila asked.

"I told you," Harlan said. "I got a little lab."

Sheila looked out her side of the van. The featureless desert stretched off toward distant mountains. There weren't any buildings, much less a biological laboratory. She began to worry about how many marbles Harlan McCay was dealing with beneath his shock of gray hair.

"I do have a bit of encouraging news," Harlan said. "Once you were able to give me the amino acid sequence of the enabling protein, and I was able to make some, I've developed a rather crude monoclonal antibody."

Sheila's head spun around. She studied the leathery-faced, blue-eyed, stubbled desert man with disbelief. "Are you sure?" she asked.

"Sure I'm sure," Harlan said. "But don't get bent out of shape, because it's not as specific as I'd like. But it works. The main point is that I've proven the protein is antigenic enough to elicit an antibody response in a mouse. I just have to select out a better B lymphocyte to make my hybridoma cell."

Pitt hazarded a quick glance at Sheila. Despite having had a number of advanced biology courses, Pitt had no idea what Harlan was talking about or even whether he was making sense. Yet Sheila was obviously extraordinarily impressed.

"To make a monoclonal antibody you need sophisticated reagents and materials, like a source of myeloma cells," Sheila said.

"No doubt," Harlan said. "Take a right up here, Pitt, just beyond that cactus."

"But there's no road," Pitt said.

"A mere technicality," Harlan said. "Turn anyway."

CASSY AWOKE FROM A SHORT NAP, GOT UP FROM THE BED, and went to the large, multipaned window. She was in a guest room on the second floor of the mansion facing south. To the left she could see a line of pedestrian traffic coming and going on the driveway. Directly ahead, her view of the grounds was limited by a tall, leafy tree. To the right she could see the tip of the terrace that surrounded the pool as

well as about a hundred yards of lawn before it butted up
against a pine forest.

She looked at her watch. She wondered when she would
start feeling ill. She tried to remember the interval that Beau
had experienced between being stung and his first symptoms, but she couldn't. All he'd told her was that he'd been
in class. She didn't know which class.

Returning to the door, she gave the knob another twist.
It was still locked as securely as when she'd been put in
the room. Turning around, she leaned against the door and
surveyed her surroundings. It was a generous bedroom with
a high ceiling, but except for the bed, it was completely
empty. And the bed itself consisted of a bare mattress on
a box spring.

The short nap had revived Cassy to a point. She felt a
mixture of depression and anger. She thought about lying
back on the bed but didn't think she could sleep. Instead
she returned to the window.

Noticing there was no lock, she tried the sash. To her
surprise it opened with ease. Leaning out the window, she
looked down. About twenty feet below was a flagstone
walkway that connected the back terrace with the front. It
was edged with a limestone balustrade. It would be a very
hard landing if she tried to jump, but she gave the idea
serious thought. Death might be preferable to becoming one
of them. The problem was, a twenty-foot fall would probably only maim, not kill.

Cassy raised her eyes and looked more carefully at the
tree. One stout branch in particular caught her attention. It
grew out of the main trunk, arched directly toward the window, then angled off to the right. Her interest was directed
at a short horizontal section that was about six or seven
feet away from where she was standing.

The question went through Cassy's mind whether she
could leap from the window, catch the branch, and hold
on. She didn't know. She'd never done anything like it in
her life and was surprised the idea even occurred to her.
Yet these were hardly normal circumstances, and she
quickly became intrigued. After all it seemed possible, es-

pecially with all the working out with weights she'd been doing over the last six months with Beau's encouragement.

Besides, Cassy thought, what if she missed? Her present prospects were dismal. Dashing herself against the balustrade didn't seem much worse and might do more than injure.

Climbing up on the windowsill, Cassy pushed the sash up to its full height to create an opening about five feet square. From that position the ground looked dramatically farther away.

She closed her eyes. Her heart was pounding, and she was breathing rapidly. Her courage vacillated. She recalled going to a circus as a child and seeing the trapeze artists and thinking she could never do anything like that. But then she thought of Eugene and Jesse and what Beau was becoming. She thought of the horror of losing her identity.

With sudden resolve, Cassy opened her eyes and leapt out into the air.

It seemed forever before she made contact. Perhaps drawing on some arboreal instincts she didn't realize she possessed, Cassy had judged the distance perfectly. Her hands made proper contact with the branch, and she grabbed on. Now the question became whether she could hold on as her legs swung beneath her.

There was a few moments of terror before her swinging came to a halt. She'd done it! But it wasn't over. She was still twenty feet off the ground, although now she was suspended over lawn, not flagstone.

Swinging her legs to help her, Cassy moved along the branch until she came to a point where she could get her right foot on a lower branch. From there it was relatively easy to work her way down the tree and eventually jump onto the grass.

The moment her feet touched the ground, Cassy was up and walking. She resisted the temptation to run out across the expansive lawn, knowing full well that it would only draw attention to herself. Instead she forced herself to assume a leisurely pace after climbing over the low balustrade. She followed the walkway to the front of the house.

Mimicking the smiles, the blank staring into the middle distance, and the relaxed walk, Cassy melded into the crowd of infected people heading out the driveway. Her heart was in her throat and she was terrified, but it worked. No one paid her any attention. The hardest part was forcing herself not to look around her, especially not at the dogs.

"HOW DO YOU KNOW WHERE WE ARE GOING?" PITT asked. They had traveled miles on a track that in places was barely discernable from the desert itself.

"We're almost there," Harlan said.

"Oh, please!" Sheila said impatiently. "We're in the middle of the damned desert. Without the paved road this is more Godforsaken than the area around that deserted gas station. Is this some kind of joke?"

"No joke," Harlan said. "Be patient! I'm giving you all a chance to help save the human race."

Sheila glanced over at Pitt, but his attention was glued to the track. Sheila sighed loudly. Just when she'd started feeling good about Harlan, it was becoming apparent he was taking them on a wild-goose chase. There was no lab out there in the desert. The whole situation was absurd.

"Okay," Harlan said. "Stop up there next to that flowering cactus."

Pitt did as he was told. He pulled on the brake and cut the engine.

"All right," Harlan said. "Everybody out." He opened the slider and stepped out onto the sand. Jonathan followed at his heels.

"Come on," Harlan encouraged the others.

Sheila and Pitt rolled their eyes for each other's benefit. They were parked in the middle of the desert. Except for a few scattered boulders, a handful of cacti, and some low rolling sand hills, there was nothing around them.

Harlan had walked about twenty feet away before turning back. He was surprised no one was following him. Jonathan had gotten out of the van, but since the others hadn't, he'd hesitated.

"For chrissake!" Harlan complained. "What d'ya need, a special invitation?"

Sheila sighed and alighted from the vehicle. Pitt followed suit. Then all three trudged after Harlan, who was striking out into nowhere land.

Sheila wiped her brow. "I don't know what to make of this," she whispered. "One minute this guy seems like a godsend, the next like a crackpot. And on top of that it's hotter than Hades."

Harlan stopped and waited for the others to catch up to him. He pointed down to the ground and said: "Welcome to the Washburn-Kraft Biological Warfare Reaction Laboratory."

Before anyone could respond to this preposterous statement, Harlan bent down and grasped a camouflaged ring. He pulled up and a circular portion of the desert floor lifted up. Beneath was a round opening lined with stainless steel. Just the tip of a ladder was visible.

Harlan made a sweeping gesture with his hand. "This whole area around here all the way to within a few miles of Paswell is honeycombed with underground facilities. It was supposed to be a big secret, but the Native Americans knew about it."

"It's an operational lab?" Sheila questioned. This indeed was too good to be true.

"It had been mothballed in kind of suspended animation," Harlan said. "It was built back in the height of the cold war but then deemed superflucus when the threat of germ warfare coming to the USA diminished. Except for a few bureaucrats who kept the thing stocked, it was pretty much forgotten about; at least that's my take on the situation. Anyway, after all this trouble started, I got into it and cranked it up to speed. So to answer your question: yes, it is an operational lab."

"And this is the entrance?" Sheila questioned. She leaned out over the rim of the opening and looked down. There were lights below. The ladder went straight down about thirty feet.

"No, this is an emergency exit plus an air vent," Harlan

said. "The real entrance is closer to Paswell, but I'm afraid to use that lest I be seen by some of my former patients."

"Can we go inside?" Sheila asked.

"Hey, that's what we're here for," Harlan said. "But before a tour I want to cover the van with a camouflage tarp."

They all climbed down the ladder to a white, high-tech corridor illuminated by banks of fluorescent lights. From a storage locker at the base of the ladder, Harlan got out the tarp he'd mentioned. Pitt returned topside with Harlan to give him a hand.

"Pretty cool," Jonathan said to Sheila while they waited. The corridor seemed to stretch off in either direction to infinity.

"Better than cool," Sheila said. "It's a godsend. And to think it was built to help thwart a germ-warfare attack by the Russians and instead is to be used to do the same thing for aliens is truly ironic."

When Harlan and Pitt returned back down, Harlan led them off in what he said was a northerly direction.

"It will take you a while to orient yourselves," he said. "Until then I recommend you stick together."

"Where are the people that kept this place up?" Sheila asked.

"They came in shifts like the guys that used to man the underground missile silos," Harlan said. "But after they got infected, I guess they either forgot about it or went off someplace. The talk in Paswell was that a lot of people were going to Santa Fe for some reason. Anyway they're not around, and by now I don't expect them."

They came to an air lock. Harlan opened it and had everybody climb into a chamber. Inside the chamber were showers and blue jump suits. Harlan closed the door, then twisted some dials. Air was heard entering the lock.

"This was to make sure none of the biological warfare agents got into the lab except in biohazard containers," Harlan said. "Obviously that's not our worry now."

"Where does the power come from?" Sheila asked.

"Nuclear," Harlan said. "It's kinda like a nuclear submarine. The whole place is independent of what's going on topside."

Everybody had to clear their ears as the pressure built up. When it was equalized with the interior of the lab, Harlan opened the inner door.

Sheila was flabbergasted. She'd never seen such a laboratory in her entire life. It was a series of three large rooms with walk-in incubators and freezers. Adding to her astonishment was the fact that all the equipment was state-of-the-art.

"These freezers are a little scary," Harlan said, tapping one of the stainless steel doors. "They contain just about every known potential biological agent, both bacterial and viral." He then pointed toward another door with large bolts like a walk-in safe. "In there is a library of chemical agents. One of James Bond's villians would have had a ball down here."

"What's through those doors?" Sheila asked, pointing to pressure-sealed hatches with round porthole windows.

"That goes into confinement rooms and a sick bay," Harlan said. "My guess is that they considered such a facility necessary in case any of the people working in here succumbed to whatever they were trying to vanquish."

"Look!" Jonathan said, pointing toward a row of black discs positioned beneath an exhaust hood.

"Don't touch those!" Harlan said anxiously.

"Don't worry," Jonathan said. "We know about them."

Everyone walked over and looked at the collection.

"They can do more than infect people," Sheila said.

"Don't I know," Harlan said. "Come with me. Let me show you something."

Harlan led everyone to a short corridor off of which were several X-ray rooms as well as an MRI scanner. He opened the door to the first X-ray room. Inside the machine had been twisted out of shape as if it had been melted and pulled inward.

"My God!" Sheila said. "This looks just like what happened in a room in the student overnight ward. Do you know how this happened?"

"I think so," Harlan said. "I tried to X-ray one of those black discs, and it didn't like it. This may sound crazy, but I think it created a miniature black hole. My guess is that's how they get here and how they leave."

"Cool," Jonathan said. "How can they do that?"

"I wish I knew," Harlan said. "But I'll tell you how I explained it to myself. Somehow they have the ability to generate enough internal energy to create an instantaneous huge gravitational field so they subatomically implode."

"So where do they go?" Jonathan asked.

"Now you have to go way out on a limb," Harlan said. "And perhaps subscribe to the wormhole theory of the cosmos. In that scenario they'd be in another parallel universe."

"Wow," Jonathan said.

"That's a bit too much for me," Pitt said.

"Me too," Sheila said. "Let's get back to the lab." As they returned she asked: "And there's mice and myeloma cells available down here for monoclonal antibody production?"

"We've got more than mice," Harlan said. "We've got rats, guinea pigs, rabbits, and even a few monkeys. In fact, half my time is taken up feeding the guys."

"What about living quarters?" Sheila asked. As tired and dirty as she was, she couldn't help but think about the pleasure of a shower and a nap.

"This way," Harlan said. He lead them out into the main corridor and through a pair of double doors. The first room they came to was a gigantic living room, complete with a large screen TV and an entire wall filled with books. Next to the living room was a dining area adjacent to a modern kitchen. Beyond the dining room and leading off a central corridor were multiple guest rooms, each with its own bath.

"Hey, this is okay," Jonathan said, seeing that each bedroom had its own computer terminal.

"This is good," Pitt said, eyeing the bed. "This is very good."

•   •   •

ONCE CASSY HAD GOTTEN AWAY FROM THE INSTITUTE, she'd been able to find a car with ease. There were hundreds of them simply abandoned as if many of the infected people weren't interested in them any longer. The people seemed to prefer walking.

As soon as she got to a phone she'd tried calling the cabin. After letting the phone ring twenty times, she'd given up. Obviously no one was there which could only mean one thing: they'd been discovered. Such a realization had been heartbreaking for Cassy, and for over an hour she'd sat in her commandeered car feeling depressed to the point of paralysis. Her wish to at least speak once more with Pitt and the others had been thwarted.

What finally pulled Cassy from the depths of her torpor was a sudden stinging sensation in her nose followed by a series of violent sneezes. Instantly she knew what was happening; the symptoms of the alien flu were starting.

Cassy went back to the telephone, and despite knowing it was in vain, tried calling the cabin again. As she'd expected, there was still no answer. But as the phone rang she thought that there was at least a small possibility that even if the cabin had been discovered, one or more might have gotten away. That was when she thought about what Jonathan had been so patient to teach her: logging onto the Internet.

By the time Cassy got back to the car, the discomfort she felt in her nose had spread down to her throat, and she began to cough. At first it was only a clearing of her throat, but it quickly progressed to a cough.

Cassy drove into the town. There was still some traffic, but it was slight. In contrast there were thousands of people walking about and busily involved with all the necessities of life. A lot of people were gardening. Everyone was smiling, and there was little conversation.

Cassy parked the car and got out onto the sidewalk. Although many businesses were still functioning, others were deserted as if the employees had just stood up at some arbitrary time and walked out the door. Nothing was locked.

One of the empty businesses was a dry-cleaning store. Cassy went inside but didn't find what she was looking for. Instead she found it next door in a copying concern. What she wanted was a computer connected to a modem.

Cassy sat down and activated the screen. When the employees had left they hadn't even turned the equipment off. Remembering Jonathan's Internet name, Jumpin Jack Flash, Cassy began typing.

"THIS IS ALL YOU HAVE?" SHEILA ASKED HARLAN. SHE was holding a small vial of clear fluid.

"That's it for now," Harlan said. "But I got a batch of mice with the hybridoma cells implanted in their peritoneal cavities as well as a bunch of cell cultures cooking in the incubator. We can certainly extract more of this monoclonal antibody. But it's only weakly active. I'd much rather try to find a more avid antibody-producing cell."

Sheila, Pitt, and Jonathan had taken showers and rested briefly, but were too wired to sleep. Sheila was especially anxious to get working and had urged Harlan to show her everything he'd done.

Jonathan and Pitt had tagged along. Pitt was having trouble following Harlan's explanations, whereas Jonathan didn't even try. Since he hadn't had much biology, it all sounded like Greek to him. Instead Jonathan ignored the others, sat down at one of the many terminals available, and started typing.

"I'll show you two the process used to select B lymphocytes from emulsified mouse spleen," Harlan said. "Provided you show me the virions you and Jonathan's mother isolated."

"We're not positive the virions are in the tissue culture," Sheila said. "We just suspect they are. We were just about ready to isolate them."

"Well, we can find out simply enough," Harlan said.

"Oh my God!" Jonathan called out suddenly.

Shocked by this outburst, everyone looked across at Jonathan. His eyes were glued to the monitor.

"What's the matter?" Pitt asked nervously.

"It's a message from Cassy!" Jonathan cried.

Pitt practically vaulted over a lab bench to get to Jonathan's side. He stared at the monitor with wide eyes.

"She's typing into the mail drop this instant," Jonathan said. "I mean this is a real-time phenomenon."

"This is fantastic," Pitt managed.

"What a cool girl," Jonathan said. "She's doing just like I taught her."

"What's she saying?" Sheila asked. "Is she saying where she is?"

"Oh no!" Jonathan said. "She says she's been infected."

"Damn!" Pitt agonized, gritting his teeth.

"She says she's already experiencing the first symptoms of the flu," Jonathan continued. "She wants to wish us good luck."

"Contact her!" Pitt shouted. "Now, live, before she signs off."

"Pitt, it's no use," Sheila said. "It will just make it more difficult. She's infected!"

"She might be infected, but obviously she's still Cassy," Pitt said. "Otherwise she wouldn't be wishing us good luck." He forcibly nudged Jonathan aside and started typing furiously.

Jonathan looked up at Sheila. Sheila shook her head. Although she knew it was wrong, she didn't have the heart to stop him.

FOR CASSY THE IMAGE ON THE MONITOR WAS INTERMITtently blurry. As she'd typed the tears had come. Closing her eyes for a moment and wiping them with the back of her hand, she tried to get herself under control. She wanted to leave one last message for Pitt. She wanted to tell him that she loved him.

Opening her eyes and returning her hands to the keyboard, Cassy was about to type her last sentence when a live message popped onto her screen. She gazed at it in astonishment. It said: "Cassy, it's me, Pitt. Where are you?"

• • •

IT WAS THE LONGEST FEW SECONDS OF PITT'S LIFE. HE GOG-gled at the monitor and willed it to respond. Then as if answering a prayer, the black characters began popping out of the luminous background.

"Yes!" Pitt shouted while punching the air with a fist. "I caught her. She knows I'm here."

"What is she saying?" Sheila ventured. She was afraid to ask because she was sure this contact was going to lead to heartache and trouble.

"She's saying she's not too far from here," Pitt said. "I'm going to tell her to meet me."

"Pitt, no!" Sheila shouted. "Even if she's not one of them now, she will be shortly. You can't take the chance. You certainly can't expose this lab."

Pitt looked over at Sheila. His emotional pain was palpable. His breaths were coming in short gasps. "I can't abandon her," he said. "I just can't."

"You must," Sheila said. "You saw what happened to Beau."

Pitt's fingers were poised above the keyboard. He'd never felt such heart-wrenching indecision.

"Wait," Harlan said suddenly. "Ask her how long it has been since she was stung."

"What difference does that make?" Sheila said angrily. She felt irritated that Harlan would interfere at such a moment.

"Just do it," Harlan said. He walked over to stand behind Pitt.

Pitt typed the question. The answer came back instantly: about four hours. Harlan looked at his watch and bit the inside of his cheek while thinking.

"What is going on inside your head?" Sheila demanded, looking Harlan in the eye.

"I have a little confession to make," Harlan said. "I wasn't telling the whole truth about those black discs. One of them did sting me when I was out collecting the last batch."

"Then you are one of them!" Sheila said with horror.

"No, at least I don't think so," Harlan said. "I tied my weak monoclonal antibody to the enabling protein, and I've been giving myself shots ever since. I've had the sniffles but no flu."

"That's fantastic," Pitt said. "Let me tell Cassy."

"Wait!" Sheila commanded. "How long after you were stung did you give yourself the antibody?"

"That's my only concern," Harlan said. "There was a three-hour interval. I was in Paswell at the time it happened. It took me three hours to get back here."

"Cassy has already been four," Sheila said. "What do you think?"

"I think it's worth a try," Harlan said. "We can put her in one of the containment rooms and see what happens. If it doesn't work out, there's no way she can get out of there. They're like dungeons."

Pitt didn't need any more encouragement. Without another word he began telling Cassy they had an antibody to the protein and giving her directions to the deserted gas station.

"Why didn't you tell us you'd been stung?" Sheila questioned. She didn't know whether to be angry or encouraged by this new development.

"To be honest," Harlan said, "I was afraid you wouldn't trust me that I was okay. I was going to tell you sooner or later. Actually the fact that it has seemingly worked makes me feel a bit optimistic."

"Well, I should say so!" Sheila said. "It's the first positive piece of information so far."

Pitt finished his communication with Cassy and came over to Sheila and Harlan.

"I hope you were as discreet as possible with the directions," Harlan said. "We certainly don't want a truckload of infected people to be there at the station waiting for you when you arrive."

"I tried to be," Pitt said. "But at the same time I wanted to make sure Cassy found the place. It is so isolated."

"Actually the risk is probably pretty small," Harlan said. "My feeling is that the infected people aren't using the Net.

They don't seem to need it since they appear to know what
each other are thinking."

"Aren't you coming with me?" Pitt asked Harlan.

"I don't think I'd better," Harlan said. "There's only a
partial dose of my antibody left. I'll have to get busy extracting more so that it's available when your friend gets
here. That means you'll have to find your own way. Think
you can do it?"

"Sounds like I don't have much choice," Pitt said.

Harlan handed Pitt the vial of what antibody he had
along with a syringe. "I hope you know how to give an
injection," he said.

Pitt commented that he thought he could do it because
he'd been clerking in the hospital for three years.

"You'd better give it IV," Harlan said. "But be prepared for some mouth to mouth if she has an anaphylatic
reaction."

Pitt visibly gulped, but he nodded.

"And you might as well take this," Harlan said, un-
buckling his holstered Colt .45. "My advice is to use it if
you have to. Remember, the infected people feel very
strongly about you being infected if they sense you aren't."

"What about me?" Jonathan asked. "I'll go with Pitt.
He might have trouble finding his way back here, and four
eyes will be better than two."

"I think you'd better stay here," Sheila said. "We can
find plenty for you to do." She rolled up her sleeves. "And
we are going to be very busy."

ONCE CASSY HAD BEEN LOCATED, BROUGHT TO THE INSTI-
tute, and subsequently infected, progress on the Gateway
speeded up. Although the thousands of workers didn't have
to be individually told what to do, ultimately their instructions came from Beau. Consequently it was necessary for
Beau to spend a good deal of time in the vicinity of the
construction and for his mind to be clear of extraneous
thoughts. With Cassy upstairs and soon to be one of the
infected, Beau found it easy to fulfill his responsibilities.

Progress had even reached a point where it was possible

to energize briefly a portion of the electrical grids. The test was a success although it did indicate that portions of the system needed further shielding. With those instructions communicated, Beau took a break.

He climbed the main stairs in a normal bipedal fashion, although he was conscious of the fact that it would probably be easier for him now to hop up, taking six or eight steps at a time. There had been considerable augmentation of his quadriceps.

Reaching the upper hall he sensed something was wrong. He hadn't felt it downstairs because the level of unspoken communication about the Gateway was so intense. But now that he was alone, it was different. By this time he should have been getting stirrings of Cassy's developing collective consciousness. Since there was none at all he feared she'd died.

Beau quickened his pace. His fear was that perhaps Cassy had been harboring some disastrous gene that had yet to express itself. In that case the virus would have self-destructed.

With a sense of panic that he didn't understand, Beau struggled to open the locked door. Bracing himself to see her lifeless body draped across the mattress, he was even more surprised to find the room empty.

Beau gazed at the open window. He walked over to it and looked down at the ground outside. He saw the walkway and the balustrade. Then his eyes went up the tree, and he looked at the branch. Suddenly he knew. She'd fled.

Letting out a shriek that echoed through the huge mansion, he rushed from the room and charged down the stairs. He was overcome with anger, and anger wasn't healthy for the collective good. The collective consciousness had rarely experienced anger, and it didn't know how to handle it.

Beau entered the ballroom and instantly all work came to a halt. All eyes turned to Beau, feeling the same anger but having no idea why. Beau's nostrils flared as his eyes searched for Alexander. He spotted him at the command control console.

Boldly Beau strode over to his lieutenant and clamped down on his arm with his snakelike fingers. "She is gone! I want her found! Now!"

19

PITT KICKED A FEW OF THE PEBBLES IN THE DRIVEWAY OF the old gas station. He bent down and picked up others and threw them absently at the ancient pumps. The stones clanged against the rusting metal.

Shielding his eyes from the sun, which was now significantly more formidable in its heat and intensity then two hours earlier, Pitt scanned the two-lane road to its vanishing point on the horizon. He began to worry. He'd thought she would have been there already.

Just when he was about to retreat back to the shade of the porch, his eye caught the glint of sunlight off a windshield. A vehicle was coming.

Unconsciously Pitt's hand slipped down to envelop the butt of the Colt. There was always the worry that it wasn't Cassy.

As the vehicle got closer, Pitt could make out that it was a late-model recreational vehicle with large tires and a built-in luggage rack on the top. It was coming fast.

For a moment Pitt contemplated hiding inside the building the way Harlan had done, but he dismissed the idea. After all, Jesse's van was sitting right there in plain sight.

The vehicle pulled into the station. Pitt wasn't sure it

was Cassy until she opened the door and called out to him. The windows were heavily tinted.

Pitt got to the vehicle in time to help Cassy down. She was coughing and her eyes were red-rimmed.

"Maybe you shouldn't get too close," Cassy said in a deeply nasal voice. "We don't know for sure whether this can spread person to person like an infection."

Ignoring her comment, Pitt enveloped her in an enthusiastic embrace. The only reason he let go of her was concern about her getting the antibody.

"I brought some of the medicine I mentioned on the Internet with me," Pitt said. "Obviously we think it is best to get it into your system as soon as possible and that means intravenous."

"Where should we do it?" Cassy asked.

"In the van," he said.

They walked around the vehicle to its slider.

"How are you feeling?" Pitt asked.

"Terrible," Cassy admitted. "I couldn't get comfortable in that four-by-four; the ride is so stiff. All my muscles ache. I've also got a fever. A half hour ago I was shivering, if you can believe it in this heat."

Pitt opened the van door. He had Cassy lie down on the van's seat. He prepared the syringe, but then, after putting on the tourniquet, he admitted his inexperience at venipuncture.

"I don't want to hear it," Cassy said, looking off in the opposite direction. "Just do it. I mean, you're going to be a doctor."

Pitt had seen medication administered IV thousands of times but never had tried it himself. The idea of puncturing another person's skin was daunting, much less a person he loved. But the consequences of not doing it overwhelmed any timidity he had. Ultimately it went well, and Cassy told him as much.

"You're just being a good sport," Pitt said.

"No, really," Cassy said. "I hardly felt it." No sooner had she complimented him that she had an explosive bout of coughing that left her gasping.

Pitt was momentarily terrified she was having a reaction to the shot as Harlan had warned. Although Pitt had had CPR training, he'd never actually done that, either. Anxiously he held her wrist to feel her pulse. Thankfully it stayed strong and regular.

"Sorry," Cassy managed when she could get her breath.

"Are you okay?" Pitt asked.

Cassy nodded.

"Thank God!" Pitt said. He swallowed to relieve a dry throat. "You stay here on the backseat. We've got about a twenty-minute drive."

"Where are we going?" Cassy asked.

"To a place that's like an answer to a prayer," Pitt said. "It's an underground lab built to deal with a biological or chemical warfare attack. It's perfect for what we have to do. I mean, if we can't do it there, then we can't do it. It's that good. Plus it has a sick bay where we can take care of you."

Pitt started to climb into the front seat when Cassy took hold of his arm. "What if this antibody doesn't work?" she said. "I mean, you warned me it was weak and very preliminary. What will you do with me if I turn into one of them? I don't want to jeopardize what you all are doing."

"Don't worry," Pitt said. "There's a doctor there named Harlan McCay who was stung and is still fine after getting the antibody. But if worst comes to worst, there are what he calls containment rooms. But everything is going to be fine." Pitt gave her shoulder a pat.

"Save the clichés, Pitt," Cassy said. "With everything that has happened, it can't turn out fine."

Pitt shrugged. He knew she was right.

Pitt got behind the wheel, started the van, and pulled out into the road. Cassy remained lying on the backseat. "I hope there's some aspirin where we're going," she said. She was as sick as she'd ever felt in her life.

"I'm sure there is," Pitt said. "If the sick bay is like the rest of the place, it's got everything."

They rode in silence for a few miles. Pitt was concen-

trating on the driving for fear of missing the turnoff. On
his way out he'd built a small cairn of rocks to mark it, but
now he was afraid it wouldn't help. The rocks had been
small and everything was the same color.

"I can't help but worry that my coming here was a bad
idea," Cassy said after another coughing spell.

"Don't talk that way!" Pitt said. "I don't want to hear
it."

"It's been more than six hours now," Cassy said.
"Maybe even more. I wasn't all that sure of the time when
I was stung. So much has been happening."

"What happened to Nancy and Jesse?" Pitt asked. It was
a question he'd avoided, but he wanted to change the subject.

"Nancy was stung," Cassy said. "They infected her in
my presence. I couldn't figure out why they didn't do it to
me until later. Jesse was a different story. I believe the same
thing happened to him as to Eugene. But I'm not sure. I
didn't see it. I just heard it, and there was a flash of light.
Nancy said it was the same as before."

"Harlan thinks those black discs can create miniature
black holes," Pitt said.

Cassy shuddered. The idea of disappearing down a black
hole seemed like the epitome of destruction. Even one's
atoms would be gone from the universe.

"I saw Beau again," Cassy said.

Pitt turned to glance at Cassy before looking back at the
road. It was the last thing he expected her to say.

"How was he?" Pitt asked.

"Horrid," Cassy said. "And he's changed visibly. He's
mutating progressively. Last time I saw him it was only a
patch of skin behind his ear. Now it's most of his body.
It's strange because the other infected people didn't seem
to be changing. I don't know if they will or if it has something to do with Beau being the first. He's definitely a
leader. They all do what he wants."

"Did he have anything to do with your being stung?"
Pitt asked.

"I'm afraid so," Cassy said. "He did it himself."

Pitt shook his head imperceptibly. He couldn't believe that his best friend could do such a thing, but then again he was no longer his best friend. He was an alien.

"The most horrid part for me was that there was still some of the old Beau inside," Cassy said. "He even told me that he missed me and that he loved me. Can you believe it?"

"No," Pitt said simply, while fuming that Beau, even as an alien, was still trying to take Cassy away from him.

BEAU WAS STANDING TO THE SIDE IN THE SHADOWS BEHIND the command control unit of the Gateway. His eyes were glowing fiercely. It was hard for him to concentrate on the problems at hand, but he had to. Time was running out.

"Maybe we should try to charge some of the electrical grids again," Randy called over to Beau. Randy was sitting at the controls. A minor glitch had developed, and as of yet, Beau had not suggested a solution.

Yanked from a daydream about Cassy, Beau tried to think. The problem from the beginning had been to create enough energy to turn the powerful, instantaneous gravity of a group of black discs working in concert into antigravity and still have the Gateway stay together. The reaction would only have to last a nanosecond as it sucked matter from a parallel universe into the current one. Suddenly the answer came to Beau; more shielding was needed.

"All right," Randy said, pleased to get some direction. He in turn alerted the thousands of workers who immediately swarmed back up into the superstructure on the gigantic construct.

"Do you think this will work?" Randy called over to Beau.

Beau communicated that he thought it would. He advised to power up all the electrical grids for an instant as soon as the augmented shielding was completed.

"What worries me is that you told me the first visitors are due tonight," Randy said. "It would be a calamity if we weren't ready. The individuals would be lost in the void as mere primary particles."

Beau grunted. He was more interested that Alexander had entered the room. Beau watched him approach. Beau didn't like the vibrations. He could tell they hadn't found her.

"We followed her spoor," Alexander reported. He purposefully stayed out of Beau's reach. "It led us to where she'd taken a vehicle. Now we're looking for the vehicle."

"You will find her!" Beau snarled.

"We will find her," Alexander repeated soothingly. "By now her consciousness should be expanding, and that will help us a great deal."

"Just find her," Beau said.

"YOU KNOW, I DON'T HAVE ANY EXPLANATION," SHEILA said.

She and Harlan were seated on laboratory stools on wheels that allowed them to zip from bench to bench.

Harlon had his chin cradled in his hand and was chewing the inside of his cheek. It was a habit he'd developed that indicated he was deep in thought.

"Could we have done something stupid?" Sheila asked.

Harlan shook his head. "We've been over our protocol several times. It wasn't technique. It has to be a real finding."

"Let's go over it once again," Sheila said. "Nancy and I had taken a tissue culture of human nasopharyngeal cells and added the enabling protein."

"What was the vehicle for the protein?" Harlan asked.

"Normal tissue culture medium," Sheila said. "The protein is fully soluble in an aqueous solution."

"All right, what next?" Harlan said.

"We simply let the culture incubate," Sheila said. "We could tell that the virus had been activated because of the rapid synthesis of DNA over and above what was needed for cell replication."

"How did you assay that?" Harlan asked.

"We used inactivated adenovirus to carry DNA probes labeled with fluorescein into the cells."

"What next?" Harlan asked.

"That was as far as we got," Sheila said. "We put the cultures aside to incubate further, hoping to get viruses."

"Well, you got them all right," Harlan said.

"Yeah, but look at this image. Under the scanning electron microscope the virus looks like it's been through a miniature meat grinder. This virus is noninfective. Something killed it, but there was nothing in the culture capable of doing that. It doesn't make sense."

"It doesn't make sense, but my gut instinct is that it is trying to tell us something," Harlan said. "We're just too stupid to see it."

"Maybe we should just try it again," Sheila said. "Maybe the culture got too hot riding in the car."

"You'd packed it well," Harlan said. "I don't think that's the answer. But fine, let's do it again. Also, I have some mice that I have been infecting. I suppose we could try to isolate the virus from them."

"Great idea!" Sheila said. "That might be even easier."

"Don't count on it," Harlan said. "The infected mice are amazingly strong and incredibly smart. I have to keep them apart and under lock and key."

"Good Lord," Sheila said. "Are you suggesting the mice are becoming alien too?"

"I'm afraid that's right," Harlan said. "In some form or fashion. My supposition is that if there were enough infected mice all in one location they could collectively act as an intelligent, single individual."

"Maybe we better stick to tissue cultures for the time being," Sheila said. "One way or the other we've got to isolate live, infective virus. It has to be the next step if we're going to do anything about this infestation."

The hiss of the air lock pressurizing sounded.

"That must be Pitt," Jonathan shouted. He ran out to the air lock door and peered through the porthole. "It is Pitt, and Cassy is with him!" he shouted back to the others.

Harlan picked up a vial of newly extracted monoclonal antibody. "I think I'd better put on my physican hat for a little while," he said.

Sheila reached out and motioned for him to give her the vial. "Emergency medicine is my specialty," she said. "We need you as the immunologist."

Harlan handed it over. "Gladly," he said. "I've always been a better researcher than clinician."

The air lock opened. Jonathan helped Cassy step through the hatch. She was pale and feverish. Jonathan's excitement moderated. She was sicker than he'd realized. Still, he couldn't help but ask where his mother was.

Cassy put her hand on his shoulder. "I'm sorry," she said. "We were separated very quickly after we were caught in the supermarket. I don't know where she is."

"Was she stung?" Jonathan asked.

"I'm afraid so," Cassy said.

"Come on!" Sheila said. "We have work to do." She put Cassy's arm over her shoulder. "Let's get you into the infirmary."

With Sheila on one side and Pitt on the other they walked Cassy through the lab to the sick bay. She was introduced to Harlan en route. He held open the door for them.

"I think it best if she occupies one of the containment rooms," Harlan said. He pushed past the group and led the way.

The room looked like a regular hospital room except for its entrance, which had an air lock so the room could be kept at a lower pressure than the rest of the complex. The inner door was also lockable and the glass in the porthole was an inch thick.

Everyone crowded into the room. With help from both Sheila and Pitt, Cassy stretched out on the bed and sighed with relief.

Sheila went right to work. With practiced deftness she started an IV, then gave a sizable dose of the monoclonal antibody. She injected it into the intravenous port on the IV line.

"Did you have any adverse reaction to the first shot?" Sheila asked as she momentarily sped up the IV to carry the last of the antibody into Cassy's system.

Cassy shook her head.

"There was no problem," Pitt said. "Except for a coughing spell which scared me. But I don't think it was related to the medication."

Sheila attached Cassy to a cardiac monitor. The beats were normal and the rhythm regular.

"Have you felt any different since that first shot?" Harlan asked.

"Not that I can tell," Cassy said.

"That's not surprising," Sheila said. "The symptoms are mainly from your own lymphokines, which we know shoot up in the early stages."

"I want to thank you all for letting me come here," Cassy said. "I know you are taking a risk."

"We're glad to have you," Harlan said, giving her knee a squeeze. "Who knows, like me you may be a valuable experimental subject."

"I wish," Cassy said.

"Are you hungry?" Sheila asked.

"Not in the slightest," Cassy said. "But I could certainly use some aspirin."

Sheila looked at Pitt. "I think I'll turn that over to Dr. Henderson," she said with a wry smile. "Meanwhile the rest of us have to get back to work."

Harlan was the first to leave. Sheila paused with one leg into the air lock. Looking back she waved to Jonathan. "Come on. Let's leave the patient to her doctor."

Jonathan reluctantly followed.

"You were right," Cassy said. "This place is unbelievable."

"It's just what the doctor ordered," Pitt said. "Let me get you that aspirin."

It took Pitt a few minutes to find the pharmacy and a few more to locate the aspirin. When he returned to the confinement room, he found that Cassy had been sleeping.

"I don't want to bother you," Pitt said.

"No bother," Cassy said. She took the aspirin, then lay back. She patted the bedside. "Sit down for a minute," she said. "I've got to tell you what I learned from Beau. This nightmare is about to get worse."

• • •

THE TRANQUILITY OF THE DESERT WAS SUDDENLY SHAT-
tered by the repetitive concussion of the rotor blades and
the roar of the Huey military jet engine as the copter swept
low across the barren landscape. Inside Vince Garbon held
a pair of binoculars to his eyes. He'd told the pilot to follow
a strip of black tarmac that cut across the sand from horizon
to horizon. In the backseat were two former police officers
from Vince's old unit.

"The last word we have is that the vehicle came out this
road," Vince shouted to the pilot over the sound of the
engine. The pilot nodded.

"I see something coming up," Vince said. "It looks like
an old gas station, but there's a vehicle and it fits the description."

The pilot slowed the forward progress. Vince held the
binoculars as steady as he could.

"Yup," he said. "I think it's the one. Let's go down
and have a look."

The helicopter lowered to the earth, kicking up a horren-
dous swirl of sand and dust in the process. When the skids
were firmly on the ground, the pilot cut the engine. The
heavy rotors slowed and came to a stop. Vince climbed out
of the cab.

The first thing Vince checked was the vehicle. He opened
the door and could immediately sense that Cassy had been
in it. He looked in the luggage space. It was empty.

Motioning toward the building, the two former policemen went inside. Vince stayed outside and let his eyes roam
around the horizon. It was so hot that he could see heat
rising in the air.

The policemen came out quickly and shook their heads.
She wasn't in there.

Vince motioned back to the copter. He was close. He
could sense it. After all, how far could she get on foot in
that heat?

PITT CAME INTO THE LAB. EVERYONE WAS WORKING SO
intently that they didn't even raise their heads.

"She's finally sleeping," he said.

"Did you lock the outer door?" Harlan asked.

"No," Pitt said. "Do you think I should?"

"Absolutely," Sheila said. "We don't want any surprises."

"I'll be right back," Pitt said. He returned to the air lock and looked in at Cassy. She was still sleeping peacefully. Her coughing had significantly abated. Pitt locked the door.

Returning to the lab, he took a seat. Again no one acknowledged him. Sheila was engrossed, inoculating tissue cultures with the enabling protein. Harlan was extracting more antibody. Jonathan was at a computer terminal wearing earphones and working a joystick.

Pitt asked Jonathan what he was doing. Jonathan took off the earphones. "It's really cool," he said. "Harlan showed me how to connect with all the monitoring equipment topside. There are cameras hidden in fake cacti which can be directed with this joystick. There's also listening devices and motion sensors. Want to try it?"

Pitt declined. Instead he told the others that Cassy had described to him some astounding and disturbing things about the aliens.

"Like what?" Sheila asked while continuing to work.

"The worst thing," Pitt said, "is that they have the infected people building a huge futuristic machine they call a Gateway."

"And what's this Gateway supposed to do?" Sheila asked, while gently swirling a tissue culture flask.

"It's some kind of transporter," Pitt said. "She was told that it will bring all sorts of alien creatures to Earth from distant planets."

"Jesus H. Christ!" Sheila exclaimed. She put down the flask. "We can't face any more adversaries. Maybe we'd better just give up."

"When is this Gateway going to be operational?" Harlan asked.

"I asked the same question," Pitt said. "Cassy didn't know, but she had the impression it was imminent. Beau

told her it was almost finished. Cassy said there were
thousands of people working on it.''

Sheila exhaled noisily in exasperation. ''What other
charming news did she tell you?''

''Some interesting facts,'' Pitt said. ''For instance, the
alien virus first came to earth three billion years ago. That's
when it inserted its DNA into the evolving life.''

Sheila's eyes narrowed. ''Three billion years ago?'' she
questioned.

Pitt nodded. ''That's what Beau told her. He also told
her that the aliens have sent the enabling protein every hundred million Earth years or so to 'awaken' the virus to see
what kind of life has evolved here and whether it was worth
inhabiting. What he meant by Earth years she didn't ask.''

''Maybe that relates to their ability to go from one universe to another,'' Harlan said. ''Here in ours we are caught
in a space/time freeze. But from the point of view of another universe, what's a billion years here, might only be
ten years there. Everything's relative.''

Harlan's explanation brought on a moment of silence.
Pitt shrugged. ''Well, I can't say it makes much sense to
me,'' he said.

''It's like a fifth dimension,'' Harlan said.

''Whatever,'' Pitt said. ''But getting back to what Cassy
was telling me, apparently this alien virus is responsible for
the mass extinctions the Earth has witnessed. Every time
they came back here, the creatures they infested weren't
suitable, so they left.''

''And all the creatures they'd infected died?'' Sheila
asked.

''That's how I understand it,'' Pitt said. ''The virus must
have made some lethal change in the DNA causing the
disappearance of entire species. That created an opportunity
for new creatures to evolve. She told me that Beau had
specifically mentioned this with regard to the dinosaurs.''

''Well, I'll be,'' Harlan said. ''So much for the asteroid
or comet theory.''

''How did the creatures die?'' Sheila asked. ''I mean,
what was the specific cause of death?''

"I don't think she knew that," Pitt said. "At least she didn't tell me. But I can ask her later."

"It might be important," Sheila said. She stared off into the middle distance with unseeing eyes. Her mind was churning. "And the virus supposedly came to Earth three billion Earth years ago?"

"That's what she said."

"What are you thinking?" Harlan asked.

"Is there any anaerobic bacteria available in the lab?" Sheila asked.

"Yeah, sure," Harlan said.

"Let's get some and infect it with the enabling protein," Sheila said with mounting excitement.

"Okay," Harlan said agreeably. He stood up. "But what's on your mind? Why do you want bacteria that grows without oxygen?"

"Humor me," Sheila said. "Just get it while I prepare some more enabling protein."

BEAU THREW OPEN THE FRENCH DOORS LEADING FROM THE sitting room to the terrace surrounding the pool. He stepped out and strode across the terrace. Alexander hurried after him.

"Beau, please!" Alexander said. "Don't go! We need you here."

"They found her car," Beau said. "She's lost in the desert. Only I can find her. By now she should be far on her way to becoming one with us."

Beau descended the few steps from the terrace to the lawn and struck out toward the waiting helicopter. Alexander stayed at his heels.

"Surely this woman cannot be so important," Alexander said. "You can have any woman you want. This is not the time to leave the Gateway. We've not even tested the grids to full power. What if we are not ready?"

Beau spun around. His narrow lips were pulled back in fury. "This woman is driving me mad. I must find her. I'll be back. Until then, carry on without me."

"Why not wait until tomorrow?" Alexander persisted.

"By then the Arrival will have occurred. Then you can go look for her. There'll be plenty of time."

"If she's lost in the desert she will be dead by tomorrow," Beau said. "It's decided."

Beau turned back to the copter and quickly closed the distance. For the last few feet he had to duck under the rotating blade. He climbed into the front seat next to the pilot, nodded a greeting to Vince in the backseat, then motioned for the pilot to lift off.

"HOW LONG HAS IT BEEN?" SHEILA ASKED.

"About an hour," Harlan said.

"That should be enough time," Sheila said impatiently. "One of the first things we learned was how fast the enabling protein functioned once it was absorbed into a cell. Now let's give the culture a slight dose of soft X-rays."

Harlan looked askance at Sheila. "I'm beginning to get the drift of what's going on in that brain of yours," he said. "You're treating this virus like a provirus, which it is. And now you want to change it from its latent form into its lytic form. But why the anaerobic bacteria? Why no oxygen?"

"Let's see what happens before I explain," Sheila said. "Just keep your fingers crossed. This could be what we are looking for. An alien Achilles' heel."

They gave the infected bacterial culture the dose of X-rays without disturbing its atmosphere of carbon dioxide. As they made mounts for the scanning electron microscope, Sheila found her hands trembling with excitement. She hoped with all her heart that they were on the brink of discovery.

WITH ONE OF HIS POWERFUL LEGS, BEAU KICKED THE DOOR of the deserted gas station. The blow tore it from its hinges and sent it crashing into the far wall of the room. Stepping into the dim interior, Beau's eyes glowed intensely. The helicopter ride had done little to temper his fury.

He stood in the semidarkness for several seconds, then turned around and walked back out into the bright sunshine.

"She was never in there," Beau said.

"I didn't think so," Vince said. He was bending down in the sand on the opposite side of the aged gas pumps. "There are some other fresh tire tracks here." He stood up and looked toward the east. "There must have been a second vehicle. Maybe they picked her up."

"What do you suggest?" Beau asked.

"Apparently she hasn't appeared in any town," Vince said. "Otherwise we would have heard. That means she's out here in the desert. We know there are isolated groups of 'runners' hiding out in the area who've so far avoided infection. Maybe she joined up with one of them."

"But she's infected," Beau said.

"I know," Vince said. "That part is a mystery. Anyway, I think we should head east along this road and see if we can find any tracks going off into the desert. There must be some kind of camp."

"All right," Beau said. "Let's do it. Time is running out."

They climbed back into the helicopter and lifted off. The pilot was ordered to fly high enough to keep from kicking up too much sand and dust yet low enough to see any tracks heading away from the road.

"MY GOSH, THERE IT IS," HARLAN SAID. THEY HAD FO-cused in on a virion at sixty thousand times magnification. It was a large filamentous virus that looked like a filoviridae with tiny, cilialike projections.

"It's awesome to think that we are looking at a highly intelligent alien life form," Sheila said. "We've always thought of viruses and bacteria as primitive."

"I don't think it is the alien per se," Pitt said. "Cassy mentioned that the viral form was what enabled the alien to withstand space travel and infest other life forms in the galaxy. Apparently Beau didn't know what the original alien form looked like."

"Maybe that's what the Gateway is for," Jonathan said. "Maybe the virus likes it here so much, the aliens themselves are coming."

"Could be," Pitt said.

"All right," Harlan said to Sheila. "So this little trick with the anaerobic bacteria worked. We've seen the virus. What was your mysterious point?"

"The point is that this virus came to Earth three billion years ago," Sheila said. "At that time the Earth was a very different place. There was very little oxygen in the primitive atmosphere. Since then things have changed. The virus is still fine when it is in the latent form or even when it has been enabled and has transformed the cell. But if it is induced to form virions, it's destroyed by oxygen."

"Interesting idea," Harlan said. He looked down at the culture whose top was now off, exposing its surface to room air. "If that's the case then we'll see damaged, uninfective virus if we make another mount."

"That's exactly what I'm hoping," Sheila said.

Without wasting any time, Sheila and Harlan set to work creating a second sample. Pitt helped as best he could. Jonathan went back to playing with the computer-run security system.

When Harlan focused in on the new mount, it was immediately apparent that Sheila was right. The viruses appeared as if they had been partially eaten.

Sheila and Harlan jumped up from their seats and enthusiastically high-fived and then embraced each other. They were ecstatic.

"What a brilliant idea," Harlan said. "You're to be congratulated. It's a joy to see science in action."

"If we were doing real science," Sheila said, "we'd go back and exhaustively prove this hypothesis. For now, we'll just take it at face value."

"Oh, I agree," Harlan said. "But it makes such sense. It's amazing how toxic oxygen is and how few laypeople know it."

"I don't think I understand," Pitt said. "How does this help us?"

The smiles faded from Sheila's and Harlan's faces. They regarded each other for a beat, then retook their seats. Both were lost in thought.

"I'm not sure how this discovery is going to help us,"

Sheila said finally. "But it has to. I mean, it must be the alien Achilles' heel."

"It must have been the way that they killed off the dinosaurs," Harlan said. "Once they decided to end the infestation, the viruses all went from being latent to being virions. Then bam! They hit the oxygen and all hell broke loose."

"That doesn't sound very scientific," Sheila said with a smile.

Harlan laughed. "I agree," he said. "But it gives us a hint. We have to induce the virus in the infected people to go from being latent to coming out of the cell."

"How is a latent virus induced?" Pitt asked.

Harlan shrugged. "A lot of ways," he said. "In tissue culture it's usually done with electromagnetic radiation like ultraviolet light or soft X rays like we used with the anaerobic bacterial culture."

"There are some chemicals that can do it," Sheila said.

"That's true," Harlan. "Some of the antimetabolites and other cellular poisons. But that doesn't help us. Neither do X rays. I mean it's not as if we could suddenly X-ray the planet."

"Are there regular viruses that are latent like the alien virus?" Pitt asked.

"Plenty," Sheila said.

"Absolutely," Harlan agreed. "Like the AIDS virus."

"Or the whole herpes viral group," Sheila said. "They can hide out for life or cause intermittent problems."

"You mean like cold sores?" Pitt asked.

"That's right," Sheila said. "That's herpes simplex. It stays latent in certain neurons."

"So when you get a cold sore it means that a latent virus has been induced to form virus particles?" Pitt asked.

"That's right," Sheila said with a touch of exasperation.

"I get cold sores every time I get a cold," Pitt said. "I suppose that's why they're called cold sores."

"Very clever," Sheila said sarcastically. "Pitt, maybe you should leave us alone while we brainstorm. This isn't supposed to be a teaching session."

"Wait a second," Harlan said. "Pitt just gave me an idea."

"I did?" Pitt questioned innocently.

"You know what is the best viral induction agent?" Harlan asked rhetorically. "Another viral infection."

"How is that going to help us?" Sheila asked.

Harlan pointed to the large freezer door across the room. "In there we've got all sorts of viruses. I'm starting to think that we should fight fire with fire!"

"You mean start some kind of epidemic?" Sheila asked.

"That's exactly what I'm thinking," Harlan said. "Something extraordinarily infectious."

"But that freezer is full of viruses designed to be used as biological warfare agents. That will be like going from the frying pan into the fire."

"Hell, that freezer has everything from nuisance viruses to the most deadly," Harlan said. "We just have to pick one that's suitable."

"Well . . ." Sheila mused. "It is true our original tissue culture was probably induced by the adenoviral vehicle we used for the DNA assay."

"Come on!" Harlan said. "Let me show you the inventory."

Sheila stood up. She was very dubious about fighting fire with fire, but she wasn't about to dismiss the idea out of hand.

Next to the freezer was a desk with a bookshelf over it. On the bookshelf were three large, black looseleaf notebooks. Harlan handed one each to Sheila and Pitt. He cracked open the third himself.

"It's like a wine list at a fancy restaurant," Harlan quipped. "Remember, we need something infectious."

"What do you mean, 'infectious'?" Pitt asked.

"Capable of being spread from person to person," Harlan said. "And we need the route to be airborne, not like AIDS or hepatitis. We want a worldwide epidemic."

"God!" Pitt commented, looking at the index of his volume. "I never thought there were so many different viruses. Here's filoviridae. Wow! There's Ebola in there."

"Too virulent," Harlan said. "We want an illness that doesn't kill by itself so that an infected individual can spread it to as many others as possible. The rapidly fatal diseases, believe it or not, tend to be self-limiting."

"Here's arenoviridae," Sheila said.

"Still too virulent," Harlan said.

"How about orthomyxoviridae?" Pitt said. "Influenza is certainly infectious. And there's been some worldwide epidemics."

"That has possibilities," Harlan admitted. "But it has a relatively long incubation period, and it can be fatal. I'd really like to find something rapidly infectious and a bit more benign. Here we go . . . This is what I'm looking for."

Harlan plopped the looseleaf he'd been holding onto the desktop. It was open to page 99. Sheila and Pitt bent over to look at it.

"Picornaviridae," Pitt read, struggling with the pronunciation. "What do they cause?"

"It's this genus that I'm interested in," Harlan said. He pointed to one of the subgroups.

"Rhinovirus," Pitt read.

"Exactly," Harlan said. "The common cold. Wouldn't it be ironic if the common cold were to save mankind?"

"But not everybody gets a cold when it goes around," Pitt said.

"True," Harlan said. "Everyone has different levels of immunity to the hundreds of different strains that exist. But let's see what our microbiologists employed by the Pentagon have come up with."

Harlan flipped through the pages until he came to the rhinovirus section. It comprised thirty-seven pages. The first page had an index of the serotypes plus a short summary section.

Everyone read the summary silently. It suggested that rhinoviruses had limited utility as biological warfare agents. The reason given was that although the upper respiratory infections would affect the performance of a modern army, it would not be to a significant degree, and certainly not as much as an enterovirus causing diarrheal disease.

"Sounds like they were not so high on rhinoviruses," Pitt said.

"True," Harlan said. "But we're not trying to incapacitate an army. We just want the virus to get in there and stir up metabolic trouble to bring the alien virus out in the open."

"Here's something that sounds interesting," Sheila said, pointing to a subsection in the index. It was *artifical rhinoviruses*.

"That's what we need," Harlan said enthusiastically. He flipped through the pages until he came to the section. He read rapidly. Pitt tried to do the same, but the text might as well have been inscribed in Sanskrit. It was all highly technical jargon.

"This is perfect! Absolutely perfect!" Harlan said. He looked at Sheila. "It's tailor-made, both literally and figuratively. They've put together a rhinovirus that has never seen the light of day, meaning no one has any immunity to it. It's a serotype that no one has ever been exposed to so everybody will catch it. It's . . . made to order!"

"Seems to me we're making a rather large leap of faith here," Sheila said. "Don't you think we should somehow test this hypothesis?"

"Absolutely," Harlan said with great excitment. He reached over and put his hand on the latch to the freezer door. "I'll get a sample of the virus for us to grow out. Then we'll test it on those mice that I had infected. Boy, am I glad I did that." Harlan opened the freezer and disappeared inside.

Pitt looked at Sheila. "Do you think it will work?" he asked.

Sheila shrugged. "He seems pretty optimistic," she said.

"If it does work, will it kill the person?" Pitt asked. He was thinking about Cassy and even Beau.

"There's no way to know," Sheila said. "For as much as we know, at this point we're stumbling around in the dark."

•   •   •

"HOLD UP!" VINCE SAID. HE HAD THE BINOCULARS pressed against his eyes. "I think I see some tracks leading off toward the south."

"Where?" Beau asked.

Vince pointed.

Beau nodded. "Take us down to the ground," he told the pilot.

The pilot set the helicopter down on the tarmac. Still, a tremendous amount of sand and dust swirled up into the air.

"I hope all this dirt doesn't cover the tracks," Vince said.

"We're far enough away," the pilot said. He turned off the engine and the rotors came to a halt. Vince and the policeman sitting next to him, named Robert Sherman, immediately got out and jogged up the road to where the tracks were. Beau and the pilot climbed out of the cab as well, but they stayed next to the copter.

Beau was breathing heavily through his mouth with his tongue hanging out like a panting dog. The alien skin was not equipped with sweat glands, and he was beginning to overheat. He looked around for shade, but there was no escape from the merciless sun.

"I want to get back into the chopper," Beau said.

"It'll be too hot in there," the pilot said.

"I want you to start the engine," Beau said.

"But that will make it difficult for the others to return," the pilot said.

"The engine will be started!" Beau growled.

The pilot nodded and did as he was told. The air conditioning came on and quickly lowered the temperature.

Outside the slowly rotating blades kicked up a miniature sandstorm. They could barely see the two men a hundred yards ahead as they bent over to examine the ground.

The radio activated and the pilot slipped on his headset. Beau glanced off at the featureless horizon to the south. Along with his anger he was feeling progressively anxious. He hated these human emotions.

"It's a message from the institute," the pilot told Beau.

"There's a problem. They cannot go to full power on the electrical grids. The system trips the circuit breakers."

Beau's long snakelike fingers intertwined to form tight, knotlike fists. His pulse quickened. His head pounded.

"What should I tell them?" the pilot asked.

"Tell them I'll be back soon," Beau said.

After signing off, the pilot removed his headphones. He was experiencing a trace of Beau's mental state via the collective consciousness, and he fidgeted in his seat. He was relieved when he saw the others returning.

Vince and Robert had to cover their faces against the stinging sand as they ducked under the rotating blades to climb into the copter. They didn't try to talk until the door was closed.

"It's the same tracks that were at the old gas station," he said. "They head south. What do you want to do?"

"Follow them!" Beau said.

WITH GREAT DIFFICULTY HARLAN, SHEILA, PITT, AND JON-athan had managed to get six of the infected mice into a type III biological safety cabinet.

"It's a good thing they weren't rats," Pitt said. "If they had been any larger than mice, I don't think we could have handled them."

Harlan was letting Sheila put disinfectant and bandages on several of the bites he'd gotten. "I knew they were going to be trouble," he said.

"What are we going to do now?" Jonathan asked. He'd become intrigued by the experiment.

"We're going to introduce the virus," Harlan said. "It's in that tissue culture flask that's already inside the hood."

"Where does this cabinet vent?" Sheila asked. "We don't want this virus getting out if it's not going to work."

"The exhaust is irradiated," Harlan said. "No worry there."

Harlan stuck his bandaged hands into the thick rubber gloves that penetrated the front of the cabinet. He grasped the tissue culture flask, pulled out the stopper, and poured the medium out in a flat dish. "There," he said. "That will vaporize rapidly, and then our little furry friends will be breathing in the artificial virus.''

"What are the black dots on the back of each mouse?" Jonathan asked.

"Each dot represents how many days ago the mouse was infected," Harlan said. "I was infecting them sequentially so that I could follow the infestation process physiologically. Now I'm glad I did it. There might be a different reaction depending on how much the enabled virus had expressed itself."

For a few minutes all four people stood in front of the cabinet and watched the mice race around the cage.

"Nothing is happening," Jonathan complained.

"Nothing on the level of the entire organism," Harlan said. "But my intuition tells me a lot is happening on a molecular/cellular level."

A few minutes later Jonathan yawned. "Wow," he said. "This is like watching paint dry. I'm going back to the computer."

A few minutes later Pitt broke the silence. "What is interesting is how they are seemingly working together. Look how they are forming a pyramid to explore up the glass."

Sheila grunted. She'd seen the phenomenon but wasn't interested. She wanted to see something physical happen to the mice. Since their level of activity hadn't changed, she was beginning to feel progressively nervous. If this experiment didn't work, they'd be back to square one.

As if reading Sheila's thoughts, Harlan said: "We shouldn't have long to wait. My guess is that it will only take the induction of one cell to initiate a cascade. My only worry is that we didn't test the viability of the virus. Maybe we should do that."

Harlan turned away to do what he'd suggested when Sheila grabbed his arm. "Wait!" she cried. "Look at that mouse with the three dots."

Harlan followed Sheila's pointing finger. Pitt crowded in behind, looking over Harlan's shoulder. The mouse in question had suddenly stopped its incessant rapid wandering around the cage to sit back on its haunches and repeatedly wipe its eyes with its front paws. Then it jerked a few times.

The three observers exchanged glances.

"Are those mouse sneezes?" Sheila asked.

"Damned if I know," Harlan said.

The mouse then swayed and toppled over.

"Is it dead?" Pitt asked.

"No," Sheila said. "It's still plainly breathing, but it doesn't look so good. Look at that foamlike stuff coming out of its eyes."

"And mouth," Harlan said. "And there's another mouse starting to have symptoms. I think it is working!"

"They are all having symptoms," Pitt said. "Look at that one with the most dots. It looks like it is having a seizure."

Hearing the commotion Jonathan returned and managed to squeeze his head between the others. He caught a quick glance at the ailing mice. "Ugh," he said. "The foam has a greenish tinge."

Harlan put his hands back into the gloves and picked up the first mouse. In contrast to its earlier belligerent behavior, it did not resist. It lay calmly in the palm of his hand breathing shallowly. Harlan put the animal down and reached for the one that had had the seizure.

"This one is dead," Harlan said. "Since it had been infected for the longest time, I guess that's telling us something."

"It's probably telling us how the dinosaurs died," Sheila said. "It was certainly rapid."

Harlan put the dead animal down and withdrew his hands. He rubbed them together enthusiastically. "Well, the first part of this experiment has gone very nicely, I'd say. Now that the animal trials are over, I think it's time for the human trials to begin."

"You mean release the virus?" Sheila said. "Like open the door and throw it out."

"No, we're not yet ready for clinical fieldwork," Harlan said with a twinkle in his eye. "I was thinking about the next stage being more close to home. I was thinking about me being the experimental subject."

"Now wait . . ." Sheila protested.

Harlan held up his hand. "There's a long history of famous medical people using themselves as the proverbial guinea pigs," he said. "This is a perfect opportunity to follow suit. I've been infected, and even though it has been a number of days, I've kept the infestation to a minimum by the monoclonal antibody. It's now time for me to rid myself of the virus altogether. So rather than thinking of myself as a sacrificial lamb, I think of myself as a beneficiary of our collective wit."

"How do you propose to do this?" Sheila asked. It was one thing to experiment with mice, quite another with a fellow human being.

"Come on," Harlan said. He grabbed one of the tissue cultures inoculated with the artificial rhinovirus and headed for the sick bay. "We'll do this the same way we did it with the mice. The difference is that you'll lock me into one of the containment rooms."

"Maybe we should use another animal first," Sheila said.

"Nonsense," Harlan said. "It's not as if we have the luxury of a lot of time. Remember that Gateway situation."

Everyone trooped after Harlan, who was obviously intent on using himself as an experimental subject. Sheila tried to talk him out of it all the way to the containment room. Harlan was not to be deterred.

"Just promise me you'll lock the door," Harlan said. "If something really weird were to happen, I don't want to jeopardize all of you."

"What if you need medical attention?" Sheila said. "Like, God forbid, CPR."

"That's a chance I have to take," Harlan said fatalistically. "Now get, so I can catch my cold in peace."

Sheila hesitated for a moment while trying to think of some other way to talk Harlan out of what she thought was a premature folly. Finally she stepped back through the air lock hatch and dogged it closed. She looked through the glass as Harlan gave her a thumbs-up sign.

Admiring Harlan's courage Sheila returned the gesture.

"What's he doing?" Pitt asked from the hallway. The air lock was only big enough for one person.

"He's taking the stopper out of the tissue culture flask," Sheila said.

"I'm going back to the computer," Jonathan said. The tension was making him feel uncomfortable.

Pitt stepped into the neighboring air lock and looked through the porthole at Cassy. She was still sleeping peacefully.

Pitt returned to the air lock occupied by Sheila. "Anything happening?"

"Not yet," Sheila said. "He's just lying down making faces at me. He's acting like he's twelve years old."

Pitt wondered how he'd behave if the situation were reversed, and he was the one in the room. He thought he'd be terrified and unable to joke around like Harlan.

"WAIT A SECOND!" VINCE SAID EXCITEDLY. "TURN around so I can see where we just passed over."

The pilot banked the copter to the left in a wide circle.

Vince snapped the binoculars to his eyes. The terrain below looked as featureless as it had looked for the previous hour. It had turned out to be extraordinarily difficult to follow the tire tracks from the air, and they'd taken many wrong turns.

"There's something down there," Vince said.

"What is it?" Beau growled. His mood had darkened. What he'd thought was going to be a simple matter of plucking Cassy out of the desert, was turning into a fiasco.

"I can't tell," Vince said. "But it is worth taking a look at. I'd recommend we go down."

"Land!" Beau snarled.

The helicopter settled down in the middle of its own sandstorm. It was worse than earlier, without the tarmac. As the air cleared everyone immediately saw what had attracted Vince's attention. It was a van with a camouflage cover partially blown off by the wind generated by the rotor blades.

"Finally something positive," Beau snapped as he

alighted from the helicopter. He strode over to the van. Grasping the tarp he ripped it off. He opened the front passenger-side door.

"She was in here," he said. He looked in the back of the van, then turned to survey the area.

"Beau, there's another communication from the institute," the pilot called out. He'd remained next to the helicopter. "They want you to know that they'd received word that the Arrival is expected in five Earth hours from now. And they want to remind you that the Gateway is not ready. What should I tell them?"

Beau gripped his head with his long fingers and pressed his temples in an attempt to relieve his tension. He breathed out slowly. Ignoring the pilot he yelled to Vince that Cassy was nearby. "I can sense it," Beau added. "But it is strangely weak."

Vince and Robert had wandered away from the van in ever widening circles. Suddenly Vince had stopped and bent down. Straightening up he called for Beau to come over.

Beau joined the two men.

Vince pointed to the ground. "It's a camouflaged hatch," he said. "It's locked from within."

Beau's fingers snaked under the edge. Progressively he applied an upward force until the hatch snapped up into the air. Vince and Beau leaned over and peered down at the lighted corridor below. Then their eyes met.

"She's down there," Beau said.

"I know," Vince said.

"HOLY SHIT!" JONATHAN CRIED. HIS EYES BULGED FROM their sockets. Then he screamed at the top of his lungs: "Pitt, Sheila, somebody, get over here!"

Pitt slammed down a syringe of antibody he'd been preparing for Cassy and dashed out of the sick bay into the hall en route to the lab where Jonathan was. Pitt had no idea what had happened but there'd been desperation in Jonathan's voice. Pitt heard Sheila running behind him.

They found Jonathan sitting at the computer. His eyes

were glued to the monitor, and his face was pale as an ivory cue ball.

"What's the matter?" Pitt demanded as he rushed up to Jonathan.

Jonathan was momentarily tongue-tied. All he could do was motion toward the computer screen. Pitt looked at it and his hand reflexly slapped across his open mouth.

"What is it?" Sheila urged as she arrived at Pitt's side.

"It's a freak!" Jonathan managed.

Sheila sucked in a breath of air when she caught sight of what was on the screen.

"It's Beau!" Pitt said with horror. "Cassy said he'd been mutating, but I had no idea . . ."

"Where is he?" Sheila asked, forcing herself to be practical despite Beau's grotesque appearance.

"It was an alarm that drew my attention," Jonathan said. "Then the computer automatically activated the appropriate minicam."

"I want to know where he is," Sheila repeated frantically.

Jonathan fumbled with the keyboard and managed to bring up a schematic of the facility. A red arrow was blinking at one of the emergency/exhaust vents.

"I think that's the one where we entered," Pitt said.

"I think you're right," Sheila said. "What does the alarm mean, Jonathan?"

"It says 'hatch cover unsealed,' " Jonathan said. "I guess that means they've got the hatch open."

"Good God!" Sheila said. "They'll be coming in."

"What should we do?" Pitt asked.

Sheila ran an anxious hand through her unfettered blond hair; her green eyes darted erratically around the room. She felt like a cornered deer.

"Pitt, go see if you can lock the door to the air lock," she sputtered. "That might delay them for a time."

Pitt dashed from the room.

"Where's Harlan's pistol?" Jonathan asked.

"I don't know," Sheila snapped. "Look for it, Jonathan."

Sheila started for the sick bay.

"Where are you going?" Jonathan called out to Sheila.

"I've got to get Harlan and Cassy out of those containment rooms," Sheila said.

"WHAT DO YOU WANT ME TO DO, BEAU?" VINCE ASKED, breaking what had seemed to be a long silence.

"What do you think this place is?" Beau asked, pointing down the hatch at the gleaming, white, high-tech interior.

"I haven't the slightest idea," Vince said.

Beau glanced back at the helicopter. The pilot was dutifully standing by. Beau returned his gaze down the hatch. His mind was in a turmoil and his emotions frayed.

"I want you and your co-worker to go down in this strange hole and find Cassy," Beau said. He spoke slowly and deliberately as if he were making great effort to restrain himself from flying into a rage. "When you find her, I want you to bring her to me. I must go back to the institute, but I will send the copter back for you."

"As you wish," Vince said warily. He was afraid of saying the wrong thing. The fragility of Beau's emotions was obvious.

Beau reached into his pocket and drew out a black disc. He handed it to Vince. "Use it as you see fit," he said. "But do not harm Cassy!" Then he turned and strode back to the waiting aircraft.

20

WITH FUMBLING HANDS SHEILA UNLOCKED THE HATCH into Harlan's containment room. By the time she had it open, Harlan was standing next to it. He was surprised and irritated.

"What the hell are you doing?" he questioned. "You've contaminated yourself and the entire facility."

"It can't be helped," Sheila sputtered. "They're here!"

"Who is here?" Harlan asked. His expression rapidly changed to concern.

"Beau and at least one other infected person," Sheila blurted out. "They have the hatch open that we used to come in here. They must have followed Cassy. They'll be here any minute."

"Damn!" Harlan exclaimed. He paused for a second to think, then stepped out through the air lock.

They immediately caught up with Cassy and Pitt as the two emerged from the neighboring containment room. Although Cassy appeared sleepy and confused, her color was better than it had been earlier.

"Where's Jonathan?" Harlan barked.

"Back in the lab," Pitt said. "He was searching for your Colt."

With Harlan leading, the group rushed from the sick bay

into the lab proper. They went from room to room. They found Jonathan in the final room, crouching by the door to the corridor. He was holding the pistol in both hands.

"We're getting out of here," Harlan yelled to Jonathan. Harlan ducked into the incubator and emerged seconds later carrying an armload of tissue culture flasks containing the rhinovirus.

A loud sputtering noise was heard from the corridor. Everyone's eyes turned to the open doorway. A shower of sparks shot by as if someone were welding in the hallway. Simultaneously the pressure in the room precipitously dropped, forcing everyone to clear their ears.

"What happened?" Sheila demanded.

"They're cutting through the pressure door," Harlan yelled. "Come on! Hurry!" He motioned for everyone to retreat back toward the infirmary. But before anybody could move a black disc rounded the corner from the corridor and entered the lab. It was glowing bright red and surrounded by a hazy halo.

"It's a disc!" Sheila shouted. "Stay away from it."

"Yes!" Harlan bellowed. "When it's active it's radio-active. It's spewing out alpha particles."

The disc hovered near Jonathan, who ducked away and ran back toward the others. Harlan herded the group through the door into the next lab room. Stepping into the room himself, he slammed the heavy, two-inch-thick fire door.

"Hurry!" he commanded.

The group had gotten halfway across the second lab when the same sputtering noise they'd heard earlier reverberated around the room. There was another shower of sparks. Harlan turned to see the disc passing effortlessly through the door.

Everyone got into the third lab space and raced for the double doors into the infirmary. Harlan took the time to slam the second fire door before running after the others. Behind him he heard the sputtering again. Sparks bounced off the back of his head as he went into the infirmary. The doors swung closed behind him.

"Where to?" Sheila demanded.

"The X-ray room," Harlan barked, pointing with a hand carrying one of the tissue culture flasks. "The one that is still operational."

Jonathan was the first to arrive. He pushed open the shielded door and held it for the others. They all crowded inside.

"This is a dead end!" Sheila shrieked. "Why did you bring us in here?"

"Get over behind the shield," Harlan ordered. Quickly he handed Sheila and Pitt the tissue culture flasks. Then he activated the machine that positioned the X-ray column. He aimed the positioning light directly at the door to the hall before rushing back and crowding behind the screen with the others.

Harlan's hands rapidly flipped switches and spun dials on the X-ray machine's control panel as sparking and sputtering commenced at the door. With the lead shielding it took the disc a few more seconds to burn through the X-ray room door than it had the fire doors. When it emerged inside the room, its red color had slightly paled.

Harlan flipped the switch that sent the high voltage built up in the machine to the X-ray source. There was an electronic buzzing noise and the overhead light dimmed. "These are the hardest X-rays this machine is capable of producing," he explained.

Bombarded with the X-rays, the disc's color instantly changed from pale red to luminous white. The pale halo intensified, expanded, and quickly engulfed the disc. The sound of an enormous furnace igniting was immediately cut off with a thump. At the same instant most of the X-ray machine, the X-ray table, an instrument tray, part of the door, and the light fixture were all pulled out of shape as if they had been sucked toward the point where the disc had been. Even the people had experienced this sudden imploding force and had instinctively braced themselves and grabbed onto whatever they could.

A pall of acrid smoke hung over the room.

Everyone was momentarily dazed.

"Is everyone okay?" Harlan asked.

"My watch exploded," Sheila said.

"So did the wall clock," Harlan said. He pointed up to the institutional clock on the wall. Its glass had been shattered, and its hands were nowhere to be seen.

"That was a miniature black hole," Harlan said.

A loud thump out in the lab shocked everybody back to reality.

"Obviously they've gotten through the air lock," Harlan said. "Come on!" He took the gun away from Jonathan and gave him a tissue culture flask to carry instead. Cassy and Pitt picked up the rest of the flasks. Harlan led everyone from behind the distorted shield toward the door.

"Don't touch anything," he warned. "There still might be some radiation."

It took all three men to get the twisted door open. Harlan leaned out. He could see down to the double doors leading to the lab. There was a small scorched hole in the right one. He looked the other way. It was clear.

"To the left," he barked. "Down through the door at the end and across into the living room. Got it?"

Everyone nodded.

"Go!" Harlan said. He kept his eye on the double doors until the last person had cleared the corridor. He was about to follow them when one of the double doors opened in the opposite direction.

Harlan fired one shot from the huge Peacemaker. The noise was deafening in the hallway. The bullet hit the closed double door and shattered its porthole-like window. The door that had been opened swung shut.

Harlan raced out into the hall and ran its length on legs that had suddenly gone rubbery. He staggered into the living room.

"Harlan?" Sheila questioned. "Have you been shot?" They had all heard the gun go off.

Harlan shook his head. A small amount of foam bubbled out of his mouth and oozed from his eyes. "I think it's the rhinovirus kicking out the alien virus," he managed. He steadied himself against the wall. "It's happening. Unfortunately it's a rather inconvenient time."

Pitt rushed to Harlan's side and draped Harlan's arm over his shoulder. He took the gun from Harlan's limp hand.

"Give me the gun," Sheila commanded. Pitt handed it over.

"How are we going to get out of here?" Sheila asked Harlan.

The sound of breaking glass drifted back from the lab.

"We'll use the main entrance," Harlan said. "My Range Rover should be there. I'd been afraid to go out that way for fear of discovery. Now it doesn't make any difference."

"All right," Sheila said. "How do we get there?"

"We go out in the main hall and turn right," Harlan said. "We pass the storerooms and there'll be another air lock. Then there is a long corridor with electric carts. The exit comes up inside a building that looks like a farmhouse."

Sheila cracked the door to the hall and began slowly to lean her head out to look back toward the lab rooms. She felt the bullet before she heard a distant gun go off. The slug had come so close to her that it had singed some of her hair before burrowing into the partially open door.

She pulled back inside the living room.

"Obviously they know where we are," she said. She wiped her forehead with her hand and examined it. She wouldn't have been surprised to see blood. "Is there another way to get to the exit? We're surely not going to be able to use the hall."

"We have to use the hall," Harlan said.

"Oh screw!" Sheila mumbled. She looked at the gun in her hand, wondering whom she thought she was kidding. She'd never even fired a gun in practice much less gotten into a battle with one.

"We can use the fire system," Harlan said. He pointed toward the security panel on the living-room wall. "If you pull the fire lever, the whole place fills up with fire retardant. The intruders won't be able to breathe very well, if at all."

"Oh that's clever," Sheila said sarcastically. "And, of course, we just walk out holding our breaths."

"No, no," Harlan said. "In the cabinet below the panel are rebreathers that are good for a least a half hour."

Sheila went over to the cabinet and pulled it open. It was filled with gas mask–like apparatuses. She took out five and handed them around. The directions on the long, tubular proboscis were to break the seal, shake, and then don.

"Everybody okay with this?" Sheila asked.

"It's not as if we have a lot of choice," Pitt said.

They all activated their units and then strapped them on. When everyone gave a thumbs-up sign, Sheila yanked down on the fire lever.

An immediate clanging was heard followed by an automated voice that repeated "Fire in the facility" over and over again. A minute later the sprinkler system was activated, sending out billows of fluid that rapidly vaporized. The room filled up with a smoglike haze.

"We have to stick together," Sheila yelled. It was hard to talk in the gas mask, and it was getting hard to see as well. Sheila opened the door to the hall and was pleased to see the hall was as hazy as the living room. She leaned out and looked toward the labs. She couldn't see for more than four or five feet.

Sheila stepped out into the hall. There were no gun shots. "Let's go," she called to the others. "Pitt, you and Harlan go ahead so that we know where we are going. Cassy and Jonathan, you carry the tissue culture flasks."

In a tight group they moved down the hallway. In the haze the corridor seemed interminable. Finally they came to the air lock and climbed in. Sheila pulled the door behind them. Pitt opened the outer door.

Beyond the air lock, the atmosphere progressively cleared, especially when they got on the electric cart. By the time they came to the exit stairs, they could remove their breathing apparatuses.

It was six flights up to the surface. They emerged through a trap door the size of a scatter rug into the living room of a farmhouse. When the trap door was closed, no one would have suspected what it concealed.

"My car should be in the barn," Harlan said. He took his arm off Pitt's shoulder. "Thanks, Pitt," he said. "I don't think I could have made it without you, but I feel a bit better already." He blew his nose noisily.

"Let's get a move on," Sheila said. "Those people who were after us might have found rebreathers as well."

The group exited the house via the front door and walked back toward the barn. The sun had set and the desert heat was rapidly dissipating. There was a blood-red smear along the edge of the western horizon. The rest of the sky was an inverted bowl of indigo blue. A few stars twinkled overhead.

As Harlan had hoped, his Range Rover was still safely parked in the barn. He put all the tissue culture flasks in the back storage area before getting behind the wheel. He took the Colt from Sheila and slipped it into the door pocket.

"Are you sure you feel up to driving?" Sheila asked. She was amazed at his recovery.

"No problem," Harlan said. "I feel completely different than I did just fifteen minutes ago. The only symptoms I have now are of garden-variety cold. I'd say our human trial was an unmitigated success!"

Sheila got into the front passenger seat. Cassy, Pitt, and Jonathan climbed into the back. Pitt put his arm around Cassy, and she snuggled up against him.

Harlan started the car and backed out of the barn. He made a U-turn and drove to the road.

"This alien infestation certainly has cut down on traffic," he said. "Look at this. Not a car in sight and we're only fifteen minutes out of Paswell."

Harlan turned right and accelerated.

"Where are we going?" Sheila asked.

"I don't think we have a lot of choice," Harlan said. "My sense is that the rhinovirus is going to take care of the infestation. The problem then boils down to the Gateway thing. We got to try to do something about it."

Cassy straightened up. "The Gateway!" she said. "Pitt has told you about it."

"He certainly did," Harlan said. "He said you thought it was almost operational. Did you get any idea when they might use it?"

"I wasn't told specifically," Cassy said. "But my sense is that it will be used as soon as it is finished."

"There you go," Harlan said. "We'll just have to hope we can get there in time and figure out a way to throw a monkey wrench into the works."

"What's this about a rhinovirus?" Cassy asked.

"Some rather good news," Harlan said, glancing at Cassy in the rearview mirror. "Particularly for you and me."

Cassy was then told the whole sequence of events that led to the discovery of a way to rid the human race of the alien viral scourge. Both Harlan and Sheila credited Cassy for the information that she'd given Pitt.

"It was the fact that the alien virus had come here three billion years ago that was so important," Sheila said. "Otherwise we wouldn't have thought about its being sensitive to oxygen."

"Maybe I should be breathing some of that rhinovirus now?" Cassy said.

"No need," Harlan said. "Just riding in the car means all of you are being adequately infected. I imagine it only takes a couple of virions since no one has any immunity to it."

Cassy settled back and snuggled against Pitt. "Only a few hours ago I thought all was lost. It's a shock to be hopeful again."

Pitt squeezed her shoulder. "We've been incredibly lucky."

They arrived at the outskirts of Santa Fe a few minutes after eleven o'clock at night. They had driven straight through, stopping only once at an abandoned service station to fill up the gas tank. They'd also helped themselves to candy and peanuts from a vending machine. There was plenty of change in the cash register.

Cassy had stayed in the car. By then she'd been in the middle of the period of weakness, malaise, and foaming at the mouth and eyes that Harlan had experienced as they'd left the underground laboratory. Harlan had been ecstatic, taking Cassy's temporary misery as further evidence of the efficacy of the "rhino-cure," as he called it.

Skirting the center of Santa Fe, they followed Cassy's directions and drove directly to the Institute for a New Beginning. At this time of night the outer gate was brightly illuminated with flood lights. The daily protesters were gone, but there was a significant number of infected people leaving the grounds.

Harlan pulled over to the side of the road and stopped. He leaned forward and surveyed the scene. "Where's the mansion?" he asked.

En route Cassy had explained to everyone everything she'd been able to remember about the institute's layout particularly the fact that the Gateway was located in the ballroom on the first floor to the right of the front entrance.

"The main building is behind that line of trees," Cassy said. "You can't see it from here."

"Which way did the ballroom windows face?" Harlan asked.

"I believe to the back of the house," Cassy said. "But I'm not positive because they had been boarded up."

"So much for the idea of breaking through the windows," Harlan said.

"Considering what the Gateway is supposed to do," Pitt said, "it must use a lot of energy, and that's got to be electric. Maybe we could unplug it."

"A wonderfully droll suggestion," Harlan quipped. "But to transport aliens through time and space I can't imagine they'll be relying on the same energy as we use to power toasters. Seeing what a single, relatively tiny black disc can do, think of what a whole bunch of them might accomplish if they were working in concert."

"It was just an idea," Pitt said. He felt stupid and decided to keep his thoughts to himself.

"How far is the mansion from the gate?" Sheila asked.

"Quite a ways," Cassy said. "A couple of hundred yards or more. The driveway goes through trees first and then crosses a stretch of wide-open lawn."

"Well, I think that's our first problem," Sheila said. "We have to get to the house if we're going to do anything."

"Good point," Harlan said.

"What about sneaking over the fence somewhere in the back?" Jonathan said. "There are lights here at the gate but I don't see others elsewhere."

"There are big dogs patrolling the grounds," Cassy said. "They're infected just like the people, and they work together. I'm afraid trying to approach the house across the lawn would be dangerous."

Suddenly the night sky above the trees lit up with undulating bands of energy that gave the impression of the northern lights. They formed a sphere and began expanding and contracting, reminiscent of an organism breathing. But each successive expansion was larger so the phenomenon was growing by the second.

"Uh oh," Sheila said. "I have a feeling we're too late. It's starting."

"All right, everybody out of the car!" Harlan commanded.

"What do you mean?" Sheila questioned.

"I want everybody out," Harlan said. "I'm going to do something impulsive. I'm going to drive in there and run this car into the ballroom. I can't let this go on."

"Well, you're not doing it alone," Sheila said.

"Suit yourself," Harlan said. "I don't have time to argue. But the rest of you, out!"

"There's not really anyplace to go," Cassy said. She glanced at Pitt and then Jonathan. Their nods told her she was speaking for them. "I think we're into this thing together."

"Oh for chrissake!" Harlan complained as he put his Range Rover into low range for off roading. "Just what the human race needs: an entire car full of goddamn martyrs." He revved the engine and told everyone to cinch up his seat belt. Harlan yanked his own as tight as he could make it. Then he put on the CD player and selected his favorite: Stravinsky's *Rite of Spring*. He advanced it to a part he especially liked; it was where the kettle drums resound. With the volume at near full blast, he pulled out into the road.

"What are you going to tell the men at the gate?" Sheila yelled.

"I'm going to tell them to eat my dust!" Harlan yelled back.

There was a black-and-white, weighted wooden gate across the driveway. The pedestrian traffic walked around it. Harlan hit it at about forty-five miles per hour and the Rover's bush bars made mincemeat of it. The smiling guards dove out of the way to either side.

Sheila spun around and looked out the back of the car. The guards had recovered and were running after them. Also in pursuit was a pack of wildly barking dogs. Gatekeepers and dogs quickly disappeared as Harlan negotiated an S-curve around some virgin conifers.

The Range Rover rocketed out of the trees. The huge mansion loomed before them in the night. The entire building was glowing, particularly the windows. The undulating bands of light that were rhythmically expanding up into the night sky appeared to be coming from the roof like gigantic flames.

"Aren't you going to slow down a little?" Sheila yelled. The engine was whining like a jet turbine and the kettle drums were pounding. It sounded as if the entire orchestra was inside the car. Sheila reached up and grasped the handle above the passenger-side door to steady herself.

Harlan didn't answer. His expression was one of intense concentration. Up until that moment he'd been steering the vehicle within the confines of the driveway. Now that he had the house in sight, he drove straight toward it across the lawn to avoid the pedestrians. People were streaming from the mansion in single file on the way out of the property.

About a hundred feet from the wide, sweeping steps that

led up to the front terrace, Harlan downshifted despite the
fact that the engine's RPMs were already close to the red
area on the gauge. The car responded by slowing considerably. At the same time significant power was directed to
the rear wheels.

"Holy shit!" Jonathan yelled as the distance closed to
the front steps. People could be seen diving blindly over
the limestone handrails to get away from the three tons of
steel hurtling at them.

The Range Rover hit the first step and the front kicked
up, launching the entire vehicle into the air. The tires made
contact with the earth again at the rear of the front terrace
ten feet from the double French door entry. Multipaned side
lights surrounded the front door on both sides as well as
the top.

Everyone but Harlan squeezed their eyes shut when the
collision with the house occurred. There was a muted sound
of shattering glass that could be heard above the classical
music, but there was surprisingly little effect on the car's
forward momentum. Harlan hit the brakes and threw the
steering wheel to the right. He was intent on avoiding the
grand staircase which was directly ahead.

The car skidded on the black-and-white checkered marble floor, brushed past a large crystal chandelier, and then
collided with a marble console table and an interior plastered wall. There was a crunching sound and everyone was
thrown against their seat belts. The passenger-side airbag
inflated and pressed a startled Sheila back into her seat.

Harlan fought the steering wheel as the car bounced over
the crushed table and broken two-by-four studding. The final collision was with a metal and wooden structure draped
with electrical cable. The car came to a halt against a steel
girder that shattered the windshield, splintering it into a
thousand pieces of tempered glass.

Outside the car there was sputtering and sparking as well
as a strange mechanical hum that could be felt more than
heard over the booming classical music.

"Is everybody okay?" Harlan asked as he disconnected
his fingers from the steering wheel. He'd been holding it

so tight as to preclude circulation. Both his hands and forearms were stiff. He turned down the volume on the CD
player.

Sheila fought with the collapsing airbag. It had abraded
her cheek and forearms.

Everyone responded that they had weathered the crash
surprisingly well.

Harlan glanced out through the broken front windshield.
All he could see were wires and twisted debris. "Do you
think this is the ballroom, Cassy?" he asked.

"I do," Cassy said.

"Then mission accomplished," Harlan said. "With all
these wires, it certainly appears as if we've collided with
some sort of high-tech apparatus. By the looks of all this
sparking, we've done something."

Since the Range Rover's engine was still running, Harlan
put it in reverse and gave it gas. With a good deal of scraping the car inched backward along its path of destruction.
After ten feet the car cleared the superstructure of the Gateway. Everyone could see up to a platform that appeared to
be made of Plexiglas. Oval stairs of the same material led
up to it. Standing on the platform was a hideous alien creature illuminated by the unabating electrical sparks. Its coal-
black eyes regarded those in the car with shocked disbelief.

All at once the creature threw back his head and let out
an agonizing cry of grief. Slowly he sank down to the surface of the platform and gripped his head with his hands
in utter anguish.

"My God! It's Beau," Cassy said from the backseat.

"I'm afraid it is," Pitt agreed. "Only his mutation has
been complete."

"Let me out!" Cassy said. She undid her seat belt.

"No," Pitt said.

"There're too many loose wires," Harlan said. "It's too
dangerous, especially with all this sparking going on. The
voltage must be astronomical."

"I don't care," Cassy said. She reached across Pitt and
opened the door.

"I can't let you," Pitt said.

"Let go of me," Cassy snapped. "I have to get out."

Reluctantly, Pitt let Cassy get out of the car. Gingerly she stepped over the wires and then slowly mounted the steps to the platform. As she got closer she could hear Beau moaning over the mechanical hum and the sputtering wires. She called out to him and he slowly raised his eyes.

"Cassy?" Beau questioned. "Why didn't I sense you?"

"Because I've been freed of the virus," Cassy said. "There's hope! There's hope we can get our old lives back."

Beau shook his head. "Not for me," he said. "I can't go back, and yet I can't go forward. I have failed the trust put in me. These human emotions are a terrible hindrance. They are completely unsuitable. Wanting you I have forsaken the collective good."

A sudden increase in the electrical sparking heralded a vibration. It was slight at first but rapidly gained strength.

"You must flee, Cassy," Beau said. "The electrical grid has been interrupted. There will be no force counteracting the antigravity. There'll be a dispersion."

"Come with me, Beau," Cassy said. "We have a way of ridding you of the virus."

"I am the virus," Beau said.

The vibration had reached a point where Cassy was having trouble maintaining her balance on the translucent steps.

"Go, Cassy!" Beau shouted passionately.

With one final touch of Beau's extended finger, Cassy struggled down to the floor of the ballroom. The room was now shaking as if there were an earthquake.

She managed to get back to the car. Pitt was holding the door open for her. She climbed in.

"Beau said we have to flee," Cassy yelled. "There's going to be a dispersion."

Needing little encouragement, Harlan put the car in reverse and stomped down on the accelerator. There was more bumping and shaking than when the car had come into the building, but soon they were back in the main hall.

Deftly Harlan pulled the car around so that it was facing

out through the shattered front entrance. The chandelier above was shaking so badly that bits and pieces of the crystal were flying off in various directions. Sitting in the front seat with no windshield, Sheila had to shield her face.

"Hang on, everybody," Harlan said. With wheels spinning on the slick marble, he rocketed the Range Rover out through the front door, across the terrace, and down the stairs. The jolt from hitting the driveway at the base of the stairs was as bad as the impact had been when they'd slammed into the ballroom wall.

Harlon drove back across the lawn in a beeline toward the cleft in the trees that marked the point where the driveway emerged.

"Must you drive this fast?" Sheila complained.

"Cassy said there was going to be a dispersion," Harlan said. "I figured the greater the distance we're away the better."

"What the hell is a dispersion?" Sheila asked.

"I haven't the foggiest," Harlan admitted. "But it sounds bad."

At that moment there was a tremendous explosion behind them, but without the usual noise or shock wave. Cassy happened to have turned around in time to see the house literally fly apart. There also wasn't any flash of light to indicate the point of conflagration.

At the same time everyone in the Range Rover became aware that they had literally become airborne. Without any traction the engine raced until Harlan took his foot from the accelerator.

The flying lasted only five seconds, and the return to earth was accompanied by a sudden lurch since the wheels had slowed but the forward movement of the car had not.

Bewildered by this strange phenomenon Harlan braked and brought the car to a stop. He was unnerved at having totally lost control of the vehicle even if it had been only for a few seconds.

"We were flying there for a moment," Sheila declared. "How did that happen?"

"I don't know," Harlan said. He looked at the gauges

and dials as if they might provide some answers.

"Look what happened to the house," Cassy said. "It
disappeared."

Everyone turned to look. Outside the car the pedestrian
were doing the same. There was no smoke and no debris
The house had just vanished.

"So now we know what a dispersion is," Harlan said
"It must be the opposite of a black hole. I guess whateve
is dispersed is reduced to all its primary particles, and they
are just blown away."

Cassy felt emotion well up inside of her. There was a
sudden, intense sense of loss, and a few tears rolled ou
onto her cheeks.

Out of the corner of his eye, Pitt saw Cassy's tears. He
understood immediately and put his arm around her shoul
der. "I'll miss him too," he said.

Cassy nodded. "I guess I'll always love him," she sai
wiping her eyes with a knuckle. But then she quickly
added: "But that doesn't mean I don't love you."

With a tenaciousness that took Pitt's breath away, Cassy
clasped him in an intense embrace. Tentatively at first and
then with equal ardor Pitt hugged her back.

Harlan got out of the car and went around the back. He
got out the flasks. "Come on, everybody," he said.
"We've got some of our own infecting to do."

"Holy shit," Jonathan cried. "There's my mother."

Everyone looked in the direction Jonathan was pointing."

"You know, I think you are right," Sheila said.

Jonathan alighted from the car with the intention of
sprinting across the grass. Harlan grabbed his arm and
thrust one of the flasks into his hand.

"Give her a whiff, son," Harlan said. "The sooner the
better."

ROBIN COOK
CHROMOSOME

6

PUTNAM